A LIFE OF
ROBERT
BY JOHN E

"Duty is the sublimest word in our language."
"Human virtue should be equal to human calamity."
LEE.

PART I.

LEE'S EARLY LIFE,

I.

INTRODUCTION.

The name of Lee is beloved and respected throughout the world. Men of all parties and opinions unite in this sentiment, not only those who thought and fought with him, but those most violently opposed to his political views and career. It is natural that his own people should love and honor him as their great leader and defender in a struggle of intense bitterness—that his old enemies should share this profound regard and admiration is due solely to the character of the individual. His military genius will always be conceded, and his figure remain a conspicuous landmark in history; but this does not account for the fact that his very enemies love the man. His private character is the origin of this sentiment. The people of the North, no less than the people of the South, feel that Lee was truly great; and the harshest critic has been able to find nothing to detract from this view of him. The soldier was great, but the man himself was greater. No one was ever simpler, truer, or more honest. Those who knew him best loved him the most. Reserved and silent, with a bearing of almost austere dignity, he impressed many persons as cold and unsympathetic, and his true character was long in revealing itself to the world. To-day all men know what his friends knew during his life—that under the grave exterior of the soldier, oppressed with care and anxiety, beat a warm and kindly heart, full of an even extraordinary gentleness and sweetness; that the man himself was not cold, or stiff, or harsh, but patient, forbearing, charitable under many trials of his equanimity, and magnanimous without effort, from the native impulse of his heart. Friend and foe thus to-day regard him with much the same sentiment, as a genuinely honest man, incapable of duplicity in thought or deed, wholly good and sincere, inspired always under all temptations by that *prisca fides* which purifies and ennobles, and resolutely bent, in the dark hour, as in the bright, on the full performance of his duty. "Duty is the sublimest word in our language," he wrote to his son; and, if we add that other august maxim, "Human virtue should be equal to human calamity," we shall have in a few words a summary of the principles which inspired Lee.

The crowning grace of this man, who was thus not only great but good, was the humility and trust in God, which lay at the foundation of his character. Upon this point we shall quote the words of a gentleman of commanding intellect, a bitter opponent of the South in the war:

"Lee is worthy of all praise. As a man, he was fearless among men. As a soldier, he had no superior and no equal. In the course of Nature my career on earth may soon terminate. God grant that, When the day of my death shall come, I may look up to Heaven with that confidence and faith which the life and character of Robert E. Lee gave him. He died trusting in God as a good man, with a good life, and a pure conscience."

He had lived, as he died, with this supreme trust in an overruling and merciful Providence; and this sentiment, pervading his whole being, was the origin of that august calmness with which he greeted the most crushing disasters of his military career. His faith and humble trust sustained him after the war, when the woes of the South wellnigh broke his great spirit; and he calmly expired, as a weary child falls asleep, knowing that its father is near.

Of this eminent soldier and man whose character offers so great an example, a memoir is attempted in this volume. The work will necessarily be "popular" rather than full and elaborate, as the public and private correspondence of Lee are not at this time accessible. These will throw a fuller light on the subject; but sufficient material is at the disposal of the writer to enable him to present an accurate likeness of Lee, and to narrate clearly the incidents of his career. In doing so, the aim of the author is to measure out full justice to all—not to arouse old enmities, which should be allowed to slumber, but to treat his subject with the judicial moderation of the student of history.

A few words will terminate this preface. The volume before the reader was begun in 1866. The writer first, however, informed General Lee of his design, and had the honor to receive from him in reply the assurance that the work "would not interfere with any he might have in contemplation; he had not written a line of any work as yet, and might never do so; but, should he write a history of the campaigns of the Army of Northern Virginia, the proposed work would be rather an assistance than a hinderance."

As the writer had offered promptly to discontinue the work if it were not agreeable to General Lee, this reply was regarded in the light of an assurance that he did not disapprove of it. The composition was, however, interrupted, and the work laid aside. It is now resumed and completed at a time when the death of the illustrious soldier adds a new and absorbing interest to whatever is connected with his character or career.

II.

THE LEES OF VIRGINIA.

The Lees of Virginia spring from an ancient and respectable family of Essex, in England.

Of some members of the family, both in the Old World and the New, a brief account will be given. The origin of an individual explains much that is striking and peculiar in his own character; and it will be found that General Lee inherited many of the traits of his ancestors, especially of some eminent personages of his name in Virginia.

The family pedigree is traced back by Lee, in the life of his father, to Launcelot Lee, of London, in France, who accompanied William the Conqueror to England. After the battle of Hastings, which subjected England to the sway of the Normans, Launcelot Lee, like others, was rewarded by lands wrested from the subdued Saxons. His estate lay in Essex, and this is all that is known concerning him. Lionel Lee is the next member of the family of whom mention is made. He lived during the reign of Richard Coeur de Lion, and, when the king went on his third crusade, in the year 1192, Lionel Lee raised a company of gentlemen, and marched with him to the Holy Land. His career there was distinguished; he displayed special gallantry at the siege of Acre, and for this he received a solid proof of King Richard's approbation. On his return he was made first Earl of Litchfield; the king presented him with the estate of "Ditchley," which became the name afterward of an estate of the Lees in Virginia; and, when he died, the armor which he had worn in the Holy Land was placed in the department of "Horse Armory" in the great Tower of London.

The name of Richard Lee is next mentioned as one of the followers of the Earl of Surrey in his expedition across the Scottish border in 1542. Two of the family about this period were "Knights Companions of the Garter," and their banners, with the Lee arms above, were suspended in St. George's Chapel in Windsor Castle. The coat-of-arms was a shield "band sinister battled and embattled," the crest a closed visor surmounted by a squirrel holding a nut. The motto, which may be thought characteristic of one of General Lee's traits as a soldier, was, "*Non incautus futuri*"

Such are the brief notices given of the family in England. They seem to have been persons of high character, and often of distinction. When Richard Lee came to Virginia, and founded the family anew there, as Launcelot, the first Lee, had founded it in England, he brought over in his veins some of the best and most valiant blood of the great Norman race.

This Richard Lee, the *princeps* of the family in Virginia, was, it seems, like the rest of his kindred, strongly Cavalier in his sentiments; indeed, the Lees seem always to have been Cavalier. The reader will recall the stately old representative of the family in Scott's "Woodstock"—Sir Henry Lee of Ditchley—who is seen stalking proudly through the great apartments of the palace, in his laced doublet, slashed boots, and velvet cloak, scowling darkly at the Puritan intruders. Sir Henry was not a fanciful person, but a real individual; and the political views attributed to him were those of the Lee family, who remained faithful to the royal cause in all its hours of adversity.

It will be seen that Richard Lee, the first of the Virginia Lees, was an ardent monarchist. He came over during the reign of Charles I., but returned to England, bequeathing all his lands to his servants; he subsequently came back to Virginia, however, and lived and died there. In his will he styles himself "Richard Lee, of Strafford Langton, in the County of Essex, Esquire." It is not certainly known whether he sought refuge in Virginia after the failure of the king's cause, or was tempted to emigrate with a view to better his fortunes in the New World. Either may have been the impelling motive. Great numbers of Cavaliers "came over" after the overthrow of Charles at Naseby; but a large emigration had already taken place, and took place afterward, induced by the salubrity of the country, the ease of living, and the cheapness and fertility of the lands on the great rivers, where families impoverished or of failing fortunes in England might "make new settlements" and build on a new foundation. This would amply account for the removal of Richard Lee to Virginia, and for the ambition he seems to have been inspired with, to build and improve, without attributing to him any apprehension of probable punishment for his political course. Very many families had the first-named motives, and commenced to build great manor-houses, which were never finished, or were too costly for any one of their descendants to possess. The abolition of primogeniture, despite the opposition of Pendleton and others, overthrew all this; and the Lees, like other families, now possess few of the broad acres which their ancestors acquired.

To return, however, to Richard Lee. He had already visited Virginia in some official capacity under the royal governor, Sir William Berkeley, and had been so much pleased with the soil and climate of the country, that he, as we have said, emigrated finally, and cast his lot in the new land. He brought a number of followers and servants, and, coming over to Westmoreland

County, in the Northern Neck of Virginia, "took up" extensive tracts of land there, and set about building manor-houses upon them.

Among these, it is stated, was the original "Stratford" House, afterward destroyed by fire. It was rebuilt, however, and became the birthplace of Richard Henry Lee, and afterward of General Robert E. Lee. We shall speak of it more in detail after finishing, in a few words, our notice of Richard Lee, its founder, and the founder of the Lee family in Virginia. He is described as a person of great force of character and many virtues—as "a man of good stature, comely visage, enterprising genius, sound head, vigorous spirit, and generous nature." This may be suspected to partake of the nature of epitaph; but, of his courage and energy, the proof remains in the action taken by him in connection with Charles II. Inheriting, it would seem, in full measure, the royalist and Cavalier sentiments of his family, he united with Sir William Berkeley, the royal governor, in the irregular proclamation of Charles II. in Virginia, a year or two before his reinstallment on the English throne. He had already, it is reported on the authority of well-supported tradition, made a voyage across the Atlantic to Breda, where Charles II. was then in exile, and offered to erect his standard in Virginia, and proclaim him king there. This proposition the young monarch declined, shrinking, with excellent good sense, from a renewal, under less favorable circumstances, of the struggle which terminated at Worcester. Lee was, therefore, compelled to return without having succeeded in his enterprise; but he had made, it seems, a very strong impression in favor of Virginia upon the somewhat frivolous young monarch. When he came to his throne again, Charles II. graciously wore a coronation-robe of Virginia silk, and Virginia, who had proved so faithful to him in the hour of his need, was authorized, by royal decree, to rank thenceforward, in the British empire, with England, Scotland, and Ireland, and bear upon her shield the motto, "*En dat Virginia quartam.*"

Richard Lee returned, after his unsuccessful mission, to the Northern Neck, and addressed himself thenceforward to the management of his private fortunes and the affairs of the colony. He had now become possessed of very extensive estates between the Potomac and Rappahannock Rivers and elsewhere. Besides Stratford, he owned plantations called "Mocke Neck," "Mathotick," "Paper-Maker's Neck," "War Captain's Neck," "Bishop's Neck," and "Paradise," with four thousand acres besides, on the Potomac, lands in Maryland, three islands in Chesapeake Bay, an interest in several trading-vessels, and innumerable indented and other servants. He became a member of the King's Council, and lived in great elegance and comfort. That he was a man of high character, and of notable piety for an age of free living and worldly tendencies, his will shows. In that document he bequeaths his soul "to that good and gracious God that gave it me, and to my blessed Redeemer, Jesus Christ, assuredly trusting, in and by His meritorious death and passion, to receive salvation."

The attention of the reader has been particularly called to the character and career of Richard Lee, not only because he was the founder of the family in Virginia, but because the traits of the individual reappear very prominently in the great soldier whose life is the subject of this volume. The coolness, courage, energy, and aptitude for great affairs, which marked Richard Lee in the seventeenth century, were unmistakably present in the character of Robert E. Lee in the nineteenth century.

We shall conclude our notice of the family by calling attention to that great group of celebrated men who illustrated the name in the days of the Revolution, and exhibited the family characteristics as clearly. These were Richard Henry Lee, of Chantilly, the famous orator and statesman, who moved in the American Congress the Declaration of Independence; Francis Lightfoot Lee, a scholar of elegant attainments and high literary accomplishments, who signed, with his more renowned brother, the Declaration; William Lee, who became Sheriff of London, and ably seconded the cause of the colonies; and Arthur Lee, diplomatist and representative of America abroad, where he displayed, as his diplomatic correspondence indicates, untiring energy and devotion to the interests of the colonies. The last of these brothers was Philip Ludwell Lee, whose daughter Matilda married her second cousin, General Henry Lee. This gentleman, afterward famous as "Light-Horse Harry" Lee, married a second time, and from this union sprung the subject of this memoir.

III.

GENERAL "LIGHT-HORSE HARRY" LEE.

This celebrated soldier, who so largely occupied the public eye in the Revolution, is worthy of notice, both as an eminent member of the Lee family, and as the father of General Robert E. Lee.

He was born in 1756, in the county of Westmoreland—which boasts of being the birthplace of Washington, Monroe, Richard Henry Lee, General Henry Lee, and General Robert E. Lee, Presidents, statesmen, and soldiers—and, after graduating at Princeton College, entered the army, in 1776, as captain of cavalry, an arm of the service afterward adopted by his more

3

celebrated descendant, in the United States army. He soon displayed military ability of high order, and, for the capture of Paulus's Hook, received a gold medal from Congress. In 1781 he marched with his "Legion" to join Greene in the Carolinas, carrying with him the high esteem of Washington, who had witnessed his skilful and daring operations in the Jerseys. His career in the arduous campaigns of the South against Cornwallis, and the efficient commander of his cavalry arm. Colonel Tarleton, may be best understood from General Greene's dispatches, and from his own memoirs of the operations of the army, which are written with as much modesty as ability. From these it is apparent that the small body of the "Legion" cavalry, under its active and daring commander, was the "eye and ear" of Greene's army, whose movements it accompanied everywhere, preceding its advances and covering its retreats. Few pages of military history are more stirring than those in Lee's "Memoirs" describing Greene's retrograde movement to the Dan; and this alone, if the hard work at the Eutaws and elsewhere were left out, would place Lee's fame as a cavalry officer upon a lasting basis. The distinguished soldier under whose eye the Virginian operated did full justice to his courage and capacity. "I believe," wrote Greene, "that few officers, either in Europe or America, are held in so high a position of admiration as you are. Everybody knows I have the highest opinion of you as an officer, and you know I love you as a friend. No man, in the progress of the campaign, had equal merit with yourself." The officer who wrote those lines was not a courtier nor a diplomatist, but a blunt and honest soldier who had seen Lee's bearing in the most arduous straits, and was capable of appreciating military ability. Add Washington's expression of his "love and thanks," in a letter written in 1789, and the light in which he was regarded by his contemporaries will be understood.

His "Memoirs of the War in the Southern Department" is a valuable military history and a very interesting book. The movements of Greene in face of Cornwallis are described with a precision which renders the narrative valuable to military students, and a picturesqueness which rivets the attention of the general reader. From these memoirs a very clear conception of the writer's character may be derived, and everywhere in them is felt the presence of a cool and dashing nature, a man gifted with the *mens aequa in arduis*, whom no reverse of fortune could cast down. The fairness and courtesy of the writer toward his opponents is an attractive characteristic of the work,[1] which is written with a simplicity and directness of style highly agreeable to readers of judgment.[2]

[Footnote 1: See his observations upon the source of his successes over Tarleton, full of the generous spirit of a great soldier. He attributes them in no degree to his own military ability, but to the superior character of his large, thorough-bred horses, which rode over Tarleton's inferior stock. He does not state that the famous "Legion" numbered only two hundred and fifty men, and that Tarleton commanded a much larger force of the best cavalry of the British army.]

[Footnote 2: A new edition of this work, preceded by a life of the author, was published by General Robert E. Lee in 1869.]

After the war General Henry Lee served a term in Congress; was then elected Governor of Virginia; returned in 1799 to Congress; and, in his oration upon the death of Washington, employed the well-known phrase, "First in war, first in peace, and first in the hearts of his countrymen." He died in Georgia, in the year 1818, having made a journey thither for the benefit of his health.

General Henry Lee was married twice; first, as we have said, to his cousin Matilda, through whom he came into possession of the old family estate of Stratford; and a second time, June 18,1793, to Miss Anne Hill Carter, a daughter of Charles Carter, Esq., of "Shirley," on James River.

The children of this second marriage were three sons and two daughters—Charles Carter, *Robert Edward*, Smith, Ann, and Mildred.

[Illustration: "STRATFORD HOUSE." The Birthplace of Gen. Lee.]

IV.

STRATFORD.

Robert Edward Lee was born at Stratford, in Westmoreland County, Virginia, on the 19th of January, 1807.[1]

[Footnote 1: The date of General Lee's birth has been often given incorrectly. The authority for that here adopted is the entry in the family Bible, in the handwriting of his mother.]

Before passing to Lee's public career, and the narrative of the stormy scenes of his after-life, let us pause a moment and bestow a glance upon this ancient mansion, which is still standing—a silent and melancholy relic of the past—in the remote "Northern Neck." As the birthplace of a great man, it would demand attention; but it has other claims still, as a venerable memorial of the past and its eminent personages, one of the few remaining monuments of a state of society that has disappeared or is disappearing.

The original Stratford House is supposed, as we have said, to have been built by Richard Lee, the first of the family in the New World. Whoever may have been its founder, it was destroyed in the time of Thomas Lee, an eminent representative of the name, early in the eighteenth century. Thomas Lee was a member of the King's Council, a gentleman of great popularity; and, when it was known that his house had been burned, contributions were everywhere made to rebuild it. The Governor, the merchants of the colony, and even Queen Anne in person, united in this subscription; the house speedily rose again, at a cost of about eighty thousand dollars; and this is the edifice still standing in Westmoreland. The sum expended in its construction must not be estimated in the light of to-day. At that time the greater part of the heavy work in house-building was performed by servants of the manor; it is fair, indeed, to say that the larger part of the work thus cost nothing in money; and thus the eighty thousand dollars represented only the English brick, the carvings, furniture, and decorations.

The construction of such an edifice had at that day a distinct object. These great old manor-houses, lost in the depths of the country, were intended to become the headquarters of the family in all time. In their large apartments the eldest son was to uphold the name. Generation after generation was to pass, and some one of the old name still live there; and though all this has passed away now, and may appear a worn-out superstition, and, though some persons may stigmatize it as contributing to the sentiment of "aristocracy," the strongest opponents of that old system may pardon in us the expression of some regret that this love of the hearthstone and old family memories should have disappeared. The great man whose character is sought to be delineated in this volume never lost to the last this home and family sentiment. He knew the kinships of every one, and loved the old country-houses of the old Virginia families—plain and honest people, attached, like himself, to the Virginia soil. We pass to a brief description of the old house in which Lee was born.

Stratford, the old home of the Lees, but to-day the property of others, stands on a picturesque bluff on the southern bank of the Potomac, and is a house of very considerable size. It is built in the form of the letter H. The walls are several feet in thickness; in the centre is a saloon thirty feet in size; and surmounting each wing is a pavilion with balustrades, above which rise clusters of chimneys. The front door is reached by a broad flight of steps, and the grounds are handsome, and variegated by the bright foliage of oaks, cedars, and maple-trees. Here and there in the extensive lawn rises a slender and ghostly old Lombardy poplar—a tree once a great favorite in Virginia, but now seen only here and there, the relic of a past generation.

Within, the Stratford House is as antique as without, and, with its halls, corridors, wainscoting, and ancient mouldings, takes the visitor back to the era of powder and silk stockings. Such was the mansion to which General Harry Lee came to live after the Revolution, and the sight of the old home must have been dear to the soldier's heart. Here had flourished three generations of Lees, dispensing a profuse and open-handed hospitality. In each generation some one of the family had distinguished himself, and attracted the "best company" to Stratford; the old walls had rung with merriment; the great door was wide open; everybody was welcome; and one could see there a good illustration of a long-passed manner of living, which had at least the merit of being hearty, open-handed, and picturesque. General Harry Lee, the careless soldier, partook of the family tendency to hospitality; he kept open house, entertained all comers, and hence, doubtless, sprung the pecuniary embarrassments embittering an old age which his eminent public services should have rendered serene and happy.

Our notice of Stratford may appear unduly long to some readers, but it is not without a distinct reference to the subject of this volume. In this quiet old mansion—and in the very apartment where Richard Henry and Francis Lightfoot Lee first saw the light—Robert E. Lee was born. The eyes of the child fell first upon the old apartments, the great grounds, the homely scenes around the old country-house—upon the tall Lombardy poplars and the oaks, through which passed the wind bearing to his ears the murmur of the Potomac.

He left the old home of his family before it could have had any very great effect upon him, it would seem; but it is impossible to estimate these first influences, to decide the depth of the impression which the child's heart is capable of receiving. The bright eyes of young Robert Lee must have seen much around him to interest him and shape his first views. Critics charged him with family pride sometimes; if he possessed that virtue or failing, the fact was not strange. Stratford opened before his childish eyes a memorial of the old splendor of the Lees. He saw around him old portraits, old plate, and old furniture, telling plainly of the ancient origin and high position of his family. Old parchments contained histories of the deeds of his race; old genealogical trees traced their line far back into the past; old servants, grown gray in the house, waited upon the child; and, in a corner of one of the great apartments, an old soldier, gray, too, and shattered in health, once the friend of Washington and Greene, was writing the history of the battles in which he had drawn his sword for his native land.

Amid these scenes and surroundings passed the first years of Robert E. Lee. They must have made their impression upon his character at a period when the mind takes every new influence, and grows in accordance with it; and, to the last, the man remained simple, hearty, proud, courteous—the *country Virginian* in all the texture of his character. He always rejoiced to visit the country; loved horses; was an excellent rider; was fond of plain country talk, jests, humorous anecdote, and chit-chat—was the plain country gentleman, in a word, preferring grass and trees and streams to all the cities and crowds in the world. In the last year of his life he said to a lady: "My visits to Florida and the White Sulphur have not benefited me much; but it did me good to go to the White House, and see *the mules walking round, and the corn growing.*"

We notice a last result of the child's residence now, or visits afterward to the country, and the sports in which he indulged—the superb physical health and strength which remained unshaken afterward by all the hardships of war. Lee, to the last, was a marvel of sound physical development; his frame was as solid as oak, and stood the strain of exhausting marches, loss of sleep, hunger, thirst, heat, and cold, without failing him.

When he died, it was care which crushed his heart; his health was perfect.

V.

LEE'S EARLY MANHOOD AND CAREER IN THE UNITED STATES ARMY.

Of Lee's childhood we have no memorials, except the words of his father, long afterward. "*Robert was always good,*" wrote General Henry Lee.[1]

[Footnote 1: To C.C. Lee, February 9, 1817.]

That is all; but the words indicate much—that the good man was "always good." It will be seen that, when he went to West Point, he never received a demerit. The good boy was the good young officer, and became, in due time, the good commander-in-chief.

In the year 1811 General Henry Lee left Stratford, and removed with his family to Alexandria, actuated, it seems, by the desire of affording his children facilities for gaining their education. After his death, in 1818, Mrs. Lee continued to reside in Alexandria; was a communicant of Christ Church; and her children were taught the Episcopal catechism by young William Meade, eventually Bishop of Virginia. We shall see how Bishop Meade, long afterward, recalled those early days, when he and his pupil, young Robert Lee, were equally unknown—how, when about to die, just as the war began in earnest, he sent for the boy he had once instructed, now the gray-haired soldier, and, when he came to the bedside, exclaimed: "God bless you, Robert! I can't call you 'general'—I have heard you your catechism too often!"

Alexandria continued to be the residence of the family until the young man was eighteen years of age, when it was necessary for him to make choice of a profession; and, following the bent of his temperament, he chose the army. Application was made for his appointment from Virginia as a cadet at West Point. He obtained the appointment, and, in 1825, at the age of eighteen, entered the Military Academy. His progress in his studies was steady, and it is said that, during his stay at West Point, he was never reprimanded, nor marked with a "demerit." He graduated, in July, 1829, second in his class, and was assigned to duty, with the rank of lieutenant, in the corps of Engineers.

[Illustration: R.E. LEE, AS A YOUNG OFFICER New York D Apololay & Co.]

He is described, by those who saw him at this time, as a young man of great personal beauty; and this is probably not an exaggeration, as he remained to the last distinguished for the elegance and dignity of his person. He had not yet lost what the cares of command afterward banished—his gayety and *abandon*—and was noted, it is said, for the sweetness of his smile and the cordiality of his manners. The person who gave the writer these details added, "He was a perfect gentleman." Three years after graduating at West Point—in the year 1832—he married Mary Custis, daughter of Mr. George Washington Parke Custis, of Arlington, the adopted son of General Washington; and by this marriage he came into possession of the estate of Arlington and the White House—points afterward well known in the war.

The life of Lee up to the beginning of the great conflict of 1861-'65 is of moderate interest only, and we shall not dwell at length upon it. He was employed on the coast defences, in New York and Virginia; and, in 1835, in running the boundary line between the States of Ohio and Michigan. In September, 1836, he was promoted to the rank of first lieutenant; in July, 1838, to a captaincy; in 1844 he became a member of the Board of Visitors to the Military Academy; in 1845 he was a member of the Board of Engineers; and in 1846, when the Mexican War broke out, was assigned to duty as chief engineer of the Central Army of Mexico, in which capacity he served to the end of the war.

Up to the date of the Mexican War, Captain Lee had attracted no public attention, but had impressed the military authorities, including General Winfield Scott, with a favorable opinion of his ability as a topographical engineer. For this department of military science he exhibited endowments of the first class—what other faculties of the soldier he possessed, it remained for events to show. This opportunity was now given him in the Mexican War; and the efficient character of his services may be seen in Scott's Autobiography, where "Captain Lee, of the Engineers," is mentioned in every report, and everywhere with commendation. From the beginning of operations, the young officer seems to have been summoned to the councils of war, and General Scott particularly mentions that held at Vera Cruz—so serious an affair, that "a death-bed discussion could hardly have been more solemn." The passages in which the lieutenant-general mentions Lee are too numerous, and not of sufficient interest to quote, but two entries will exhibit the general tenor of this "honorable mention." After Cerro Gordo, Scott writes, in his official report of the battle: "I am compelled to make special mention of Captain R.E. Lee, engineer. This officer greatly distinguished himself at the siege of Vera Cruz; was again indefatigable during these operations, in reconnoissance as daring, as laborious, and of the utmost value." After Chapultepec, he wrote: "Captain Lee, so constantly distinguished, also bore important orders for me (September 13th), until he fainted from a wound, and the loss of two nights' sleep at the batteries."

We may add here the statement of the Hon. Reverdy Johnson, that he "had heard General Scott more than once say that his success in Mexico was largely due to the skill, valor, and undaunted energy of Robert E. Lee."

For these services Lee received steady promotion. For meritorious conduct at Cerro Gordo, he was made brevet major; for the same at Contreras and Cherubusco, brevet lieutenant-colonel; and, after Chapultepec, he received the additional brevet of colonel—distinctions fairly earned by energy and courage.

When the war ended, Lee returned to his former duties in the Engineer Corps of the U.S.A., and was placed in charge of the works, then in process of construction, at Fort Carroll, near Baltimore. His assignment to the duty of thus superintending the military defences of Hampton Roads, New York Bay, and the approaches to Baltimore, in succession, would seem to indicate that his abilities as engineer were highly esteemed. Of his possession of such ability there can be no doubt. The young officer was not only thoroughly trained in this high department of military science, but had for his duties unmistakable natural endowments. This fact was clearly indicated on many occasions in the Confederate struggle—his eye for positions never failed him. It is certain that, had Lee never commanded troops in the field, he would have left behind him the reputation of an excellent engineer.

In 1855 he was called for the first time to command men, for his duties hitherto had been those of military engineer, astronomer, or staff-officer. The act of Congress directing that two new cavalry regiments should be raised excited an ardent desire in the officers of the army to receive appointments in them, and Lee was transferred from his place of engineer to the post of lieutenant-colonel in the Second Cavalry, one of the regiments in question. The extraordinary number of names of officers in this regiment who afterward became famous is worthy of notice. The colonel was Albert Sydney Johnston; the lieutenant-colonel, R.E. Lee; the senior major, William J. Hardee; the junior major, George H. Thomas; the senior captain, Earl Van Dorn; the next ranking captain, Kirby Smith; the lieutenants, Hood, Fields, Cosby, Major, Fitzhugh Lee, Johnson, Palmer, and Stoneman, all of whom became general officers afterward on the Southern side, with the exception of Thomas, and the three last named, who became prominent generals in the Federal army. It is rare that such a constellation of famous names is found in the list of officers of a single regiment. The explanation is, nevertheless simple. Positions in the new regiments were eagerly coveted by the best soldiers of the army, and, in appointing the officers, those of conspicuous ability only were selected. The Second Regiment of cavalry thus became the *corps d'élite* of the United States Army; and, after Albert Sydney Johnston, Robert E. Lee was the ranking officer.

Lee proceeded with his regiment to Texas, remaining there for several years on frontier duty, and does not reappear again until 1859.

Such was the early career in the army of the soldier soon to become famous on a greater theatre—that of a thoroughly-trained, hard-working, and conscientious officer. With the single exception of his brief record in the Mexican War, his life had been passed in official duties, unconnected with active military operations. He was undoubtedly what is called a "rising man," but he had had no opportunity to display the greatest faculties of the soldier. The time was coming now when he was to be tested, and the measure of his faculties taken in one of the greatest wars which darken the pages of history.

A single incident of public importance marks the life of Lee between 1855 and 1861. This was what is known to the world as the "John Brown raid"—an incident of the year 1859, and preluding the approaching storm. This occurrence is too well known to require a minute account in these pages, and we shall accordingly pass over it briefly, indicating simply the part borne in the affair by Lee. He was in Washington at the time—the fall of 1859—on a visit to his family, then residing at Arlington, near the city, when intelligence came that a party of desperadoes had attacked and captured Harper's Ferry, with the avowed intent of arming and inciting to insurrection the slaves of the neighborhood and entire State. Lee was immediately, thereupon, directed by President Buchanan to proceed to the point of danger and arrest the rioters. He did so promptly; found upon his arrival that Brown and his confederates had shut themselves up in an engine-house of the town, with a number of their prisoners. Brown was summoned to surrender, to be delivered over to the authorities for civil trial—he refused; and Lee then proceeded to assault, with a force of marines, the stronghold to which Brown had retreated. The doors were driven in, Brown firing upon the assailants and killing or wounding two; but he and his men were cut down and captured; they were turned over to the Virginia authorities, and Lee, having performed the duty assigned him returned to Washington, and soon afterward to Texas.

He remained there, commanding the department, until the early spring of 1861. He was then recalled to Washington at the moment when the conflict between the North and the South was about to commence.

VI.

LEE AND SCOTT.

Lee found the country burning as with fever, and the air hot with contending passions. The animosity, long smouldering between the two sections, was about to burst into the flame of civil war; all men were taking sides; the war of discussion on the floor of Congress was about to yield to the clash of bayonets and the roar of cannon on the battle-field.

Any enumeration of the causes which led to this unhappy state of affairs would be worse than useless in a volume like the present. Even less desirable would be a discussion of the respective blame to be attached to each of the great opponents in inaugurating the bitter and long-continued struggle. Such a discussion would lead to nothing, and would probably leave every reader of the same opinion as before. It would also be the repetition of a worn-out and wearisome story. These events are known of all men; for the political history of the United States, from 1820, when the slavery agitation began, on the question of the Missouri restriction, to 1861, when it ended in civil convulsion, has been discussed, rediscussed, and discussed again, in every journal, great and small, in the whole country. The person who is not familiar, therefore, with the main points at issue, must be ignorant beyond the power of any writer to enlighten him. We need only say that the election of Abraham Lincoln, the nominee of the Republican party, had determined the Gulf States to leave the Union. South Carolina accordingly seceded, on the 20th of December, 1860; and by the 1st of February, 1861, she had been followed by Mississippi, Florida, Alabama, Georgia, Louisiana, and Texas. The struggle thus approached. Military movements began at many points, like those distant flashes of lightning and vague mutterings which herald the tempest. Early in February Jefferson Davis, of Mississippi, was elected President of the Confederate States, at Montgomery. On the 13th of April Fort Sumter surrendered to General Beauregard, and on the next day, April 14, 1861, President Lincoln issued his proclamation declaring the Gulf States in rebellion, and calling upon the States which had not seceded for seventy-five thousand men to enforce the Federal authority.

Tip to this time the older State of Virginia had persistently resisted secession. Her refusal to array herself against the General Government had been based upon an unconquerable repugnance, it seemed, for the dissolution of that Union which she had so long loved; from real attachment to the flag which she had done so much to make honorable, and from a natural indisposition to rush headlong into a conflict whose whole fury would burst upon and desolate her own soil. The proclamation of President Lincoln, however, decided her course. The convention had obdurately refused, week after week, to pass the ordinance of secession. Now the naked question was, whether Virginia should fight with or against her sisters of the Gulf States. She was directed to furnish her quota of the seventy-five thousand troops called for by President Lincoln, and must decide at once. On the 17th of April, 1861, accordingly, an ordinance of secession passed the Virginia Convention, and that Commonwealth cast her fortunes for weal or woe with the Southern Confederacy.

Such is a brief and rapid summary of the important public events which had preceded, or immediately followed, Lee's return to Washington in March, 1861. A grave, and to him a very solemn, question demanded instant decision. Which side should he espouse—the side of the United States or that of the South? To choose either caused him acute pain. The attachment of the soldier to his flag is greater than the civilian can realize, and Lee had before him the brightest military prospects. The brief record which we have presented of his military career in Mexico conveys a very inadequate idea of the position which he had secured in the army. He was regarded by the authorities at Washington, and by the country at large, as the ablest and most promising of all the rising class of army officers. Upon General Winfield Scott, Commander-in-Chief of the Federal Army, he had made an impression which is the most striking proof of his great merit. General Scott was enthusiastic in his expressions of admiration for the young Virginian; and with the death of that general, which his great age rendered a probable event at any moment, Lee was sure to become a candidate for the highest promotion in the service. To this his great ability gave him a title at the earliest possible moment; and other considerations operated to advance his fortunes. He was conceded by all to be a person of the highest moral character; was the descendant of an influential and distinguished family, which had rendered important services to the country in the Revolution; his father had been the friend of Washington, and had achieved the first glories of arms, and the ample estates derived from his wife gave him that worldly prestige which has a direct influence upon the fortunes of an individual. Colonel Lee could thus look forward, without the imputation of presumption, to positions of the highest responsibility and honor under the Government. With the death of Scott, and other aged officers of the army, the place of commander-in-chief would fall to the most deserving of the younger generation; and of this generation there was no one so able and prominent as Lee.[1]

[Footnote 1: "General Scott stated his purpose to recommend Lee as his successor in the chief command of the army."—*Hon. Reverdy Johnson.*]

The personal relations of Lee with General Scott constituted another powerful temptation to decide him against going over to the Southern side. We have referred to the great admiration which the old soldier felt for the young officer. He is said to have exclaimed on one occasion: "It would be better for every officer in the army, including myself, to die than Robert Lee." There seems no doubt of the fact that Scott looked to Lee as his ultimate successor in the supreme command, for which his character and military ability peculiarly fitted him. Warm personal regard gave additional strength to his feelings in Lee's favor; and the consciousness of this regard on the part of his superior made it still more difficult for Lee to come to a decision.

VII.

LEE RESIGNS.

It is known that General Scott used every argument to persuade Lee not to resign. To retain him in the service, he had been appointed, on his arrival at Washington, a full colonel, and in 1860 his name had been sent in, with others, by Scott, as a proper person to fill the vacancy caused by the death of Brigadier-General Jessup. To these tempting intimations that rapid promotion would attend his adherence to the United States flag, Scott added personal appeals, which, coming from him, must have been almost irresistible.

"For God's sake, don't resign, Lee!" the lieutenant-general is said to have exclaimed. And, in the protracted interviews which took place between the two officers, every possible argument was urged by the elder to decide Lee to remain firm.

The attempt was in vain. Lee's attachment to the flag he had so long fought under, and his personal affection for General Scott, were great, but his attachment to his native State was still more powerful. By birth a Virginian, he declared that he owed his first duty to her and his own people. If she summoned him, he must obey the summons. As long as she remained in the Union he might remain in the United States Army. When she seceded from the Union, and took part with the Gulf States, he must follow her fortunes, and do his part in defending her. The struggle had been bitter, but brief. "My husband has wept tears of blood," Mrs. Lee wrote to a friend, "over this terrible war; but he must, as a man and a Virginian, share the destiny of his State, which has solemnly pronounced for independence."

The secession of Virginia, by a vote of the convention assembled at Richmond, decided Lee in his course. He no longer hesitated. To General Scott's urgent appeals not to send in his resignation, he replied: "I am compelled to. I cannot consult my own feelings in this matter." He accordingly wrote to General Scott from Arlington, on the 20th of April, enclosing his resignation. The letter was in the following words:

GENERAL: Since my interview with you, on the 18th instant, I have felt that I ought not longer to retain my commission in the army. I therefore tender my resignation, which I request you will recommend for acceptance. It would have been presented at once but for the struggle it has cost me to separate myself from a service to which I have devoted all the best years of my life, and all the ability I possessed.

During the whole of that time—more than a quarter of a century—I have experienced nothing but kindness from my superiors, and the most cordial friendship from my comrades. To no one, general, have I been as much indebted as to yourself for uniform kindness and consideration, and it has always been my ardent desire to merit your approbation. I shall carry to the grave the most grateful recollections of your kind consideration, and your name and fame will always be dear to me.

Save in defence of my native State, I never desire again to draw my sword. Be pleased to accept my most earnest wishes for the continuance of your happiness and prosperity, and believe me, most truly yours,

R.E. LEE. LIEUTENANT-GENERAL WINFIELD SCOTT, *Commanding United States Army.*

In this letter, full of dignity and grave courtesy, Lee vainly attempts to hide the acute pain he felt at parting from his friend and abandoning the old service. Another letter, written on the same day, expresses the same sentiment of painful regret:

ARLINGTON, VIRGINIA, *April 20,1861.*

MY DEAR SISTER: I am grieved at my inability to see you … I have been waiting "for a more convenient season," which has brought to many before me deep and lasting regret. Now we are in a state of war which will yield to nothing. The whole South is in a state of revolution, into which Virginia, after a long struggle, has been drawn, and, *though I recognize no necessity for this state of things,* and would have forborne and pleaded to the end for redress of grievances, real or supposed, yet in my own person I had to meet the question, *whether I should take part against my native State.* With all my devotion to the Union, and the feeling of loyalty and duty of an American citizen, I have not been able to make up my mind to raise my hand against my relatives, my children, my home. I have, therefore, resigned my commission in the army, and, save in defence of my native State, with the sincere hope that my poor services may never be needed, I hope I may never be called on to draw my sword.

I know you will blame me, but you must think as kindly of me as you can, and believe that I have endeavored to do what I thought right. To show you the feeling and struggle it has cost me, I send a copy of my letter to General Scott, which accompanied my letter of resignation. I have no time for more…. May God guard and protect you and yours, and shower upon you every blessing, is the prayer of your devoted brother,

R.E. LEE.

The expression used in this letter—"though I recognize no necessity for this state of things"—conveys very clearly the political sentiments of the writer. He did not regard the election of a Republican President, even by a strictly sectional vote, as sufficient ground for a dissolution of the Union. It may be added here, that such, we believe, was the opinion of a large number of Southern officers at that time. Accustomed to look to the flag as that which they were called upon to defend against all comers, they were loath to admit the force of the reasoning which justified secession, and called upon them to abandon it. Their final action seems to have been taken from the same considerations which controlled the course of Lee. Their States called them, and they obeyed.

In resigning his commission and going over to the South, Lee sacrificed his private fortunes, in addition to all his hopes of future promotion in the United States Army. His beautiful home, Arlington, situated upon the heights opposite Washington, must be abandoned forever, and fall into the hands of the enemy. This old mansion was a model of peaceful loveliness and attraction. "All around here," says a writer, describing the place, "Arlington Heights presents a lovely picture of rural beauty. The 'General Lee house,' as some term it, stands on a grassy lot, surrounded with a grove of stately trees and underwood, except in front, where is a verdant sloping ground for a few rods, when it descends into a valley, spreading away in beautiful and broad expanse to the lovely Potomac. This part of the splendid estate is apparently a highly-cultivated meadow, the grass waving in the gentle breeze, like the undulating bosom of Old Atlantic. To the south, north, and west, the grounds are beautifully diversified into hill and valley, and richly stored with oak, willow, and maple, though the oak is the principal wood. The view from the height is a charming picture. Washington, Georgetown, and the intermediate Potomac, are all before you in the foreground."

In this old mansion crowning the grassy hill, the young officer had passed the happiest moments of his life. All around him were spots associated with his hours of purest enjoyment. Each object in the house—the old furniture and very table-sets—recalled the memory of Washington, and were dear to him. Here were many pieces of the "Martha Washington china," portions of the porcelain set presented to Mrs. Washington by Lafayette and others—in the centre of each piece the monogram "M.W." with golden rays diverging to the names of the old thirteen States. Here were also fifty pieces, remnants of the set of one thousand, procured from China by the Cincinnati Society, and presented to Washington—articles of elaborate decoration in blue and gold, "with the coat-of-arms of the society, held by Fame, with a blue ribbon, from which is suspended the eagle of the order, with a green wreath about its neck, and on its breast a shield representing the inauguration of the order." Add to these the tea-table used by Washington and one of his bookcases; old portraits, antique furniture, and other memorials of the Lee family from Stratford—let the reader imagine the old mansion stored with these priceless relics, and he will understand with what anguish Lee must have contemplated what came duly to pass, the destruction, by rude hands, of objects so dear to him. That he must have foreseen the fate of his home is certain. To take sides with Virginia was to give up Arlington to its fate.

There is no proof, however, that this sacrifice of his personal fortunes had any effect upon him. If he could decide to change his flag, and dissolve every tie which bound him to the old service, he could sacrifice all else without much regret. No one will be found to say that the hope of rank or emolument in the South influenced him. The character and whole career of the man contradict the idea. His ground of action may be summed up in a single sentence. He went with his State because he believed it was his duty to do so, and because, to ascertain what was his duty, and perform it, was the cardinal maxim of his life.

VIII.

HIS RECEPTION AT RICHMOND.

No sooner had intelligence of Lee's resignation of his commission in the United States Army reached Richmond, than Governor Letcher appointed him major-general of the military forces of Virginia. The appointment was confirmed by the convention, rather by acclamation than formal vote; and on the 23d of April, Lee, who had meanwhile left Washington and repaired to Richmond, was honored by a formal presentation to the convention.

The address of President Janney was eloquent, and deserves to be preserved. Lee stood in the middle aisle, and the president, rising, said:

"MAJOR-GENERAL LEE: In the name of the people of our native State, here represented, I bid you a cordial and heart-felt welcome to this hall, in which we may almost yet hear the echoes of the voices of the statesmen, the soldiers, and sages of by-gone days, who have borne your name, and whose blood now flows in your veins.

"We met in the month of February last, charged with the solemn duty of protecting the rights, the honor, and the interests of the people of this Commonwealth. We differed for a time as to the best means of accomplishing that object, but there never was, at any moment, a shade of difference among us as to the great object itself; and now, Virginia having taken her position, as far as the power of this convention extends, we stand animated by one impulse, governed by one desire and one determination, and that is, that she shall be defended, and that no spot of her soil shall be polluted by the foot of an invader.

"When the necessity became apparent of having a leader for our forces, all hearts and all eyes, by the impulse of an instinct which is a surer guide than reason itself, turned to the old county of Westmoreland. We knew how prolific she had been in other days of heroes and statesmen. We knew she had given birth to the Father of his Country, to Richard Henry Lee, to Monroe, and, last, though not least, to your own gallant father, and we knew well, by your deeds, that her productive power was not yet exhausted.

"Sir, we watched with the most profound and intense interest the triumphal march of the army led by General Scott, to which you were attached, from Vera Cruz to the capital of Mexico. We read of the sanguinary conflicts and the blood-stained fields, in all of which victory perched upon our own banners. We knew of the unfading lustre that was shed upon the American arms by that campaign, and we know, also, what your modesty has always disclaimed, that no small share of the glory of those achievements was due to your valor and your military genius.

"Sir, one of the proudest recollections of my life will be the honor that I yesterday had of submitting to this body confirmation of the nomination, made by the Governor of this State, of you as commander-in-chief of the military and naval forces of this Commonwealth. I rose to put the question, and when I asked if this body would advise and consent to that appointment, there rushed from the hearts to the tongues of all the members an affirmative response, which told with an emphasis that could leave no doubt of the feeling whence it emanated. I put the negative of the question, for form's sake, but there was an unbroken silence.

"Sir, we have, by this unanimous vote, expressed our convictions that you are at this day, among the living citizens of Virginia, 'first in war.' We pray to God most fervently that you may so conduct the operations committed to your Charge that it may soon be said of you that you are 'first in peace,' and when that time comes you will have earned the still prouder distinction of being 'first in the hearts of your countrymen.'"

The president concluded by saying that Virginia on that day intrusted her spotless sword to Lee's keeping, and Lee responded as follows:

"MR. PRESIDENT AND GENTLEMEN OF THE CONVENTION: Profoundly impressed with the solemnity of the occasion, for which I must say I was not prepared, I accept the position assigned me by your partiality. I would have much preferred had your choice fallen upon an abler man. Trusting in Almighty God, an approving conscience, and the aid of my fellow-citizens, I devote myself to the service of my native State, in whose behalf alone will I ever again draw my sword."

Such were the modest and dignified expressions of Lee in accepting the great trust. The reply is brief and simple, but these are very great merits on such an occasion. No portion of the address contains a phrase or word denunciatory of the Federal Government, or of the motives of the opponents of Virginia; and this moderation and absence of all rancor characterized the utterances of Lee, both oral and written, throughout the war. He spoke, doubtless, as he felt, and uttered no expression of heated animosity, because he cherished no such sentiment. His heart was bleeding still from the cruel trial it had undergone in abruptly tearing away from the old service to embark upon civil war; with the emotions of the present occasion, excited by the great ovation in his honor, no bitterness mingled—or at least, if there were such bitterness in his heart, he did not permit it to rise to his lips. He accepted the trust confided to him in terms of dignity and moderation, worthy of Washington; exchanged grave salutations with the members of the convention; and then, retiring from the hall where he had solemnly consecrated his life to his native Commonwealth, proceeded at once to energetic work to get the State in a posture of defence.

The sentiment of the country in reference to Lee was even warmer than that of the convention. For weeks, reports had been rife that he had determined to adhere to the Federal Government in the approaching struggle. Such an event, it was felt by all, would be a public calamity to Virginia; and the general joy may be imagined when it was known that Lee had resigned and come to fight with his own people. He assumed command, therefore, of all the Virginia forces, in the midst of universal public rejoicing; and the fact gave strength and consistency to the general determination to resist the Federal Government to the last.

IX.

LEE IN 1861.

At this time—April, 1861—General Lee was fifty-four years of age, and may be said to have been in the ripe vigor of every faculty. Physically and intellectually he was "at his best," and in the bloom of manhood. His figure was erect, and he bore himself with the brief, somewhat stiff air of command derived from his military education and service in the army. This air of the professional soldier, which characterized generally the graduates of West Point, was replaced afterward by a grave dignity, the result of high command and great responsibilities. In April, 1861, however, he was rather the ordinary army officer in bearing than the commander-in-chief.

He had always been remarkable for his manly beauty, both of face and figure, and the cares of great command had not yet whitened his hair. There was not a gray hair in his head, and his mustache was dark and heavy. The rest of his face was clean-shaven, and his cheeks had that fresh, ruddy hue which indicates high physical health. This was not at that time or afterward the result of high living. Of all the prominent personages of his epoch. Lee was, perhaps, the most temperate. He rarely drank even so much as a single glass of wine, and it was a matter of general notoriety in the army afterward, that he cared not what he ate. The ruddy appearance which characterized him from first to last was the result of the most perfectly-developed physical health, which no species of indulgence had ever impaired. He used no tobacco then or afterward, in any shape—that seductive weed which has been called "the soldier's comfort"—and seemed, indeed, superior to all those small vices which assail men of his profession. Grave, silent, with a military composure of bearing which amounted at times, as we have said, to stiffness, he resembled a machine in the shape of a man. At least this was the impression which he produced upon those who saw him in public at this time.

The writer's design, here, is to indicate the personal appearance and bearing of General Lee on the threshold of the war. It may be said, by way of summing up all, that he was a full-blooded "West-Pointer" in appearance; the *militaire* as distinguished from the civilian; and no doubt impressed those who held official interviews with him as a personage of marked reserve. The truth and frankness of the man under all circumstances, and his great, warm heart, full of honesty and unassuming simplicity, became known only in the progress of the war. How simple and true and honest he was, will appear from a letter to his son, G.W. Custis Lee, written some time before:

"You must study," he wrote, "to be frank with the world; frankness is the child of honesty and courage. Say just what you mean to do on every occasion, and take it for granted you mean to do right. If a friend asks a favor, you should grant it, if it is reasonable; if not, tell him plainly why you cannot: you will wrong him and wrong yourself by equivocation of any kind. Never do a wrong thing to make a friend or keep one; the man who requires you to do so, is dearly purchased at a sacrifice. Deal kindly, but firmly, with all your classmates; you will find it the policy which wears best. Above all, do not appear to others what you are not. If you have any fault to find with any one, tell him, not others, of what you complain; there is no more dangerous experiment than that of undertaking to be one thing before a man's face and another behind his back. We should live, act, and say, nothing to the injury of any one. It is not only best as a matter of principle, but it is the path to peace and honor.

"In regard to duty, let me, in conclusion of this hasty letter, inform you that, nearly a hundred years ago, there was a day of remarkable gloom and darkness—still known as 'the dark day'—a day when the light of the sun was slowly extinguished, as if by an eclipse. The Legislature of Connecticut was in session, and, as its members saw the unexpected and unaccountable darkness coming on, they shared in the general awe and terror. It was supposed by many that the last day—the day of judgment—had come. Some one, in the consternation of the hour, moved an adjournment. Then there arose an old Puritan legislator, Davenport, of Stamford, and said that, if the last day had come, he desired to be found at his place doing his duty, and, therefore, moved that candles be brought in, so that the House could proceed with its duty. There was quietness in that man's mind, the quietness of heavenly wisdom and inflexible willingness to obey present duty. Duty, then, is the sublimest word in our language. Do your duty in all things, like the old Puritan. You cannot do more, you should never wish to do less. Never let me and your mother wear one gray hair for any lack of duty on your part."

The maxims of this letter indicate the noble and conscientious character of the man who wrote it. "Frankness is the child of honesty and courage." "Say just what you mean to do on every occasion." "Never do a wrong thing to make a friend or keep one." "Duty is the sublimest word in our language ... do your duty in all things ... you cannot do more." That he lived up to these great maxims, amid all the troubled scenes and hot passions of a stormy epoch, is Lee's greatest glory. His fame as a soldier, great as it is, yields to the true glory of having placed duty before his eyes always as the supreme object of life. He resigned his commission from a sense of duty to his native State; made this same duty his sole aim in every portion of his subsequent career; and, when all had failed, and the cause he had fought for was overthrown, it was the consciousness of having performed conscientiously, and to his utmost, his whole duty, which took the sting from defeat, and gave him that noble calmness which the whole world saw and admired. "Human virtue should be equal to human calamity," were his august words when all was lost, and men's minds were sinking under the accumulated agony of defeat and despair. Those words could only have been uttered by a man who made duty the paramount object of living—the performance of it, the true glory and crown of virtuous manhood. It may be objected by some critics that he mistook his duty in espousing the Southern cause. Doubtless many persons will urge that objection, and declare that the words here written are senseless panegyric. But that will not affect the truth or detract from Lee's great character. He performed at least what in his inmost soul *he* considered his duty, and, from the beginning of his career, when all was so bright, to its termination, when all was so dark, it will be found that his controlling sentiment was, first, last, and all the time, this performance of duty. The old Puritan, whose example he admired so much, was not more calm and resolute. When "the last day" of the cause he fought for came—in the spring of 1865—it was plain to all who saw the man, standing unmoved in the midst of the general disaster, that his sole desire was to be "found at his place, and doing his duty."

From this species of digression upon the moral constituents of the individual, we pass to the record of that career which made the great fame of the soldier. The war had already begun when Lee took command of the provisional forces of Virginia, and the collisions in various portions of the Gulf States between the Federal and State authorities were followed by overt acts in Virginia, which all felt would be the real battle-ground of the war. The North entered upon the struggle with very great ardor and enthusiasm. The call for volunteers to enforce obedience to the Federal authority was tumultuously responded to throughout the entire North, and troops were hurried forward to Washington, which soon became an enormous camp. The war began in Virginia with the evacuation and attempted destruction of the works at Harper's Ferry, by the Federal officer in command there. This was on the 19th of April, and on the next day reinforcements were thrown into Fortress Monroe; and the navy-yard at Norfolk, with the shipping, set on fire and abandoned.

Lee thus found the Commonwealth in a state of war, and all his energies were immediately concentrated upon the work of placing her in a condition of defence. He established his headquarters in the custom-house at Richmond; orderlies were seen coming and going; bustle reigned throughout the building, and by night, as well as by day, General Lee labored incessantly to organize the means of resistance. From the first moment, all had felt that Virginia, from her geographical position, adjoining the Federal frontier and facing the Federal capital, would become the arena of the earliest, longest, and most determined struggle. Her large territory and moral influence, as the oldest of the Southern States, also made her the chief object of the Federal hostility. It was felt that if Virginia were occupied, and her people reduced under the Federal authority again, the Southern cause would be deprived of a large amount of its prestige and strength. The authorities of the Gulf States accordingly hurried forward to Richmond all available troops; and from all parts of Virginia the volunteer regiments, which had sprung up like magic, were in like manner forwarded by railway to the capital. Every train brought additions to this great mass of raw war material; large camps rose around Richmond, chief among which was that named "Camp Lee;" and the work of drilling and moulding this crude material for the great work before it was ardently proceeded with under the supervision of Lee.

An Executive Board, or Military Council, had been formed, consisting of Governor Letcher and other prominent officials; but these gentlemen had the good sense to intrust the main work of organizing an army to Lee. As yet the great question at Richmond was to place Virginia in a state of defence—to prepare that Commonwealth for the hour of trial, by enrolling her own people. It will be remembered that Lee held no commission from the Confederate States; he was major-general of the Provisional Army of Virginia, and to place this Provisional Army in a condition to take the field was the first duty before him. It was difficult, not from want of ardor in the population, but from the want of the commonest material necessary in time of war. There were few arms, and but small supplies of ammunition. While the Federal Government entered upon the war with the amplest resources, the South found herself almost entirely destitute of the munitions essential to her protection. All was to be organized and put at once into operation—the quartermaster, commissary, ordnance, and other departments. Transportation, supplies of rations, arms, ammunition, all were to be collected immediately. The material existed, or could be supplied, as the sequel clearly showed; but as yet there was almost nothing. And it was chiefly to the work of organizing these departments, first of all, that General Lee and the Military Council addressed themselves with the utmost energy.

The result was, that the State found herself very soon in a condition to offer a determined resistance. The troops at the various camps of instruction were successively sent to the field; others took their places, and the work of drilling the raw material into soldiers went on; supplies were collected, transportation found, workshops for the construction of arms and ammunition sprung up; small-arms, cannon, cartridges, fixed and other ammunition, were produced in quantities; and, in a time which now seems wholly inadequate for such a result, the Commonwealth of Virginia was ready to take the field against the Federal Government.

X.

THE WAR BEGINS.

Early in May, Virginia became formally a member of the Southern Confederacy, and the troops which she had raised a portion of the Confederate States Army. When Richmond became the capital soon afterward, and the Southern Congress assembled, five brigadier-generals were appointed, Generals Cooper, Albert S. Johnston, Lee, J.E. Johnston, and Beauregard. Large forces had been meanwhile raised throughout the South; Virginia became the centre of all eyes, as the scene of the main struggle; and early in June occurred at Bethel, in Lower Virginia, the first prominent affair, in which General Butler, with about four thousand men, was repulsed and forced to retire.

The affair at Bethel, which was of small importance, was followed by movements in Northern and Western Virginia—the battles at Rich Mountain and Carrick's Ford; Johnston's movements in the Valley; and the advance of the main Federal army on the force under Beauregard, which resulted in the first battle of Manassas. In these events, General Lee bore no part, and we need not speak of them further than to present a summary of the results. The Federal design had been to penetrate Virginia in three columns. One was to advance from the northwest under General McClellan; a second, under General Patterson, was to take possession of the Valley; and a third, under General McDowell, was to drive Beauregard back from Manassas on Richmond. Only one of these columns—that of McClellan—succeeded in its undertaking. Johnston held Patterson in check in the Valley until the advance upon Manassas; then by a flank march the Confederate general hastened to the assistance of Beauregard. The battle of Manassas followed on Sunday, the 21st of July. After an unsuccessful attempt to force the Confederate right, General McDowell assailed their left, making for that purpose a long *détour*—and at first carried all before him. Reënforcements were hurried forward, however, and the Confederates fought with the energy of men defending their own soil. The obstinate stand made by Evans, Bee, Bartow, Jackson, and their brave associates, turned the fortunes of the day, and, when reënforcements subsequently reached the field under General Kirby Smith and General Early, the Federal troops retreated in great disorder toward Washington.

XI.

LEE'S ADVANCE INTO WESTERN VIRGINIA.

General Lee nowhere appears, as we have seen, in these first great movements and conflicts. He was without any specific command, and remained at Richmond, engaged in placing that city in a state of defence. The works which he constructed proved subsequently of great importance to the city, and a Northern officer writes of Lee: "While the fortifications of

Richmond stand, his name will evoke admiration; the art of war is unacquainted with any defence so admirable."

Lee's first appearance in the war, as commander of troops in the field, took place in the fall of 1861, when he was sent to operate against the forces under General Rosecrans in the fastnesses of Western Virginia. This indecisive and unimportant movement has been the subject of various comment; the official reports were burned in the conflagration at Richmond, or captured, and the elaborate plans drawn up by Lee of his intended movement against General Reynolds, at Cheat Mountain, have in the same manner disappeared. Under these circumstances, and as the present writer had no personal knowledge of the subject, it seems best to simply quote the brief statement which follows. It is derived from an officer of high rank and character, whose statement is only second in value to that of General Lee himself:

"After General Garnett's death, General Lee was sent by the President to ascertain what could be done in the trans-Alleghany region, and to endeavor to harmonize our movements, etc., in that part of the State. He was not ordered to take command of the troops, nor did he do so, during the whole time he was there.

"Soon after his arrival he came to the decided conclusion that *that* was not the line from which to make an offensive movement. The country, although not hostile, was not friendly; supplies could not be obtained; the enemy had possession of the Baltimore and Ohio Railroad, from which, and the Ohio River as a base, he could operate with great advantage against us, and our only chance was to drive him from the railroad, take possession, and use it ourselves. We had not the means of doing this, and consequently could only try to hold as much country as possible, and occupy as large a force of the enemy as could be kept in front of us. The movement against Cheat Mountain, which failed, was undertaken with a view of causing the enemy to contract his lines, and enable us to unite the troops under Generals Jackson (of Georgia) and Loring. After the failure of this movement on our part, General Rosecrans, feeling secure, strengthened his lines in that part of the country, and went with a part of his forces to the Kanawha, driving our forces across the Gauley. General Lee then went to that line of operations, to endeavor to unite the troops under Generals Floyd and Wise, and stop the movements under Rosecrans. General Loring, with a part of his force from Valley Mountain, joined the forces at Sewell Mountain. Rosecrans's movement was stopped, and, the season for operations in that country being over, General Lee was ordered to Richmond, and soon afterward sent to South Carolina, to meet the movement of the enemy from Port Royal, etc. He remained in South Carolina until shortly before the commencement of the campaign before Richmond, in 1862."

The months spent by General Lee in superintending the coast defences of South Carolina and Georgia, present nothing of interest, and we shall therefore pass to the spring of 1862, when he returned to Richmond. His services as engineer had been highly appreciated by the people of the South, and a writer of the period said: "The time will yet come when his superior abilities will be vindicated, both to his own renown and the glory of his country." The time was now at hand when these abilities, if the individual possessed them, were to have an opportunity to display themselves.

XII.

LEE'S LAST INTERVIEW WITH BISHOP MEADE.

A touching incident of Lee's life belongs to this time—the early spring of 1862. Bishop Meade, the venerable head of the Episcopal Church in Virginia, lay at the point of death, in the city of Richmond. When General Lee was informed of the fact, he exhibited lively emotion, for the good bishop, as we have said in the commencement of this narrative, had taught him his catechism when he was a boy in Alexandria. On the day before the bishop's death. General Lee called in the morning to see him, but such was the state of prostration under which the sick man labored, that only a few of his most intimate friends were permitted to have access to his chamber. In the evening General Lee called again, and his name was announced to Bishop Meade. As soon as he heard it, he said faintly, for his breathing had become much oppressed, and he spoke with great difficulty: "I must see him, if only for a few moments."

General Lee was accordingly introduced, and approached the dying man, with evidences of great emotion in his countenance. Taking the thin hand in his own, he said:

"How do you feel, bishop?"

"Almost gone," replied Bishop Meade, in a voice so weak that it was almost inaudible; "but I wanted to see you once more."

He paused for an instant, breathing heavily, and looking at Lee with deep feeling.

"God bless you! God bless you, Robert!" he faltered out, "and fit you for your high and responsible duties. I can't call you 'general'—I must call you 'Robert;' I have heard you your catechism too often."

General Lee pressed the feeble hand, and tears rolled down his cheeks.

"Yes, bishop—very often," he said, in reply to the last words uttered by the bishop.

A brief conversation followed, Bishop Meade making inquiries in reference to Mrs. Lee, who was his own relative, and other members of the family. "He also," says the highly-respectable clergyman who furnishes these particulars, "put some pertinent questions to General Lee about the state of public affairs and of the army, showing the most lively interest in the success of our cause."

It now became necessary to terminate an interview which, in the feeble condition of the aged man, could not be prolonged. Much exhausted, and laboring under deep emotion, Bishop Meade shook the general by the hand, and said:

"Heaven bless you! Heaven bless you! and give you wisdom for your important and arduous duties!"

These were the last words uttered during the interview. General Lee pressed the dying man's hand, released it, stood for several minutes by the bedside motionless and in perfect silence, and then went out of the room.

On the next morning Bishop Meade expired.

[Illustration: Environs of Richmond.]

PART II.

IN FRONT OF RICHMOND.

I.

PLAN OF THE FEDERAL CAMPAIGN.

The pathetic interview which we have just described took place in the month of March, 1862.

By the latter part of that month, General McClellan, in command of an army of more than one hundred thousand men, landed on the Peninsula between the James and York Rivers, and after stubbornly-contested engagements with the forces of General Johnston, advanced up the Peninsula—the Confederates slowly retiring. In the latter part of May, a portion of the Federal forces had crossed the Chickahominy, and confronted General Johnston defending Richmond.

Such was the serious condition of affairs in the spring of 1862. The Federal sword had nearly pierced the heart of Virginia, and, as the course of events was about to place Lee in charge of her destinies, a brief notice is indispensable of the designs of the adversaries against whom he was to contend on the great arena of the State.

While the South had been lulled to sleep, as it were, by the battle of Manassas, the North, greatly enraged at the disaster, had prepared to prosecute the war still more vigorously. The military resources of the South had been plainly underestimated. It was now obvious that the North had to fight with a dangerous adversary, and that the people of the South were entirely in earnest. Many journals of the North had ridiculed the idea of war; and one of them had spoken of the great uprising of the Southern States from the Potomac to the Gulf of Mexico as a mere "local commotion" which a force of fifty thousand men would be able to put down without difficulty. A column of twenty-five thousand men, it was said, would be sufficient to carry all before it in Virginia, and capture Richmond, and the comment on this statement had been the battle of Manassas, where a force of more than fifty thousand had been defeated and driven back to Washington.

It was thus apparent that the war was to be a serious struggle, in which the North would be compelled to exert all her energies. The people responded to the call upon them with enthusiasm. All the roving and adventurous elements of Northern society flocked to the Federal standard, and in a short time a large force had once more assembled at Washington. The work now was to drill, equip, and put it in efficient condition for taking the field. This was undertaken with great energy, the Congress coöperating with the Executive in every manner. The city of Washington resounded with the wheels of artillery and the tramp of cavalry; the workshops were busy night and day to supply arms and ammunition; and the best officers devoted themselves, without rest, to the work of drilling and disciplining the mass.

By the spring of 1862 a force of about two hundred thousand men was ready to take the field in Virginia. General Scott was not to command in the coming campaigns. He had retired in the latter part of the year 1861, and his place had been filled by a young officer of rising reputation—General George B. McClellan, who had achieved the successes of Rich Mountain and Carrick's Ford in Western Virginia. General McClellan was not yet forty, but had impressed the authorities with a high opinion of his abilities. A soldier by profession, and enjoying the distinction of having served with great credit in the Mexican War, he had been sent as United States military commissioner to the Crimea, and on his return had written a book of marked ability on the military organizations of the powers of Europe. When the struggle between the North and South approached, he was said—with what truth we know not—to have hesitated, before determining upon his course; but it is probable that the only question with him was

16

whether he should fight for the North or remain neutral. In his politics he was a Democrat, and the war on the South is said to have shocked his State-rights view. But, whatever his sentiments had been, he accepted command, and fought a successful campaign in Western Virginia. From that moment his name became famous; he was said to have achieved "two victories in one day," and he received from the newspapers the flattering name of "the Young Napoleon."

The result of this successful campaign, slight in importance as it was, procured for General McClellan the high post of commander-in-chief of the armies of the United States. Operations in every portion of the South were to be directed by him; and he was especially intrusted with the important work of organizing the new levies at Washington. This he performed with very great ability. Under his vigorous hand, the raw material soon took shape. He gave his personal attention to every department; and the result, as we have said, in the early spring of 1862, was an army of more than two hundred thousand men, for operations in Virginia alone.

The great point now to be determined was the best line of operations against Richmond. President Lincoln was strongly in favor of an advance by way of Manassas and the Orange and Alexandria Railroad, which he thought would insure the safety of the Federal capital. This was always, throughout the whole war, a controlling consideration with him; and, regarded in the light of subsequent events, this solicitude seems to have been well founded. More than once afterward, General Lee—to use his own expression—thought of "swapping queens," that is to say, advancing upon Washington, without regard to the capture of Richmond; and President Lincoln, with that excellent good sense which he generally exhibited, felt that the loss of Washington would prove almost fatal to the Federal cause.—Such was the origin of the President's preference for the Manassas line. General McClellan did not share it. He assented it seems at first, but soon resolved to adopt another plan—an advance either from Urbanna on the Rappahannock, or from West Point on the York. Against his views and determination, the President and authorities struggled in vain. McClellan treated their arguments and appeals with a want of ceremony amounting at times nearly to contempt; he adhered to his own plan resolutely, and in the end the President gave way. In rueful protest against the continued inactivity of General McClellan, President Lincoln had exclaimed, "If General McClellan does not want to use the army, I would like to borrow it;" and "if something is not soon done, the bottom will be out of the whole affair."

At last General McClellan carried his point, and an advance against Richmond from the Peninsula was decided upon. In order to assist this movement, General Fremont was to march through Northwestern Virginia, and General Banks up the Valley; and, having thus arranged their programme, the Federal authorities began to move forward to the great work. To transport an army of more than one hundred thousand men by water to the Peninsula was a heavy undertaking; but the ample resources of the Government enabled them to do so without difficulty. General McClellan, who had now been removed from his post of commander-in-chief of the armies of the United States, and assigned to the command only of the army to operate against Richmond, landed his forces on the Peninsula, and, after several actions of an obstinate description, advanced toward the Chickahominy, General Johnston, the Confederate commander, deliberately retiring. Johnston took up a position behind this stream, and, toward the end of May, McClellan crossed a portion of his forces and confronted him.

II.

JOHNSTON IS WOUNDED.

The army thus threatening the city which had become the capital of the Confederacy was large and excellently equipped. It numbered in all, according to General McClellan's report, one hundred and fifty-six thousand eight hundred and thirty-eight men, of whom one hundred and fifteen thousand one hundred and two were effective troops—that is to say, present and ready for duty as fighting-men in the field.

Results of such magnitude' were expected from this great army, that all the resources of the Federal Government had been taxed to bring it to the highest possible state of efficiency. The artillery was numerous, and of the most approved description; small-arms of the best patterns and workmanship were profusely supplied; the ammunition was of the finest quality, and almost inexhaustible in quantity; and the rations for the subsistence of the troops, which were equally excellent and abundant, were brought up in an unfailing stream from the White House, in General McClellan's rear, over the York River Railroad, which ran straight to his army.

Such was the admirable condition of the large force under command of General McClellan. It would be difficult to imagine an army better prepared for active operations; and the position which it held had been well selected. The left of the army was protected by the wellnigh impassable morass of the White-oak Swamp, and all the approaches from the direction of Richmond were obstructed by the natural difficulties of the ground, which had been rendered still more forbidding by an abattis of felled trees and earthworks of the best description. Unless the right of McClellan, on the northern bank of the Chickahominy, were turned by the Confederates, his communications with his base at the White House and the safety of his army were assured. And even the apparently improbable contingency of such an assault on his right had been provided for. Other bodies of Federal troops had advanced into Virginia to coöperate with the main force on the Peninsula. General McDowell, the able soldier who had nearly defeated the Confederates at Manassas, was at Fredericksburg with a force of about forty thousand men, which were to advance southward without loss of time and unite with General McClellan's right. This would completely insure the communications of his army from interruption; and it was no doubt expected that Generals Fremont and Banks would coöperate in the movement also. Fremont was to advance from Northwestern Virginia, driving before him the small Confederate force, under Jackson, in the Valley; and General Banks, then at Winchester, was to cross the Blue Ridge Mountains, and, posting his forces along the Manassas Railroad, guard the approaches to Washington when McDowell advanced from Fredericksburg to the aid of General McClellan. Thus Richmond would be half encircled by Federal armies. General McClellan, if permitted by the Confederates to carry out his plan of operations, would soon be in command of about two hundred thousand men, and with this force it was anticipated he would certainly be able to capture Richmond.

Such was the Federal programme of the war in Virginia. It promised great results, and ought, it would seem, to have succeeded. The Confederate forces in Virginia did not number in all one hundred thousand men; and it is now apparent that, without the able strategy of Johnston, Lee, and Jackson, General McClellan would have been in possession of Richmond before the summer.

Prompt action was thus necessary on the part of the sagacious soldier commanding the army at Richmond, and directing operations throughout the theatre of action in Virginia. The officer in question was General Joseph E. Johnston, a Virginian by birth, who had first held General Patterson in check in the Shenandoah Valley, and then hastened to the assistance of General Beauregard at Manassas, where, in right of his superior rank, he took command. Before the enemy's design to advance up the Peninsula had been developed, Johnston had made a masterly retreat from Manassas. Reappearing with his force of about forty thousand men on the Peninsula, he had obstinately opposed McClellan, and only retired when he was compelled by numbers to do so, with the resolution, however, of fighting a decisive battle on the Chickahominy. In face, figure, and character, General Johnston was thoroughly the soldier. Above the medium height, with an erect figure, in a close-fitting uniform buttoned to the chin; with a ruddy face, decorated with close-cut gray side-whiskers, mustache, and tuft on the chin; reserved in manner, brief of speech, without impulses of any description, it seemed, General Johnston's appearance and bearing were military to stiffness; and he was popularly compared to "a gamecock," ready for battle at any moment. As a soldier, his reputation was deservedly high; to unshrinking personal courage he added a far-reaching capacity for the conduct of great operations. Throughout his career he enjoyed a profound public appreciation of his abilities as a commander, and was universally respected as a gentleman and a patriot.

General Johnston, surveying the whole field in Virginia, and penetrating, it would seem, the designs of the enemy, had hastened to direct General Jackson, commanding in the Valley, to begin offensive operations, and, by threatening the Federal force there—with Washington in perspective—relieve the heavy pressure upon the main arena. Jackson carried out these instructions with the vigor which marked all his operations. In March he advanced down the Valley in the direction of Winchester, and, coming upon a considerable force of the enemy at Kernstown, made a vigorous assault upon them; a heavy engagement ensued, and, though Jackson was defeated and compelled to retreat, a very large Federal force was retained in the Valley to protect that important region. A more decisive diversion soon followed. Jackson advanced in May upon General Banks, then at Strasburg, drove him from that point to and across the Potomac; and such was the apprehension felt at Washington, that President Lincoln ordered General McDowell, then at Fredericksburg with about forty thousand men, to send twenty thousand across the mountains to Strasburg in order to pursue or cut off Jackson.

Thus the whole Federal programme in Virginia was thrown into confusion. General Banks, after the fight at Kernstown, was kept in the Valley. After Jackson's second attack upon him, when General Banks was driven across the Potomac and Washington threatened, General McDowell was directed to send half his army to operate against Jackson. Thus General McClellan, waiting at Richmond for McDowell to join him, did not move; with a portion of his army on one side of the stream, and the remainder on the other side, he remained inactive, hesitating and unwilling, as any good soldier would have been, to commence the decisive assault.

His indecision was brought to an end by General Johnston. Discovering that the force in his front, near "Seven Pines," on the southern bank of the Chickahominy, was only a portion of the Federal army, General Johnston determined to attack it. This resolution was not in consequence of the freshet in the Chickahominy, as has been supposed, prompting Johnston to attack while the Federal army was cut in two, as it were. His resolution, he states, had already been taken, and was, with or without reference to the rains, that of a good soldier. General Johnston struck at General McClellan on the last day of May, just at the moment, it appears, when the Federal commander designed commencing his last advance upon the city. The battle which took place was one of the most desperate and bloody of the war. Both sides fought with obstinate courage, and neither gained a decisive advantage. On the Confederate right, near "Seven Pines," the Federal line was broken and forced back; but, on the left, at Fair Oaks Station, the Confederates, in turn, were repulsed. Night fell upon a field where neither side could claim the victory. The most that could be claimed by the Southerners was that McClellan had received a severe check; and they sustained a great misfortune in the wound received by General Johnston. He was struck by a fragment of shell while superintending the attack at Fair Oaks, and the nature of his wound rendered it impossible for him to retain command of the army. He therefore retired from the command, and repaired to Richmond, where he remained for a long time an invalid, wholly unable to continue in service in the field.

This untoward event rendered it necessary to find a new commander for the army without loss of time. General Lee had returned some time before from the South, and to him all eyes were turned. He had had no opportunity to display his abilities upon a conspicuous theatre—the sole command he had been intrusted with, that in trans-Alleghany Virginia, could scarcely be called a real command—and he owed his elevation now to the place vacated by General Johnston, rather to his services performed in the old army of the United States, than to any thing he had effected in the war of the Confederacy. The confidence of the Virginia people in his great abilities had never wavered, and there is no reason to suppose that the Confederate authorities were backward in conceding his merits as a soldier. Whatever may have been the considerations leading to his appointment, he was assigned on the 3d day of June to the command of the army, and thus the Virginians assembled to defend the capital of their State found themselves under the command of the most illustrious of their own countrymen.

III.

LEE ASSIGNED TO THE COMMAND—HIS FAMILY AT THE WHITE HOUSE.

Lee had up to this time effected, as we have shown, almost nothing in the progress of the war. Intrusted with no command, and employed only in organizing the forces, or superintending the construction of defences, he had failed to achieve any of those successes in the field which constitute the glory of the soldier. He might possess the great abilities which his friends and admirers claimed for him, but he was yet to show the world at large that he did really possess them.

The decisive moment had now arrived which was to test him. He was placed in command of the largest and most important army in the Confederacy, and to him was intrusted the defence of the capital not only of Virginia, but of the South. If Richmond were to fall, the Confederate Congress, executive, and heads of departments, would all be fugitives. The evacuation of Virginia might or might not follow, but, in the very commencement of the conflict, the enemy would achieve an immense advantage. Recognition by the European powers would be hopeless in such an event, and the wandering and fugitive government of the Confederacy would excite only contempt.

Such were the circumstances under which General Lee assumed command of the "Army of Northern Virginia," as it was soon afterward styled. The date of his assignment to duty was June 3, 1862—three days after General Johnston had retired in consequence of his wound. Thirty days afterward the great campaign around Richmond had been decided, and to the narrative of what followed the appointment of Lee we shall at once proceed, after giving a few words to another subject connected with his family.

When General Lee left "Washington to repair to Richmond," he removed the ladies of his family from Arlington to the "White House" on the Pamunkey, near the spot where that river unites with the Mattapony to form the York River. This estate, like the Arlington property, had come into possession of General Lee through his wife, and as Arlington was exposed to the enemy, the ladies had taken refuge here, with the hope that they would be safe from intrusion or danger. The result was unfortunate. The White House was a favorable "base" for the Federal army, and intelligence one day reached Mrs. Lee and her family that the enemy were approaching. The ladies therefore hastened from the place to a point of greater safety, and before her departure Mrs. Lee is said to have affixed to the door a paper containing the following words:

"Northern soldiers who profess to reverence Washington, forbear to desecrate the home of his first married life, the property of his wife, now owned by her descendants.

"A GRAND-DAUGHTER OF MRS. WASHINGTON."

When the Federal forces took possession of the place, a Northern officer, it is said, wrote beneath this:

"A Northern officer has protected your property, in sight of the enemy, and at the request of your overseer."

The resolute spirit of Mrs. Lee is indicated by an incident which followed. She took refuge with her daughters in a friend's house near Richmond, and, when a Federal officer was sent to search the house, handed to him a paper addressed to "the general in command," in which she wrote:

"Sir: I have patiently and humbly submitted to the search of my house, by men under your command, who are satisfied that there is nothing here which they want. All the plate and other valuables have long since been removed to Richmond, and are now beyond the reach of any Northern marauders who may wish for their possession.

"WIFE OF ROBERT LEE, GENERAL C.S.A."

The ladies finally repaired for safety to the city of Richmond, and the White House was burned either before or when General McClellan retreated. The place was not without historic interest, as the scene of Washington's first interview with Martha Custis, who afterward became his wife. He was married either at St. Peter's Church near by, or in the house which originally stood on the site of the one now destroyed by the Federal forces. Its historic associations thus failed to protect the White House, and, like Arlington, it fell a sacrifice to the pitiless hand of war.

From this species of digression we come back to the narrative of public events, and the history of the great series of battles which were to make the banks of the Chickahominy historic ground. On taking command, Lee had assiduously addressed himself to the task of increasing the efficiency of the army: riding incessantly to and fro, he had inspected with his own eyes the condition of the troops; officers of the commissary, quartermaster, and ordnance departments were held to a strict accountability; and, in a short time, the army was in a high state of efficiency.

"What was the amount of the Confederate force under command of Lee?" it may be asked. The present writer is unable to state this number with any thing like exactness. The official record, if in existence, is not accessible, and the matter must be left to conjecture. It is tolerably certain, however, that, even after the arrival of Jackson, the army numbered less than seventy-five thousand. Officers of high rank and character state the whole force to have been sixty or seventy thousand only.

It will thus be seen that the Federal army was larger than the Confederate; but this was comparatively an unimportant fact. The event was decided rather by generalship than the numbers of the combatants.

IV

LEE RESOLVES TO ATTACK.

General Lee assumed command of the army on the 3d of June. A week afterward, Jackson finished the great campaign of the Valley, by defeating Generals Fremont and Shields at Port Republic.

Such had been the important services performed by the famous "Stonewall Jackson," who was to become the "right arm" of Lee in the greater campaigns of the future. Retreating, after the defeat of General Banks, and passing through Strasburg, just as Fremont from the west, and the twenty thousand men of General McDowell from the east, rushed to intercept him, Jackson had sullenly fallen back up the Valley, with all his captured stores and prisoners, and at Cross Keys and Port Republic had achieved a complete victory over his two adversaries. Fremont was checked by Ewell, who then hastened across to take part in the attack on Shields. The result was a Federal defeat and retreat down the Valley. Jackson was free to move in any direction; and his army could unite with that at Richmond for a decisive attack upon General McClellan.

The attack in question had speedily been resolved on by Lee. Any further advance of the Federal army would bring it up to the very earthworks in the suburbs of the city; and, unless the Confederate authorities proposed to undergo a siege, it was necessary to check the further advance of the enemy by a general attack.

How to attack to the best advantage was now the question. The position of General McClellan's army has been briefly stated. Advancing up the Peninsula, he had reached and passed the Chickahominy, and was in sight of Richmond. To this stream, the natural line of defence of the city on the north and east, numerous roads diverged from the capital, including the York River Railroad, of which the Federal commander made such excellent use; and General McClellan had thrown his left wing across the stream, advancing to a point on the railroad four or five miles from the city. Here he had erected heavy defences to protect that wing until the right wing crossed in turn. The tangled thickets of the White-oak Swamp, on his left flank, were a natural defence; but he had added to these obstacles, as we have stated, by felling trees, and guarding every approach by redoubts. In these, heavy artillery kept watch against an approaching enemy; and any attempt to attack from that quarter seemed certain to result in repulse. In front, toward Seven Pines, the chance of success was equally doubtful. The excellent works of the Federal commander bristled with artillery, and were heavily manned. It seemed thus absolutely necessary to discover some other point of assault; and, as the Federal right beyond the Chickahominy was the only point left, it was determined to attack, if possible, in that quarter.

An important question was first, however, to be decided, the character of the defences, if any, on General McClellan's right, in the direction of Old Church and Cold Harbor. A reconnoissance in force was necessary to acquire this information, and General Lee accordingly directed General Stuart, commanding the cavalry of the army, to proceed with a portion of his command to the vicinity of Old Church, in the Federal rear, and gain all the information possible of their position and defences.

V.
STUART'S "RIDE AROUND McCLELLAN."

General James E.B. Stuart, who now made his first prominent appearance upon the theatre of the war, was a Virginian by birth, and not yet thirty years of age. Resigning his commission of lieutenant in the United States Cavalry at the beginning of the war, he had joined Johnston in the Valley, and impressed that officer with a high opinion of his abilities as a cavalry officer; proceeded thence to Manassas, where he charged and broke a company of "Zouave" infantry; protected the rear of the army when Johnston retired to the Rappahannock, and bore an active part in the conflict on the Peninsula. In person he was of medium height; his frame was broad and powerful; he wore a heavy brown beard flowing upon his breast, a huge mustache of the same color, the ends curling upward; and the blue eyes, flashing beneath a "piled-up" forehead, had at times the dazzling brilliancy attributed to the eyes of the eagle. Fond of movement, adventure, bright colors, and all the pomp and pageantry of war, Stuart had entered on the struggle with ardor, and enjoyed it as the huntsman enjoys the chase. Young, ardent, ambitious, as brave as steel, ready with jest or laughter, with his banjo-player following him, going into the hottest battles humming a song, this young Virginian was, in truth, an original character, and impressed powerfully all who approached him. One who knew him well wrote: "Every thing striking, brilliant, and picturesque, seemed to centre in him. The war seemed to be to Stuart a splendid and exciting game, in which his blood coursed joyously, and his immensely strong physical organization found an arena for the display of all its faculties. The affluent life of the man craved those perils and hardships which flush the pulses and make the heart beat fast. He swung himself into the saddle at the sound of the bugle as the hunter springs on horseback; and at such moments his cheeks glowed and his huge mustache curled with enjoyment. The romance and poetry of the hard trade of arms seemed first to be inaugurated when this joyous cavalier, with his floating plume and splendid laughter, appeared upon the great arena of the war in Virginia." Precise people shook their heads, and called him frivolous, undervaluing his great ability. Those best capable of judging him were of a different opinion. Johnston wrote to him from the west: "How can I eat or sleep in peace without *you* upon the outpost?" Jackson said, when he fell at Chancellorsville: "Go back to General Stuart, and tell him to act upon his own judgment, and do what he thinks best, I have implicit confidence in him." Lee said, when he was killed at Yellow Tavern: "I can scarcely think of him without weeping." And the brave General Sedgwick, of the United States Army, said: "Stuart is the best cavalry officer ever *foaled* in North America!"

In the summer of 1862, when we present him to the reader, Stuart had as yet achieved little fame in his profession, but he was burning to distinguish himself. He responded ardently, therefore, to the order of Lee, and was soon ready with a picked force of about fifteen hundred cavalry, under some of his best officers. Among them were Colonels William H.F. Lee and Fitz-Hugh Lee—the first a son of General Lee, a graduate of West Point, and an officer of distinction afterward; the second, a son of Smith Lee, brother of the general, and famous subsequently in the most brilliant scenes of the war as the gay and gallant "General Fitz Lee," of the cavalry. With his picked force, officered by the two Lees, and other excellent lieutenants, Stuart set out on his adventurous expedition to Old Church. He effected more than he anticipated, and performed a daring feat of arms in addition. Driving the outposts from Hanover Court-House, he charged and broke a force of Federal cavalry near Old Church; pushed on to the York River Railroad, which he crossed, burning or capturing all Federal stores met with, including enormous wagon-camps; and then, finding the way back barred against him, and the Federal army on the alert, he continued his march with rapidity, passed entirely around General McClellan's army, and, building a bridge over the Chickahominy, safely reëntered the Confederate lines just as a large force made its appearance in his rear. The temporary bridge was destroyed, however, and Stuart hastened to report to his superiors. His information was important. General McClellan's right and rear were unprotected by works of any strength. If the Confederate general desired to attack in that quarter, there was nothing to prevent.

The results of Stuart's famous "ride around McClellan," as the people called it, determined General Lee to make the attack on the north bank of the stream, if he had not already so decided. It was necessary now to bring Jackson's forces from the Valley without delay, and almost equally important to mask the movement from General McClellan. To this end a very simple *ruse* was adopted. On the 11th of June, Whiting's division was embarked on the cars of the Danville Railroad at Richmond, and moved across the river to a point near Belle Isle, where at that moment a considerable number of Federal prisoners were about to be released and sent down James River. Here the train, loaded with Confederate troops, remained for some time, and *the secret* was discovered by the released prisoners. General Lee was reënforcing Jackson, in order that the latter might march on Washington. Such was the report carried to General McClellan, and it seems to have really deceived him. [Footnote: "I have no doubt Jackson has been reënforced from here."—*General McClellan to President Lincoln, June 20th.*] Whiting's division reached Lynchburg, and was thence moved by railway to Charlottesville—Jackson marched and countermarched with an elaborate pretence of advancing down the Valley—at last, one morning, the astute Confederate, who kept his own counsels, had disappeared; he was marching rapidly to join Lee on the Chickahominy. Not even his own soldiers knew what direction they were taking. They were forbidden by general order to inquire even the names of the towns they passed through; directed to reply "I don't know" to every question; and it is said that when Jackson demanded the name and regiment of a soldier robbing a cherry-tree, he could extract from the man no reply but "I don't know."

Jackson advanced with rapidity, and, on the 25th of June, was near Ashland. Here he left his forces, and rode on rapidly to Richmond. Passing unrecognized through the streets, after night, he went on to General Lee's headquarters, at a house on the "Nine-mile road," leading from the New Bridge road toward Fair Oaks Station; and here took place the first interview, since the commencement of the war, between Lee and Jackson.

What each thought of the other will be shown in the course of this narrative. We shall proceed now with the history of the great series of battles for which Jackson's appearance was the signal.

PART III.

ON THE CHICKAHOMINY.

I.

THE TWO ARMIES.

The Chickahominy, whose banks were now to be the scene of a bitter and determined conflict between the great adversaries, is a sluggish and winding stream, which, rising above Richmond, describes a curve around it, and empties its waters into the James, far below the city. Its banks are swampy, and thickly clothed with forest or underwood. From the nature of these banks, which scarcely rise in many places above the level of the water, the least freshet produces an overflow, and the stream, generally narrow and insignificant, becomes a sort of lake, covering the low grounds to the bases of the wooded bluffs extending upon each side. Numerous bridges cross the stream, from Bottom's Bridge, below the York River Railroad, to Meadow Bridge, north of the city. Of these, the Mechanicsville Bridge, about four miles from the city, and the New Bridge, about nine miles, were points of the greatest importance.

General McClellan's position has been repeatedly referred to. He had crossed a portion of his army east of Richmond, and advanced to within four or five miles of the city. The remainder, meanwhile, lay on the north bank of the stream, and swept round, in a sort of crescent, to the vicinity of Mechanicsville, where it had been anticipated General McDowell would unite with it, thereby covering its right flank, and protecting the communications with the Federal base at the White House. That this disposition of the Federal troops was faulty, in face of adversaries like Johnston and Lee, there could be no doubt. But General McClellan was the victim, it seems, of the shifting and vacillating policy of the authorities at Washington. With the arrival of the forty thousand men under McDowell, his position would have been a safe one. General McDowell did not arrive; and this unprotected right flank—left unprotected from the fact that McDowell's presence was counted on—became the point of the Confederate attack.

The amount of blame, if any, justly attributable to General McClellan, first for his inactivity, and then for his defeat by Lee, cannot be referred to here, save in a few brief sentences. A sort of feud seems to have arisen between himself and General Halleck, the commander-in-chief, stationed at Washington; and General Halleck then and afterward appears to have regarded McClellan as a soldier without decision or broad generalship. And yet McClellan does not seem to have merited the censure he received. He called persistently for reinforcements, remaining inactive meanwhile, because he estimated the Confederate army before him at two hundred thousand men, and was unwilling to assail this force, under command of soldiers like Johnston and Lee, until his own force seemed adequate to the undertaking. Another consideration was, the Confederate position in front of the powerful earthworks of the city. These works would double the Confederate strength in case of battle in front of them; and, believing himself already outnumbered, the Federal commander was naturally loath to deliver battle until reënforced. The faulty disposition of his army, divided by a stream crossed by few bridges, has been accounted for in like manner—he so disposed the troops, expecting reënforcements. But Jackson's energy delayed these. Washington was in danger, it was supposed, and General McDowell did not come. It thus happened that General McClellan awaited attack instead of making it, and that his army was so posted as to expose him to the greatest peril.

A last point is to be noted in vindication of this able soldier. Finding, at the very last moment, that he could expect no further assistance from the President or General Halleck, he resolved promptly to withdraw his exposed right wing and change his base of operations to James River, where at least his communications would be safe. This, it seems, had been determined upon just before the Confederate attack; or, if he had not then decided, General McClellan soon determined upon that plan.

To pass now to the Confederate side, where all was ready for the great movement. General Lee's army lay in front of Richmond, exactly corresponding with the front of General McClellan. The divisions of Magruder and Huger, supported by those of Longstreet and D.H. Hill, were opposite McClellan's left, on the Williamsburg and York River roads, directly east of the city. From Magruder's left, extended the division of General A.P. Hill, reaching thence up the river toward Mechanicsville; and a brigade, under General Branch lay on Hill's left near the point where the Brook Turnpike crosses the Chickahominy north of Richmond. The approaches from the east, northeast, and north, were thus carefully guarded. As the Confederates held the interior line, the whole force could be rapidly concentrated, and was thoroughly in hand, both for offensive or defensive movements.

The army thus held in Lee's grasp, and about to assail its great Federal adversary, was composed of the best portion of the Southern population. The rank and file was largely made up of men of education and high social position. And this resulted from the character of the struggle. The war was a war of invasion on the part of the North; and the ardent and high-spirited youth of the entire South threw themselves into it with enthusiasm. The heirs of ancient families and great wealth served as privates. Personal pride, love of country, indignation at the thought that a hostile section had sent an army to reduce them to submission, combined to draw into the Confederate ranks the flower of the Southern youth, and all the best fighting material. Deficient in discipline, and "hard to manage," this force was yet of the most efficient character. It could be counted on for hard work, and especially for offensive operations. And the officers placed over it shared its character.

Among these, General A.P. Hill, a Virginian by birth, was soon to be conspicuous as commander of the "Light Division," and representative of the spirit and dash and enthusiasm of the army. Under forty years of age, with a slender figure, a heavily-bearded face, dark eyes, a composed and unassuming bearing, characterized when off duty by a quiet cordiality, he was personally popular with all who approached him, and greatly beloved, both as man and commander. His chief merit as a soldier was his dash and impetus in the charge. A braver heart never beat in human breast; throughout the war he retained the respect and admiration of the army and the country; and a strange fact in relation to this eminent soldier is, that his name was uttered by both Jackson and Lee as they expired.

Associated with him in the battles of the Chickahominy, and to the end, was the able and resolute Longstreet—an officer of low and powerful stature, with a heavy, brown beard reaching to his breast, a manner marked by unalterable composure, and a countenance whose expression of phlegmatic tranquillity never varied in the hottest hours of battle. Longstreet was as famous for his bull-dog obstinacy, as Hill for his dash and enthusiasm. General Lee styled him his "old war-horse," and depended upon him, as will be seen, in some of the most critical operations of the war.

Of the young and ardent Virginian, General Magruder, the brave and resolute North-Carolinian, D.H. Hill, and other officers who subsequently acquired great reputations in the army, we have no space at present to speak. All were to coöperate in the assault on General McClellan, and do their part.

On the night of the 25th of June, all was ready for the important movement, and the troops rested on their arms, ready for the coming battle.

23

II.
LEE'S PLAN OF ASSAULT.

General Lee had been hitherto regarded as a soldier of too great caution, but his plan for the assault on General McClellan indicated the possession of a nerve approaching audacity.

Fully comprehending his enemy's strength and position, and aware that a large portion of the Federal army had crossed the Chickahominy, and was directly in his front, he had resolved to pass to the north bank of the stream with the bulk of his force, leaving only about twenty-five thousand men to protect the city, and deliver battle where defeat would prove ruinous. This plan indicated nothing less than audacity, as we have already said; but, like the audacity of the flank movement at Chancellorsville afterward, and the daring march, in disregard of General Hooker, to Pennsylvania in 1864, it was founded on profound military insight, and indicated the qualities of a great soldier.

Lee's design was to attack the Federal right wing with a part of his force, while Jackson, advancing still farther to the left, came in on their communications with the White House, and assailed them on their right and rear. Meanwhile Richmond was to be protected by General Magruder with his twenty-five thousand men, on the south bank; if McClellan fell back down the Peninsula, this force was to cross and unite with the rest; thus the Federal army would be driven from all its positions, and the fate of the whole campaign against Richmond would be decided.

Lee's general order directing the movement of the troops is here given. It possesses interest as a clear and detailed statement of his intended operations; and it will be seen that what was resolved on by the commander in his tent, his able subordinates translated detail by detail, with unimportant modifications, into action, under his eyes in the field:

HEADQUARTERS ARMY OF NORTHERN VIRGINIA,
June 24, 1862.
GENERAL ORDERS No. 75.

I. General Jackson's command will proceed to-morrow from Ashland toward the Slash Church, and encamp at some convenient point west of the Central Railroad. Branch's brigade, of A.P. Hill's division, will also, to-morrow evening, take position on the Chickahominy, near Half Sink. At three o'clock Thursday morning, 26th instant, General Jackson will advance on the road leading to Pale Green Church, communicating his march to General Branch, who will immediately cross the Chickahominy, and take the road leading to Mechanicsville. As soon as the movements of these columns are discovered, General A.P. Hill, with the rest of his division, will cross the Chickahominy near Meadow Bridge, and move direct upon Mechanicsville. To aid his advance, the heavy batteries on the Chickahominy will at the proper time open upon the batteries at Mechanicsville. The enemy being driven from Mechanicsville, and the passage across the bridge opened, General Longstreet, with his division and that of General D.H. Hill, will cross the Chickahominy at or near that point—General D.H. Hill moving to the support of General Jackson, and General Longstreet supporting General A.P. Hill—the four divisions keeping in communication with each other, and moving in *echelon* on separate roads, if practicable; the left division in advance, with skirmishers and sharp-shooters extending in their front, will sweep down the Chickahominy and endeavor to drive the enemy from his position above New Bridge; General Jackson, bearing well to his left, turning Beaver Dam Creek, and taking the direction toward Cold Harbor. They will then press forward toward York River Railroad, closing upon the enemy's rear and forcing him down the Chickahominy. Any advance of the enemy toward Richmond will be prevented by vigorously following his rear, and crippling and arresting his progress.

II. The divisions under Generals Huger and Magruder will hold their positions in front of the enemy against attack, and make such demonstrations, Thursday, as to discover his operations. Should opportunity offer, the feint will be converted into a real attack; and, should an abandonment of his intrenchments by the enemy be discovered, he will be closely pursued.

III. The Third Virginia cavalry will observe the Charles City road. The Fifth Virginia, the First North Carolina, and the Hampton Legion cavalry will observe the Darbytown, Varina, and Osborne roads. Should a movement of the enemy, down the Chickahominy, be discovered, they will close upon his flank, and endeavor to arrest his march.

IV. General Stuart, with the First, Fourth, and Ninth Virginia cavalry, the cavalry of Cobb's Legion, and the Jeff Davis Legion, will cross the Chickahominy, to-morrow, and take position to the left of General Jackson's line of march. The main body will be held in reserve, with scouts well extended to the front and left. General Stuart will keep General Jackson informed of the movements of the enemy on his left, and will coöperate with him in his advance. The Sixteenth Virginia cavalry, Colonel Davis, will remain on the Nine-mile road.

V. General Ransom's brigade, of General Holmes's command, will be placed in reserve on the Williamsburg road, by General Huger, to whom he will report for orders.

VI. Commanders of divisions will cause their commands to be provided with three days' cooked rations. The necessary ambulances and ordinance-trains will be ready to accompany the divisions, and receive orders from their respective commanders. Officers in charge of all trains will invariably remain with them. Batteries and wagons will keep on the right of the road. The Chief-Engineer, Major Stevens, will assign engineer officers to each division, whose duty it will be to make provision for overcoming all difficulties to the progress of the troops. The staff-departments will give the necessary instructions to facilitate the movements herein directed.

By command of General LEE: R.H. CHILTON, *A.A. General.*

This order speaks for itself, and indicates Lee's plan of battle in all its details. Further comment is unnecessary; and we proceed to narrate the events which followed. In doing so, we shall strive to present a clear and intelligible account of what occurred, rather than to indulge in the warlike splendors of style which characterized the "army correspondents" of the journals during the war. Such a treatment of the subject is left to others, who write under the influence of partisan afflatus, rather than with the judicious moderation of the historian. Nor are battles themselves the subjects of greatest interest to the thoughtful student. The combinations devised by great commanders are of more interest than the actual struggles. We have therefore dwelt at greater length upon the plans of Generals Lee and McClellan than we shall dwell upon the actual fighting of their armies.

III.

THE BATTLE OF THE CHICKAHOMINY.

On the morning of the 26th of June, 1862, all was ready for the great encounter of arms between the Confederates and the Federal forces on the Chickahominy. General Jackson had been delayed on his march from the mountains, and had not yet arrived; but it was known that he was near, and would soon make his appearance; and, in the afternoon, General Lee accordingly directed that the movement should commence. At the word, General A.P. Hill moved from his camps to Meadow Bridge, north of Richmond; crossed the Chickahominy there, and moved rapidly on Mechanicsville, where a small Federal force, behind intrenchments, guarded the head of the bridge. This force was not a serious obstacle, and Hill soon disposed of it. He attacked the Federal works, stormed them after a brief struggle, and drove the force which had occupied them back toward Beaver Dam Creek, below. The Mechanicsville bridge was thus cleared; and, in compliance with his orders from Lee, General Longstreet hastened to throw his division across. Hill had meanwhile pressed forward on the track of the retreating enemy, and, a mile or two below, found himself in front of a much more serious obstruction than that encountered at the bridge, namely, the formidable position held by the enemy on Beaver Dam Creek.

The ground here is of a peculiar character, and admirably adapted for a defensive position against an enemy advancing from above. On the opposite side of a narrow valley, through which runs Beaver Dam Creek, rises a bold, almost precipitous, bluff, and the road which the Confederates were compelled to take bends abruptly to the right when near the stream, thus exposing the flank of the assaulting party to a fire from the bluff. As Hill's column pushed forward to attack this position, it was met by a determined fire of artillery and small-arms from the crest beyond the stream, where a large force of riflemen, in pits, were posted, with infantry supports. Before this artillery-fire, raking his flanks and doing heavy execution, Hill was compelled to fall back. It was impossible to cross the stream in face of the fusillade and cannon. The attack ended after dark with the withdrawal of the Confederates; but at dawn Hill resumed the struggle, attempting to cross at another point, lower down the stream. This attempt was in progress when the Federal troops were seen rapidly falling back from their strong position; and intelligence soon came that this was in consequence of the arrival of Jackson, who had passed around the Federal right flank above, and forced them to retire toward the main body of the Federal army below.

No time was now lost. The memorable 27th of June had dawned clear and cloudless, and the brilliant sunshine gave promise of a day on which no interference of the elements would check the bloody work to be performed. Hill advanced steadily on the track of the retiring Federal forces, who had left evidences of their precipitate retreat all along the road, and, about noon, came in front of the very powerful position of the main body of the enemy, near Cold Harbor.

General McClellan had drawn up his forces on a ridge along the southern bank of Powhite Creek, a small water-course which, flowing from the northeast, empties below New Bridge into the Chickahominy. His left, nearest the Chickahominy, was protected by a deep ravine in front, which he had filled with sharp-shooters; and his right rested upon elevated ground, near the locality known as Maghee's House. In front, the whole line of battle, which described a curve backward to cover the bridges in rear, was protected by difficult approaches. The ground was either swampy, or covered with tangled undergrowth, or both. The ridge held by the Federal forces had been hastily fortified by breastworks of felled trees and earth, behind which the long lines of infantry, supported by numerous artillery, awaited the attack.

The amount of the Federal force has been variously stated. The impression of the Confederates differed from the subsequent statements of Federal writers. "The principal part of the Federal army," says General Lee, in his report, "was now on the north side of the Chickahominy." The force has been placed by Northern writers at only thirty, or at most thirty-five thousand. If this was the whole number of troops engaged, from first to last, in the battle, the fact is highly creditable to the Federal arms, as the struggle was long doubtful. No doubt the exact truth will some day be put upon record, and justice will be done to both the adversaries.

The Federal force was commanded by the brave and able General Fitz-John Porter, with General Morell commanding his right, General Sykes his left, and General McCall forming a second line. Slocum's division, and the brigades of Generals French and Meagher, afterward reënforced Porter, who now prepared, with great coolness, for the Confederate attack.

The moment had come. A.P. Hill, pressing forward rapidly, with Longstreet's division on the right, reached Cold Harbor, in front of the Federal centre, about noon. Hill immediately attacked, and an engagement of the most obstinate character ensued. General Lee, accompanied by General Longstreet, had ridden from his headquarters, on the Nine-mile road, to the scene of action, and now witnessed in person the fighting of the troops, who charged under his eye, closing in in a nearly hand-to-hand conflict with the enemy. This was, no doubt, the first occasion on which a considerable portion of the men had seen him—certainly in battle—and that air of supreme calmness which always characterized him in action must have made a deep impression upon them. He was clad simply, and wore scarcely any badges of rank. A felt hat drooped low over the broad forehead, and the eyes beneath were calm and unclouded. Add a voice of measured calmness, the air of immovable composure which marked the erect military figure, evidently at home in the saddle, and the reader will have a correct conception of General Lee's personal appearance in the first of the great battles of his career.

Hill attacked with that dash and obstinacy which from this time forward characterized him, but succeeded in making no impression on the Federal line. In every assault he was repulsed with heavy loss. The Federal artillery, which was handled with skill and coolness, did great execution upon his column, as it rushed forward, and the infantry behind their works stood firm in spite of the most determined efforts to drive them from the ridge. Three of Hill's regiments reached the crest, and fought hand to hand over the breastworks, but they were speedily repulsed and driven from the crest, and, after two hours' hard fighting, Hill found that he had lost heavily and effected nothing.

It was now past two o'clock in the afternoon, and General Lee listened with anxiety for the sound of guns from the left, which would herald the approach of General Jackson. Nothing was heard from that quarter, however, and affairs were growing critical. The Confederate attack had been repulsed—the Federal position seemed impregnable—and "it became apparent," says General Lee, "that the enemy was gradually gaining ground." Under these circumstances, General McClellan might adopt either one of the two courses both alike dangerous to the Confederates. He might cross a heavy force to the assistance of General Porter, thus enabling that officer to assume the offensive; or, finding Lee thus checked, he might advance on Magruder, crush the small force under him, and seize on Richmond, which would be at his mercy. It was thus necessary to act without delay, while awaiting the appearance of Jackson. General Lee, accordingly, directed General Longstreet, who had taken position to the right of Cold Harbor, to make a feint against the Federal left, and thus relieve the pressure on Hill. Longstreet proceeded with promptness to obey the order; advanced in face of a heavy fire, and with a cross-fire of artillery raking his right from over the Chickahominy, and made the feint which had been ordered by General Lee. It effected nothing; and, to attain the desired result, it was found necessary to turn the feint into a real attack. This Longstreet proceeded to do, first dispersing with a single volley a force of cavalry which had the temerity to charge his infantry. As he advanced and attacked the powerful position before him, the roar of guns, succeeded by loud cheers, was heard on the left of Lee's line.

Jackson had arrived and thrown his troops into action without delay. He then rode forward to Cold Harbor, where General Lee awaited him, and the two soldiers shook hands in the midst of tumultuous cheering from the troops, who had received intelligence that Jackson's corps had joined them. The contrast between the two men was extremely striking. We have presented a brief sketch of Lee's personal appearance upon the occasion—of the grave commander-in-chief, with his erect and graceful seat in the saddle, his imposing dignity of demeanor, and his calm and measured tones, as deliberate as though he were in a drawing-room. Jackson was a very different personage. He was clad in a dingy old coat, wore a discolored cadet-cap, tilted almost upon his nose, and rode a rawboned horse, with short stirrups, which raised his knees in the most ungraceful manner. Neither in his face nor figure was there the least indication of the great faculties of the man, and a more awkward-looking personage it would be impossible to imagine. In his hand he held a lemon, which he sucked from time to time, and his demeanor was abstracted and absent.

As Jackson approached, Lee rode toward him and greeted him with a cordial pressure of the hand.

"Ah, general," said Lee, "I am very glad to see you. I hoped to be with you before!"

Jackson made a twitching movement of his head, and replied in a few words, rather jerked from the lips than deliberately uttered.

Lee had paused, and now listened attentively to the long roll of musketry from the woods, where Hill and Longstreet were engaged; then to the still more incessant and angry roar from the direction of Jackson's own troops, who had closed in upon the Federal forces.

"That fire is very heavy," said Lee. "Do you think your men can stand it?"

Jackson listened for a moment, with his head bent toward one shoulder, as was customary with him, for he was deaf, he said, in one ear, "and could not hear out of the other," and replied briefly:

"They can stand almost any thing! They can stand that!"

He then, after receiving General Lee's instructions, immediately saluted and returned to his corps—Lee remaining still at Cold Harbor, which was opposite the Federal centre.

[Illustration: Lee and Jackson at Cold harbor.]

The arrival of Jackson changed in a moment the aspect of affairs in every part of the field. Whitney's division of his command took position on Longstreet's left; the command of General D.H. Hill, on the extreme right of the whole line, and Ewell's division, with part of Jackson's old division, supported A.P. Hill. No sooner had these dispositions been made, than General Lee ordered an attack along the whole line. It was now five or six o'clock, and the sun was sinking. From that moment until night came, the battle raged with a fury unsurpassed in any subsequent engagement of the war. The Texan troops, under General Hood, especially distinguished themselves. These, followed by their comrades, charged the Federal left on the bluff, and, in spite of a desperate resistance, carried the position. "The enemy were driven," says General Lee, "from the ravine to the first line of breastworks, over which one impetuous column dashed, up to the intrenchments on the crest." Here the Federal artillery was captured, their line driven from the hill, and in other parts of the field a similar success followed the attack. As night fell, their line gave way in all parts, and the remnants of General Porter's command retreated to the bridges over the Chickahominy.

The first important passage of arms between General McClellan and General Lee—and it may be added the really decisive one—had terminated in a great success on the side of the Confederates.

IV.

THE RETREAT.

The battle of Cold Harbor—or, as General Lee styles it in his report, the "battle of the Chickahominy"—was the decisive struggle between the great adversaries, and determined the fate of General McClellan's campaign against Richmond.

This view is not held by writers on the Northern side, who represent the battle in question as only the first of a series of engagements, all of pretty nearly equal importance, and mere incidents attending General McClellan's change of base to the shores of the James River. Such a theory seems unfounded. If the battle at Cold Harbor had resulted in a Federal victory, General McClellan would have advanced straight on Richmond, and the capture of the city would inevitably have followed. But at Cold Harbor he sustained a decisive defeat. His whole campaign was reversed, and came to naught, from the events occurring between noon and nightfall on the 27th of June. The result of that obstinate encounter was not a Federal success, leading to the fall of Richmond, but a Federal defeat, which led to the retreat to the James River, and the failure of the whole campaign against the Confederate capital.

It is conceded that General McClellan really intended to change his base; but after the battle of Cold Harbor every thing had changed. He no longer had under him a high-spirited army, moving to take up a stronger position, but a weary and dispirited multitude of human beings, hurrying along to gain the shelter of the gunboats on the James River, with the enemy pursuing closely, and worrying them at every step. To the condition of the Federal army one of their own officers testifies, and his expressions are so strong as wellnigh to move the susceptibilities of an opponent. "We were ordered to retreat," says General Hooker, "and it was like the retreat of a whipped army. We retreated like a parcel of sheep; everybody on the road at the same time; and a few shots from the rebels would have panic-stricken the whole command."[1]

Such was the condition of that great army which had fought so bravely, standing firm so long against the headlong assaults of the flower of the Southern troops. It was the battle at Cold Harbor which had produced this state of things, thereby really deciding the result of the campaign. To attribute to that action, therefore, no more importance than attached to the engagements on the retreat to James River, seems in opposition to the truth of history.

We shall present only a general narrative of the famous retreat which reflected the highest credit upon General McClellan, and will remain his greatest glory. He, at least, was too good a soldier not to understand that the battle of the 27th was a decisive one. He determined to retreat, without risking another action, to the banks of the James River, where the Federal gunboats would render a second attack from the Confederates a hazardous undertaking; and, "on the evening of the 27th of June," as he says in his official report, "assembled the corps commanders at his headquarters, and informed them of his plan, its reasons, and his choice of route, and method of execution." Orders were then issued to General Keyes to move with his corps across the White-Oak Swamp Bridge, and, taking up a position with his artillery on the opposite side, cover the passage of the rest of the troops; the trains and supplies at Savage Station, on the York River Railroad, were directed to be withdrawn; and the corps commanders were ordered to move with such provisions, munitions, and sick, as they could transport, on the direct road to Harrison's Landing.

These orders were promptly carried out. Before dawn on the 29th the Federal army took up the line of march, and the great retrograde movement was successfully begun. An immense obstacle to its success lay in the character of the country through which it was necessary to pass. White Oak Swamp is an extensive morass, similar to that skirting the banks of the Chickahominy, and the passage through it is over narrow, winding, and difficult roads, which furnish the worst possible pathways for wagons, artillery, or even troops. It was necessary, however, to use these highways or none, and General McClellan resolutely entered upon his critical movement.

General Lee was yet in doubt as to his opponent's designs, and the fact is highly creditable to General McClellan. A portion of the Federal army still remained on the left bank of the Chickahominy, and it might be the intention of McClellan to push forward reënforcements from the Peninsula, fight a second battle for the protection of his great mass of supplies at the White House, or, crossing his whole army to the left bank of the Chickahominy by the lower bridges, retreat down the Peninsula by the same road followed in advancing. All that General Lee could do, under these circumstances, was to remain near Cold Harbor with his main body, send a force toward the York River road, on the eastern bank of the Chickahominy, to check any Federal attempt to cross there, and await further developments.

It was not until the morning of the 29th that General McClellan's designs became apparent. It was then ascertained that he had commenced moving toward James River with his entire army, and Lee issued prompt orders for the pursuit. While a portion of the Confederate army followed closely upon the enemy's rear, other bodies were directed to move by the Williamsburg and Charles City roads, and intercept him, or assail his flanks. If these movements were promptly made, and no unnecessary delay took place, it was expected that the Federal army would be brought to bay in the White-Oak Swamp, and a final victory be achieved by the Confederates.

These complicated movements were soon in full progress, and at various points on the line of retreat fierce fighting ensued. General Magruder, advancing to Savage Station, an important depot of Federal stores, on the York River Railroad, encountered on the 29th, the powerful Federal rear-guard, which fought obstinately until night, when it retired. Next day Generals Longstreet and A.P. Hill had pushed down the Long Bridge road, and on the next day (June 30th) came on the retreating column which was vigorously engaged. From the character of the ground, little, however, was effected. The enemy fought with obstinate courage, and repulsed every assault. The battle raged until after nightfall, when the Federal army continued to retreat.

These actions were the most important, and in both the Confederates had failed to effect any important results.

Even Jackson, who had been delayed, by the destruction of the Chickahominy bridges, in crossing to the south bank from the vicinity of Cold Harbor, and had followed in rear of the rest of the army, found himself checked by General McClellan's admirable disposition for the protection of his rear. Jackson made every effort to strike a decisive blow at the Federal rear in the White-Oak Swamp, but he found a bridge in his front destroyed, the enemy holding the opposite side in strong force, and, when he endeavored to force a passage, the determined fire from their artillery rendered it impossible for him to do so. General McClellan had thus foiled the generalship of Lee, and the hard fighting of Stonewall Jackson. His excellent military judgement had defeated every attempt made to crush him. On the 1st of July he had successfully passed the terrible swamp, in spite of all his enemies, and his army was drawn up on the wellnigh impregnable heights of Malvern Hill.

A last struggle took place at Malvern Hill, and the Confederate assault failed at all points. Owing to the wooded nature of the ground, and the absence of accurate information in regard to it, the attack was made under very great difficulties and effected nothing. The Federal troops resisted courageously, and inflicted heavy loss upon the assailing force, which advanced to the muzzles of the Federal cannon, but did not carry the heights; and at nightfall the battle ceased, the Confederates having suffered a severe repulse.

On the next morning, General McClellan had disappeared toward Harrison's Landing, to which he conducted his army safely, without further molestation, and the long and bitter struggle was over.

V.

RICHMOND IN DANGER—LEE'S VIEWS.

We have presented a sufficiently full narrative of the great battles of the Chickahominy to enable the reader to form his own opinion of the events, and the capacity of the two leaders who directed them. Full justice has been sought to be done to the eminent military abilities of General McClellan, and the writer is not conscious that he has done more than justice to General Lee.

Lee has not escaped criticism, and was blamed by many persons for not putting an end to the Federal army on the retreat through White-Oak Swamp. To this criticism, it may be said in reply, that putting an end to nearly or quite one hundred thousand men is a difficult undertaking; and that in one instance, at least, the failure of one of his subordinates in arriving promptly, reversed his plans at the most critical moment of the struggle. General Lee himself, however, states the main cause of failure: "Under ordinary circumstances," he says, "the Federal army should have been destroyed. Its escape is due to the causes already stated. Prominent among them is the want of timely and correct information. This fact, attributed chiefly to the character of the country, enabled General McClellan skilfully to conceal his retreat, and to add much to the obstruction with which Nature had beset the way of our pursuing columns. But regret that more was not accomplished, gives way to gratitude to the Sovereign Ruler of the Universe for the results achieved."

The reader will form his own opinion whether Lee was or was not to blame for this want of accurate information, which would seem, however, to be justly attributable to the War Department at Richmond, rather than to an officer who had been assigned to command only three or four weeks before. Other criticisms of Lee referred to his main plan of operations, and the danger to which he exposed Richmond by leaving only twenty-five thousand men in front of it, when he began his movement against General McClellan's right wing, beyond the Chickahominy. General Magruder, who commanded this force of twenty-five thousand men left to guard the capital, expressed afterward, in his official report, his views of the danger to which the city had been exposed. He wrote:

"From the time at which the enemy withdrew his forces to this side of the Chickahominy, and destroyed the bridges, to the moment of his evacuation, that is, from Friday night until Saturday morning, I considered the situation of our army as extremely critical and perilous. The larger portion of it was on the opposite side of the Chickahominy. The bridges had been all destroyed; but one was rebuilt—the New Bridge—which was commanded fully by the enemy's guns from Goulding's; and there were but twenty-five thousand men between his army of one hundred thousand and Richmond…. Had McClellan massed his whole force in column, and advanced it against any point of our line of battle, as was done at Austerlitz under similar circumstances by the greatest captain of any age, though the head of his column would have suffered greatly, its momentum would have insured him success, and the occupation of our works about Richmond, and consequently the city, might have been his reward. His failure to do so is the best evidence that our wise commander fully understood the character of his opponent."

To this portion of General Magruder's report General Lee appended the following "Remarks" in forwarding it:

"General Magruder is under a misapprehension as to the separation of troops operating on the north side of the Chickahominy from those under himself and General Huger on the south side. He refers to this subject on pages 2, 3, 4, 5, 6, and 7, of his report.

"The troops on the two sides of the river were only separated until we succeeded in occupying the position near what is known as New Bridge, which occurred before twelve o'clock M. on Friday, June 27th, and before the attack on the enemy at Gaines's Mill.

"From the time we reached the position referred to, I regarded communication between the two wings of our army as reëstablished.

"The bridge referred to, and another about three-quarters of a mile above, were ordered to be repaired before noon on Friday, and the New Bridge was sufficiently rebuilt to be passed by artillery on Friday night, and the one above it was used for the passage of wagons, ambulances, and troops, early on Saturday morning.

"Besides this, all other bridges above New Bridge, and all the fords above that point, were open to us."

To this General Magruder subsequently responded as follows:

"New Bridge was finished on Friday evening, the 27th, instead of Saturday, 28th of June.

"I wrote from memory in reference to the time of its being finished.

"It was reported to me that the bridge three-quarters of a mile above was attempted to be crossed by troops (I think Ransom's brigade), on Saturday morning, from the south to the north side, but that, finding the bridge or the approach to it difficult, they came down and crossed at New Bridge on the same morning.

"My statement in regard to these bridges was not intended as a criticism on General Lee's plan, but to show the position of the troops, with a view to the proper understanding of my report, and to prove that the enemy might have reasonably entertained a design, after concentrating his troops, to march on Richmond."

We shall not detain the reader by entering upon a full discussion of the interesting question here raised. General Lee, as his observations on General Magruder's report show, did not regard Richmond as exposed to serious danger, and was confident of his ability to recross the Chickahominy and go to its succor in the event of an attack on the city by General McClellan. Had this prompt recrossing of the stream here, even, been impracticable, it may still be a question whether General Lee did not, in his movement against the Federal right wing with the bulk of his army, follow the dictates of sound generalship. In war, something must be risked, and occasions arise which render it necessary to disregard general maxims. It is one of the first principles of military science that a commander should always keep open his line of retreat; but the moment may come when his best policy is to burn the bridges behind him. Of Lee's movement against General McClellan's right, it may be said that it was based on the broadest good sense and the best generalship. The situation of affairs rendered an attack in some quarter essential to the safety of the capital, which was about to be hemmed in on all sides. To attack the left of General McClellan, promised small results. It had been tried and had failed; his right alone remained. It was possible, certainly, that he would mass his army, and, crushing Magruder, march into Richmond; but it was not probable that he would make the attempt. The Federal commander was known to be a soldier disposed to caution rather than audacity. The small amount of force under General Magruder was a secret which he could not be expected to know. That General Lee took these facts into consideration, as General Magruder intimates, may or may not have been the fact; and the whole discussion may be fairly summed up, perhaps, by saying that success vindicated the course adopted. "Success, after all, is the test of merit," said the brave Albert Sydney Johnston, and Talleyrand compressed much sound reasoning in the pithy maxim, "Nothing succeeds like success."

On the 2d of July the campaign was over, and General McClellan must have felt, in spite of his hopeful general orders to the troops, and dispatches to his Government, that the great struggle for Richmond had virtually ended. A week before, he had occupied a position within a few miles of the city, with a numerous army in the highest spirits, and of thorough efficiency. Now, he lay on the banks of James River, thirty miles away from the capital, and his army was worn out by the tremendous ordeal it had passed through, and completely discouraged. We have not dwelt upon the horrors of the retreat, and the state of the army, which Northern writers painted at the time in the gloomiest colors. For the moment, it was no longer the splendid war-engine it had been, and was again afterward. Nothing could be done with it, and General McClellan knew the fact. Without fresh troops, a renewed advance upon Richmond was a mere dream.

No further attack was made by General Lee, who remained for some days inactive in the hot forests of Charles City. His reasons for refraining from a new assault on General McClellan are summed up in one or two sentences of his report: "The Federal commander," he says, "immediately began to fortify his position, which was one of great natural strength, flanked on each side by a creek, and the approach to his front commanded by the heavy guns of his shipping, in addition to those mounted in his intrenchments. It was deemed inexpedient to attack him, and in view of the condition of our troops, who had been marching and fighting almost incessantly for seven days under the most trying circumstances, it was determined to withdraw, in order to afford them the repose of which they stood so much in need."

On the 8th of July, General Lee accordingly directed his march back toward Richmond, and the troops went into camp and rested.

30

VI.

LEE AND McCLELLAN—THEIR IDENTITY OF OPINION.

General Lee had thus, at the outset of his career, as commander of the Confederate army, saved the capital by a blow at the enemy as sudden as it was resistless. The class of persons who are never satisfied, and delight in fault-finding under all circumstances, declared that a great general would have crushed the enemy on their retreat; these certainly were in a minority; the people at large greeted Lee as the author of a great deliverance worked out for them, and, on his return to Richmond, he was received with every mark of gratitude and honor. He accepted this public ovation with the moderation and dignity which characterized his demeanor afterward, under all circumstances, either of victory or defeat. It was almost impossible to discover in his bearing at this time, as on other great occasions, any evidences whatever of elation. Success, like disaster, seemed to find him calm, collected, and as nearly unimpressible as is possible for a human being.

The character of the man led him to look upon success or failure with this supreme composure, which nothing seemed able to shake; but in July, 1862, he probably understood that the Confederate States were still as far as ever from having achieved the objects of the war. General McClellan had been defeated in battle, but the great resources of the United States Government would enable it promptly to put other and larger armies in the field. Even the defeated army was still numerous and dangerous, for it consisted, according to McClellan's report, of nearly or quite ninety thousand men; and the wise brain of its commander had devised a plan of future operations which promised far greater results than the advance on Richmond from the Chickahominy.

We shall touch, in passing, on this interesting subject, but shall first ask the reader's attention to a communication addressed, by General McClellan, at this time to President Lincoln. It is one of those papers which belong to history, and should be placed upon record. It not only throws the clearest light on the character and views of General Lee's great adversary, but expresses with admirable lucidity the sentiments of a large portion of the Federal people at the time. The President had invited a statement of General McClellan's views on the conduct of the war, and on July 7th, in the very midst of the scenes of disaster at Harrison's Landing, McClellan wrote these statesmanlike words:

"This rebellion has assumed the character of a war; as such it should be regarded, and it should be conducted upon the highest principles know to Christian civilization. It should not be a war looking to the subjugation of the people of any State in any event. It should not be at all a war upon population, but against armed forces and political organization. Neither confiscation of property, political executions, territorial organizations of States, nor forcible abolition of slavery, should be contemplated for a moment. In prosecuting the war all private property and unarmed persons should be strictly protected, subject only to the necessity of military operations. All private property taken for military use should be paid or receipted for; pillage and waste should be treated as high crimes; all unnecessary trespass sternly prohibited, and offensive demeanor by the military toward citizens promptly rebuked. Military arrests should not be tolerated, except in places where active hostilities exist, and oaths not required by enactments constitutionally made should be neither demanded nor received. Military government should be confined to the preservation of public order and the protection of political right. Military power should not be allowed to interfere with the relations of servitude, either by supporting or impairing the authority of the master, except for repressing disorder, as in other cases. Slaves contraband under the Act of Congress, seeking military protection, should receive it. The right of the Government to appropriate permanently to its own service claims to slave-labor should be asserted, and the right of the owner to compensation therefor should be recognized.

"This principle might be extended upon grounds of military necessity and security to all the slaves of a particular State, thus working manumission in such State; and in Missouri, perhaps in Western Virginia also, and possibly even in Maryland, the expediency of such a measure is only a question of time.

"A system of policy thus constitutional, and pervaded by the influences of Christianity and freedom, would receive the support of almost all truly loyal men, would deeply impress the rebel masses and all foreign nations, and it might be humbly hoped that it would commend itself to the favor of the Almighty.

"Unless the principles governing the future conduct of our struggle shall be made known and approved, the effort to obtain requisite forces will be almost hopeless. A declaration of radical views, especially upon slavery, will rapidly disintegrate our present armies.

"The policy of the Government must be supported by concentrations of military power. The national forces should not be dispersed in expeditions, posts of occupation, and numerous armies; but should be mainly collected into masses, and brought to bear upon the armies of the

31

Confederate States. Those armies thoroughly defeated, the political structure which they support would soon cease to exist.

"In carrying out any system of policy which you may form, you will require a commander-in-chief of the army—one who possesses your confidence, understands your views, and who is competent to execute your orders, by directing the military forces of the nation to the accomplishment of the objects by you proposed. I do not ask that place for myself. I am willing to serve you in such positions as you may assign me, and I will do so as faithfully as ever subordinate served superior. I may be on the brink of eternity, and, as I hope forgiveness from my Maker, I have written this letter with sincerity toward you, and from love for my country."

This noble and earnest exposition of his opinion, upon the proper mode of conducting the war, will reflect honor upon General McClellan when his military achievements are forgotten. It discusses the situation of affairs, both from the political and military point of view, in a spirit of the broadest statesmanship, and with the acumen of a great soldier. That it had no effect, is the clearest indication upon which the war was thenceforward to be conducted.

The removal of General McClellan, as holding views opposed to the party in power, is said to have resulted from this communication. It certainly placed him in open antagonism to General Halleck, the Federal Secretary of War, and, as this antagonism had a direct effect upon even connected with the subject of our memoir, we shall briefly relate now it was now displayed.

Defeated on the Chickahominy, and seeing little to encourage an advance, on the left bank of the James, upon Richmond, General McClellan proposed to cross that river and operate against the capital and its communications, near Petersburg. The proof of McClellan's desire to undertake this movement, which afterward proved so successful under General Grant, is found in a memorandum, by General Halleck himself, of what took place on a visit paid by him to McClellan, at Harrison's Landing, on July 25, 1862.

"I stated to him," says General Halleck, "that the object of my visit was to ascertain from him his views and wishes in regard to future operations. He said that he proposed to cross the James River at that point, attack Petersburg, and cut off the enemy's communications by that route South, making no further demonstration for the present against Richmond. I stated to him very frankly my views in regard to the manner and impracticability of the plan;" and nothing further, it seems, was said of this highly "impracticable" plan of operations. It became practicable afterward under General Grant; McClellan was not permitted to essay it in July, 1862, from the fact that it had been resolved to relieve him from command, or from General Halleck's inability to perceive its good sense.

General Lee's views upon this subject coincided completely with those of General McClellan. He expressed at this time, to those in his confidence, the opinion that Richmond could be assailed to greater advantage from the South, as a movement of the enemy in that direction would menace her communications with the Gulf States; and events subsequently proved the soundness of this view. Attacks from all other quarters failed, including a repetition by General Grant of McClellan's attempt from the side of the Chickahominy. When General Grant carried out his predecessor's plan of assailing the city from the direction of Petersburg, he succeeded in putting an end to the war.

PART IV.

THE WAR ADVANCES NORTHWARD

I.

LEE'S PROTEST.

General Lee remained in front of Richmond, watching General McClellan, but intelligence soon reached him from the upper Rappahannock that another army was advancing in that quarter, and had already occupied the county of Culpepper, with the obvious intention of capturing Gordonsville, the point of junction of the Orange and Alexandria and Virginia Central Railroads, and advancing thence upon Richmond.

The great defeat on the Chickahominy had only inspired the Federal authorities with new energy. Three hundred thousand new troops were called for, large bounties were held out as an inducement to enlistment, negro-slaves in regions occupied by the United States armies were directed to be enrolled as troops, and military commanders were authorized to seize upon whatever was "necessary or convenient for their commands," without compensation to the owners. This indicated the policy upon which it was now intended to conduct the war, and the army occupying Culpepper proceeded to carry out the new policy in every particular.

This force consisted of the troops which had served under Generals Banks, McDowell, and Fremont—a necleus—and reënforcements from the army of McClellan, together with the troops under General Burnside, were hastening to unite with the newly-formed army. It was styled the "Army of Virginia," and was placed under command of Major-General John Pope, who had hitherto served in the West. General Pope had procured the command, it is said, by impressing the authorities with a high opinion of his energy and activity. In these qualities, General McClellan was supposed to be deficient; and the new commander, coming from a region where the war was conducted on a different plan, it was said, would be able to infuse new life into the languid movements in Virginia. General Pope had taken special pains to allay the fears of the Federal authorities for the safety of Washington. He intended to "lie off on the flanks" of Lee's army, he said, and render it impossible for the rebels to advance upon the capital while he occupied that threatening position. When asked if, with an army like General McClellan's, he would find any difficulty in marching through the South to New Orleans, General Pope replied without hesitation, "I should suppose not."

This confident view of things seems to have procured General Pope his appointment, and it will soon be seen that he proceeded to conduct military operations upon principles very different from those announced by General McClellan. War, as carried on by General Pope, was to be war *à l'outrance.* General McClellan had written: "The war should not be at all a war upon population, but against armed forces … all private property, taken for military use, should be paid for; pillage and waste should be treated as high crimes; all unnecessary trespass sternly prohibited, and offensive demeanor by the military toward citizens promptly rebuked." The new commander intended to act upon a very different principle, and to show that he possessed more activity and resolution than his predecessor.

General Pope's assumption of the command was signalized by much pomp and animated general orders. He arrived in a train decked out with streamers, and issued an order in which he said to the troops: "I desire you to dismiss from your minds certain phrases which I am sorry to find much in vogue among you. I hear constantly of taking strong positions and holding them, *of lines of retreat and bases of supplies.* Let us discard such ideas. The strongest position which a soldier should desire to occupy is the one from which he can most easily advance upon the enemy. Let us study the probable line of retreat of our opponents, *and leave our own to take care of itself. Let us look before, and not behind. Disaster and shame look in the rear.*" The result, as will be seen, furnished a grotesque commentary upon that portion of General Pope's order which we have italicized. In an address to the army, he added further: "I have come to you from the West, where we have always seen the backs of our enemies—from an army whose business it has been to seek the adversary, and beat him when found—where policy has been attack, and not defence. I presume I have been called here to pursue the same system."

Such was the tenor of General Pope's orders on assuming command—orders which were either intended seriously as an announcement of his real intentions, or as a blind to persuade the Confederates that his force was large.

Unfortunately for the region in which he now came to operate, General Pope did not confine himself to these flourishes of rhetoric. He proceeded to inaugurate a military policy in vivid contrast to General McClellan's. His "expatriation orders" directed that all male citizens disloyal to the United States should be immediately arrested; the oath of allegiance to the United States Government should be proffered them, and, "if they furnished sufficient security for its observance," they should be set free again. If they refused the oath, they should be sent beyond the Federal lines; and, if afterward found within his lines, they should be treated as spies, "and shot, their property to be seized and applied to the public use." All communication with persons living within the Southern lines was forbidden; such communication should subject the individual guilty of it to be treated as *a spy*. Lastly, General Pope's subordinates were directed to arrest prominent citizens, and hold them as hostages for the good behavior of the population. If his soldiers were "bushwhacked"—that is to say, attacked on their foraging expeditions—the prominent citizens thus held as hostages were to *suffer death*.

It is obvious that war carried on upon such principles is rapine. General Pope ventured, however, upon the new programme; and a foreign periodical, commenting upon the result, declared that this commander had prosecuted hostilities against the South "in a way that cast mankind two centuries back toward barbarism." We shall not pause to view the great outrages committed by the Federal troops in Culpepper. They have received thus much comment rather to introduce the following communication to the Federal authorities, from General Lee, than to record what is known now to the Old World as well as the New. Profoundly outraged and indignant at these cruel and oppressive acts, General Lee, by direction of the Confederate authorities, addressed, on the 2d of August, the following note to General Halleck:

HEADQUARTERS ARMY OF THE C.S., /
NEAR RICHMOND, VA., *August* 2, 1862.;
To the General commanding the U.S. Army, Washington:
GENERAL: In obedience to the order of his Excellency, the President of the Confederate States, I have the honor to make you the following communication:

On the 22d of July last a cartel for a general exchange of prisoners was signed by Major-General John A. Dix, on behalf of the United States, and by Major-General D.H. Hill, on the part of this government. By the terms of that cartel it is stipulated that all prisoners of war hereafter taken shall be discharged on parole until exchanged. Scarcely had the cartel been signed, when the military authorities of the United States commenced a practice changing the character of the war, from such as becomes civilized nations, into a campaign of indiscriminate robbery and murder.

A general order issued by the Secretary of War of the United States, in the city of Washington, on the very day that the cartel was signed in Virginia, directs the military commanders of the United States to take the property of our people, for the convenience and use of the army, without compensation.

A general order issued by Major-General Pope, on the 23d of July last, the day after the date of the cartel, directs the murder of our peaceful citizens as spies, if found quietly tilling their farms in his rear, even outside of his lines.

And one of his brigadier-generals, Steinwehr, has seized innocent and peaceful inhabitants, to be held as hostages, to the end that they may be murdered in cold blood if any of his soldiers are killed by some unknown persons whom he designates as "bushwhackers." Some of the military authorities seem to suppose that their end will be better attained by a savage war in which no quarter is to be given, and no age or sex is to be spared, than by such hostilities as are alone recognized to be lawful in modern times. We find ourselves driven by our enemies by steady progress toward a practice which we abhor, and which we are vainly struggling to avoid.

Under these circumstances, this Government has issued the accompanying general order, which I am directed by the President to transmit to you, recognizing Major-General Pope and his commissioned officers to be in the position which they have chosen for themselves—that of robbers and murderers, and not that of public enemies, entitled, if captured, to be treated as prisoners of war. The President also instructs me to inform you that we renounce our right of retaliation on the innocent, and will continue to treat the private soldiers of General Pope's army as prisoners of war; but if, after notice to your Government that they confine repressive measures to the punishment of commissioned officers who are willing to participate in these crimes, the savage practices threatened in the orders alluded to be persisted in, we shall reluctantly be forced to the last resort of accepting the war on the terms chosen by our enemies, until the voice of an outraged humanity shall compel a respect for the recognized usages of war. While the President considers that the facts referred to would justify a refusal on our part to execute the cartel by which we have agreed to liberate an excess of prisoners of war in our hands, a sacred regard for plighted faith, which shrinks from the semblance of breaking a promise, precludes a resort to such an extremity, nor is it his desire to extend to any other forces of the United States the punishment merited by General Pope and such commissioned officers as choose to participate in the execution of his infamous order.

I have the honor to be, very respectfully, your obedient servant,

R.E. LEE, *General commanding.*

This communication requires no comment. It had the desired effect, although General Halleck returned it as couched in language too insulting to be received. On the 15th of August, the United States War Department so far disapproved of General Pope's orders as to direct that "no officer or soldier might, without proper authority, leave his colors or ranks to take private property, or to enter a private house for the purpose, under penalty of death."

II.

LEE'S MANOEUVRES.

General Pope had promptly advanced, and his army lay in Culpepper, the right reaching toward the Blue Ridge, and the left extending nearly to the Rapidan.

The campaign now became a contest of brains between Lee and the Federal authorities. Their obvious aim was to leave him in doubt whether a new advance was intended under McClellan from James River, or the real movement was to be against Richmond from the North. Under these circumstances, General Lee remained with the bulk of his army in front of Richmond; but, on the 13th of July, sent Jackson with two divisions in the direction of Gordonsville. The game of wits had thus begun, and General Lee moved cautiously, looking in both directions, toward James River and the Upper Rappahannock. As yet the real design of the enemy was undeveloped. The movement of General Pope might or might not be a real advance. But General McClellan remained inactive, and, on the 27th of July, A.P. Hill's division was sent up to reënforce Jackson—while, at the same time, General D.H. Hill, commanding a force on the south bank of the James River, was directed to make demonstrations against McClellan's communications by opening fire on his transports.

The moment approached now when the game between the two adversaries was to be decided. On the 2d of August, Jackson assumed the offensive, by attacking the enemy at Orange Court-House; and, on the 5th, General McClellan made a prompt demonstration to prevent Lee from sending him further reinforcements. A large Federal force advanced to Malvern Hill, and was drawn up there in line of battle, with every indication on the part of General McClellan of an intention to advance anew upon Richmond. Lee promptly went to meet him, and a slight engagement ensued on Curl's Neck. But, on the next morning, the Federal army had disappeared, and the whole movement was seen to have been a feint.

This state of indecision continued until nearly the middle of August. An incident then occurred which clearly indicated the enemy's intentions. General Burnside was known to have reached Hampton Roads from the Southern coast with a considerable force, and the direction which his flotilla now took would show the design of the Federal authorities. If a new advance was intended from the James, the flotilla would ascend that river; if General Pope's army was looked to for the real movement, General Burnside would go in that direction. The secret was discovered by the afterward celebrated Colonel John S. Mosby, then a private, and just returned, by way of Fortress Monroe, from prison in Washington. He ascertained, when he disembarked, that Burnside's flotilla was about to move toward the Rappahannock, and, aware of the importance of the information, hastened to communicate it to General Lee. He was admitted, at the headquarters of the latter near Richmond, to a private interview, and when General Lee had finished his conversation with the plain-looking individual, then almost unknown, he was in possession of the information necessary to determine his plans. The Rappahannock, and not the James, was seen to be the theatre of the coming campaign, and General Lee's whole attention was now directed to that quarter.

Jackson had already struck an important blow there, coöperating vigorously, as was habitual with him, in the general plan of action. General McClellan had endeavored by a feint to hold Lee at Richmond. By a battle now, Jackson hastened the retreat of the army under McClellan from James River. With his three divisions, Jackson crossed the Rapidan, and, on the 9th of August, attacked the advance force of General Pope at Cedar Mountain. The struggle was obstinate, and at one time Jackson's left was driven back, but the action terminated at nightfall in the retreat of the Federal forces, and the Confederate commander remained in possession of the field. He was too weak, however, to hold his position against the main body of the Federal army, which was known to be approaching; he accordingly recrossed the Rapidan to the vicinity of Gordonsville, and here he was soon afterward joined by General Lee, with the great bulk of the Confederate army.

Such were the events which succeeded the battles of the Chickahominy, transferring hostilities to a new theatre, and inaugurating the great campaigns of the summer and autumn of 1862 in Northern Virginia and Maryland.

III.
LEE ADVANCES FROM THE RAPIDAN.

General Lee, it will thus be seen, had proceeded in his military manoeuvres with the utmost caution, determined to give his adversaries no advantage, and remain in front of the capital until it was free from all danger. But for the daring assault upon General McClellan, on the Chickahominy, his critics would no doubt have charged him with weakness and indecision now; but, under any circumstances, it is certain that he would have proceeded in the same manner, conducting operations in the method which his judgment approved.

At length the necessity of caution had disappeared. General Burnside had gone to reënforce General Pope, and a portion of McClellan's army was believed to have followed. "It therefore seemed," says General Lee, "that active operations on the James were no longer contemplated," and he wisely concluded that "the most effectual way to relieve Richmond from any danger of attack from that quarter would be to reënforce General Jackson, and advance upon General Pope." In commenting upon these words, an able writer of the North exclaims: "Veracious prophecy, showing that *insight* which is one of the highest marks of generalship!" The movement, indeed, was the right proceeding, as the event showed; and good generalship may be defined to be the power of seeing what is the proper course, and the decision of character which leads to its adoption.

General Lee exhibited throughout his career this mingled good judgment and daring, and his cautious inactivity was now succeeded by one of those offensive movements which, if we may judge him, by his subsequent career, seemed to be the natural bent of his character. With the bulk of his army, he marched in the direction of General Pope; the rest were speedily ordered to follow, and active operations began for driving the newly-formed Federal "Army of Virginia" back toward Washington.

We have presented Lee's order for the attack on General McClellan, and here quote his order of march for the advance against General Pope, together with a note addressed to Stuart, commanding his cavalry, for that officer's guidance.

HEADQUARTERS ARMY NORTHERN VIRGINIA,
August 19, 1862.
SPECIAL ORDER No. 185.

I. General Longstreet's command, constituting the right wing of the army, will cross the Rapidan at Raccoon Ford, and move in the direction of Culpepper Court-House. General Jackson's command, constituting the left wing, will cross at Summerville Ford, and move in the same direction, keeping on the left of General Longstreet. General Anderson's division will cross at Summerville Ford, follow the route of General Jackson, and act in reserve. The battalion of light artillery, under Colonel S.D. Lee, will take the same route. The cavalry, under General Stuart, will cross at Morton's Ford, pursue the route by Stevensburg to Rappahannock Station, destroy the railroad bridge, cut the enemy's communications, telegraph line, and, operating toward Culpepper Court-House, will take position on General Longstreet's right.

II. The commanders of each wing will designate the reserve for their commands. Medical and ammunition wagons will alone follow the troops across the Rapidan. The baggage and supply trains will be parked under their respective officers, in secure positions on the south side, so as not to embarrass the different roads.

III. Cooked rations for three days will be carried in the haversacks of the men, and provision must be made for foraging the animals. Straggling from the ranks is strictly prohibited, and commanders will make arrangements to secure and punish the offenders.

IV. The movements herein directed will commence to-morrow, 20th instant, at dawn of day.

By command of General R.E. Lee:
A.P. MASON, *A.A. G.*
HEADQUARTERS CRENSHAW'S FARM,} *August* 19, 1862.}
General J.E.B. Stuart, commanding Cavalry:

General: I desire you to rest your men to-day, refresh your horses, prepare rations and every thing for the march to-morrow. Get what information you can of fords, roads, and position of the enemy, so that your march can be made understandingly and with vigor. I send to you Captain Mason, an experienced bridge-builder, etc., whom I think will be able to aid you in the destruction of the bridge, etc. When that is accomplished, or when in train of execution, as circumstances permit, I wish you to operate back toward Culpepper Court-House, creating such confusion and consternation as you can, without unnecessarily exposing your men, till you feel Longstreet's right. Take position there on his right, and hold yourself in reserve, and act as circumstances may require. I wish to know during the day how you proceed in your preparations. They will require the personal attention of all your officers. The last reports from the signal-stations yesterday evening were, that the enemy was breaking up his principal encampments, and moving in direction of Culpepper Court-House.

Very respectfully, etc., R.E. LEE, *General.*

These orders indicate General Lee's design—to reach the left flank of the enemy, prevent his retreat by destroying the bridges on the Rappahannock, and bring him to battle in the neighborhood of Culpepper Court-House. The plan failed in consequence of a delay of two days, which took place in its execution—a delay, attributed at that time, we know not with what justice, to the unnecessarily deliberate movements of the corps commanded by General Longstreet. This delay enabled the enemy to gain information of the intended movement; and when General Lee advanced on the 20th of August, instead of on the 18th, as he had at first determined to do, it was found that General Pope had broken up his camps, and was in rapid retreat. Lee followed, and reached the Rappahannock only to find that the Federal army had passed that stream. General Pope, who had promised to conduct none but offensive operations, and never look to the rear, had thus hastened to interpose the waters of the Rappahannock between himself and his adversary, and, when General Lee approached, he found every crossing of the river heavily defended by the Federal infantry and artillery.

In face of this large force occupying a commanding position on the heights, General Lee made no effort to cross. He determined, he says, "not to attempt the passage of the river at that point with the army," but to "seek a more favorable place to cross, higher up the river, and thus gain the enemy's right." This manoeuvre was intrusted to Jackson, whose corps formed the Confederate left wing. Jackson advanced promptly to the Warrenton Springs Ford, which had been selected as the point of crossing, drove away a force of the enemy posted at the place, and immediately began to pass the river with his troops. The movement was however interrupted by a severe rain-storm, which swelled the waters of the Rappahannock, and rendered a further prosecution of it impracticable. General Lee was thus compelled to give up that plan, and ordered Jackson to withdraw the force which had crossed. This was done, and General Lee was now called upon to adopt some other method of attack; or to remain inactive in face of the enemy.

But to remain inactive was impossible. The army must either advance or retire; information which had just reached the Confederate general rendered one of these two proceedings indispensable. The information referred to had been obtained by General Stuart. The activity and energy of this officer, especially in gaining intelligence, now proved, as they proved often afterward, of the utmost importance to Lee. Stuart had been directed by General Lee to make an attack, with a cavalry force, on the Orange and Alexandria Railroad, in the enemy's rear; he had promptly carried out his orders by striking the Federal communications at Catlett's Station, had destroyed there all that he found, and torn up the railroad, but, better than all, had captured a box containing official papers belonging to General Pope. These papers, which Stuart hastened—marching day and night, through storm and flood—to convey to General Lee, presented the clearest evidence of the enemy's movements and designs. Troops were hastening from every direction to reënforce General Pope, the entire force on James River especially was to be brought rapidly north of the Rappahannock, and any delay in the operations of the Confederates would thus expose them to attack from the Federal forces concentrated from all quarters in their front.

[Illustration: Map—Upper Rappahannock]

IV.

JACKSON FLANKS GENERAL POPE.

It was thus necessary to act with decision, and General Lee resolved upon a movement apparently of the most reckless character. This was to separate his army into two parts, and, while one remained confronting the enemy on the Rappahannock, send the other by a long circuit to fall on the Federal rear near Manassas. This plan of action was opposed to the first rule of the military art, that a general should never divide his force in the face of an enemy. That Lee ventured to do so on this occasion can only be explained on one hypothesis, that he did not highly esteem the military ability of his opponent. These flank attacks undoubtedly, however, possessed a great attraction for him, as they did for Jackson, and, in preferring such movement, Lee was probably actuated both by the character of the troops on both sides and by the nature of the country. The men of both armies were comparatively raw levies, highly susceptible to the influence of "surprise," and the appearance of an enemy on their flanks, or in their rear, was calculated to throw them into disorder. The wooded character of the theatre of war generally rendered such movements practicable, and all that was requisite was a certain amount of daring in the commander who was called upon to decide upon them. This daring Lee repeatedly exhibited, and the uniform success of the movements indicates his sound generalship.

To command the force which was now to go on the perilous errand of striking General Pope's rear, General Lee selected Jackson, who had exhibited such promptness and decision in the campaigns of the Valley of Virginia. Rapidity of movement was necessary above all things, and, if any one could be relied upon for that, it was the now famous Stonewall Jackson. To him the operation was accordingly intrusted, and his corps was at once put in motion. Crossing the Rappahannock at an almost forgotten ford, high up and out of view of the Federal right, Jackson pushed forward day and night toward Manassas, reached Thoroughfare Gap, in the Bull Run Mountain, west of that place, passed through, and completely destroyed the great mass of supplies in the Federal depot at Manassas. The whole movement had been made with such rapidity, and General Stuart, commanding the cavalry, had so thoroughly guarded the flank of the advancing column from observation, that Manassas was a mass of smoking ruins almost before General Pope was aware of the real danger. Intelligence soon reached him, however, of the magnitude of the blow aimed by Lee, and, hastily breaking up his camps on the Rappahannock, he hurried to attack the force assailing his communications.

The first part of General Lee's plan had thus fully succeeded. General Pope, who had occupied every ford of the Rappahannock, so as to render the passage difficult, if not impossible, had disappeared suddenly, to go and attack the enemy in his rear. General Lee promptly moved in his turn, with the great corps under Longstreet, and pushed toward Manassas, over nearly the same road followed by Jackson.

[Illustration: T.J. Jackson]

V.

LEE FOLLOWS.

The contest of generalship had now fully begun, and the brain of General Lee was matched against the brain of General Pope. It is no part of the design of the writer of this volume to exalt unduly the reputation of Lee, and detract from the credit due his adversaries.

Justice has been sought to be done to General McClellan; the same measure of justice will be dealt out to his successors on the Federal side; nor is it calculated to elevate the fame of Lee, to show that his opponents were incapable and inefficient. Of General Pope, however, it must be said that he suffered himself to be outgeneralled in every particular; and the pithy comment of General Lee, that he "did not appear to be aware of his situation," sums up the whole subject.

It is beyond our purpose to enter upon any thing resembling a detailed narrative of the confused and complicated movements of the various corps of the army under General Pope. These have been the subject of the severest criticism by his own followers. We shall simply notice the naked events. Jackson reached Manassas on the night of August 26th, took it, and on the next day destroyed the great depot. General Pope was hastening to protect it, but was delayed by Ewell at Bristoe, and a force sent up from Washington, under the brave General Taylor, was driven off with loss. Then, having achieved his aim, Jackson fell back toward Sudley.

If the reader will look at the map, he will now understand the exact condition of affairs. Jackson had burned the Federal depot of supplies, and retired before the great force hastening to rescue them. He had with him about twenty thousand men, and General Pope's force was probably triple that number. Thus, the point was to hold General Pope at arm's-length until the arrival of Lee; and, to accomplish this great end, Jackson fell back beyond Groveton. There he formed line of battle, and waited.

It is obvious that, under these circumstances, the true policy of General Pope was to obstruct Thoroughfare Gap, the only road by which Lee could approach promptly, and then crush Jackson. On the night of the 27th, General McDowell was accordingly sent thither with forty thousand men; but General Pope ordered him, on the next morning, to Manassas, where he hoped to "bag the whole crowd," he said—that is to say, the force under Jackson. This was the fatal mistake made by General Pope. Thoroughfare Gap was comparatively undefended. While General Pope was marching to attack Jackson, who had disappeared, it was the next thing to a certainty that General Lee would attack *him*.

All parties were thus moving to and fro; but the Confederates enjoyed the very great advantage over General Pope of knowing precisely how affairs stood, and of having determined upon their own plan of operations. Jackson, with his back to the mountain, was waiting for Lee. Lee was approaching rapidly, to unite the two halves of his army. General Pope, meanwhile, was marching and countermarching, apparently ignorant of the whereabouts of Jackson,[1]

General Lee, in personal command of Longstreet's corps, reached the western end of Thoroughfare Gap about sunset, on the 28th, and the sound of artillery from the direction of Groveton indicated that Jackson and General Pope had come in collision. Jackson had himself brought on this engagement by attacking the flank of one of General Pope's various columns, as it marched across his front, over the Warrenton road, and this was the origin of the sound wafted to General Lee's ears as he came in sight of Thoroughfare. It was certainly calculated to excite his nerves if they were capable of being excited. Jackson was evidently engaged, and the disproportion between his forces and those of General Pope rendered such an engagement extremely critical. Lee accordingly pressed forward, reached the Gap, and the advance force suddenly halted: the Gap was defended. The Federal force posted here, at the eastern opening of the Gap, was small, and wholly inadequate for the purpose; but this was as yet unknown to General Lee. His anxiety under these circumstances must have been great. Jackson might be crushed before his arrival. He rode up to the summit of the commanding hill which rises just west of the Gap, and dismounting directed his field-glass toward the shaggy defile in front.

[Footnote 1: "Not knowing at the time where was the enemy."—*General Porter.*] and undecided what course to pursue.

[Illustration: Lee Reconnoitring at Throughfare Gap.]

The writer of these pages chanced to be near the Confederate commander at this moment, and was vividly impressed by the air of unmoved calmness which marked his countenance and demeanor. Nothing in the expression of his face, and no hurried movement, indicated excitement or anxiety. Here, as on many other occasions, Lee impressed the writer as an individual gifted with the most surprising faculty of remaining cool and unaffected in the midst of circumstances calculated to arouse the most phlegmatic. After reconnoitring for some moments without moving, he closed his glass slowly, as though he were buried in reflection, and deliberating at his leisure, and, walking back slowly to his horse, mounted and rode down the hill.

The attack was not delayed, and flanking columns were sent to cross north of the Gap and assail the enemy's rear. But the assault in front was successful. The small force of the enemy at the eastern opening of the Gap retired, and, by nine o'clock at night, General Longstreet's corps was passing through.

All the next morning (August 29th), Longstreet's troops were coming into position on the right of Jackson, under the personal supervision of Lee. By noon the line of battle was formed.[1]

Lee's army was once more united. General Pope had not been able to crush less than one-half that army, for twenty-four hours nearly in his clutches, and it did not seem probable that he would meet with greater success, now that the whole was concentrated and held in the firm hand of Lee.

[Footnote 1: The hour of Longstreet's arrival has been strangely a subject of discussion. The truth is stated in the reports of Lee, Longstreet, Jones, and other officers. But General Pope was ignorant of Longstreet's presence *at five in the evening*; and General Porter, his subordinate, was dismissed from the army for not at that hour attacking Jackson's right, declared by General Pope to be undefended. Longstreet was in line of battle by noon.]

VI.

THE SECOND BATTLE OF MANASSAS.

Lee's order of battle for the coming action was peculiar. It resembled an open V, with the opening toward the enemy—Jackson's corps forming the left wing, and extending from near Sudley, to a point in rear of the small village of Groveton, Longstreet's corps forming the right wing, and reaching from Jackson's right to and beyond the Warrenton road which runs to Stonebridge.

The field of battle was nearly identical with that of July 21, 1861. The only difference was, that the Confederates occupied the ground formerly held by the Federal troops, and that the latter attacked, as Johnston and Beauregard had attacked, from the direction of Manassas, and the tableland around the well-known Henry House.

The Southern order of battle seems to have contemplated a movement on one or both of General Pope's flanks while he attacked in front. An assault on either wing would expose him to danger from the other, and it will be seen that the fate of the battle was decided by this judicious arrangement of the Confederate commander.

The action began a little after noon, when the Federal right, consisting of the troops of Generals Banks, Sigel, and others, advanced and made a vigorous attack on Jackson's left, under A.P. Hill. An obstinate conflict ensued, the opposing lines fighting almost bayonet to bayonet, "delivering their volleys into each other at the distance of ten paces." At the first charge, an interval between two of Hill's brigades was penetrated by the enemy, and that wing of Jackson's corps was in great danger of being driven back. This disaster was, however, prevented by the prompt stand made by two or three regiments; the enemy was checked, and a prompt counter-charge drove the Federal assaulting columns back into the woods.

The attempt to break Jackson's line at this point was not, however, abandoned. The Federal troops returned again and again to the encounter, and General Hill reported "six separate and distinct assaults" made upon him. They were all repulsed, in which important assistance was rendered by General Early. That brave officer attacked with vigor, and, aided by the fire of the Confederate artillery from the elevated ground in Jackson's rear, drove the enemy before him with such slaughter that one of their regiments is said to have carried back but three men.

This assault of the enemy had been of so determined a character, that General Lee, in order to relieve his left, had directed Hood and Evans, near his centre, to advance and attack the left of the assaulting column. Hood was about to do so, when he found a heavy force advancing to charge his own line. A warm engagement followed, which resulted in the repulse of the enemy, and Hood followed them a considerable distance, inflicting heavy loss.

It was now nearly nine o'clock at night, and the darkness rendered further operations impossible. The troops which had driven the enemy were recalled from their advanced position, the Southern line was reformed on the same ground occupied at the commencement of the action, and General Lee prepared for the more decisive struggle of the next day.

Morning came (August 30th), but all the forenoon passed without a resumption of the battle. Each of the adversaries seemed to await some movement on the part of the other, and the Federal commander made heavy feints against both the Confederate right and left, with the view of discovering some weak point, or of inducing Lee to lay himself open to attack. These movements had, however, no effect. Lee remained obstinately in his strong position, rightly estimating the advantage it gave him, and no doubt taking into consideration the want of supplies General Pope must labor under, a deficiency which rendered a prompt assault on his part indispensable. The armies thus remained in face of each other, without serious efforts upon either side, until nearly or quite the hour of three in the afternoon.

General Pope then resumed the assault on Lee's left, under Jackson, with his best troops. The charge was furious, and a bloody struggle ensued; but Jackson succeeded in repulsing the force. It fell back in disorder, but was succeeded by a second and a third line, which rushed forward at the "double-quick," in a desperate attempt to break the Southern line. These new attacks were met with greater obstinacy than at first, and, just as the opponents had closed in, a heavy fire was directed against the Federal column by Colonel S.D. Lee, commanding the artillery at Lee's centre. This fire, which was of the most rapid and destructive character, struck the enemy in front and flank at once, and seemed to sweep back the charging brigades as they came. The fire of the cannon was then redoubled, and Jackson's line advanced with cheers. Before this charge, the Federal line broke, and Jackson pressed forward, allowing them no respite.

General Lee then threw forward Longstreet, who, knowing what was expected of him, was already moving. The enemy were pressed thus in front and on their flank, as Lee had no doubt intended, in forming his peculiar line. The corps of Jackson and Longstreet closed in like two iron arms; the Federal forces were driven from position to position; the glare of their cannon, more and more distant, indicated that they had abandoned further contest, and at ten at night the darkness put an end to the battle and pursuit. General Pope was retreating with his defeated forces toward Washington.

On the next day, Lee dispatched Jackson to turn Centreville and cut off the retreat of General Pope. The result was a severe engagement near Germantown, which was put an end to by a violent storm. General Pope, now reënforced by the commands of Generals Sumner and Franklin, had been enabled to hold his ground until night. When, on the next day (September 2d), the Confederates advanced to Fairfax Court-House, it was found that the entire Federal army was in rapid retreat upon Washington.

Such had been the fate of General Pope.

PART V.

LEE INVADES MARYLAND.

I.

HIS DESIGNS.

The defeat of General Pope opened the way for movements not contemplated, probably, by General Lee, when he marched from Richmond to check the advance in Culpepper. His object at that time was doubtless simply to arrest the forward movement of the new force threatening Gordonsville. Now, however, the position of the pieces on the great chess-board of war had suddenly changed, and it was obviously Lee's policy to extract all the advantage possible from the new condition of things.

He accordingly determined to advance into Maryland—the fortifications in front of Washington, and the interposition of the Potomac, a broad stream easily defended, rendering a movement in that direction unpromising. On the 3d of September, therefore, and without waiting to rest his army, which was greatly fatigued with the nearly continuous marching and fighting since it had left the Rapidan, General Lee moved toward Leesburg, crossed his forces near that place, and to the music of the bands playing the popular air, "Maryland, my Maryland," advanced to Frederick City, which he occupied on the 7th of September.

Lee's object in invading Maryland has been the subject of much discussion, one party holding the view that his sole aim was to surround and capture a force of nine or ten thousand Federal troops stationed at Harper's Ferry; and another party maintaining that he proposed an invasion of Pennsylvania as far as the Susquehanna, intending to fight a decisive battle there, and advance thereafter upon Philadelphia, Baltimore, or Washington. The course pursued by an army commander is largely shaped by the progress of events. It can only be said that General Lee, doubtless, left the future to decide his ultimate movements; meanwhile he had a distinct and clearly-defined aim, which he states in plain words.

His object was to draw the Federal forces out of Virginia first. The movement culminating in the victory over the enemy at Manassas had produced the effect of paralyzing them in every quarter. On the coast of North Carolina, in Western Virginia, and in the Shenandoah Valley, had been heard the echo of the great events in Middle and Northern Virginia. General Burnside's force had been brought up from the South, leaving affairs at a stand-still in that direction; and, contemporaneously with the retreat of General Pope, the Federal forces at Washington and beyond had fallen back to the Potomac. This left the way open, and Lee's farther advance, it was obvious, would now completely clear Virginia of her invaders. The situation of affairs, and the expected results, are clearly stated by General Lee:

"The war was thus transferred," he says, "from the interior to the frontier, and the supplies of rich and productive districts made accessible to our army. To prolong a state of affairs in every way desirable, and not to permit the season for active operations to pass without endeavoring to inflict other injury upon the enemy, the best course appeared to be the transfer of the army into Maryland."

The state of things in Maryland was another important consideration. That great Commonwealth was known to be sectionally divided in its sentiment toward the Federal Government, the eastern portion adhering generally to the side of the South, and the western portion generally to the Federal side. But, even as high up as Frederick, it was hoped that the Southern cause would find adherents and volunteers to march under the Confederate banner. If

40

this portion of the population had only the opportunity to choose their part, unterrified by Federal bayonets, it was supposed they would decide for the South. In any event, the movement would be important. The condition of affairs in Maryland, General Lee says, "encouraged the belief that the presence of our army, however inferior to that of the enemy, would induce the Washington Government to retain all its available force to provide for contingencies which its course toward the people of that State gave it reason to apprehend," and to cross the Potomac "might afford us an opportunity to aid the citizens of Maryland in any efforts they might be disposed to make to recover their liberty."

It may be said, in summing up on this point, that Lee expected volunteers to enroll themselves under his standard, tempted to do so by the hope of throwing off the yoke of the Federal Government, and the army certainly shared this expectation. The identity of sentiment generally between the people of the States of Maryland and Virginia, and their strong social ties in the past, rendered this anticipation reasonable, and the feeling of the country at the result afterward was extremely bitter.

Such were the first designs of Lee; his ultimate aim seems as clear. By advancing into Maryland and threatening Baltimore and Washington, he knew that he would force the enemy to withdraw all their troops from the south bank of the Potomac, where they menaced the Confederate communications with Richmond; when this was accomplished, as it clearly would be, his design was, to cross the Maryland extension of the Blue Ridge, called there the South Mountain, advance by way of Hagerstown into the Cumberland Valley, and, by thus forcing the enemy to follow him, draw them to a distance from their base of supplies, while his own communications would remain open by way of the Shenandoah Valley. This was essentially the same plan pursued in the campaign of 1863, which terminated in the battle of Gettysburg. General Lee's movements now indicated similar intentions. He doubtless wished, in the first place, to compel the enemy to pursue him—then to lead them as far as was prudent—and then, if circumstances were favorable, bring them to decisive battle, success in which promised to open for him the gates of Washington or Baltimore, and end the war.

It will now be seen how the delay caused by the movement of Jackson against Harper's Ferry, and the discovery by General McClellan of the entire arrangement devised by Lee for that purpose, caused the failure of this whole ulterior design.

[Illustration: Map—Map of the MARYLAND CAMPAIGN.]

II.

LEE IN MARYLAND.

The Southern army was concentrated in the neighborhood of Frederick City by the 7th of September, and on the next day General Lee issued an address to the people of Maryland.

We have not burdened the present narrative with Lee's army orders and other official papers; but the great force and dignity of this address render it desirable to present it in full:

HEADQUARTERS ARMY OF NORTHERN VIRGINIA,}
NEAR FREDERICKTOWN, *September* 8, 1862.}

To the People of Maryland:

It is right that you should know the purpose that has brought the army under my command within the limits of your State, so far as that purpose concerns yourselves.

The people of the Confederate States have long watched with the deepest sympathy the wrongs and outrages that have been inflicted upon the citizens of a Commonwealth allied to the States of the South by the strongest social, political, and commercial ties.

They have seen, with profound indignation, their sister State deprived of every right, and reduced to the condition of a conquered province. Under the pretence of supporting the Constitution, but in violation of its most valuable provisions, your citizens have been arrested and imprisoned upon no charge, and contrary to all forms of law. The faithful and manly protest against this outrage, made by the venerable and illustrious Marylanders—to whom in better days no citizen appealed for right in vain—was treated with scorn and contempt. The government of your chief city has been usurped by armed strangers; your Legislature has been dissolved by the unlawful arrest of its members; freedom of the press and of speech have been suppressed; words have been declared offences by an arbitrary desire of the Federal Executive, and citizens ordered to be tried by military commission for what they may dare to speak.

Believing that the people of Maryland possessed a spirit too lofty to submit to such a government, the people of the South have long wished to aid you in throwing off this foreign yoke, to enable you again to enjoy the inalienable rights of freemen, and restore independence and sovereignty to your State.

In obedience to this wish, our army has come among you, and is prepared to assist you, with the power of its arms, in regaining the rights of which you have been despoiled. This, citizens of Maryland, is our mission, so far as you are concerned. No constraint upon your free will is intended—no intimidation will be allowed. Within the limits of this army, at least, Marylanders shall once more enjoy their ancient freedom of thought and speech. We know no enemies among you, and will protect all of every opinion. It is for you to decide your destiny, freely, and without constraint. This army will respect your choice, whatever it may be; and, while the Southern people will rejoice to welcome you to your natural position among them, they will only welcome you when you come of your own free will.

R.E. LEE, *General commanding.*

This address, full of grave dignity, and highly characteristic of the Confederate commander, was in vivid contrast with the harsh orders of General Pope in Culpepper. The accents of friendship and persuasion were substituted for the "rod of iron." There would be no coercive measures; no arrests, with the alternative presented of an oath to support the South, or instant banishment. No intimidation would be permitted. In the lines of the Southern army, at least, Marylanders should enjoy freedom of thought and speech, and every man should "decide his destiny freely, and without constraint."

This address, couched in terms of such dignity, had little effect upon the people. Either their sentiment in favor of the Union was too strong, or they found nothing in the condition of affairs to encourage their Southern feelings. A large Federal force was known to be advancing; Lee's army, in tatters, and almost without supplies, presented a very uninviting appearance to recruits, and few joined his standard, the population in general remaining hostile or neutral.

The condition of the army was indeed forlorn. It was worn down by marching and fighting; the men had scarcely shoes upon their feet; and, above the tattered figures, flaunting their rags in the sunshine, were seen gaunt and begrimed faces, in which could be read little of the "romance of war." The army was in no condition to undertake an invasion; "lacking much of the material of war, feeble in transportation, poorly provided with clothing, and thousands of them destitute of shoes," is Lee's description of his troops. Such was the condition of the better portion of the force; on the opposite side of the Potomac, scattered along the hills, could be seen a weary, ragged, hungry, and confused multitude, who had dragged along in rear of the rest, unable to keep up, and whose miserable appearance said little for the prospects of the army to which they belonged.

From these and other causes resulted the general apathy of the Marylanders, and Lee soon discovered that he must look solely to his own men for success in his future movements. He faced that conviction courageously; and, without uttering a word of comment, or indulging in any species of crimination against the people of Maryland, resolutely commenced his movements looking to the capture of Harper's Ferry and the invasion of Pennsylvania.[1]

[Footnote 1: The reader will perceive that the intent to *invade* Pennsylvania is repeatedly attributed in these pages to General Lee. His own expression is, "by *threatening* Pennsylvania, to induce the enemy," etc. That he designed invasion, aided by the recruits anticipated in Maryland, seems unquestionable; since, even after discovering the lukewarmness of the people there by the fact that few joined his standard, he still advanced to Hagerstown, but a step from the Pennsylvania line. These facts have induced the present writer to attribute the design of actual invasion to Lee with entire confidence; and all the circumstances seem to him to support that hypothesis.]

The promises of his address had been kept. No one had been forced to follow the Southern flag; and now, when the people turned their backs upon it, closing the doors of the houses in the faces of the Southern troops, they remained unmolested. Lee had thus given a practical proof of the sincerity of his character. He had promised nothing which he had not performed; and in Maryland, as afterward in Pennsylvania, in 1863, he remained firm against the temptation to adopt the harsh course generally pursued by the commanders of invading armies. He seems to have proceeded on the principle that good faith is as essential in public affairs as in private, and to have resolved that, in any event, whether of victory or disaster, his enemies should not have it in their power to say that he broke his plighted word, or acted in a manner unbecoming a Christian gentleman.

Prompt action was now necessary. The remnants of General Pope's army, greatly scattered and disorganized by the severe battle of Manassas, had been rapidly reformed and brought into order again, and to this force was added a large number of new troops, hurried forward from the Northern States to Washington. This new army was not to be commanded by General Pope, who had been weighed and found wanting in ability to contend with Lee. The force was intrusted to General McClellan, in spite of his unpopularity with the Federal authorities; and the urgent manner in which he had been called upon to take the head of affairs and protect the Federal capital, is the most eloquent of all commentaries upon the position which he held in the eyes of the country and the army. It was felt, indeed, by all that the Federal ship was rolling in the storm, and an experienced pilot was necessary for her guidance. General McClellan was accordingly directed, after General Pope's defeat, to take command of every thing, and see to the safety of Washington; and, finding himself at length at the head of an army of about one hundred thousand men, he proceeded, after the manner of a good soldier, to protect the Federal capital by advancing into upper Maryland in pursuit of Lee.

III.

MOVEMENTS OF THE TWO ARMIES.

General Lee was already moving to the accomplishment of his designs, the capture of Harper's Ferry, and an advance into the Cumberland Valley.

His plan to attain the first-mentioned object was simple, and promised to be successful. Jackson was to march around by way of "Williamsport and Martinsburg," and thus approach from the south. A force was meanwhile to seize upon and occupy the Maryland Heights, a lofty spot of the mountain across the Potomac, north of the Ferry. In like manner, another body of troops was to cross the Potomac, east of the Blue Ridge, and occupy the Loudon Heights, looking down upon Harper's Ferry from the east. By this arrangement the retreat of the enemy would be completely cut off in every direction. Harper's Ferry must be captured, and, having effected that result, the whole Confederate force, detached for the purpose, was to follow the main body of this army in the direction of Hagerstown, to take part in the proposed invasion of Pennsylvania.

This excellent plan failed, as will be seen, from no fault of the great soldier who devised it, but in consequence of unforeseen obstacles, and especially of one of those singular incidents which occasionally reverse the best-laid schemes and abruptly turn aside the currents of history.

Jackson and the commanders coöperating with him moved on September 10th. General Lee then with his main body crossed the South Mountain, taking the direction of Hagerstown. Meanwhile, General McClellan had advanced cautiously and slowly, withheld by incessant dispatches from Washington, warning him not to move in such a manner as to expose that city to danger. Such danger existed only in the imaginations of the authorities, as the army in advancing extended its front from the Potomac to the Baltimore and Ohio Railroad. General McClellan, nevertheless, moved with very great precaution, feeling his way, step by step, like a man in the dark, when on reaching Frederick City, which the Confederates had just evacuated, good fortune suddenly came to his assistance. This good fortune was the discovery of a copy of General Lee's orders of march for the army, in which his whole plan was revealed. General McClellan had therein the unmistakable evidence of his opponent's intentions, and from that moment his advance was as rapid as before it had been deliberate.

The result of this fortunate discovery was speedily seen. General Lee, while moving steadily toward Hagerstown, was suddenly compelled to turn his attention to the mountain-passes in his rear. It had not been the intention of Lee to oppose the passage of the enemy through the South Mountain, as he desired to draw General McClellan as far as possible from his base, but the delay in the fall of Harper's Ferry now made this necessary. It was essential to defend the mountain-defiles in order to insure the safety of the Confederate troops at Harper's Ferry; and Lee accordingly directed General D.H. Hill to oppose the passage of the enemy at Boonsboro Gap, and Longstreet was sent from Hagerstown to support him.

An obstinate struggle now ensued for the possession of the main South Mountain Gap, near Boonsboro, and the roar of Jackson's artillery from Harper's Ferry must have prompted the assailants to determined efforts to force the passage. The battle continued until night (September 14th), and resulted in heavy loss on both sides, the brave General Reno, of the United States army, among others, losing his life. Darkness put an end to the action, the Federal forces not having succeeded in passing the Gap; but, learning that a column of the enemy had crossed below and threatened him with an attack in flank, General Lee determined to retire in the direction of Sharpsburg, where Jackson and the forces coöperating with him could join the main body of the army. This movement was effected without difficulty, and Lee notices the skill and efficiency of General Fitz Lee in covering the rear with his cavalry. The Federal army failed to press forward as rapidly as it is now obvious it should have done. The head of the column did not appear west of the mountain until eight o'clock in the morning (September 15th), and, nearly at the same moment ("the attack began at dawn; in about two hours the garrison surrendered," says General Lee), Harper's Ferry yielded to Jackson.

Fast-riding couriers brought the welcome intelligence of Jackson's success to General Lee, as the latter was approaching Sharpsburg, and official information speedily came that the result had been the capture of more than eleven thousand men, thirteen thousand small-arms, and seventy-three cannon. It was probably this large number of men and amount of military stores falling into the hands of the Confederates which afterward induced the opinion that Lee's sole design in invading Maryland had been the reduction of Harper's Ferry.

General McClellan had thus failed, in spite of every effort which he had made, to relieve Harper's Ferry,[1] and no other course remained now but to follow Lee and bring him to battle. The Federal army accordingly moved on the track of its adversary, and, on the afternoon of the same day (September 15th), found itself in sight of Lee's forces drawn up on the western side of Antietam Creek, near the village of Sharpsburg.

[Footnote 1: All along the march he had fired signal-guns to inform the officer in command at Harper's Ferry of his approach.]

At last the great opponents were in face of each other, and a battle, it was obvious, could not long be delayed.

IV.

THE PRELUDE TO SHARPSBURG.

General Lee had once more sustained a serious check from the skill and soldiership of the officer who had conducted the successful retreat of the Federal army from the Chickahominy to James River.

The defeat and dispersion of the army of General Pope on the last day of August seemed to have opened Pennsylvania to the Confederates. On the 15th of September, a fortnight afterward, General McClellan, at the head of a new army, raised in large measure by the magic of his name, had pursued the victorious Confederate, checked his further advance, and, forcing him to abandon his designs of invasion, brought him to bay a hundred miles from the capital. This was generalship, it would seem, in the true acceptation of the term, and McClellan, harassed and hampered by the authorities, who looked but coldly upon him, could say, with Coriolanus, "Alone I did it."

Lee was thus compelled to give up his movement in the direction of Pennsylvania, and concentrate his army to receive the assault of General McClellan. Jackson, marching with his customary promptness, joined him with a portion of the detached force on the next day (September 16th), and almost immediately those thunders which prelude the great struggles of history began.

General Lee had drawn up his army on the high ground west of the Antietam, a narrow and winding stream which flows, through fields dotted with homesteads and clumps of fruit and forest trees, to the Potomac. Longstreet's corps was posted on the right of the road from Sharpsburg to Boonsboro, his right flank guarded by the waters of the stream, which here bends westward; on the left of the Boonsboro road D.H. Hill's command was stationed; two brigades under General Hood were drawn up on Hill's left; and when Jackson arrived Lee directed him to post his command on the left of Hood, his right resting on the Hagerstown road, and his left extending backward obliquely toward the Potomac, here making a large bend, where Stuart with his cavalry and horse-artillery occupied the ground to the river's bank.

This arrangement of his troops was extremely judicious, as the sequel proved. It was probable that General McClellan would direct his main attack against the Confederate left, with the view of turning that flank and hemming in the Southern army, or driving it into the river. By retiring Jackson's left, Lee provided for this contingency, and it will be seen that the design attributed by him to his adversary was that determined upon.

General McClellan occupied the ground on the eastern bank of the Antietam. He had evidently massed his forces opposite the Confederate left, but a heavy order of battle stood opposite the centre and right of Lee, where bridges crossed the stream.

The respective numbers of the adversaries can be stated with accuracy. "Our forces at the battle of Antietam," said General McClellan, when before the committee of investigation afterward, "were, total in action, eighty-seven thousand one hundred and sixty-four."

General Lee says in his report: "This great battle was fought by less than forty thousand men on our side."

Colonel Walter H. Taylor, a gentleman of the highest character, and formerly adjutant-general of the army, makes the Confederate numbers somewhat less. In a memorandum before the writer, he says:

Our strength at Sharpsburg. I think this is correct:

Jackson (*including A.P. Hill*) 10,000
Longstreet 12,000
  D.H. Hill and Walker 7,000

———

Effective infantry 29,000
  Cavalry and artillery 8,000

———

Total of all arms 37,000

This disproportion was very great, amounting, as it did, to more than two for one. But this was unavoidable. The Southern army had been worn out by their long marching and fighting. Portions of the command were scattered all over the roads of Northern Virginia, wearily dragging their half-clothed limbs and shoeless feet toward Winchester, whither they were directed to repair. This was the explanation of the fact that, in spite of the ardent desire of the whole army to participate in the great movement northward, Lee had in line of battle at Sharpsburg "less than forty thousand men."

General McClellan made a demonstration against his adversary on the evening of the 16th, before the day of the main struggle. He threw his right, commanded by General Hooker, across the Antietam at a point out of range of fire from the Confederates, and made a vigorous attack on Jackson's two divisions lying near the Hagerstown road running northward, and thus parallel with Lee's line of battle. A brief engagement took place in the vicinity of the "Dunker Church," in a fringe of woods west of the road, but it was too late to effect any thing of importance; night fell, and the engagement ceased. General Hooker retaining his position on the west side of the stream.

The opposing lines then remained at rest, waiting for the morning which all now saw would witness the commencement of the more serious conflict.

V.

THE BATTLE OF SHARPSBURG.

The battle of Sharpsburg, or Antietam, for it is known by both names, began at early dawn on the 17th of September.

General McClellan had obviously determined to direct his main assault against the Confederate left, a movement which General Lee had foreseen and provided for,[1] and at dawn commenced a rapid fire of artillery upon that portion of the Confederate line. Under cover of this fire, General Hooker then advanced his infantry and made a headlong assault upon Jackson's line, with the obvious view of crushing that wing of Lee's army, or driving it back on Sharpsburg and the river. The Federal force making this attack, or advancing promptly to support it, consisted of the corps of Generals Hooker, Mansfield, and Sumner, and numbered, according to General Sumner, forty thousand men, of whom eighteen thousand belonged to General Hooker's corps.

[Footnote 1: "In anticipation of a movement to turn the line of Antietam, Hood's two brigades had been transferred from the right to the left," etc.—*Lee.*]

Jackson's whole force was four thousand men. Of the truth of this statement of the respective forces, proof is here given:

"I have always believed," said General Sumner afterward, before the war committee, "that, instead of sending these troops into that action in driblets, had General McClellan authorized me to march *there forty thousand men* on the left flank of the enemy," etc.

"Hooker formed his corps of *eighteen thousand* men," etc., says Mr. Swinton, the able and candid Northern historian of the war.

Jackson's force is shown by the Confederate official reports. His corps consisted of Ewell's division and "Jackson's old division." General Jones, commanding the latter, reported: "The division at the beginning of the fight numbered not over one thousand six hundred men." Early, commanding Ewell's division,[1] reported the three brigades to number:

Lawton's 1,150
Hayes's 550
Walker's 700
2,400
"Old Division," as above 1,600
Jackson's corps 4,000
[Footnote 1: After General Lawton was disabled.]

This was the entire force carried by General Jackson into the fight, and these four thousand men, as the reader will perceive, bore the brunt of the first great assault of General McClellan.

Just as the light broadened in the east above the crest of mountains rising in rear of the Federal lines. General Hooker made his assault. His aim was plainly to drive the force in his front across the Hagerstown road and back on the Potomac, and in this he seemed about to succeed. Jackson had placed in front Ewell's division of twenty-four hundred men. This force received General Hooker's charge, and a furious struggle followed, in which the division was nearly destroyed. A glance at the casualties will show this. They were remarkable. General Lawton, division commander, was wounded and carried from the field; Colonel Douglas, brigade commander, was killed; Colonel Walker, also commanding brigade, was disabled; Lawton's brigade lost five hundred and fifty-four killed and wounded out of eleven hundred and fifty, and five out of six regimental commanders. Hayes's brigade lost three hundred and twenty-three out of five hundred and fifty, and all the regimental commanders. Walker's brigade lost two hundred and twenty-eight out of less than seven hundred, and three out of four regimental commanders; and, of the staff-officers of the division, scarcely one remained.

In an hour after dawn, this heavy slaughter had been effected in Ewell's division, and the detailed statement which we have given will best show the stubborn resistance offered by the Southern troops. Still, they were unable to hold their ground, and fell back at last in disorder before General Hooker, who pressed forward to seize the Hagerstown road and crush the whole Confederate left. He was met, however, by Jackson's Old Division of sixteen hundred men, who had been held in reserve; and General Lee hastened to the point threatened Hood's two small brigades, one of which, General Hood states, numbered but eight hundred and sixty-four men. With this force Jackson now met the advancing column of General Hooker, delivering a heavy fire from the woods upon the Federal forces. In face of this fire they hesitated, and Hood made a vigorous charge, General Stuart opening at the same time a cross-fire on the enemy with his horse-artillery. The combined fire increased their disorganization, and it now turned into disorder. Jackson seized the moment, as always, throwing forward his whole line, and the enemy were first checked, and then driven back in confusion, the Confederates pursuing and cheering.

The first struggle had thus resulted in favor of the Confederates—with about six thousand they had repulsed eighteen thousand—and it was obvious to General McClellan that, without reinforcements, his right could not hold its ground. He accordingly, just at sunrise, sent General Mansfield's corps to the aid of General Hooker, and at nine o'clock General Sumner's corps was added, making in all forty thousand men.

The appearance of affairs at this moment was discouraging to the Federal commander. His heavy assaulting column had been forced back with great slaughter; General Hooker had been wounded and borne from the field; General Mansfield, while forming his line, had been mortally wounded; and now, at nine o'clock, when the corps of General Sumner arrived, the prospect was depressing. Of the condition of the Federal forces, General Sumner's own statement conveys a very distinct conception: "On going upon the field," said General Sumner, before the war committee, "I found that General Hooker's corps had been dispersed and routed. I passed him some distance in the rear, where he had been carried wounded, but I saw nothing of his corps at all, as I was advancing with my command on the field. I sent one of my staff-officers to find where they were, and General Ricketts, the only officer we could find, stated that he could not raise three hundred men of the corps." General Mansfield's corps also had been checked, and now "began to waver and break."

Such had been the result of the great Federal assault, and it was highly creditable to the Confederate arms. With a comparatively insignificant force, Jackson had received the attack of the entire Federal right wing, and had not only repulsed, but nearly broken to pieces, the large force in his front.

The arrival of General Sumner, however, completely changed the face of affairs, and, as his fresh troops advanced, those which had been so roughly handled by Jackson had an opportunity to reform. This was rapidly effected, and, having marshalled his troops, General Sumner, an officer of great dash and courage, made a vigorous charge. From this moment the battle began to rage with new fury. General Lee had sent to the left the brigades of Colquitt, Ripley, and McRae, and with these, the troops of Hood, and his own shattered division, Jackson presented a stubborn front, but his loss was heavy. General Starke, of the Old Division, was killed; the brigade, regimental, and company officers fell almost without an exception, and the brigades dwindled to mere handfuls.

Under the great pressure, Jackson was at length forced back. One of General Sumner's divisions drove the right of the Confederates beyond the Hagerstown road, and, at this moment the long struggle seemed ended; the great wrestle in which the adversaries had so long staggered to and fro, advancing and retreating in turn, seemed at last virtually decided in favor of the Federal arms.

This was undoubtedly the turning-point of the battle of Sharpsburg, and General Lee had witnessed the conflict upon his left with great anxiety. It was impossible, however, to send thither more troops than he had already sent. As will be seen in a moment, both his centre and right were extremely weak. A.P. Hill and General McLaws had not arrived from Harper's Ferry. Thus the left had been reënforced to the full extent of Lee's ability, and now that portion of his line seemed about to be crushed.

Fortunately, however, General McLaws, who had been delayed longer than was expected by General Lee, at last arrived, and was hurried to the left. It was ten o'clock, and in that one hour the fighting of an entire day seemed to have been concentrated. Jackson was holding his ground with difficulty when the divisions of McLaws and Walker were sent to him. As soon as they reached the field, they were thrown into action, and General Lee had the satisfaction of witnessing a new order of things. The advance—it might rather be called the onward rush—of the Federal line was checked. Jackson's weary men took fresh heart; that great commander promptly assumed the offensive, and, advancing his whole line, drove the enemy before him until he reoccupied the ground from which General Sumner had forced him to retire.

From the ground thus occupied, the Federal forces were unable to dislodge him, and the great struggle of "the left at Sharpsburg" was over. It had begun at dawn and was decided by ten or eleven o'clock, and the troops on both sides had fought as resolutely as in any other action of the war. The event had been decided by the pertinacity of the Southern troops, and by the prompt movement of reënforcements by General Lee from his right and centre. Posted near his centre, he had surveyed at one glance the whole field of action; the design of General McClellan to direct his main assault upon the Confederate left was promptly penetrated, and the rapid concentration of the Southern forces in that quarter had, by defeating this movement, decided the result of the battle.

Attacks on the Confederate centre and right followed that upon the left. In the centre a great disaster was at one time imminent. Owing to a mistake of orders, the brave General Rhodes had drawn back his brigade posted there—this was seen by the enemy—and a sudden rush was made by them with the view of piercing Lee's centre. The promptness and courage of a few officers and a small body of troops defeated this attempt. General D.H. Hill rallied a few hundred men, and opened fire with a single gun, and Colonel Cooke faced the enemy with his regiment, "standing boldly in line," says General Lee, "without a cartridge." The stand made by this small force saved the army from serious disaster; the Federal line retired, but a last assault was soon begun, this time against the Confederate right. It continued in a somewhat desultory manner until four in the evening, when, having massed a heavy column under General Burnside, opposite the bridge in front of Lee's right wing, General McClellan forced the bridge and carried the crest beyond.

The moment was critical, as the Confederate force at this point was less than three thousand men. But, fortunately, reënforcements arrived, consisting of A.P. Hill's forces from Harper's Ferry. These attacked the enemy, drove him from the hill across the Antietam again; and so threatening did the situation at that moment appear to General McClellan, that he is said to have sent General Burnside the message: "Hold your ground! If you cannot, then the bridge, to the last man. Always the bridge! If the bridge is lost, all is lost!"

The urgency of this order sufficiently indicates that the Federal commander was not without solicitude for the safety of his own left wing. Ignorant, doubtless, of the extremely small force which had thus repulsed General Burnside, in all four thousand five hundred men, he feared that General Lee would cross the bridge, assail his left, and that the hard-fought day might end in disaster to his own army. That General Lee contemplated this movement, in spite of the disproportion of numbers, is intimated in his official report. "It was nearly dark," he says, "and the Federal artillery was massed to defend the bridge, with General Porter's corps, consisting of fresh troops, behind it. Under these circumstances," he adds, "it was deemed injudicious to push our advantage further in the face of fresh troops of the enemy much exceeding our own."

The idea of an advance against the Federal left was accordingly abandoned, and a movement of Jackson's command, which Lee directed, with the view of turning the Federal right, was discontinued from the same considerations. Night had come, both sides were worn out, neither of the two great adversaries cared to risk another struggle, and the bitterly-contested battle of Sharpsburg was over.

The two armies remained facing each other throughout the following day. During the night of this day, Lee crossed with his army back into Virginia. He states his reasons for this: "As we could not look for a material increase of strength," he says, "and the enemy's force could be largely and rapidly augmented, it was not thought prudent to wait until he should be ready again to offer battle."

General McClellan does not seem to have been able to renew the struggle at that time. "The next morning," he says, referring to the day succeeding the battle, "I found that our loss had been so great, and there was so much disorganization in some of the commands, that I did not consider it proper to renew the attack that day."

This decision of General McClellan's subjected him subsequently to very harsh criticism from the Federal authorities, the theory having obtained at Washington that he had had it in his power, by renewing the battle, to cut Lee to pieces. Of the probability of such a result the reader will form his own judgment. The ground for such a conclusion seems slight. The loss and disorganization were, it would seem, even greater on the Federal than on the Confederate side, and Lee would have probably been better able to sustain an attack than General McClellan to make it. It will be seen that General Meade afterward, under circumstances more favorable still, declined to attack Lee at Williamsport. If one of the two commanders be greatly censured, the other must be also, and the world will be always apt to conclude that they knew what could be effected better than the civilians.

But General McClellan did make an attempt to "crush Lee," such as the authorities at Washington desired, and its result may possibly throw light on the point in discussion.

On the night of the 19th, Lee having crossed the Potomac on the night of the 18th, General McClellan sent a considerable force across the river near Shepherdstown, which drove off the Confederate artillery there, and at daylight formed line of battle on the south bank, protected by their cannon north of the river. Of the brief but bloody engagement which followed—an incident of the war little dwelt upon in the histories—General A.P. Hill, who was sent by Lee to repulse the enemy, gives an animated account. "The Federal artillery, to the number of seventy pieces," he says, "lined the opposite heights, and their infantry was strongly posted on the crest of the Virginia hills. When he advanced with his division, he was met by the most tremendous fire of artillery he ever saw," but the men continued to move on without wavering, and the attack resulted in the complete rout of the enemy, who were "driven pell-mell into the river," the current of which was "blue with floating bodies." General Hill chronicles this incident in terms of unwonted eloquence, and declares that, by the account of the enemy themselves, they lost "three thousand men killed and drowned from one brigade," which appears to be an exaggeration. His own loss was, in killed and wounded, two hundred and sixty-one.

This repulse was decisive, and General McClellan made no further attempt to pursue the adversary, who, standing at bay on the soil of Virginia, was still more formidable than he had been on the soil of Maryland. As we have intimated on a preceding page, the result of this attempt to pursue would seem to relieve General McClellan from the criticism of the Washington authorities. If he was repulsed with heavy slaughter in his attempt to strike at Lee on the morning of September 20th, it is not probable that an assault on his adversary on September 18th would have had different results.

No further crossing at that time was undertaken by the Federal commander. His army was moved toward Harper's Ferry, an important base for further operations, and Lee's army went into camp along the banks of the Opequan.

VI.

LEE AND McCLELLAN—THEIR MERITS IN THE MARYLAND CAMPAIGN.

General Lee and his adversary had displayed conspicuous merit in the campaign thus terminated, and we shall pause for a moment to glance back upon this great passage at arms.

To give precedence to General McClellan, he had assembled an army, after the defeat at Manassas, with a promptness for which only his own great personal popularity can adequately account, had advanced to check Lee, and had fully succeeded in doing so; and had thus not only protected the fertile territory of Pennsylvania from invasion, but had struck a death-blow for the time to any designs General Lee might have had to advance on the Federal capital. If the situation of affairs at that moment be attentively considered, the extreme importance of these results will not fail to appear. It may perhaps be said with justice, that General McClellan had saved the Federal cause from decisive defeat. There was no army to protect Washington but the body of troops under his command; these were largely raw levies, which defeat would have broken to pieces, and thus the way would have been open for Lee's march upon Washington or toward Philadelphia—a movement whose probable result would have been a treaty of peace and the independence of the Southern Confederacy. All these hopes were reversed by McClellan's rapid march and prompt attack. In the hours of a single autumn day, on the banks of the Antietam, the triumphant advance of the Confederates was checked and defeated. And, if the further fact be considered that the adversary thus checkmated was Lee, the military ability of General McClellan must be conceded. It is the fashion, it would appear, in some quarters, to deny him this quality. History will decide.

The merit of Lee was equally conspicuous, and his partial failure in the campaign was due to circumstances over which he had no control. His plan, as was always the case with him, was deep-laid, and every contingency had been provided for. He was disappointed in his aim by three causes which he could not foresee. One was the great diminution of his force, owing to the rapidity of his march, and the incessant fighting; another, the failure in obtaining recruits in Maryland; and a third, the discovery by General McClellan of the "lost dispatch," as it is called, which revealed Lee's whole plan to his adversary. In consequence of the "finding" of the order of march, McClellan advanced with such rapidity that the laggards of the Southern army on the hills north of Leesburg had no opportunity of joining the main body. The gaps in the ranks of the army thus made were not filled up by Maryland recruits; Lee fell back, and his adversary followed, no longer fearful of advancing too quickly; Jackson had no time after reducing Harper's Ferry to rejoin Lee at Hagerstown; thus concentration of his troops, and a battle somewhere near Sharpsburg, were rendered a necessity with General Lee.

In this tissue of adverse events, the discovery of the order of march by General McClellan occupies a very prominent place. This incident resembles what the French call a fatality. Who was to blame for the circumstance still remains a mystery; but it may be said with entire certainty that the brave officer upon whom it was charged was entirely guiltless of all fault in the matter.

[Footnote: The officer here referred to is General D.H. Hill. General McClellan said in his testimony afterward, before the congressional committee: "When at Frederick, we found the original order issued to D.H. Hill," etc. The inference was thus a natural one that General Hill was to blame, but that officer has proved clearly that he had nothing to do with the affair. He received but one copy of the order, which was handed to him by General Jackson in person, and, knowing its great importance, he placed it in his pocket-book, and still retains it in his possession. This fact is conclusive, since General Hill could not have "lost" what he continues to hold in his hands. This mystery will be cleared up at some time, probably; at present, but one thing is certain, that General Hill was in no manner to blame. The present writer desires to make this statement as explicit as possible, as, in other accounts of these transactions, he was led by General McClellan's language to attribute blame to General Hill where he deserved none.]

Whatever may have been the secret history of the "lost dispatch," however, it certainly fell into General McClellan's hands, and largely directed the subsequent movements of the opposing armies.

From what is here written, it will be seen that Lee was not justly chargeable with the result of the Maryland campaign. He had provided for every thing as far as lay in his power. Had he not been disappointed in events to be fairly anticipated, it seemed his force would have received large accessions, his rear would have closed up, and the advance into Pennsylvania would have taken place. Instead of this, he was forced to retire and fight a pitched battle at Sharpsburg; and this action certainly exhibited on Lee's part military ability of the highest order. The force opposed to him had been at least double that of his own army, and the Federal troops had fought with a gallantry unsurpassed in any other engagement of the war. That their assault on Lee failed, was due to the fighting qualities of his troops and his own generalship. His army had been manoeuvred with a rapidity and precision which must have excited even the admiration of the distinguished soldier opposed to him. He had promptly concentrated his forces opposite every threatened point in turn, and if he had not been able to carry out the axiom of Napoleon, that a commander should always be superior to the enemy at the point of contact, he had at least done all that was possible to effect that end, and had so far succeeded as to have repulsed if not routed his adversary. This is the main feature to be noticed in Lee's handling of his troops at Sharpsburg. An unwary or inactive commander would have there suffered decisive defeat, for the Confederate left wing numbered, throughout the early part of the battle, scarcely more than four thousand men, while the column directed against it amounted first to eighteen thousand, and in all to forty thousand men. To meet the impact of this heavy mass, not only desperate fighting, but rapid and skilful manoeuvring, was necessary. The record we have presented will enable the reader to form his own opinion whether Lee was equal to this emergency involving the fate of his army.

Military critics, examining this great battle with fair and candid eyes, will not fail, we think, to discern the truth. That the Southern army, of less than forty thousand men, repulsed more than eighty thousand in the battle of Sharpsburg, was due to the hard fighting of the smaller force, and the skill with which its commander manoeuvred it.

VII.

LEE AND HIS MEN.

General Lee and his army passed the brilliant days of autumn in the beautiful valley of the Shenandoah. This region is famous for its salubrity and the beauty of its scenery. The mountain winds are pure and invigorating, and the forests, which in the season of autumn assume all the colors of the rainbow, inspire the mind with the most agreeable sensations. The region, in fact, is known as the "Garden of Virginia," and the benign influence of their surroundings was soon seen on the faces of the troops.

A Northern writer, who saw them at Sharpsburg, describes them as "ragged, hungry, and in all ways miserable;" but their forlorn condition, as to clothing and supplies of every description, made no perceptible difference in their demeanor now. In their camps along the banks of the picturesque little stream called the Opequan, which, rising south of Winchester, wanders through beautiful fields and forests to empty into the Potomac, the troops laughed, jested, sang rude camp-ballads, and exhibited a joyous indifference to their privations and hardships, which said much for their courage and endurance. Those who carefully considered the appearance and demeanor of the men at that time, saw that much could be effected with such tough material, and had another opportunity to witness, under circumstances calculated to test it, the careless indifference, to the past as well as the future, peculiar alike to soldiers and children. These men, who had passed through a campaign of hard marches and nearly incessant battles, seemed to have forgotten all their troubles and sufferings. The immense strain upon their energies had left them apparently as fresh and efficient as when the campaign begun. There was no want of rebound; rather an excessive elasticity and readiness to undertake new movements. They had plainly acquired confidence in themselves, rightly regarding the event of the battle of Sharpsburg, where they were so largely outnumbered, as highly honorable to them, and they had acquired still greater confidence in the officers who commanded them.

We shall hereafter speak more particularly of the sentiment of the troops toward General Lee at this period of his connection with the army. The great events of the war continually modified the relations between him and his men; as they came to know him better and better, he steadily rose in their admiration and regard. At this time—the autumn of 1862—it may be said that the troops had already begun to love their leader, and had bestowed upon him as an army commander their implicit confidence.

Without this confidence on the part of his men, a general can effect little; with it, he may accomplish almost any thing. The common soldier is a child, and feels that the directing authority is above him; that he should look upon that authority with respect and confidence is the first necessity of effecting military organization. Lee had already inspired the troops with this sentiment, and it was mainly the secret of his often astounding successes afterward. The men universally felt that their commander was equal to any and every emergency. Such a repute cannot be usurped. Troops measure their leaders with instinctive acumen, and a very astonishing accuracy. They form their opinions for themselves on the merits of the question; and Lee had already impressed the army with a profound admiration for his soldiership. From this to the sentiment of personal affection the transition was easy; and the kindness, consideration, and simplicity of the man, made all love him. Throughout the campaign, Lee had not been heard to utter one harsh word; a patient forbearance and kindness had been constantly exhibited in all his dealings with officers and men; he was always in front, indifferent plainly to personal danger, and the men looked now with admiring eyes and a feeling of ever-increasing affection on the erect, soldierly figure in the plain uniform, with scarce any indication of rank, and the calm face, with its expression of grave dignity and composure, which remained unchanged equally on the march and in battle. It may be said that, when he assumed command of the army before Richmond, the troops had taken him on trust; now they had come to love him, and when he appeared the camps buzzed, the men ran to the road, called out to each other: "There goes Mas' Robert!" or "Old Uncle Robert!" and cheers followed him as he rode by.

The country generally seemed to share the opinion of the army. There was exhibited, even at this early period of the war, by the people at large, a very great admiration and affection for General Lee. While in the Shenandoah Valley, where Jackson was beloved almost beyond expression, Lee had evidences of the position which he occupied in the eyes of the people, which must have been extremely gratifying to him. Gray-haired men came to his camp and uttered prayers for his health and happiness as the great leader of the South; aged ladies greeted him with faltering expressions full of deep feeling and pathetic earnestness; and, wherever he went, young girls and children received him with their brightest smiles. The august fame of the great soldier, who has now passed away, no doubt renders these memories of personal interviews with him dear to many. Even the most trifling incidents are cherished and kept fresh by repetition; and the writer of these pages recalls at the moment one of these trifles, which may possibly interest some readers. There stood and still stands an ancient and hospitable homestead on the south bank of the Opequan, the hearts of whose inmates, one and all, were ardently with the South in her struggle. Soon after Sharpsburg, General Lee one day visited the old manor-house crowning the grassy hill and overshadowed by great oaks; Generals Jackson, Longstreet, and Stuart, accompanied him, and the reception which he met with, though we cannot describe it, was such as would have satisfied the most exacting. The children came to him and held out their small hands, the ladies divided their attention between him and the beloved "hero of the Valley," Jackson; and the lady of the manor could only express her sense of the great honor of receiving such company, by declaring, with a smile, that the dinner resembled the famous *breakfast at Tillietudlem* in Scott's "Old Mortality." General Lee highly enjoyed this, and seemed disposed to laugh when the curious fact was pointed out to him that he had seated himself at table in a chair with an open-winged *United States eagle* delineated upon its back. The result of this visit, it appeared afterward, was a sentiment of great regard and affection for the general personally by all at the old country-house. Old and young were charmed by his grave sweetness and mild courtesy, and doubtless he inspired the same sentiment in other places.

His headquarters were at this time in a field some miles from Winchester. An Englishman, who visited him there, described the general and his surroundings with accuracy, and, from the account printed in *Blackwood's Magazine*, we quote the following sentences:

"In visiting the headquarters of the Confederate generals, but particularly those of General Lee, any one accustomed to see European armies in the field cannot fail to be struck with the great absence of all the 'pomp and circumstance of war' in and around their encampments. Lee's headquarters consisted of about seven or eight pole-tents, pitched with their backs to a stake fence, upon a piece of ground so rocky that it was unpleasant to ride over it, its only recommendation being a little stream of good water which flowed close by the general's tent. In front of the tents were some three four-wheeled wagons, drawn up without any regularity, and a number of horses roamed loose about the field. The servants, who were, of course, slaves, and the mounted soldiers, called 'couriers,' who always accompany each general of division in the field, were unprovided with tents, and slept in or under the wagons. Wagons, tents, and some of the horses, were marked 'U.S.,' showing that part of that huge debt in the North has gone to furnishing even the Confederate generals with camp equipments. No guard or sentries were to be seen in the vicinity; no crowd of aides-de-camp loitering about, making themselves agreeable to visitors, and endeavoring to save their generals from receiving those who had no particular business. A large farm-house stands close by, which, in any other army, would have been the general's residence *pro tem.*, but, as no liberties are allowed to be taken with personal property in Lee's army, he is particular in setting a good example himself. His staff are crowded together, two or three in a tent; none are allowed to carry more baggage than a small box each, and his own kit is but very little larger. Every one who approaches him does so with marked respect, although there is none of that bowing and flourishing of forage caps which occurs in the presence of European generals; and, while all honor him, and place implicit faith in his courage and ability, those with whom he is most intimate feel for him the affection of sons to a father. Old General Scott was correct in saying that, when Lee joined the Southern cause, it was worth as much as the accession of twenty thousand men to the 'rebels.' Since then every injury that it was possible to inflict, the Northerners have heaped upon him. Notwithstanding all these personal losses, however, when speaking of the Yankees, he neither evinced any bitterness of feeling, nor gave utterance to a single violent expression, but alluded to many of his former friends and companions among them in the kindest terms. He spoke as a man proud of the victories won by his country, and confident of ultimate success, under the blessing of the Almighty, whom he glorified for past successes, and whose aid he invoked for all future operations."

The writer adds that the troops "regarded him in the light of infallible love," and had "a fixed and unshakable faith in all he did—a calm confidence of victory when serving under him." The peculiarly interesting part of this foreign testimony, however, is that in which the writer speaks of General Lee's religious sentiment, of his gratitude for past mercies, and prayers for the assistance of the Almighty in the hours of conflict still to come. This point we shall return to, endeavoring to give it that prominence which it deserves. At present we shall leave the subject of General Lee, in his private and personal character, and proceed to narrate the last campaign of the year 1862.

VIII.

LEE PASSES THE BLUE RIDGE

From the central frontier of his headquarters, near Winchester, the key of the lower Valley, General Lee was able to watch at once the line of the Potomac in his front, beyond which lay General McClellan's army, and the gaps of the Blue Ridge on his right, through which it was possible for the enemy, by a rapid movement, to advance and attack his flank and rear.

If Lee had at any time the design of recrossing into Maryland, he abandoned it. General McClellan attributed that design to him. "I have since been confirmed in the belief," he wrote, "that if I had crossed the Potomac below Harper's Ferry in the early part of October, General Lee would have recrossed into Maryland." Of Lee's ability to thus reënter Maryland there can be no doubt. His army was rested, provisioned, and in high spirits; the "stragglers" had rejoined their commands, and it is certain that the order for a new advance would have been hailed by the mercurial troops with enthusiasm. No such order was, however, issued, and soon the approach of winter rendered the movement impossible.

More than a month thus passed, the two armies remaining in face of each other. No engagement of any importance occurred during this period of inactivity, but once or twice the Federal commander sent heavy reconnoitring forces across the Potomac; and Stuart, now mounting to the zenith of his reputation as a cavalry-officer, repeated his famous "ride around McClellan," on the Chickahominy.

The object of General Lee in directing this movement of the cavalry was the ordinary one, on such occasions, of obtaining information and inflicting injury upon the enemy. Stuart responded with ardor to the order. He had conceived a warm affection for General Lee, mingled with a respect for his military genius nearly unbounded, and at this time, as always afterward, received the orders of his commander for active operations with enthusiasm. With about eighteen hundred troopers and four pieces of horse-artillery, Stuart crossed the Potomac above Williamsport, marched rapidly to Chambersburg, in Pennsylvania, where he destroyed the machine-shops, and other buildings containing a large number of arms and military stores; and continued his way thence toward Frederick City, with the bold design of completely passing around the Federal army, and recrossing the river east of the Blue Ridge. In this he succeeded, thanks to his skill and audacity, in spite of every effort of the enemy to cut off and destroy him. Reaching White's Ford, on the Potomac, north of Leesburg, he disposed his horse-artillery so as to cover this movement, cut his way through the Federal cavalry disputing his passage, and recrossed into Virginia with a large number of captured horses, and without losing a man.

This expedition excited astonishment, and a prominent officer of the Federal army declared that he would not have believed that "horse-flesh could stand it," as the distance passed over in about forty-eight hours, during which considerable delay had occurred at Chambersburg, was nearly or quite one hundred miles. General McClellan complained that his orders had not been obeyed, and said that after these orders he "did not think it possible for Stuart to recross," and believed "the destruction or capture of his entire force perfectly certain."

Soon afterward the Federal commander attempted reconnoissances in his turn. A considerable force of infantry, supported by artillery, crossed the Potomac and advanced to the vicinity of the little village of Leetown, but on the same evening fell back rapidly, doubtless fearful that Lee would interpose a force between them and the river and cut off their retreat. This was followed by a movement of the Federal cavalry, which crossed at the same spot and advanced up the road leading toward Martinsburg. These were met and subsequently driven back by Colonel W.H.F. Lee, son of the general. A third and more important attempt to reconnoitre took place toward the end of October. General McClellan then crossed a considerable body of troops both at Shepherdstown and Harper's Ferry; the columns advanced to Kearneysville and Charlestown respectively, and near the former village a brief engagement took place, without results. General McClellan, who had come in person as far as Charlestown, then returned with his troops across the Potomac, and further hostilities for the moment ceased.

These reconnoissances were the prelude, however, of an important movement which the Federal authorities had been long urging General McClellan to make. Although the battle of Sharpsburg had been indecisive in one acceptation of the term, in another it had been entirely decisive. A drawn battle of the clearest sort, it yet decided the future movements of the opposing armies. General Lee had invaded Maryland with the design of advancing into Pennsylvania—the result of Sharpsburg was, that he fell back into Virginia. General McClellan had marched from Washington with no object but an offensive-defensive campaign to afford the capital protection; he was now enabled to undertake anew the invasion of Virginia.

To the success of such a movement the Federal commander seems rightly to have considered a full and complete equipment of his troops absolutely essential. He was directed at once, after Sharpsburg, to advance upon Lee. He replied that it was impossible, neither his men nor his horses had shoes or rations. New orders came—General Halleck appearing to regard the difficulties urged by General McClellan as imaginary. New protests followed, and then new protests and new orders again, until finally a peremptory dispatch came. This dispatch was, "Cross the Potomac and give battle to the enemy or drive him south," an order bearing the impress of the terse good sense and rough directness of the Federal President. This order it was necessary in the end to obey, and General McClellan, having decided in favor of a movement across the Potomac east instead of west of the mountain, proceeded, in the last days of October, to cross his army. His plan was excellent, and is here set forth in his own words:

"The plan of campaign I adopted during this advance," he says, "was to move the army well in hand, parallel to the Blue Ridge, taking Warrenton as the point of direction for the main army, seizing each pass on the Blue Ridge by detachments as we approached it, and guarding them after we had passed, as long as they would enable the enemy to trouble our communications with the Potomac.... We depended upon Harper's Ferry and Berlin for supplies until the Manassas Gap Railway was reached. When that occurred, the passes in our rear were to be abandoned, and the army massed ready for action or movement in any direction. It was my intention, if, upon reaching Ashby's or any other pass, the enemy were in force between it and the Potomac, in the Valley of the Shenandoah, to move into the Valley and endeavor to gain their rear."

From this statement of General McClellan it will be seen that his plan was judicious, and displayed a thorough knowledge of the country in which he was about to operate. The conformation of the region is peculiar. The Valley of the Shenandoah, in which Lee's army lay waiting, is separated from "Piedmont Virginia," through which General McClellan was about to advance, by the wooded ramparts of the Blue Ridge Mountains, passable only at certain points. These *gaps*, as they are called in Virginia, are the natural doorways to the Valley; and as long as General McClellan held them, as he proposed to do, by strong detachments, he would be able both to protect his own communications with the Potomac, and, if he thought fit to do so, enter the Valley and assail the Confederate rear. That he ever seriously contemplated the latter design is, however, extremely doubtful. It is not credible that he would have undertaken to "cut off" Lee's whole army; and, if he designed a movement of that description against any portion of the Southern army which might be detached, the opportunity was certainly presented to him by Lee, when Jackson was left, as will be seen, at Millwood.

No sooner had General McClellan commenced crossing the Potomac, east of the mountain, than General Lee broke up his camp along the Opequan, and moved to check this new and formidable advance into the heart of Virginia. It was not known, however, whether the whole of the Federal forces had crossed east of the Blue Ridge; and, to guard against a possible movement on his rear from the direction of Harper's Ferry, as well as on his flank through the gaps of the mountain, Lee sent Jackson's corps to take position on the road from Charlestown to Berryville, where he could oppose an advance of the enemy from either direction. The rest of the army then moved guardedly, but rapidly, across the mountain into Culpepper.

Under these circumstances, General McClellan had an excellent opportunity to strike a heavy blow at Jackson, who seemed to invite that movement by crossing soon afterward, in accordance with directions from Lee, one of his divisions to the east side of the mountain on the Federal rear. That General McClellan did not strike is not creditable to him as a commander. The Confederate army was certainly divided in a very tempting manner. Longstreet was in Culpepper on the 3d of November, the day after General McClellan's rear-guard had passed the Potomac, and nothing would seem to have been easier than to cut the Confederate forces by interposing between them. By seizing the Blue Ridge gaps, and thus shutting up all the avenues of exit from the Valley, General McClellan would have had it in his power, it would seem, to crush Jackson; or if that wily commander escaped, Longstreet in Culpepper was exposed to attack. General McClellan did not embrace this opportunity of a decisive blow, and Lee seems to have calculated upon the caution of his adversary. Jackson's presence in the Valley only embarrassed McClellan, as Lee no doubt intended it should. No attempt was made to strike at him. On the contrary, the Federal army continued steadily to concentrate upon Warrenton, where, on the 7th of November, General McClellan was abruptly relieved of the command.

He was in his tent, at Rectortown, at the moment when the dispatch was handed to him—brought by an officer from Washington through a heavy snow-storm then falling. General Ambrose E. Burnside was in the tent. McClellan read the dispatch calmly, and, handing it indifferently to his visitor, said, "Well, Burnside, you are to command the army."

Such was the abrupt termination of the military career of a commander who fills a large space in the history of the war in Virginia. The design of this volume is not such as to justify an extended notice of him, or a detailed examination of his abilities as a soldier. That he possessed military endowments of a very high order is conceded by most persons, but his critics add that he was dangerously prone to caution and inactivity. Such was the criticism of his enemies at Washington and throughout the North, and his pronounced political opinions had gained him a large number. It may, however, be permitted one who can have no reason to unduly commend him, to say that the retreat to James River, and the arrest of Lee in his march of invasion toward Pennsylvania, seem to indicate the possession of something more than "inactivity," and of that species of "caution" which achieves success. It will probably, however, be claimed by few, even among the personal friends of this general, that he was a soldier of the first ability—one competent to oppose Lee.

As to the personal qualities of General McClellan, there seems to be no difference of opinion. He was a gentleman of high breeding, and detested all oppression of the weak and non-combatants. Somewhat prone to *hauteur*, in presence of the importunities of the Executive and other civilians unskilled in military affairs, he was patient, mild, and cordial with his men. These qualities, with others which he possessed, seem to have rendered him peculiarly acceptable to the private soldier, and it is certain that he was, beyond comparison, the most popular of all the generals who, one after another, commanded the "Army of the Potomac."

IX.

LEE CONCENTRATES AT FREDERICKSBURG.

In returning from the Valley, General Lee had exhibited that combination of boldness and caution which indicates in a commander the possession of excellent generalship.

One of two courses was necessary: either to make a rapid march with his entire army, in order to interpose himself between General McClellan and what seemed to be his objective point, Gordonsville; or, to so manoeuvre his forces as to retard and embarrass his adversary. Of these, Lee chose the latter course, exposing himself to what seemed very great danger. Jackson was left in the Valley, and Longstreet sent to Culpepper; under these circumstances, General McClellan might have cut off one of the two detached bodies; but Lee seems to have read the character of his adversary accurately, and to have felt that a movement of such boldness would not probably be undertaken by him. Provision had nevertheless been made for this possible contingency. Jackson was directed by Lee, in case of an attack by General McClellan, to retire, by way of Strasburg, up the Valley, and so rejoin the main body. That this movement would become necessary, however, was not, as we have said, contemplated. It was not supposed by Lee that his adversary would adopt the bold plan of crossing the Blue Ridge to assail Jackson; thus, to leave that commander in the Valley, instead of being a military blunder, was a stroke of generalship, a source of embarrassment to General McClellan, and a standing threat against the Federal communications, calculated to clog the movements of their army. That Lee aimed at this is obvious from his order to Jackson to cross a division to the eastern side of the Blue Ridge, in General McClellan's rear. When this was done, the Federal commander abandoned, if he had ever resolved upon, the design of striking in between the Confederate detachments, as is claimed by his admirers to have been his determination; gave up all idea of "moving into the Valley and endeavoring to gain their rear;" and from that moment directed his whole attention to the concentration of his army near Warrenton, with the obvious view of establishing a new base, and operating southward on the line of the Orange and Alexandria Railroad.

Lee's object in these manoeuvres, besides the general one of embarrassing his adversary, seems to have been to gain time, and thus to render impossible, from the lateness of the season, a Federal advance upon Richmond. Had General McClellan remained in command, it is probable that this object would have been attained, and the battle of Fredericksburg would not have taken place. The two armies would have lain opposite each other in Culpepper and Fauquier respectively, with the Upper Rappahannock between them throughout the winter; and the Confederate forces, weary and worn by the long marches and hard combats of 1862, would have had the opportunity to rest and recover their energies for the coming spring.

The change of commanders defeated these views, if they were entertained by General Lee. On assuming command, General Burnside conceived the project, in spite of the near approach of winter, of crossing the Rappahannock at Fredericksburg, and marching on Richmond. This now proceeded to attempt, by steadily moving from Warrenton toward the Lower Rappahannock, and the result, as will be seen, was a Federal disaster to wind up this "year of battles."

We have spoken with some particularity of the character and military abilities of General McClellan, the first able commander of the Federal forces in Virginia. Of General Burnside, who appears but once, and for a brief space only, on that great theatre, it will be necessary to say only a few words. A modest and honorable soldier, cherishing for General McClellan a cordial friendship, he was unwilling to supersede that commander, both from personal regard and distrust of his own abilities. He had not sought the position, which had rather been thrust upon him. He was "surprised" and "shocked," he said, at his assignment to the command; he "did not want it, it had been offered to him twice before, and he did not feel that he could take it; he had told them that he was not competent to command such an army as this; he had said the same over and over again to the President and the Secretary of War." He was, however, directed to assume command, accepted the responsibility, and proceeded to carry out the unexpected plan of advancing upon Richmond by way of Fredericksburg.

To cover this movement, General Burnside made a heavy feint as though designing to cross into Culpepper. This does not seem to have deceived Lee, who, on the 17th of November, knew that his adversary was moving. No sooner had the fact been discovered that General Burnside was making for Fredericksburg, than the Confederate commander, by a corresponding movement, passed the Rapidan and hastened in the same direction. As early as the 17th, two divisions of infantry, with cavalry and artillery, were in motion. On the morning of the 19th, Longstreet's corps was sent in the same direction; and when, on November 20th, General Burnside arrived with his army, the Federal forces drawn up on the hills north of Fredericksburg saw, on the highlands south of the city, the red flags and gray lines of their old adversaries.

As General Jackson had been promptly directed to join the main body, and was already moving to do so, Lee would soon be able to oppose General Burnside with his whole force.

Such were the movements of the opposing armies which brought them face to face at Fredericksburg. Lee had acted promptly, and, it would seem, with good judgment; but the question has been asked, why he did not repeat against General Burnside the strategic movement which had embarrassed General McClellan, and arrest the march upon Fredericksburg by threatening, with the detachment under Jackson, the Federal rear. The reasons for not adopting this course will be perceived by a glance at the map. General Burnside was taking up a new base—Aquia Creek on the Potomac—and, from the character of the country, it was wholly impossible for Lee to prevent him from doing so. He had only to fall back before Jackson, or any force moving against his flank or rear; the Potomac was at hand, and it was not in the power of Lee to further annoy him. The latter accordingly abandoned all thought of repeating his old manoeuvre, moved Longstreet and the other troops in Culpepper toward Fredericksburg, and, directing Jackson to join him there, thus concentrated his forces directly in the Federal front with the view of fighting a pitched battle, army against army.

This detailed account of Lee's movements may appear tedious to some readers, but it was rather in grand tactics than in fighting battles that he displayed his highest abilities as a soldier. He uniformly adopted the broadest and most judicious plan to bring on battle, and personally directed, as far as was possible, every detail of his movements. When the hour came, it may be said of him that he felt he had done his best—the actual fighting was left largely in the hands of his corps commanders.

The feints and slight encounters preceding the battle of Fredericksburg are not of much interest or importance. General Burnside sent a force to Port Royal, about twenty-five miles below the city, but Lee promptly detached a portion of his army to meet it, if it attempted to cross, and that project was abandoned. No attempt was made by General Burnside to cross above, and it became obvious that he must pass the river in face of Lee or not at all.

Such was the condition of affairs at Fredericksburg in the first days of December.

X.

THE BATTLE OF FREDERICKSBURG.

To a correct understanding of the interesting battle of Fredericksburg, a brief description of the ground is essential.

The city lies on the south bank of the Rappahannock, which here makes a considerable bend nearly southward; and along the northern bank, opposite, extends a range of hills which command the city and the level ground around it. South of the river the land is low, but from the depth of the channel forms a line of bluffs, affording good shelter to troops after crossing to assail a force beyond. The only good position for such a force, standing on the defensive, is a range of hills hemming in the level ground. This range begins near the western suburbs of the city, where it is called "Marye's Hill," and sweeps round to the southward, gradually receding from the stream, until, at Hamilton's Crossing, on the Richmond and Potomac Railroad, a mile or more from the river, it suddenly subsides into the plain. This plain extends to the right, and is bounded by the deep and difficult channel of Massaponnax Creek. As Marye's Hill is the natural position for the left of an army posted to defend Fredericksburg, the crest above Hamilton's Crossing is the natural position for the right of such a line, care being taken to cover the extreme right with artillery, to obstruct the passage of the ground between the crest and the Massaponnax.

[Illustration: Map—Battle of Fredericksburg.]

Behind the hills on the north side General Burnside's army was posted, having the railroad to Aquia Creek for the transportation of their supplies. On the range of hills which we have described south of the city, General Lee was stationed, the same railroad connecting him with Richmond. Longstreet's corps composed his left wing, and extended from Marye's Hill to about the middle of the range of hills. There Jackson's line began, forming the right wing, and extending to the termination of the range at Hamilton's Crossing. On Jackson's right, to guard the plain reaching to the Massaponnax, Stuart was posted with cavalry and artillery.

The numbers of the adversaries at Fredericksburg can be stated with accuracy upon one side, but not upon the other. General Lee's force may be said to have been, in round numbers, about fifty thousand of all arms. It could scarcely have exceeded that, unless he received heavy reënforcements after Sharpsburg; and the present writer has never heard or read that he received reënforcements of any description. The number, fifty thousand, thus seems to have been the full amount of the army. That of General Burnside's forces seems to have been considerably larger. The Federal army consisted of the First, Second, Third, Fifth, Sixth, Ninth, and Eleventh Corps; the latter a corps of reserve and large. If these had been recruited to the full number reported by General McClellan at Sharpsburg, and the additional troops (Fifth and Eleventh Corps) be estimated, the Federal army must have exceeded one hundred thousand men. This estimate is borne out by Federal authorities. "General Franklin," says a Northern writer, "had now with him about one-half the whole army;" and General Meade says that Franklin's force "amounted to from fifty-five thousand to sixty thousand men," which would seem to indicate that the whole army numbered from one hundred and ten thousand to one hundred and twenty thousand men.

A strong position was obviously essential to render it possible for the Southern army, of about fifty thousand men, to successfully oppose the advance of this force of above one hundred thousand. Lee had found this position, and constructed earthworks for artillery, with the view of receiving the attack of the enemy after their crossing. He was unable to obstruct this crossing in any material degree; and he states clearly the grounds of this inability. "The plain of Fredericksburg," he says, "is so completely commanded by the Stafford heights, that no effectual opposition could be made to the construction of bridges, or the passage of the river, without exposing our troops to the destructive fire of the numerous batteries of the enemy.... Our position was, therefore, selected with a view to resist the enemy's advance after crossing, and the river was guarded only by a force sufficient to impede his movements until the army could be concentrated."

The brief description we have presented of the character of the ground around Fredericksburg, and the position of the adversaries, will sufficiently indicate the conditions under which the battle was fought. Both armies seem to have been in excellent spirits. That of General Burnside had made a successful march, during which they had scarcely seen an enemy, and now looked forward, probably, to certain if not easy victory. General Lee's army, in like manner, had undergone recently no peculiar hardships in marching or fighting; and, to whatever cause the fact may be attributed, was in a condition of the highest efficiency. The men seemed to be confident of the result of the coming conflict, and, in their bivouacs on the line of battle, in the woods fringing the ridge which they occupied, laughed, jested, cheered, on the slightest provocation, and, instead of shrinking from, looked forward with eagerness to, the moment when General Burnside would advance to attack them. This buoyant and elastic spirit in the Southern troops was observable on the eve of nearly every battle of the war. Whether it was due to the peculiar characteristics of the race, or to other causes, we shall not pause here to inquire; but the fact was plain to the most casual observation, and was never more striking than just before Fredericksburg, unless just preceding the battle of Gettysburg.

Nothing of any importance occurred, from the 20th of November, when General Burnside's army was concentrated on the heights north of Fredericksburg, until the 11th of December, when the Federal army began crossing the Rappahannock to deliver battle. Lee's reasons for not attempting to resist the passage of the river have been given above. The plain on which it would have been necessary to draw up his army, in order to do so, was too much exposed to the numerous artillery of the enemy on the northern bank. Lee resolved, therefore, not to oppose the crossing of the Federal troops, but to await their assault on the commanding ground west and south of the city.

On the morning of December 11th, before dawn, the dull boom of Lee's signal-guns indicated that the enemy were moving, and the Southern troops formed line of battle to meet the coming attack. General Burnside had made arrangements to cross the river on pontoon bridges, one opposite the city, and another a mile or two lower down the stream. General Franklin, commanding the two corps of the left Grand Division, succeeded, without trouble, in laying the lower bridge, as the ground did not permit Lee to offer material obstruction; and this large portion of the army was now ready to cross. The passage of the stream at Fredericksburg was more difficult. Although determined not to make a serious effort to prevent the enemy from crossing, General Lee had placed two regiments of Barksdale's Mississippians along the bank of the river, in the city, to act as sharp-shooters, and impede the construction of the pontoon bridges, with the view, doubtless, of thus giving time to marshal his troops. The success of this device was considerable. The workmen, busily engaged in laying the Federal pontoons, were so much interrupted by the fire of the Confederate marksmen—who directed their aim through the heavy fog by the noise made in putting together the boats—that, after losing a number of men, the Federal commander discontinued his attempt. It was renewed again and again, without success, as before, when, provoked apparently by the presence of this hornet's nest, which reversed all his plans, General Burnside, about ten o'clock, opened a furious fire of artillery upon the city. The extent of this bombardment will be understood from the statement that one hundred and forty-seven pieces of artillery were employed, which fired seven thousand three hundred and fifty rounds of ammunition, in one instance piercing a single small house with fifty round-shot. An eye-witness of this scene says: "The enemy had planted more than a hundred pieces of artillery on the hills to the northern and eastern sides of the town, and, from an early hour in the forenoon, swept the streets with round-shot, shell, and case-shot, firing frequently a hundred guns a minute. The quick puffs of smoke, touched in the centre with tongues of flame, ran incessantly along the lines of their batteries on the slopes, and, as the smoke slowly drifted away, the bellowing roar came up in one continuous roll. The town was soon fired, and a dense cloud of smoke enveloped its roofs and steeples. The white church-spires still rose serenely aloft, defying shot or shell, though a portion of one of them was torn off. The smoke was succeeded by lurid flame, and the crimson mass brought to mind the pictures of Moscow burning." The same writer says: "Men, women, and children, were driven from the town, and hundreds of ladies and children were seen wandering, homeless, and without shelter, over the frozen highway, in thin clothing, knowing not where to find a place of refuge."

[Illustration: FREDERICKSBURG]

General Lee watched this painful spectacle from a redoubt to the right of the telegraph road, not far from his centre, where a shoulder jutting out from the ridge, and now called "Lee's Hill," afforded him a clear view of the city. The destruction of the place, and the suffering of the inhabitants, aroused in him a deep melancholy, mingled with exasperation, and his comment on the scene was probably as bitter as any speech which he uttered during the whole war. Standing, wrapped in his cape, with only a few officers near, he looked fixedly at the flames rising from the city, and, after remaining for a long time silent, said, in his grave, deep voice: "These people delight to destroy the weak, and those who can make no defence; it just suits them."

General Burnside continued the bombardment for some hours, the Mississippians still holding the river-bank and preventing the laying of the pontoons, which was again begun and again discontinued. At about four in the afternoon, however, a force was sent across in barges, and by nightfall the city was evacuated by Lee, and General Burnside proceeded rapidly to lay his pontoon bridge, upon which his army then began to pass over. The crossing continued throughout the next day, not materially obstructed by the fire of Lee's artillery, as a dense fog rendered the aim of the cannoneers unreliable. By nightfall (of the 12th) the Federal army was over, with the exception of General Hooker's Centre Grand Division, which was held in reserve on the north bank. General Burnside then proceeded to form his line of battle. It stretched from the western suburbs of Fredericksburg down the river, along what is called the River road, for a distance of about four miles, and consisted of the Right Grand Division, under General Sumner, at the city, and the Left Grand Division, under General Franklin, lower down, and opposite Lee's right. General Franklin's Grand Division numbered, according to General Meade, from fifty-five to sixty thousand men; the numbers of Generals Sumner and Hooker are not known to the present writer, but are said by Federal authorities, as we have stated, to have amounted together to about the same.

At daybreak, on the morning of December 13th, a muffled sound, issuing from the dense fog covering the low ground, indicated that the Federal lines were preparing to advance.

To enable the reader to understand General Burnside's plan of attack, it is necessary that brief extracts should be presented from his orders on the occasion, and from his subsequent testimony before the committee on the conduct of the war. Despite the length of time since his arrival at Fredericksburg—a period of more than three weeks—the Federal commander had, it appears, been unable to obtain full and accurate information of the character of the ground occupied by Lee, and thus moved very much in the dark. He seems to have formed his plan of attack in consequence of information from "a colored man." His words are: "The enemy had cut a road along in the rear of the line of heights where we made our attack…. I obtained, from a colored man at the other side of the town, information in regard to this new road which proved to be correct. I wanted to obtain possession of that new road, and that was my reason for making an attack on the extreme left." It is difficult for those familiar with the ground referred to, to understand how this "new road," a mere country bridle-path, as it were, extending along in the rear of Lee's right wing, could have been regarded as a topographical feature of any importance. The road, which remains unchanged, and may be seen by any one to-day, was insignificant in a military point of view, and, in attaching such importance to seizing it, the Federal commander committed a grave error.

What seems to have been really judicious in his plan, was the turning movement determined on against Lee's right, along the old Richmond road, running from the direction of the river past the end of the ridge occupied by the Confederates, and so southward. To break through at this point was the only hope of success, and General Burnside had accordingly resolved, he declared, upon "a rapid movement down the old Richmond road" with Franklin's large command. Unfortunately, however, this wise design was complicated with another, most unwise, to send forward *a division*, first, to seize the crest of the ridge near the point where it sinks into the plain. On this crest were posted the veterans of Jackson, commanded in person by that skilful soldier. Three lines of infantry, supported by artillery, were ready to receive the Federal attack, and, to force back this stubborn obstacle, General Burnside sent a division. The proof is found in his order to General Franklin at about six o'clock on the morning of the battle: "Send out a division at least … to seize, if possible, the heights near Captain Hamilton's," which was the ground whereon Jackson's right rested.

An attack on the formidable position known as Marye's Hill, on Lee's left, west of Fredericksburg, was also directed to be made by the same small force. The order to General Sumner was to "form a column of *a division*, for the purpose of pushing in the direction of the Telegraph and Plank roads, for the purpose of seizing the heights in the rear of the town;" or, according to another version, "up the Plank road to its intersection with the Telegraph road, where they will divide, with the object of seizing the heights on both sides of those roads."

The point of "intersection" here referred to was the locality of what has been called "that sombre, fatal, terrible stone wall," just under Marye's Hill, where the most fearful slaughter of the Federal forces took place. Marye's Hill is a strong position, and its importance was well understood by Lee. Longstreet's infantry was in heavy line of battle behind it, and the crest bristled with artillery. There was still less hope here of effecting any thing with "a division" than on the Confederate right held by Jackson.

General Burnside seems, however, to have regarded success as probable. He added in his order: "Holding these heights, with the heights near Captain Hamilton's, will, I hope, compel the enemy to evacuate the whole ridge between these points." In his testimony afterward, he said that, in the event of failure in these assaults on Lee's flanks, he "proposed to make a direct attack on their front, and drive them out of their works."

These extracts from General Burnside's orders and testimony clearly indicate his plan, which was to assail both Lee's right and left, and, in the event of failure, direct a heavy blow at his centre. That the whole plan completely failed was mainly due, it would seem, to the inconsiderable numbers of the assaulting columns.

We return now to the narrative of the battle which these comments have interrupted.

General Lee was ready to receive the Federal attack, and, at an early hour of the morning, rode from his headquarters, in rear of his centre, along his line of battle toward the right, where he probably expected the main assault of the enemy to take place. He was clad in his plain, well-worn gray uniform, with felt hat, cavalry-boots, and short cape, without sword, and almost without any indications of his rank. In these outward details, he differed much from Generals Jackson and Stuart, who rode with him. The latter, as was usual with him, wore a fully-decorated uniform, sash, black plume, sabre, and handsome gauntlets. General Jackson, also, on this day, chanced to have exchanged his dingy old coat and sun-scorched cadet-cap for a new coat[1] covered with dazzling buttons, and a cap brilliant with a broad band of gold lace, in which (for him) extraordinary disguise his men scarcely knew him.

[Footnote 1: This coat was a present from Stuart.]

As Lee and his companions passed along in front of the line of battle, the troops cheered them. It was evident that the army was in excellent spirits, and ready for the hard work which the day would bring. Lee proceeded down the old Richmond, or stage road—that mentioned in General Burnside's order as the one over which his large flanking column was to move—and rode on with Stuart until he was near the River road, running toward Fredericksburg, parallel to the Federal line of battle. Here he stopped, and endeavored to make out, through the dense fog covering the plain, whether the Federal forces were moving. A stifled hum issued from the mist, but nothing could be seen. It seemed, however, that the enemy's skirmishers—probably concealed in the ditches along the River road—had sharper eyes, as bullets began to whistle around the two generals, and soon a number of black specks were seen moving forward. General Lee remained for some time longer, in spite of the exposure, conversing with great calmness and gravity with Stuart, who was all ardor. He then rode back slowly, passed along his line of battle, greeted wherever he was seen with cheers, and took his position on the eminence in his centre, near the Telegraph road, the same commanding point from which he had witnessed the bombardment of Fredericksburg.

The battle did not commence until ten o'clock, owing to the dense fog, through which the light of the sun could scarcely pierce. At that hour the mist lifted and rolled away, and the Confederates posted on the ridge saw a heavy column of infantry advancing to attack their right, near the Hamilton House. This force was Meade's division, supported by Gibbon's, with a third in reserve, General Franklin having put in action as many troops as his orders ("a division at least") permitted. General Meade was arrested for some time by a minute but most annoying obstacle. Stuart had placed a single piece of artillery, under Major John Pelham, near the point where the old Richmond and River roads meet—that is, directly on the flank of the advancing column—and this gun now opened a rapid and determined fire upon General Meade. Major Pelham—almost a boy in years—continued to hold his exposed position with great gallantry, although the enemy opened fire upon him with several batteries, killing a number of his gunners. General Lee witnessed this duel from the hill on which he had taken his stand, and is said to have exclaimed, "It is glorious to see such courage in one so young!" [Footnote: General Lee's opinion of Major Pelham appears from his report, in which he styles the young officer "the gallant Pelham," and says: "Four batteries immediately turned upon him, but he sustained their heavy fire with the unflinching courage that ever distinguished him." Pelham fell at Kelly's Ford in March, 1863.]

58

Pelham continued the cannonade for about two hours, only retiring when he received a peremptory order from Jackson to do so; and it would seem that this one gun caused a considerable delay in the attack. "Meade advanced across the plain, but had not proceeded far," says Mr. Swinton, "before he was compelled to stop and silence a battery that Stuart had posted on the Port Royal road." Having brushed away this annoying obstacle, General Meade, with a force which he states to have amounted to ten thousand men, advanced rapidly to attack the hill upon which the Confederates awaited him. He was suffered to approach within a few hundred yards, when Jackson's artillery, under Colonel Walker, posted near the end of the ridge, opened a sudden and furious fire, which threw the Federal line into temporary confusion. The troops soon rallied, however, and advanced again to the attack, which fell on Jackson's front line under A.P. Hill. The struggle which now ensued was fierce and bloody, but, a gap having been left between the brigades of Archer and Lane, the enemy pierced the opening, turning the left of one brigade and the right of the other, pressed on, attacked Gregg's brigade of Hill's reserve, threw it into confusion, and seemed about to carry the crest. Gregg's brigade was quickly rallied, however, by its brave commander, who soon afterward fell, mortally wounded; the further progress of the enemy was checked, and, Jackson's second line rapidly advancing, the enemy were met and forced back, step by step, until they were driven down the slope again. Here they were attacked by the brigades of Hoke and Atkinson, and driven beyond the railroad, the Confederates cheering and following them into the plain. The repulse had been complete, and the slope and ground in front of it were strewed with Federal dead. They had returned as rapidly as they had charged, pursued by shot and shell, and General Lee, witnessing the spectacle from his hill, murmured, in his grave and measured voice: "It is well this is so terrible! we should grow too fond of it!"

The assault on the Confederate right had thus ended in disaster, but almost immediately another attack took place, whose results were more bloody and terrible still. As General Meade fell back, pursued by the men of Jackson, the sudden roar of artillery from the Confederate left indicated that a heavy conflict had begun in that quarter. The Federal troops were charging Marye's Hill, which was to prove the Cemetery Hill of Fredericksburg. This frightful charge—for no other adjective can describe it—was made by General French's division, supported by General Hancock. The Federal troops rushed forward over the broken ground in the suburbs of the city, and, "as soon as the masses became dense enough,"[1] were received with a concentrated artillery fire from the hill in front of them. This fire was so destructive that it "made gaps that could be seen at the distance of a mile." The charging division had advanced in column of brigades, and the front was nearly destroyed. The troops continued to move forward, however, and had nearly reached the base of the hill, when the brigades of Cobb and Cooke, posted behind a stone wall running parallel with the Telegraph road, met them with a sudden fire of musketry, which drove them back in terrible disorder. Nearly half the force was killed or lay disabled on the field, and upon the survivors, now in full retreat, was directed a concentrated artillery-fire from, the hill.

[Footnote 1: Longstreet.]

In face of this discharge of cannon, General Hancock's force, supporting French, now gallantly advanced in its turn. The charge lasted about fifteen minutes, and in that time General Hancock lost more than two thousand of the five thousand men of his command. The repulse was still more bloody and decisive than the first. The second column fell back in disorder, leaving the ground covered with their dead.

General Burnside had hitherto remained at the "Phillips House," a mile or more from the Rappahannock. He now mounted his horse, and, riding down to the river, dismounted, walked up and down in great agitation, and exclaimed, looking at Marye's Hill: "That crest must be carried to-night."[1]

[Footnote 1: The authority for this incident is Mr. William Swinton, who was present.]

In spite of the murderous results of the first charges, the Federal commander determined on a third. General Hooker's reserve was ordered to make it, and, although that officer protested against it, General Burnside was immovable, and repeated his order. General Hooker sullenly obeyed, and opened with artillery upon the stone wall at the foot of the hill, in order to make a breach in it. This fire continued until nearly sunset, when Humphrey's division was formed for the charge. The men were ordered to throw aside their knapsacks, and not to load their guns, "for there was no time there to load and fire," says General Hooker. The word was given about sunset, and the division charged headlong over the ground already covered with dead. A few words will convey the result. Of four thousand men who charged, seventeen hundred and sixty were left dead or wounded on the field. The rest retreated, pursued by the fire of the batteries and infantry; and night fell on the battle-field.

This charge was the real termination of the bloody battle of Fredericksburg, but, on the Confederate right, Jackson had planned and begun to execute a decisive advance on the force in his front. This he designed to undertake "precisely at sunset," and his intention was to depend on the bayonet, his military judgment or instinct having satisfied him that the *morale* of the Federal army was destroyed. The advance was discontinued, however, in consequence of the lateness of the hour and the sudden artillery-fire which saluted him as he began to move. A striking feature of this intended advance is the fact that Jackson had placed his artillery *in front* of his line of battle, intending to attack in that manner.

As darkness settled down, the last guns of Stuart, who had defended the Confederate right flank with about thirty pieces of artillery, were heard far in advance, and apparently advancing still. The Federal lines had fallen back, wellnigh to the banks of the river, and there seems little room to doubt that the*morale* of the men was seriously impaired. "From what I knew of our want of success upon the right," says General Franklin, when interrogated on this point, "and the demoralized condition of the troops upon the right and centre, as represented to me by their commanders, I confess I believe the order to recross was a very proper one."

General Burnside refused to give the order; and, nearly overwhelmed, apparently, by the fatal result of the attack, determined to form the ninth corps in column of regiments, and lead it in person against Marye's Hill, on the next morning. Such a design, in a soldier of ability, indicates desperation. To charge Marye's Hill with a corps in column of regiments, was to devote the force to destruction. It was nearly certain that the whole command would be torn to pieces by the Southern artillery, but General Burnside seems to have regarded the possession of the hill as worth any amount of blood; and, in face of the urgent appeals of his officers, gave orders for the movement. At the last moment, however, he yielded to the entreaties of General Sumner, and abandoned his bloody design.

Still it seemed that the Federal commander was unable to come to the mortifying resolution of recrossing the Rappahannock. The battle was fought on the 13th of December, and until the night of the 15th General Burnside continued to face Lee on the south bank of the river—his bands playing, his flags flying, and nothing indicating an intention of retiring. To that resolve he had however come, and on the night of the 15th, in the midst of storm and darkness, the Federal army recrossed to the north bank of the Rappahannock.

XI FINAL MOVEMENTS OF 1862

The battle of Fredericksburg was another defeat of the Federal programme of invasion, as decisive, and in one sense as disastrous, as the second battle of Manassas. General Burnside had not lost as many men as General Pope, and had not retreated in confusion, pursued by a victorious enemy; but, brief as the conflict had been—two or three hours summing up all the real fighting—its desperate character, and the evident hopelessness of any attempt to storm Lee's position, profoundly discouraged and demoralized the Northern troops. We have quoted the statement of General Franklin, commanding the whole left wing, that from "the demoralized condition of the troops upon the right and centre, as represented to him by their commanders, he believed the order to recross was a very proper one." Nor is there any ground to suppose that the feeling of the left wing was greatly better. That wing of the army had not suffered as heavily as the right, which had recoiled with such frightful slaughter from Marye's Hill; but the repulse of General Meade in their own front had been equally decisive, and the non-success of the right must have reacted on the left, discouraging that also. Northern writers, in a position to ascertain the condition of the troops, fully bear out this view: "That the *morale* of the Army of the Potomac became seriously impaired after the disaster at Fredericksburg," says Mr. Swinton, the able and candid historian of the campaign, "was only too manifest. Indeed, it would be impossible to imagine a graver or gloomier, a more sombre or unmusical body of men than the Army of the Potomac a month after the battle. And, as the days went by, despondency, discontent, and all evil inspirations, with their natural consequent, desertion, seemed to increase rather than to diminish, until, for the first time, the Army of the Potomac could be said to be really demoralized." General Sumner noticed that a spirit of "croaking" had become diffused throughout the forces. For an army to display that tendency clearly indicates that the troops have lost the most important element of victory—confidence in themselves and their leader. And for this sentiment there was valid reason. Columns wholly inadequate in numbers had been advanced against the formidable Confederate positions, positions so strong and well defended that it is doubtful if thrice the force could have made any impression upon them, and the result was such as might have been expected. The men lost confidence in the military capacity of their commander, and in their own powers. After the double repulse at Marye's Hill and in front of Jackson, the troops, looking at the ground strewed with dead and wounded, were in no condition to go forward hopefully to another struggle which promised to be equally bloody.

The Southern army was naturally in a condition strongly in contrast with that of their adversary. They had repulsed the determined assault of the Federal columns with comparative ease on both flanks. Jackson's first line, although pierced and driven back, soon rallied, and checked the enemy until the second line came up, when General Meade was driven back, the third line not having moved from its position along the road near the Hamilton House. On the left, Longstreet had repulsed the Federal charge with his artillery and two small brigades. The loss of the Confederates in both these encounters was much less than that of their adversaries[1], a natural result of the circumstances; and thus, instead of sharing the depression of their opponents, the Southern troops were elated, and looked forward to a renewal of the battle with confidence in themselves and in their leader.

[Footnote 1: "Our loss during the operation, since the movements of the enemy began, amounts to about eighteen hundred killed and wounded."—*Lee's Report*. Federal authorities state the Northern loss at a little over twelve thousand; the larger part, no doubt, in the attack on Marye's Hill.]

It is not necessary to offer much comment upon the manner in which General Burnside had attacked. He is said, by his critics, not to have, at the time, designed the turning movement against General Lee's right, upon which point the present writer is unable to decide. That movement would seem to have presented the sole and only chance of success for the Federal arms, as the successful advance of General Franklin's fifty-five or sixty thousand men up the old Richmond road would have compelled Lee to retire his whole right wing, to protect it from an assault in flank and reverse. What dispositions he would have made under these circumstances must be left to conjecture; but, it is certain that the blow would have proved a serious one, calling for the display of all his military ability. In the event, however, that this was the main great aim of General Burnside, his method of carrying out his design insured, it would seem, its failure. Ten thousand men only were to clear the way for the flanking movement, in order to effect which object it was necessary to crush Jackson. So that it may be said that the success of the plan involved the repulse of one-half Lee's army with ten thousand men.

The assault on Marye's Hill was an equally fatal military mistake. That the position could not be stormed, is proved by the result of the actual attempt. It is doubtful if, in any battle ever fought by any troops, men displayed greater gallantry. They rushed headlong, not only once, but thrice, into the focus of a frightful front and cross fire of artillery and small-arms, losing nearly half their numbers in a few minutes; the ground was littered with their dead, and yet the foremost had only been able to approach within sixty yards of the terrible stone wall in advance of the hill. There they fell, throwing up their hands to indicate that they saw at last that the attempt to carry the hill was hopeless.

These comments seem justified by the circumstances, and are made with no intention of casting obloquy upon the commander who, displaying little ability, gave evidences of unfaltering courage. He had urged his inability to handle so large an army, but the authorities had forced the command upon him; he had accepted it and done his best, and, like a brave soldier, determined to lead the final charge in person, dying, if necessary, at the head of his men.

General Lee has not escaped criticism any more than General Burnside. The Southern people were naturally dissatisfied with the result—the safe retreat of the Federal army—and asked why they had not been attacked and captured or destroyed. The London *Times*, at that period, and a military critic recently, in the same journal, declared that Lee had it in his power to crush General Burnside, "horse, foot, and dragoons," and, from his failure to do so, argued his want of great generalship. A full discussion of the question is left by the present writer to those better skilled than himself in military science. It is proper, however, to insert here General Lee's own explanation of his action:

"The attack on the 13th," he says, "had been so easily repulsed, and by so small a part of our army, that it was not supposed the enemy would limit his efforts to one attempt, which, in view of the magnitude of his preparations, and the extent of his force, seemed to be comparatively insignificant. Believing, therefore, that he would attack us, it was not deemed expedient to lose the advantages of our position and expose the troops to the fire of his inaccessible batteries beyond the river, by advancing against him. But we were necessarily ignorant of the extent to which he had suffered, and only became aware of it when, on the morning of the 16th, it was discovered that he had availed himself of the darkness of night, and the prevalence of a violent storm of wind and rain, to recross the river."

This statement was no doubt framed by General Lee to meet the criticisms which the result of the battle occasioned. In conversing with General Stuart on the subject, he added that he felt too great responsibility for the preservation of his troops to unnecessarily hazard them. "No one knows," he said, "how *brittle* an army is."

The word may appear strange, applied to the Army of Northern Virginia, which had certainly vindicated its claim, under many arduous trials, to the virtues of toughness and endurance. But Lee's meaning was plain, and his view seems to have been founded on good sense. The enemy had in all, probably, two hundred pieces of artillery, a large portion of which were posted on the high ground north of the river. Had Lee descended from his ridge and advanced into the plain to attack, this large number of guns would have greeted him with a rapid and destructive fire, which must have inflicted upon him a loss as nearly heavy as he had inflicted upon General Burnside at Marye's Hill. From such a result he naturally shrunk. It has been seen that the Federal troops, brave as they were, had been demoralized by such a fire; and Lee was unwilling to expose his own troops to similar slaughter.

There is little question, it seems, that an advance of the description mentioned would have resulted in a conclusive victory, and the probable surrender of the whole or a large portion of the Federal army. Whether the probability of such a result was sufficient to compensate for the certain slaughter, the reader will decide for himself. General Lee did not think so, and did not order the advance. He preferred awaiting, in his strong position, the second assault which General Burnside would probably make; and, while he thus waited, the enemy secretly recrossed the river, rendering an attack upon them by Lee impossible.

General Burnside made a second movement to cross the Rappahannock—this time at Banks's Ford, above Fredericksburg—in the inclement month of January; but, as he might have anticipated, the condition of the roads was such that it was impossible to advance. His artillery, with the horses dragging the pieces, sank into the almost bottomless mud, where they stuck fast—even the foot-soldiers found it difficult to march through the quagmire—and the whole movement was speedily abandoned.

When General Burnside issued the order for this injudicious advance, two of his general officers met, and one asked:

"What do you think of it?"

"It don't seem to have the *ring*" was the reply.

"No—the bell is broken," the other added.

This incident, which is given on the authority of a Northern writer, probably conveys a correct idea of the feeling of both the officers and men of General Burnside's army. The disastrous day of Fredericksburg had seriously injured the troops.

"The Army of the Potomac," the writer adds, "was sadly fractured, and its tones had no longer the clear, inspiring ring of victory."

XII.

THE YEAR OF BATTLES.

The stormy year 1862 had terminated, thus, in a great Confederate success. In its arduous campaigns, following each other in rapid succession, General Lee had directed the movements of the main great army, and the result of the year's fighting was to gain him that high military reputation which his subsequent movements only consolidated and increased.

A rapid glance at the events of the year in their general outlines will indicate the merit due the Southern commander. The Federal plan of invasion in the spring had been extremely formidable. Virginia was to be pierced by no less than four armies—from the northwest, the Shenandoah Valley, the Potomac, and the Peninsula—the whole force to converge upon Richmond, the "heart of the rebellion." Of these, the army of General McClellan was the largest and most threatening. It advanced, with little opposition, until it reached the Chickahominy, crossed, and lay in sight of Richmond. The great force of one hundred and fifty thousand men was about to make the decisive assault, when Lee attacked it, and the battle which ensued drove the Federal army to a point thirty miles from the city, with such loss as to render hopeless any further attempt to assail the capital.

Such was the first act of the drama; the rest speedily followed. A new army was raised promptly by the Federal authorities, and a formidable advance was made against Richmond again, this time from the direction of Alexandria. Lee was watching General McClellan when intelligence of the new movement reached him. Remaining, with a portion of his troops, near Richmond, he sent Jackson to the Rapidan. The battle of Cedar Mountain resulted in the repulse of General Pope's vanguard; and, discovering at last that the real danger lay in the direction of Culpepper, Lee moved thither, drove back General Pope, flanked him, and, in the severe battle of Manassas, routed his army, which was forced to retire upon Washington.

Two armies had thus been driven from the soil of Virginia, and the Confederate commander had moved into Maryland, in order to draw the enemy thither, and, if practicable, transfer the war to the heart of Pennsylvania. Unforeseen circumstances had defeated the latter of these objects. The concentration on Sharpsburg was rendered necessary; an obstinately-fought battle ensued there; and, not defeated, but forced to abandon further movements toward Pennsylvania, Lee had retired into Virginia, where he remained facing his adversary. This was the first failure of Lee up to that point in the campaigns of the year; and an attentive consideration of the circumstances will show that the result was not fairly attributable to any error which he had committed. Events beyond his control had shaped his action, and directed all his movements;

and it will remain a question whether the extrication of his small force from its difficult position did not better prove Lee's generalship than the victory at Manassas.

The subsequent operations of the opposing armies indicated clearly that the Southern forces were still in excellent fighting condition; and the movements of Lee, during the advance of General McClellan toward Warrenton, were highly honorable to his military ability. With a force much smaller than that of his adversary, he greatly embarrassed and impeded the Federal advance; confronted them on the Upper Rappahannock, completely checking their forward movement in that direction; and, when they moved rapidly to Fredericksburg, crossed the Rapidan promptly, reappearing in their front on the range of hills opposite that city. The battle which followed compensated for the failure of the Maryland campaign and the drawn battle of Sharpsburg. General Burnside had attacked, and sustained decisive defeat. The stormy year, so filled with great events and arduous encounters, had thus wound up with a pitched battle, in which the enemy suffered a bloody repulse; and the best commentary on the decisive character of this last struggle of the year, was the fault found with General Lee for not destroying his adversary.

In less than six months Lee had thus fought four great pitched battles—all victories to his arms, with the exception of Sharpsburg, which was neither a victory nor a defeat. The result was thus highly encouraging to the South; and, had the Army of Northern Virginia had its ranks filled up, as the ranks of the Northern armies were, the events of the year 1862 would have laid the foundation of assured success. An inquiry into the causes of failure in this particular is not necessary to the subject of the volume before the reader. It is only necessary to state the fact that the Army of Northern Virginia, defending what all conceded to be the territory on which the decisive struggle must take place, was never sufficiently numerous to follow up the victories achieved by it. At the battles of the Chickahominy the army numbered at most about seventy-five thousand; at the second Manassas, about fifty thousand; at Sharpsburg, less than forty thousand; and at Fredericksburg, about fifty thousand. In the following year, it will be seen that these latter numbers were at first but little exceeded, and, as the months passed on, that they dwindled more and more, until, in April, 1865, the whole force in line of battle at Petersburg was scarcely more than thirty thousand men.

Such had been the number of the troops under command of Lee in 1862. The reader has been informed of the number of the Federal force opposed to him. This was one hundred and fifty thousand on the Chickahominy, of whom one hundred and fifteen thousand were effective; about one hundred thousand, it would seem, under General Pope, at the second battle of Manassas; eighty-seven thousand actually engaged at the battle of Sharpsburg; and at Fredericksburg from one hundred and ten to one hundred and twenty thousand.

These numbers are stated on the authority of Federal officers or historians, and Lee's force on the authority of his own reports, or of gentlemen of high character, in a situation to speak with accuracy. Of the truth of the statements the writer of these pages can have no doubt; and, if the fighting powers of the Northern and Southern troops be estimated as equal, the fair conclusion must be arrived at that Lee surpassed his adversaries in generalship.

The result, at least, of the year's fighting, had been extremely encouraging to the South, and after the battle of Fredericksburg no attempts were made to prosecute hostilities during the remainder of the year. The scheme of crossing above Fredericksburg proved a *fiasco*, beginning and ending in a day. Thereafter all movements ceased, and the two armies awaited the return of spring for further operations.

XIII.

LEE IN DECEMBER, 1862.

Before passing to the great campaigns of the spring and summer of 1863, we propose to say a few words of General Lee, in his private and personal character, and to attempt to indicate the position which he occupied at this time in the eyes of the army and the country. Unknown, save by reputation, when he assumed command of the forces in June, 1862, he had now, by the winter of the same year, become one of the best-known personages in the South. Neither the troops nor the people had perhaps penetrated the full character of Lee; and they seem to have attributed to him more reserve and less warmth and impulse than he possessed; but it was impossible for a human being, occupying so prominent a station before the general eye, to hide, in any material degree, his main great characteristics, and these had conciliated for Lee an exalted and wellnigh universal public regard. He was felt by all to be an individual of great dignity, sincerity, and earnestness, in the performance of duty. Destitute plainly of that vulgar ambition which seeks personal aggrandizement rather than the general good, and dedicated as plainly, heart and soul, to the cause for which he fought, he had won, even from those who had denounced him for the supposed hesitation in his course in April, 1861, and had afterward criticised his military operations, the repute of a truly great man, as well as of a commander of the first ability.

It was felt by all classes that the dignity of the Southern cause was adequately represented in the person and character of the commander of her most important army. While others, as brave and patriotic, no doubt, but of different temperament, had permitted themselves to become violent and embittered in their private and public utterances in reference to the North, Lee had remained calm, moderate, and dignified, under every provocation. His reports were without rhodomontade or exaggeration, and his tone uniformly modest, composed, and uninflated. After his most decisive successes, his pulse had remained calm; he had written of those successes with the air of one who sees no especial merit in any thing which he has performed; and, so marked was this tone of moderation and dignity, that, in reading his official reports to-day, it seems wellnigh impossible that they could have been written in the hot atmosphere of a war which aroused the bitterest passions of the human soul.

Upon this point of Lee's personal and official dignity it is unnecessary to dwell further, as the quality has long since been conceded by every one acquainted with the character of the individual, in the Old World and the New. It is the trait, perhaps, the most prominent to the observer, looking back now upon the individual; and it was, doubtless, this august moderation, dignity, and apparent exemption from natural infirmity, which produced the impression upon many persons that Lee was cold and unimpressible. We shall speak, in future, at greater length of his real character than is necessary in this place; but it may here be said, that the fancy that he was cold and unimpressible was a very great error. No man had stronger or warmer feelings, or regarded the invasion of the South with greater indignation, than himself. The sole difference was, that he had his feelings under greater control, and permitted no temptation to overcome his sense of that august dignity and composure becoming in the chief leader of a great people struggling for independent government.

The sentiment of the Southern people toward Lee may be summed up in the statement that they regarded him, in his personal and private character, with an admiration which was becoming unbounded, and reposed in him, as commander of the army, the most implicit confidence.

These expressions are strong, but they do not convey more than the truth. And this confidence was never withdrawn from him. It remained as strong in his hours of disaster as in his noontide of success. A few soured or desponding people might lose heart, indulge in "croaking," and denounce, under their breath, the commander of the army as responsible for failure when it occurred; but these fainthearted people were in a small minority, and had little encouragement in their muttered criticisms. The Southern people, from Virginia to the utmost limits of the Gulf States, resolutely persisted in regarding Lee as one of the greatest soldiers of history, and retained their confidence in him unimpaired to the end.

The army had set the example of this implicit reliance upon Lee as the chief leader and military head of the Confederacy. The brave fighting-men had not taken his reputation on trust, but had seen him win it fairly on some of the hardest-contested fields of history. The heavy blow at General McClellan on the Chickahominy had first shown the troops that they were under command of a thorough soldier. The rout of Pope at Manassas had followed in the ensuing month. At Sharpsburg, with less than forty thousand men, Lee had repulsed the attack of nearly ninety thousand; and at Fredericksburg General Burnside's great force had been driven back with inconsiderable loss to the Southern army. These successes, in the eyes of the troops, were the proofs of true leadership, and it did not detract from Lee's popularity that, on all occasions, he had carefully refrained from unnecessary exposure of the troops, especially at Fredericksburg, where an ambitious commander would have spared no amount of bloodshed to complete his glory by a great victory. Such was Lee's repute as army commander in the eyes of men accustomed to close scrutiny of their leaders. He was regarded as a thorough soldier, at once brave, wise, cool, resolute, and devoted, heart and soul, to the cause.

Personally, the commander-in-chief was also, by this time, extremely popular. He did not mingle with the troops to any great extent, nor often relax the air of dignity, somewhat tinged with reserve, which was natural with him. This reserve, however, never amounted to stiffness or "official" coolness. On the contrary, Lee was markedly free from the chill demeanor of the martinet, and had become greatly endeared to the men by the unmistakable evidences which he had given them of his honesty, sincerity, and kindly feeling for them. It cannot, indeed, be said that he sustained the same relation toward the troops as General Jackson. For the latter illustrious soldier, the men had a species of familiar affection, the result, in a great degree, of the informal and often eccentric demeanor of the individual. There was little or nothing in Jackson to indicate that he was an officer holding important command. He was without reserve, and exhibited none of that formal courtesy which characterized Lee. His manners, on the contrary, were quite informal, familiar, and conciliated in return a familiar regard. We repeat the word *familiar* as conveying precisely the idea intended to be expressed. It indicated the difference between these two great soldiers in their outward appearance. Lee retained about him, upon all occasions, more or less of the commander-in-chief, passing before the troops on an excellent and well-groomed horse, his figure erect and graceful in the saddle, for he was one of the best riders in the army; his demeanor grave and thoughtful; his whole bearing that of a man intrusted with great responsibilities and the general care of the whole army. Jackson's personal appearance and air were very different. His dress was generally dingy: a faded cadet-cap tilted over his eyes, causing him to raise his chin into the air; his stirrups were apt to be too short, and his knees were thus elevated ungracefully, and he would amble along on his rawboned horse with a singularly absent-minded expression of countenance, raising, from time to time, his right hand and slapping his knee. This brief outline of the two commanders will serve to show the difference between them personally, and it must be added that Jackson's eccentric bearing was the source, in some degree, of his popularity. The men admired him immensely for his great military ability, and his odd ways procured for him that familiar liking to which we have alluded.

It is not intended, however, in these observations to convey the idea that General Lee was regarded as a stiff and unapproachable personage of whom the private soldiers stood in awe. Such a statement would not express the truth. Lee was perfectly approachable, and no instance is upon record, or ever came to the knowledge of the present writer, in which he repelled the approach of his men, or received the humblest of them with any thing but kindness. He was naturally simple and kind, with great gentleness and patience; and it will not be credible, to any who knew the man, that he ever made any difference in his treatment of those who approached him from a consideration of their rank in the army. His theory, expressed upon many occasions, was, that the private soldiers—men who fought without the stimulus of rank, emolument, or individual renown—were the most meritorious class of the army, and that they deserved and should receive the utmost respect and consideration. This statement, however, is doubtless unnecessary. Men of Lee's pride and dignity never make a difference in their treatment of men, because one is humble, and the other of high rank. Of such human beings it may be said that *noblesse oblige.*

The men of the army had thus found their commander all that they could wish, and his increasing personal popularity was shown by the greater frequency with which they now spoke of him as "Marse Robert," "Old Uncle Robert," and by other familiar titles. This tendency in troops is always an indication of personal regard; these nicknames had been already showered upon Jackson, and General Lee was having his turn. The troops regarded him now more as their fellow-soldier than formerly, having found that his dignity was not coldness, and that he would, under no temptation, indulge his personal convenience, or fare better than themselves. It was said—we know not with what truth—that the habit of Northern generals in the war was to look assiduously to their individual comfort in selecting their quarters, and to take pleasure in surrounding themselves with glittering staff-officers, body-guards, and other indications of their rank, and the consideration which they expected. In these particulars Lee differed extremely from his opponents, and there were no evidences whatever, at his headquarters, that he was the commander-in-chief, or even an officer of high rank. He uniformly lived in a tent, in spite of the urgent invitations of citizens to use their houses for his headquarters; and this refusal was the result both of an indisposition to expose these gentlemen to annoyance from the enemy when he himself retired, and of a rooted objection to fare better than his troops. They had tents only, often indeed were without even that much covering, and it was repugnant to Lee's feelings to sleep under a good roof when the troops were so much exposed. His headquarters tent, at this time (December, 1862), as before and afterward, was what is called a "house-tent," not differing in any particular from those used by the private soldiers of the army in winter-quarters. It was pitched in an opening in the wood near the narrow road leading to Hamilton's Crossing, with the tents of the officers of the staff grouped near; and, with the exception of an orderly, who always waited to summon couriers to carry dispatches, there was nothing in the shape of a body-guard visible, or any indication that the unpretending group of tents was the army headquarters.

Within, no article of luxury was to be seen. A few plain and indispensable objects were all which the tent contained. The covering of the commander-in-chief was an ordinary army blanket, and his fare was plainer, perhaps, than that of the majority of his officers and men. This was the result of an utter indifference, in Lee, to personal convenience or indulgence. Citizens frequently sent him delicacies, boxes filled with turkeys, hams, wine, cordials, and other things, peculiarly tempting to one leading the hard life of the soldier, but these were almost uniformly sent to the sick in some neighboring hospital. Lee's principle in so acting seems to have been to set the good example to his officers of not faring better than their men; but he was undoubtedly indifferent naturally to luxury of all descriptions. In his habits and feelings he was not the self-indulgent man of peace, but the thorough soldier, willing to live hard, to sleep upon the ground, and to disregard all sensual indulgence. In his other habits he was equally abstinent. He cared nothing for wine, whiskey, or any stimulant, and never used tobacco in any form. He rarely relaxed his energies in any thing calculated to amuse him; but, when not riding along his lines, or among the camps to see in person that the troops were properly cared for, generally passed his time in close attention to official duties connected with the well-being of the army, or in correspondence with the authorities at Richmond. When he relaxed from this continuous toil, it was to indulge in some quiet and simple diversion, social converse with ladies in houses at which he chanced to stop, caresses bestowed upon children, with whom he was a great favorite, and frequently in informal conversation with his officers. At "Hayfield" and "Moss Neck," two hospitable houses below Fredericksburg, he at this time often stopped and spent some time in the society of the ladies and children there. One of the latter, a little curly-headed girl, would come up to him always to receive her accustomed kiss, and one day confided to him, as a personal friend, her desire to kiss General Jackson, who blushed like a girl when Lee, with a quiet laugh, told him of the child's wish. On another occasion, when his small friend came to receive his caress, he said, laughing, that she would show more taste in selecting a younger gentleman than himself, and, pointing to a youthful officer in a corner of the room, added, "There is the handsome Major Pelham!" which caused that modest young soldier to blush with confusion. The bearing of General Lee in these hours of relaxation, was quite charming, and made him warm friends. His own pleasure and gratification were plain, and gratified others, who, in the simple and kindly gentleman in the plain gray uniform, found it difficult to recognize the commander-in-chief of the Southern army.

These moments of relaxation were, however, only occasional. All the rest was toil, and the routine of hard work and grave assiduity went on month after month, and year after year, with little interruption. With the exceptions which we have noted, all pleasures and distractions seemed of little interest to Lee, and to the present writer, at least, he seemed on all occasions to bear the most striking resemblance to the traditional idea of Washington. High principle and devotion to duty were plainly this human being's springs of action, and he went through the hard and continuous labor incident to army command with a grave and systematic attention, wholly indifferent, it seemed, to almost every species of diversion and relaxation.

This attempt to show how Lee appeared at that time to his solders, has extended to undue length, and we shall be compelled to defer a full notice of the most interesting and beautiful trait of his character. This was his humble and profound piety. The world has by no means done him justice upon this subject. No one doubted during the war that General Lee was a sincere Christian in conviction, and his exemplary moral character and life were beyond criticism. Beyond this it is doubtful if any save his intimate associates understood the depth of his feeling on the greatest of all subjects. Jackson's strong religious fervor was known and often alluded to, but it is doubtful if Lee was regarded as a person of equally fervent convictions and feelings. And yet the fact is certain that faith in God's providence and reliance upon the Almighty were the foundation of all his actions, and the secret of his supreme composure under all trials. He was naturally of such reserve that it is not singular that the extent of this sentiment was not understood. Even then, however, good men who frequently visited him, and conversed with him upon religious subjects, came away with their hearts burning within them. When the Rev. J. William Jones, with another clergyman, went, in 1863, to consult him in reference to the better observance of the Sabbath in the army, "his eye brightened, and his whole countenance glowed with pleasure; and as, in his simple, feeling words, he expressed his delight, we forgot the great warrior, and only remembered that we were communing with an humble, earnest Christian." When he was informed that the chaplains prayed for him, tears started to his eyes, and he replied: "I sincerely thank you for that, and I can only say that I am a poor sinner, trusting in Christ alone, and that I need all the prayers you can offer for me."

On the day after this interview he issued an earnest general order, enjoining the observance of the Sabbath by officers and men, urging them to attend public worship in their camps, and forbidding the performance on Sunday of all official duties save those necessary to the subsistence or safety of the army. He always attended public worship, if it were in his power to do so, and often the earnestness of the preacher would "make his eye kindle and his face glow." He frequently attended the meetings of his chaplains, took a warm interest in the proceedings, and uniformly exhibited, declares one who could speak from personal knowledge, an ardent desire for the promotion of religion in the army. He did not fail, on many occasions, to show his men that he was a sincere Christian. When General Meade came over to Mine Run, and the Southern army marched to meet him, Lee was riding along his line of battle in the woods, when he came upon a party of soldiers holding a prayer-meeting on the eve of battle. Such a spectacle was not unusual in the army then and afterward—the rough fighters were often men of profound piety—and on this occasion the sight before him seems to have excited deep emotion in Lee. He stopped, dismounted—the staff-officers accompanying him did the same—and Lee uncovered his head, and stood in an attitude of profound respect and attention, while the earnest prayer proceeded, in the midst of the thunder of artillery and the explosion of the enemy's shells.[1]

[Footnote 1: These details are given on the authority of the Rev. J. William Jones, of Lexington, Va.]

[Illustration: Lee at the Soldiers' Prayer Meeting.]

Other incidents indicating the simple and earnest piety of Lee will be presented in the course of this narrative. The fame of the soldier has in some degree thrown into the background the less-imposing trait of personal piety in the individual. No delineation of Lee, however, would be complete without a full statement of his religious principles and feelings. As the commander-in-chief of the Army of Northern Virginia, he won that august renown which encircles his name with a halo of military glory, both in America and Europe. His battles and victories are known to all men. It is not known to all that the illustrious soldier whose fortune it was to overthrow, one after another, the best soldiers of the Federal army, was a simple, humble, and devoted Christian, whose eyes filled with tears when he was informed that his chaplains prayed for him; and who said, "I am a poor sinner, trusting in Christ alone, and need all the prayers you can offer for me."

PART VI.
CHANCELLORSVILLE AND GETTYSBURG
I.
ADVANCE OF GENERAL HOOKER.

Lee remained throughout the winter at his headquarters in the woods south of Fredericksburg, watching the Northern army, which continued to occupy the country north of the city, with the Potomac River as their base of supplies.

With the coming of spring, it was obviously the intention of the Federal authorities to again essay the crossing of the Rappahannock at some point either above or below Fredericksburg; and as the movement above was less difficult, and promised more decisive results, it was seen by General Lee that this would probably be the quarter from which he might expect an attack. General Stuart, a soldier of sound judgment, said, during the winter, "The next battle will take place at Chancellorsville," and the position of Lee's troops seemed to indicate that this was also his own opinion. His right remained still "opposite Fredericksburg," barring the direct approach to Richmond, but his left extended up the Rappahannock beyond Chancellorsville, and all the fords were vigilantly guarded to prevent a sudden flank movement by the enemy in that direction. As will be seen, the anticipations of Lee were to be fully realized. The heavy blow aimed at him, in the first days of spring, was to come from the quarter in which he had expected it.

The Federal army was now under command of General Joseph Hooker, an officer of dash, energy, excellent administrative capacity, and, Northern writers add, extremely prone to "self-assertion." General Hooker had harshly criticised the military operations both of General McClellan on the Chickahominy, and of General Burnside at Fredericksburg, and so strong an impression had these strictures made upon the minds of the authorities, that they came to the determination of intrusting the command of the army to the officer who made them, doubtless concluding that his own success would prove greater than that of his predecessors. This opinion seemed borne out by the first proceedings of General Hooker. He set to work energetically to reorganize and increase the efficiency of the army, did away with General Burnside's defective "grand division" arrangement, consolidated the cavalry into an effective corps, enforced strict discipline among officers and men alike, and at the beginning of spring had brought his army to a high state of efficiency. His confident tone inspired the men; the depression resulting from the great disaster at Fredericksburg was succeeded by a spirit of buoyant hope, and the army was once more that great war-engine, ready for any undertaking, which it had been under McClellan.

It numbered, according to one Federal statement, one hundred and fifty-nine thousand three hundred men; but according to another, which appears more reliable, one hundred and twenty thousand infantry and artillery, and twelve thousand cavalry; in all, one hundred and thirty-two thousand troops. The army of General Lee was considerably smaller. Two divisions of Longstreet's corps had been sent to Suffolk, south of James River, to obtain supplies in that region, and this force was not present at the battle of Chancellorsville. The actual numbers under Lee's command will appear from the following statement of Colonel Walter H. Taylor, assistant adjutant-general of the army:

Our strength at Chancellorsville:

Anderson and McLaws............................ 13,000
Jackson (Hill, Rodes, and Trimble)............ 21,000
Early (Fredericksburg)......................... 6,000

——————
40,000

Cavalry and artillery.......................... 7,000
_____

Total of all arms............................. 47,000

As the Federal infantry numbered one hundred and twenty thousand, according to the smallest estimate of Federal authorities, and Lee's infantry forty thousand, the Northern force was precisely three times as large as the Southern.

[Illustration: Map—Battle of Chancellorsville.]

General Hooker had already proved himself an excellent administrative officer, and his plan of campaign against Lee seemed to show that he also possessed generalship of a high order. He had determined to pass the Rappahannock above Fredericksburg, turn Lee's flank, and thus force him to deliver battle under this disadvantage, or retire upon Richmond. The safe passage of the stream was the first great object, and General Hooker's dispositions to effect this were highly judicious. A force of about twenty thousand men was to pass the Rappahannock at Fredericksburg, and thus produce upon Lee the impression that the Federal army was about to renew the attempt in which they had failed under General Burnside. While General Lee's attention was engaged by the force thus threatening his right, the main body of the Northern army was to cross the Rappahannock and Rapidan above Chancellorsville, and, sweeping down rapidly upon the Confederate left flank, take up a strong position between Chancellorsville and Fredericksburg. The column which had crossed at the latter point to engage the attention of the Confederate commander, was then to recross to the northern bank, move rapidly to the upper fords, which the advance of the main body would by that time have uncovered; and, a second time crossing to the southern bank, unite with the rest. Thus the whole Federal army would be concentrated on the southern bank of the Rappahannock, and General Lee would be compelled to leave his camps on the hills of the Massaponnax, and fight upon ground dictated by his adversary. If he did not thus accept battle, but one other course was left. He must fall back in the direction of Richmond, to prevent his adversary from attacking his rear, and capturing or destroying his army.

In order to insure the success of this promising plan of attack, a strong column of well-mounted cavalry was to cross in advance of the army and strike for the railroads in Lee's rear, connecting him with Richmond and the Southwest. Thus flanked or cut off, and with all his communications destroyed, it seemed probable that General Lee would suffer decisive defeat, and that the Federal army would march in triumph to the capture of the Confederate capital.

This plan was certainly excellent, and seemed sure to succeed. It was, however, open to some criticism, as the event showed. General Hooker was detaching, in the beginning of the movement, his whole cavalry force for a distant operation, and dividing his army by the *ruse* at Fredericksburg, in face of an adversary not likely to permit that great error to escape him. While advancing thus, apparently to the certain destruction of Lee, General Hooker was leaving a vulnerable point in his own armor. Lee would probably discover that point, and aim to pierce his opponent there. At most, General Hooker was wrapping in huge folds the sword of Lee, not remembering that there was danger in the *cordon* as well as to the weapon.

Such was the plan which General Hooker had devised to bring back that success of the Federal arms in the spring of 1863 which had attended them in the early spring of 1862. At this latter period a heavy cloud rested upon the Confederate cause. Donaldson and Roanoke Island, Fort Macon, and the city of New Orleans, had then fallen; at Elkhorn, Kernstown, Newbern, and other places, the Federal forces had achieved important successes. These had been followed, however, by the Southern victories on the Chickahominy, at Manassas, and at Fredericksburg. Near this last-named spot now, where the year had wound up with so mortifying a Federal failure, General Hooker hoped to reverse events, and recover the Federal glories of the preceding spring.

Operations began as early as the middle of March, when General Averill, with about three thousand cavalry, crossed the Rappahannock at Kelly's Ford, above its junction with the Rapidan, and made a determined attack upon nearly eight hundred horsemen there, under General Fitz Lee, with the view of passing through Culpepper, crossing the Rapidan, and cutting Lee's communications in the direction of Gordonsville. The obstinate stand of General Fitz Lee's small force, however, defeated this object, and General Averill was forced to retreat beyond the Rappahannock again with considerable loss, and abandon his expedition. In this engagement fell Major John Pelham, who had been styled in Lee's first report of the battle of Fredericksburg "the gallant Pelham," and whose brave stand on the Port Royal road had drawn from Lee the exclamation, "It is glorious to see such courage in one so young." Pelham was, in spite of his youth, an artillerist of the first order of excellence, and his loss was a serious one, in spite of his inferior rank.

After this action every thing remained quiet until toward the end of April—General Lee continuing to hold the same position with his right at Fredericksburg, his left at the fords near Chancellorsville, and his cavalry, under Stuart, guarding the banks of the Rappahannock in Culpepper. On the 27th of April, General Hooker began his forward movement, by advancing three corps of his army—the Fifth, Eleventh, and Twelfth—to the banks of the river, near Kelly's Ford; and, on the next day, this force was joined by three additional corps—the First, Third, and Sixth—and the whole, on Wednesday (the 29th), crossed the river without difficulty. That this movement was a surprise to Lee, as has been supposed by some persons, is a mistake. Stuart was an extremely vigilant picket-officer, and both he and General Lee were in the habit of sending accomplished scouts to watch any movements in the Federal camps. As soon as these movements—which, in a large army, cannot be concealed—took place, information was always promptly brought, and it was not possible that General Hooker could move three large army corps toward the Rappahannock, as he did on April 27th, without early knowledge on the part of his adversary of so important a circumstance.

As the Federal infantry thus advanced, the large cavalry force began also to move through Culpepper toward the Central Railroad in Lee's rear. This column was commanded by General Stoneman, formerly a subordinate officer in Lee's old cavalry regiment in the United States Army; and, as General Stoneman's operations were entirely separate from those of the infantry, and not of much importance, we shall here dismiss them in a few words. He proceeded rapidly across Culpepper, harassed in his march by a small body of horse, under General William H.F. Lee; reached the Central Railroad at Trevillian's, below Gordonsville, and tore up a portion of it; passed on to James River, ravaging the country, and attempted the destruction of the Columbia Aqueduct, but did not succeed in so doing; when, hearing probably of the unforeseen result at Chancellorsville, he hastened back to the Rapidan, pursued and harassed as in his advance, and, crossing, regained the Federal lines beyond the Rappahannock.

To return to the movements of the main Federal force, under the personal command of General Hooker. This advanced rapidly across the angle between the two rivers, with no obstruction but that offered by the cavalry under Stuart, and on Thursday, April 30th, had crossed the Rapidan at Germanna and Ely's Fords, and was steadily concentrating around Chancellorsville. At the same time the Second Corps, under General Couch, was preparing to cross at United States Ford, a few miles distant; and General Sedgwick, commanding the detached force at Fredericksburg, having crossed and threatened Lee, in obedience to orders, now began passing back to the northern bank again, in order to march up and join the main body. Thus all things seemed in train to succeed on the side of the Federal army. General Hooker was over with about one hundred thousand men—twenty thousand additional troops would soon join him. Lee's army seemed scattered, and not "in hand" to oppose him; and there was some ground for the ebullition of joy attributed to General Hooker, as he saw his great force massing steadily in the vicinity of Chancellorsville. To those around him he exclaimed: "The rebel army is now the legitimate property of the Army of the Potomac. They may as well pack up their haversacks and make for Richmond, and I shall be after them!"

In a congratulatory order to his troops, he declared that they occupied now a position so strong that "the enemy must either ingloriously fly, or come out from behind his defences and give us battle on our own ground, where certain destruction awaits him."

Such were the joyful anticipations of General Hooker, who seems to have regarded the campaign as virtually ended by the successful passage of the river. His expressions and his general order would seem to indicate an irrepressible joy, but it is doubtful if the skilful soldiers under him shared this somewhat juvenile enthusiasm. The gray cavalier at Fredericksburg was not reported to be retiring, as was expected. On the contrary, the Southern troops seemed to be moving forward with the design of accepting battle.

Lee had determined promptly upon that course as soon as Stuart sent him information of the enemy's movements. Chancellorsville was at once seen to be the point for which General Hooker was aiming, and Lee's dispositions were made for confronting him there and fighting a pitched battle. The brigades of Posey and Mahone, of Anderson's Division, had been in front of Banks's and Ely's Fords, and this force of about eight thousand men was promptly ordered to fall back on Chancellorsville. At the same time Wright's brigade was sent up to reënforce this column; but the enemy continuing to advance in great force, General Anderson, commanding the whole, fell back from Chancellorsville to Tabernacle Church, on the road to Fredericksburg, where he was joined on the next day by Jackson, whom Lee had sent forward to his assistance.

The *ruse* at Fredericksburg had not long deceived the Confederate commander. General Sedgwick, with three corps, in all about twenty-two thousand men, had crossed just below Fredericksburg on the 29th, and Lee had promptly directed General Jackson to oppose him there. Line of battle was accordingly formed in the enemy's front beyond Hamilton's Crossing;

but as, neither on that day nor the next, any further advance was made by General Sedgwick, the whole movement was seen to be a feint to cover the real operations above. Lee accordingly turned his attention in the direction of Chancellorsville. Jackson, as we have related, was sent up to reënforce General Anderson, and Lee followed with the rest of the army, with the exception of about six thousand men, under General Early, whom he left to defend the crossing at Fredericksburg.

Such were the positions of the opposing forces on the 1st day of May. Each commander had displayed excellent generalship in the preliminary movements preceding the actual fighting. At last, however, the opposing lines were facing each other, and the real struggle was about to begin.

II.

THE WILDERNESS.

The "Wilderness," as the region around Chancellorsville is called, is so strange a country, and the character of the ground had so important a bearing upon the result of the great battle fought there, that a brief description of the locality will be here presented.

The region is a nearly unbroken expanse of dense thicket pierced only by narrow and winding roads, over which the traveller rides, mile after mile, without seeing a single human habitation. It would seem, indeed, that the whole barren and melancholy tract had been given up to the owl, the whippoorwill, and the moccasin, its original tenants. The plaintive cries of the night-birds alone break the gloomy silence of the desolate region, and the shadowy thicket stretching in every direction produces a depressing effect upon the feelings. Chancellorsville is in the centre of this singular territory, on the main road, or rather roads, running from Orange Court-House to Fredericksburg, from which latter place it is distant about ten miles. In spite of its imposing name, Chancellorsville was simply a large country-house, originally inhabited by a private family, but afterward used as a roadside inn. A little to the westward the "Old Turnpike" and Orange Plank-road unite as they approach the spot, where they again divide, to unite a second time a few miles to the east, where they form the main highway to Fredericksburg. From the north come in roads from United States and Ely's Fords; Germanna Ford is northwest; from the south runs the "Brock Road" in the direction of the Rapidan, passing a mile or two west of the place.

The whole country, the roads, the chance houses, the silence, the unending thicket, in this dreary wilderness, produce a sombre effect. A writer, familiar with it, says: "There all is wild, desolate, and lugubrious. Thicket, undergrowth, and jungle, stretch for miles, impenetrable and untouched. Narrow roads wind on forever between melancholy masses of stunted and gnarled oak. Little sunlight shines there. The face of Nature is dreary and sad. It was so before the battle; it is not more cheerful to-day, when, as you ride along, you see fragments of shell, rotting knapsacks, rusty gun-barrels, bleached bones, and grinning skulls.... Into this jungle," continues the same writer, "General Hooker penetrated. It was the wolf in his den, ready to tear any one who approached. A battle there seemed impossible. Neither side could see its antagonist. Artillery could not move; cavalry could not operate; the very infantry had to flatten their bodies to glide between the stunted trees. That an army of one hundred and twenty thousand men should have chosen that spot to fight forty thousand, and not only chosen it, but made it a hundred times more impenetrable by felling trees, erecting breastworks, disposing artillery *en masse* to sweep every road and bridle-path which led to Chancellorsville—this fact seemed incredible."

It was no part of the original plan of the Federal commander to permit himself to be cooped up in this difficult and embarrassing region, where it was impossible to manoeuvre his large army. The selection of the Wilderness around Chancellorsville, as the ground of battle, was dictated by Lee. General Hooker, it seems, endeavored to avoid being thus shut up in the thicket, and hampered in his movements. Finding that the Confederate force, retiring from in front of Ely's and United States Fords, had, on reaching Chancellorsville, continued to fall back in the direction of Fredericksburg, he followed them steadily, passed through the Wilderness, and, emerging into the open country beyond, rapidly began forming line of battle on ground highly favorable to the manoeuvring of his large force in action. A glance at the map will indicate the importance of this movement, and the great advantages secured by it. The left of General Hooker's line, nearest the river, was at least five miles in advance of Chancellorsville, and commanded Banks's Ford, thereby shortening fully one-half the distance of General Sedgwick's march from Fredericksburg, by enabling him to use the ford in question as a place of crossing to the south bank, and uniting his column with the main body. The centre and right of the Federal army had in like manner emerged from the thickets of the Wilderness, and occupied cleared ground, sufficiently elevated to afford them great advantages.

This was in the forenoon of the 1st of May, when there was no force in General Hooker's front, except the eight thousand men of Anderson at Tabernacle Church. Jackson had marched at midnight from the Massaponnax Hills, with a general order from Lee to "attack and repulse the enemy," but had not yet arrived. There was thus no serious obstacle in the path of the Federal commander, who had it in his power, it would seem, to mass his entire army on the commanding ground which his vanguard already occupied. Lee was aware of the importance of the position, and, had he not been delayed by the feint of General Sedgwick, would himself have seized upon it. As it was, General Hooker seemed to have won the prize in the race, and Lee would, apparently, be forced to assail him on his strong ground, or retire in the direction of Richmond.

The movements of the enemy had, however, been so rapid that Lee's dispositions seem to have been made before they were fully developed and accurately known to him. He had sent forward Jackson, and now proceeded to follow in person, leaving only a force of about six thousand men, under Early, to defend the crossing at Fredericksburg. The promptness of these movements of the Confederate commander is noticed by Northern writers. "Lee, with instant perception of the situation," says an able historian, "now seized the masses of his force, and, with the grasp of a Titan, swung them into position, as a giant might fling a mighty stone from a sling." [Footnote: Mr. Swinton, in "Campaigns of the Army of the Potomac." Whether the force under Lee could be justly described as "mighty," however, the reader will form his own opinion.]

Such were the relative positions of the two armies on the 1st of May: General Hooker's forces well in advance of Chancellorsville, and rapidly forming line of battle on a ridge in open country; General Lee's, stretching along the whole distance, from Fredericksburg to Tabernacle Church, and certainly not in any condition to deliver or accept battle. The Federal commander seemed to have clearly outgeneralled his adversary, and, humanly speaking, the movements of the two armies, up to this time, seemed to point to a decisive Federal success.

General Hooker's own act reversed all this brilliant promise. At the very moment when his army was steadily concentrating on the favorable ground in advance of Chancellorsville, the Federal commander, for some reason which has never been divulged, sent a peremptory order that the entire force should fall back into the Wilderness. This order, reversing every thing, is said to have been received "with mingled amazement and incredulity" by his officers, two of whom sent him word that, from the great advantages of the position, it should be "held at all hazards." General Hooker's reply was, "Return at once." The army accordingly fell back to Chancellorsville.

This movement undoubtedly lost General Hooker all the advantages which up to that moment he had secured. What his motive for the order in question was, it is impossible for the present writer to understand, unless the approach of Lee powerfully affected his imagination, and he supposed the thicket around Chancellorsville to be the best ground to receive that assault which the bold advance of his opponent appeared to foretell. Whatever his motive, General Hooker withdrew his lines from the open country, fell back to the vicinity of Chancellorsville, and began to erect elaborate defences, behind which to receive Lee's attack.

In this backward movement he was followed and harassed by the forces of Jackson, the command of Anderson being in front. Jackson's maxim was to always press an enemy when he was retiring; and no sooner had the Federal forces begun to move, than he made a prompt attack. He continued to follow them up toward Chancellorsville until nightfall, when the fighting ceased, the Confederate advance having been pushed to Alrich's house, within about two miles of Chancellorsville. Here the outer line of the Federal works was found, and Jackson paused. He was unwilling at so late an hour to attempt an assault upon them with his small force, and, directing further movements to cease, awaited the arrival of the commander-in-chief.

Lee arrived, and a consultation was held. The question now was, the best manner, with a force of about thirty-five thousand, to drive the Federal army, of about one hundred thousand, beyond the Rappahannock.

III.

LEE'S DETERMINATION.

On this night, of the 1st of May, the situation of affairs was strange indeed.

General Hooker had crossed the Rappahannock with a force of one hundred and twenty thousand infantry, and had, without obstruction, secured a position so strong, he declared, that Lee must either "ingloriously fly," or fight a battle in which "certain destruction awaited him." So absolutely convinced, indeed, was the Federal commander, of the result of the coming encounter, that he had jubilantly described the Southern army as "the legitimate property of the Army of the Potomac," which, in the event of the retreat of the Confederates, would "be after them." There seemed just grounds for this declaration, whatever question may have arisen of the good taste displayed by General Hooker in making it. The force opposed to him was in all about forty-seven thousand men, but, as cavalry take small part in pitched battles, Lee's fighting force was only about forty thousand. To drive back forty thousand with one hundred and twenty thousand would not apparently prove difficult, and it was no doubt this conviction which had occasioned the joyous exclamation of General Hooker.

But his own act, and the nerve of his adversary, had defeated every thing. Instead of retreating with his small force upon Richmond, Lee had advanced to accept or deliver battle. This bold movement, which General Hooker does not seem to have anticipated, paralyzed his energies. He had not only crossed the two rivers without loss, but had taken up a strong position, where he could manoeuvre his army perfectly, when, in consequence of Lee's approach with the evident intent of fighting, he had ceased to advance, hesitated, and ended by retiring. This is a fair summary of events up to the night of the 1st of May. General Hooker had advanced boldly; he was now falling back. He had foretold that his adversary would "ingloriously fly;" and that adversary was pressing him closely. The Army of the Potomac, he had declared, would soon be "after" the Army of Northern Virginia; but, from the appearance of things at the moment, the Army of Northern Virginia seemed "after" the Army of the Potomac. We use General Hooker's own phrases—they are expressive, if not dignified. They are indeed suited to the subject, which contains no little of the grotesque. That anticipations and expressions so confident should have been met with a "commentary of events" so damaging, was sufficient, had the occasion not been so tragic, to cause laughter in the gravest of human beings.

Lee's intent was now unmistakable. Instead of falling back from the Rappahannock to some line of defence nearer Richmond, where the force under Longstreet, at Suffolk, might have rejoined him, with other reënforcements, he had plainly resolved, with the forty or fifty thousand men of his command, to meet General Hooker in open battle, and leave the event to Providence. A design so bold would seem to indicate in Lee a quality which at that time he was not thought to possess—the willingness to risk decisive defeat by military movements depending for their success upon good fortune alone. Such seemed now the only *deus ex machina* that could extricate the Southern army from disaster; and a crushing defeat at that time would have had terrible results. There was no other force, save the small body under Longstreet and a few local troops, to protect Richmond. Had Lee been disabled and afterward pressed by General Hooker, it is impossible to see that any thing but the fall of the Confederate capital could have been the result.

From these speculations and comments we pass to the narrative of actual events. General Hooker had abandoned the strong position in advance of Chancellorsville, and retired to the fastnesses around that place, to receive the Southern attack. His further proceedings indicated that he anticipated an assault from Lee. The Federal troops had no sooner regained the thicket from which they had advanced in the morning, than they were ordered to erect elaborate works for the protection of infantry and artillery. This was promptly begun, and by the next morning heavy defences had sprung up as if by magic. Trees had been felled, and the trunks interwoven so as to present a formidable obstacle to the Southern attack. In front of these works the forest had been levelled, and the fallen trunks were left lying where they fell, forming thus an *abatis* sufficient to seriously delay an assaulting force, which would thus be, at every step of the necessarily slow advance, under fire. On the roads piercing the thicket in the direction of the Confederates, cannon were posted, to rake the approaches to the Federal position. Having thus made his preparations to receive Lee's attack, General Hooker awaited that attack, no doubt confident of his ability to repulse it.

His line resembled in some degree the two sides of an oblong square—the longer side extending east and west in front, that is to say, south of Chancellorsville, and the shorter side north and south nearly, east of the place. His right, in the direction of Wilderness Tavern, was comparatively undefended, as it was not expected that Lee would venture upon a movement against that remote point. This line, it would appear, was formed with a view to the possible necessity of falling back toward the Rappahannock. A commander determined to risk everything would, it seems, have fronted Lee boldly, with a line running north and south, east of Chancellorsville. General Hooker's main front was nearly east and west, whatever may have been his object in so establishing it.

On the night of the 1st of May, as we have said, Lee and Jackson held a consultation to determine the best method of attacking the Federal forces on the next day. All the information which they had been able to obtain of the Federal positions east and south of Chancellorsville, indicated that the defences in both these quarters were such as to render an assault injudicious. Jackson had found his advance obstructed by strong works near Alrich's house, on the road running eastward from the enemy's camps; and General Stuart and General Wright, who had moved to the left, and advanced upon the enemy's front near the point called "The Furnace," had discovered the existence of powerful defences in that quarter also. They had been met by a fierce and sudden artillery-fire from Federal epaulements; and here, as to the east of Chancellorsville, the enemy had evidently fortified their position.

Under these circumstances, it was necessary to discover, if possible, some more favorable opening for an attack. There remained but one other—General Hooker's right, west of Chancellorsville; but to divide the army, as would be necessary in order to attack in that quarter, seemed an undertaking too hazardous to be thought of. To execute such a plan of assault with any thing like a hope of success, General Lee would be compelled to detach considerably more than half of his entire force. This would leave in General Hooker's front a body of troops too inconsiderable to make any resistance if he advanced his lines, and thus the movement promised to result in the certain destruction of one portion of the army, to be followed by a triumphant march of the Federal forces upon Richmond. In the council of war between Lee and Jackson, on the night of the 1st of May, these considerations were duly weighed, and the whole situation discussed. In the end, the hazardous movement against General Hooker's right, beyond Chancellorsville, was determined upon. This was first suggested, it is said, by Jackson—others have attributed the suggestion to Lee. The point is not material. The plan was adopted, and Lee determined to detach a column of about twenty-one thousand men, under Jackson, to make the attack on the next day. His plan was to await the arrival of Jackson at the point selected for attack, meanwhile engaging the enemy's attention by demonstrations in their front. When Jackson's guns gave the signal that he was engaged, the force in front of the enemy was to advance and participate in the assault; and thus, struck in front and flank at once. General Hooker, it was hoped, would be defeated and driven back across the Rappahannock.

There was another possible result, the defeat of Lee and Jackson by General Hooker. But the desperate character of the situation rendered it necessary to disregard this risk.

By midnight this plan had been determined upon, and at dawn Jackson began to move.

JACKSON'S ATTACK AND FALL.

On the morning of the 2d of May, General Lee was early in the saddle, and rode to the front, where he remained in personal command of the force facing the enemy's main line of battle throughout the day.

This force consisted of the divisions of Anderson and McLaws, and amounted to thirteen thousand men. That left at Fredericksburg, as we have said, under General Early, numbered six thousand men; and the twenty-one thousand which Jackson had taken with him, to strike at the enemy's right, made up the full body of troops under Lee, that is to say, a little over forty thousand, artillerymen included. The cavalry, numbering four or five thousand, were, like the absent Federal cavalry, not actually engaged.

In accordance with the plan agreed upon between Lee and Jackson, the force left in the enemy's front proceeded to engage their attention, and desultory fighting continued throughout the day. General Lee meanwhile awaited the sound of Jackson's guns west of Chancellorsville, and must have experienced great anxiety at this trying moment, although, with his accustomed self-control, he displayed little or none. We shall now leave this comparatively interesting portion of the field, and invite the attention of the reader to the movements of General Jackson, who was about to strike his last great blow, and lose his own life in the moment of victory.

Jackson set out at early dawn, having under him three divisions, commanded by Rhodes and Trimble, in all about twenty-one thousand men, and directed his march over the Old Mine road toward "The Furnace," about a mile or so from and in front of the enemy's main line. Stuart moved with his cavalry on the flank of the column, with the view of masking it from observation; and it reached and passed "The Furnace," where a regiment with artillery was left to guard the road leading thence to Chancellorsville, and repel any attack which might be made upon the rear of the column. Just as the rear-guard passed on, the anticipated attack took place, and the regiment thus left, the Twenty-third Georgia, was suddenly surrounded and the whole force captured. The Confederate artillery, however, opened promptly upon the assailing force, drove it back toward Chancellorsville, and Jackson proceeded on his march without further interruption. He had thus been seen, but it seems that the whole movement was regarded by General Hooker as a retreat of the Confederates southward, a bend in the road at this point toward the south leading to that supposition.

"We know the enemy is flying," General Hooker wrote, on the afternoon of this day, to General Sedgwick, "trying to save his trains; two of Sickles's divisions are among them."

Soon after leaving "The Furnace," however, Jackson, following the same wood-road, turned westward, and, marching rapidly between the walls of thicket, struck into the Brock road, which runs in a direction nearly northwest toward Germanna and Ely's Fords. This would enable him to reach, without discovery, the Orange Plank-road, or Old Turnpike, west of Chancellorsville, as the woods through which the narrow highway ran completely barred him from observation. Unless Federal spies were lurking in the covert, or their scouting-parties of cavalry came in sight of the column, it would move as secure from discovery as though it were a hundred miles distant from the enemy; and against the latter danger of cavalry-scouts, Stuart's presence with his horsemen provided. The movement was thus made without alarming the enemy, and the head of Jackson's column reached the Orange Plank-road, near which point General Fitz Lee invited Jackson to ride up to a slight elevation, from which the defences of the enemy were visible. Jackson did so, and a glance showed him that he was not yet sufficiently upon the enemy's flank. He accordingly turned to an aide and said, pointing to the Orange Plank-road: "Tell my column to cross that road."

The column did so, continuing to advance toward the Rapidan until it reached the Old Turnpike running from the "Old Wilderness Tavern" toward Chancellorsville. At this point, Jackson found himself full on the right flank of General Hooker, and, halting his troops, proceeded promptly to form line of battle for the attack. It was now past four in the afternoon, and the declining sun warned the Confederates to lose no time. The character of the ground was, however, such as to dismay any but the most resolute, and it seemed impossible to execute the intended movement with any thing like rapidity in such a jungle. On both sides of the Old Turnpike rose a wall of thicket, through which it was impossible to move a regular line of battle. All the rules of war must be reversed in face of this obstacle, and the assault on General Hooker's works seemed destined to be made in column of infantry companies, and with the artillery moving in column of pieces.

Despite these serious obstacles, Jackson hastened to form such order of battle as was possible, and with Rodes's division in front, followed by Colston (Trimble) and Hill, advanced steadily down the Old Turnpike, toward Chancellorsville. He had determined, not only to strike the enemy's right flank, but to execute, if possible, a still more important movement. This was, to extend his lines steadily to the left, swing round his left wing, and so interpose himself between General Hooker and the Rapidan. This design of unsurpassed boldness continued to burn in Jackson's brain until he fell, and almost his last words were an allusion to it.

The Federal line of works, which the Confederates thus advanced to assault, extended across the Old Turnpike near the house of Melzi Chancellor, and behind was a second line, which was covered by the Federal artillery in the earthworks near Chancellorsville. The Eleventh Corps, under General Howard, was that destined to receive Jackson's assault. This was made at a few minutes past five in the evening, and proved decisive. The Federal troops were surprised at their suppers, and were wholly unprepared. They had scarcely time to run to their muskets, which were stacked[1] near at hand, when Rodes burst upon them, stormed their works, over which the troops marched almost unresisted, and in a few minutes the entire corps holding the Federal right was in hopeless disorder. Rodes pressed on, followed by the division in his rear, and the affair became rather a hunt than a battle. The Confederates pursued with yells, killing or capturing all with whom they could come up; the Federal artillery rushed off at a gallop, striking against tree-trunks and overturning, and the army of General Hooker seemed about to be hopelessly routed. This is the account given by Northern writers, who represent the effect of Jackson's sudden attack as indescribable. It had a serious effect, as will be subsequently shown, on the *morale* both of General Hooker and his army. While opposing the heavy demonstrations of General Lee's forces on their left and in front, this storm had burst upon them from a quarter in which no one expected it; they were thus caught between two fires, and, ignorant as they were of the small number of the Confederates, must have regarded the army as seriously imperilled.

[Footnote 1: "Their arms were stacked, and the men were away from them and scattered about for the purpose of cooking their suppers."—*General Hooker.*]

Jackson continued to pursue the enemy on the road to Chancellorsville, intent now upon making his blow decisive by swinging round his left and cutting off the Federal army from the Rappahannock. It was impossible, however, to execute so important a movement until his troops were well in hand, and the two divisions which had made the attack had become mixed up in a very confused manner. They were accordingly directed to halt, and General A.P. Hill, whose division had not been engaged, was sent for and ordered to advance to the front, thus affording the disordered divisions an opportunity to reform their broken lines.

Soon after dispatching this order, Jackson rode out in front of his line, on the Chancellorsville road, in order to reconnoitre in person, and ascertain, if possible, the position and movements of the enemy, then within a few hundred yards of him. It was now between nine and ten o'clock at night. The fighting had temporarily ceased, and the moon, half-seen through misty clouds, lit up the dreary thickets, in which no sound was heard but the incessant and melancholy cries of the whippoorwills. Jackson had ridden forward about a hundred yards in advance of his line, on the turnpike, accompanied by a few officers, and had checked his horse to listen for any sound coming from the direction of Chancellorsville, when suddenly a volley was fired by his own infantry on the right of the road, apparently directed at him and his companions, under the impression that they were a Federal reconnoitring-party. Several of the party fell from their horses, and, wheeling to the left, Jackson galloped into the wood to escape a renewal of the fire. The result was melancholy. He passed directly in front of his men, who had been warned to guard against an attack of cavalry. In their excited state, so near the enemy, and surrounded by darkness, Jackson was supposed to be a Federal cavalryman. The men accordingly fired upon him, at not more than twenty paces, and wounded him in three places—twice in the left arm, and once in the right hand. At the instant when he was struck he was holding his bridle with his left hand, and had his right hand raised, either to protect his face from boughs, or in the strange gesture habitual to him in battle. As the bullets passed through his arm he dropped the bridle of his horse from his left hand, but seized it again with the bleeding fingers of his right hand, when the animal, wheeling suddenly, darted toward Chancellorsville. In doing so he passed beneath the limb of a pine-tree, which struck the wounded man in the face, tore off his cap, and threw him back on his horse, nearly dismounting him. He succeeded, however, in retaining his seat, and regained the road, where he was received in the arms of Captain Wilbourn, one of his staff-officers, and laid at the foot of a tree.

The fire had suddenly ceased, and all was again still. Only Captain Wilbourn and a courier were with Jackson, but a shadowy figure on horseback was seen in the edge of the wood near, silent and motionless. When Captain Wilbourn called to this person, and directed him to ride back and see what troops had thus fired upon them, the silent figure disappeared, and did not return. Who this could have been was long a mystery, but it appears, from a recent statement of General Revere, of the Federal army, that it was himself. He had advanced to the front to reconnoitre, had come on the group at the foot of the tree, and, receiving the order above mentioned, had thought it prudent not to reveal his real character. He accordingly rode into the wood, and regained his own lines.

A few words will terminate our account of this melancholy event in the history of the war—the fall of Jackson. He was supported to the rear by his officers, and during this painful progress gave his last order. General Pender recognized him, and stated that he feared he could not hold his position. Jackson's eye flashed, and he replied with animation, "You must hold your ground, General Pender! You must hold your ground, sir!"

He was now so weak as to be unable to walk, even leaning on the shoulders of his officers. He was accordingly placed on a litter, and borne toward the rear. Before the litter had gone far a furious artillery-fire swept the road from the direction of Chancellorsville, and the bearers lowered it to the earth and lay down beside it. The fire relaxing, they again moved, but one of the bearers stumbled over a root and let the litter fall. Jackson groaned, and as the moonlight fell upon his face it was seen to be so pale that he appeared to be about to die. When asked if he was much hurt, he opened his eyes, however, and said, "No, my friend, don't trouble yourself about me."

He was then borne to the rear, placed in an ambulance, and carried to the hospital at the Old Wilderness Tavern, where he remained until he was taken to Guinea's station, where he died.

Such was the fate of Lee's great lieutenant—the man whom he spoke of as his "right arm"—whose death struck a chill to the hearts of the Southern people from which they never recovered.

V.

THE BATTLE OF CHANCELLORSVILLE.

General Lee was not informed of the misfortune which had befallen his great lieutenant until toward daybreak on the next morning.

This fact was doubtless attributable to the difficult character of the country; the interposition of the Federal army between the two Confederate wings, which rendered a long détour necessary in reaching Lee; and the general confusion and dismay attending Jackson's fall. It would be difficult, indeed, to form an exaggerated estimate of the condition of Jackson's corps at this time. The troops had been thrown into what seemed inextricable disorder, in consequence of the darkness and the headlong advance of the Second (Calston's) Division upon the heels of Rhodes, which had resulted in a complete intermingling of the two commands; and, to make matters worse, General A.P. Hill, the second in command, had been wounded and disabled, nearly at the same moment with Jackson, by the artillery-fire of the enemy. This transferred the command, of military right, to the brave and skilful General Rhodes, the ranking officer after Hill; but Rhodes was only a brigadier-general, and had, for that reason, never come into personal contact with the whole corps, who knew little of him, and was not aware of Jackson's plans, and distrusted, under these circumstances, his ability to conduct to a successful issue so vitally important an operation as that intrusted to this great wing of the Southern army. Stuart, who had gone with his cavalry toward Ely's Ford to make a demonstration on the Federal rear, was therefore sent for, and rode as rapidly as possible to the scene of action, and the command was formally relinquished to him by General Rhodes. Jackson sent Stuart word from Wilderness Tavern to "act upon his own judgment, and do what he thought best, as he had implicit confidence in him;" but, in consequence of the darkness and confusion, it was impossible for Stuart to promptly reform the lines, and thus all things remained entangled and confused.

It was essential, however, to inform General Lee of the state of affairs, and Jackson's chief-of-staff, Colonel Pendleton, requested Captain Wilbourn, who had witnessed all the details of the painful scene in the wood, to go to General Lee and acquaint him with what had taken place, and receive his orders. From a MS. statement of this meritorious officer, we take these brief details of the interview:

Lee was found lying asleep in a little clump of pines near his front, covered with an oil-cloth to protect him from the dews of the night, and surrounded by the officers of his staff, also asleep. It was not yet daybreak, and the darkness prevented the messenger from distinguishing the commander-in-chief from the rest. He accordingly called for Major Taylor, Lee's adjutant-general, and that officer promptly awoke when he was informed of what had taken place. As the conversation continued, the sound awoke General Lee, who asked, "Who is there?" Major Taylor informed him, and, rising upon his elbow, Lee pointed to his blankets, and said: "Sit down here by me, captain, and tell me all about the fight last evening."

He listened without comment during the recital, but, when it was finished, said with great feeling: "Ah! captain, any victory is dearly bought which deprives us of the services of General Jackson, even for a short time."

From this reply it was evident that he did not regard the wounds received by Jackson as of a serious character—as was natural, from the fact that they were only flesh-wounds in the arm and hand—and believed that the only result would be a temporary absence of his lieutenant from command. As Captain Wilbourn continued to speak of the incident, Lee added with greater emotion than at first: "Ah! don't talk about it; thank God it is no worse!"

He then remained silent, but seeing Captain Wilbourn rise, as if to go, he requested him to remain, as he wished to "talk with him some more," and proceeded to ask a number of questions in reference to the position of the troops, who was in command, etc. When informed that Rhodes was in temporary command, but that Stuart had been sent for, he exclaimed: "Rhodes is a gallant, courageous, and energetic officer;" and asked where Jackson and Stuart could be found, calling for paper and pencil to write to them. Captain Wilbourn added that, from what he had heard Jackson say, he thought he intended to get possession, if possible, of the road to United States Ford in the Federal rear, and so cut them off from the river that night, or early in the morning. At these words, Lee rose quickly and said with animation, "These people must be pressed to-day."

It would seem that at this moment a messenger—probably Captain Hotchkiss, Jackson's skilful engineer—arrived from Wilderness Tavern, bringing a note from the wounded general. Lee read it with much feeling, and dictated the following reply:

GENERAL: I have just received your note informing me that you were wounded. I cannot express my regret at the occurrence. Could I have directed events, I should have chosen, for the good of the country, to have been disabled in your stead.

I congratulate you upon the victory, which is due to your skill and energy. R.E. LEE, *General.*

This was dispatched with a second note to Stuart, directing him to assume command, and press the enemy at dawn. Lee then mounted his horse, and, just as the day began to break, formed line of battle opposite the enemy's front, his line extending on the right to the plank-road running from Chancellorsville in the direction of Fredericksburg. This force, under the personal command of Lee, amounted, as we have said, originally to about thirteen thousand men; and, as their loss had not been very severe in the demonstrations made against the enemy on the preceding days, they were in good condition. The obvious course now was to place the troops in a position which would enable them, in the event of Stuart's success in driving the Federal right, to unite the left of Lee's line with the right of Stuart, and so press the Federal army back on Chancellorsville and the river. We shall now return to the left wing of the army, which, in spite of the absence of the commanding general, was the column of attack, which was looked to for the most important results.

In response to the summons of the preceding night, Stuart had come back from the direction of Ely's Ford, at a swift gallop, burning with ardor at the thought of leading Jackson's great corps into battle. The military ambition of this distinguished commander of Lee's horse was great, and he had often chafed at the jests directed at the cavalry arm, and at himself as "only a cavalry-officer." He had now presented to him an opportunity of showing that he was a trained soldier, competent by his nerve and military ability to lead any arm of the service, and greeted the occasion with delight. The men of Jackson had been accustomed to see that commander pass slowly along their lines on a horse as sedate-looking as himself, a slow-moving figure, with little of the "poetry of war" in his appearance. They now found themselves commanded by a youthful and daring cavalier on a spirited animal, with floating plume, silken sash, and a sabre which gleamed in the moonlight, as its owner galloped to and fro cheering the men and marshalling them for the coming assault As he led the lines afterward with joyous vivacity, his sabre drawn, his plume floating proudly, one of the men compared him to Henry of Navarre at the battle of Ivry. But Stuart's spirit of wild gayety destroyed the romantic dignity of the scene. He led the men of Jackson against General Hooker's breastworks bristling with cannon, singing "Old Joe Hooker, will you come out of the Wilderness!"

This sketch will convey a correct idea of the officer who had now grasped the bâton falling from the hand of the great marshal of Lee. It was probable that the advance of the infantry under such a commander would partake of the rush and rapidity of a cavalry-charge; and the sequel justified this view.

At early dawn the Southern lines began to move. Either in consequence of orders from Lee, or following his own conception, Stuart reversed the movement of Jackson, who had aimed to swing round his left and cut off the enemy. He seemed to have determined to extend his right, with the view of uniting with the left of Anderson's division under Lee, and enclosing the enemy in the angle near Chancellorsville. Lee had moved at the same moment on their front, advancing steadily over all obstacles, and a Northern writer, who witnessed the combined attack, speaks of it in enthusiastic terms: "From the large brick house which gives the name to this vicinity," says the writer, speaking of Chancellorsville, "the enemy could be seen, sweeping slowly but confidently, determinedly and surely, through the clearings which extended in front. Nothing could excite more admiration for the qualities of the veteran soldiers than the manner in which the enemy swept out, as they moved steadily onward, the forces which were opposed to them. We say it reluctantly, and for the first time, that the enemy have shown the finest qualities, and we acknowledge on this occasion their superiority in the open field to our own men. They delivered their fire with precision, and were apparently inflexible and immovable under the storm of bullets and shell which they were constantly receiving. Coming to a piece of timber, which was occupied by a division of our own men, half the number were detailed to clear the woods. It seemed certain that here they would be repulsed, but they marched right through the wood, driving our own soldiers out, who delivered their fire and fell back, halted again, fired, and fell back as before, seeming to concede to the enemy, as a matter of course, the superiority which they evidently felt themselves. Our own men fought well. There was no lack of courage, but an evident feeling that they were destined to be beaten, and the only thing for them to do was to fire and retreat."

This description of the steady advance of the Southern line applies rather to the first portion of the attack, which compelled the front line of the Federal army to retire to the stronger ground in rear. When this was reached, and the troops of Lee saw before them the last citadel, the steady advance became a rush. The divisions of Anderson and McLaws, on the right, made a determined charge upon the great force under Generals Hancock, Slocum, and others, in that quarter, and Stuart closed in on the Federal right, steadily extending his line to join on to Anderson.

The spectacle here was superb. As the troops rushed on, Stuart shouted, "Charge! and remember Jackson!" and this watchword seemed to drive the line forward. With Stuart leading them, and singing, in his joyous voice, "Old Joe Hooker, will you come out of the Wilderness!"— for courage, poetry, and seeming frivolity, were strangely mingled in this great soldier—the troops went headlong at the Federal works, and in a few moments the real struggle of the battle of Chancellorsville had begun.

From this instant, when the lines, respectively commanded in person by Lee and by Stuart, closed in with the enemy, there was little manoeuvring of any description. It was an open attempt of Lee, by hard fighting, to crush in the enemy's front, and force them back upon the river. In this arduous struggle it is due to Stuart to say that his generalship largely decided the event, and the high commendation which he afterward received from General Lee justifies the statement. As his lines went to the attack, his quick military eye discerned an elevated point on his right, from which it appeared an artillery-fire woulden filade the Federal line. About thirty pieces of cannon were at once hastened to this point, and a destructive fire opened on the lines of General Slocum, which threw his troops into great confusion. So serious was this fire that General Slocum sent word to General Hooker that his front was being swept away by it, to which the sullen response was, "I cannot make soldiers or ammunition!"

General Hooker was indeed, it seems, at this moment in no mood to take a hopeful view of affairs. The heavy assault of Jackson appears to have as much demoralized the Federal commander as his troops. During the night he had erected a semicircular line of works, in the form of a redan, in his rear toward the river, behind which new works he no doubt contemplated falling back. He now awaited the result of the Southern attack, leaning against a pillar of the porch at the Chancellorsville House, when a cannon-ball struck the pillar, throwing it down, and so stunning the general as to prevent him from retaining the command, which was delegated to General Couch.

[Illustration: Chancellorsville]

The fate of the day had now been decided. The right wing of the Southern army, under Lee, had gradually extended its left to meet the extension of Stuart's right; and this junction of the two wings having been effected, Lee took personal command of all, and advanced his whole front in a decisive assault. Before this the Federal front gave way, and the disordered troops were huddled back—now only a confused and disorganized mass—upon Chancellorsville. The Southern troops pursued with yells, leaping over the earthworks, and driving all before them. A scene of singular horror ensued. The Chancellorsville House, which had been set on fire by shell, was seen to spout flame from every window, and the adjoining woods had, in like manner, caught fire, and were heard roaring over the dead and wounded of both sides alike. The thicket had become the scene of the cruellest of all agonies for the unfortunates unable to extricate themselves. The whole spectacle in the vicinity of the Chancellorsville House, now in Lee's possession, was frightful. Fire, smoke, blood, confused yells, and dying groans, mingled to form the dark picture.

Lee had ridden to the front of his line, following up the enemy, and as he passed before the troops they greeted him with one prolonged, unbroken cheer, in which those wounded and lying upon the ground united. In that cheer spoke the fierce joy of men whom the hard combat had turned into blood-hounds, arousing all the ferocious instincts of the human soul. Lee sat on his horse, motionless, near the Chancellorsville House, his face and figure lit up by the glare of the burning woods, and gave his first attention, even at this exciting moment, to the unfortunates of both sides, wounded, and in danger of being burned to death. While issuing his orders on this subject, a note was brought to him from Jackson, congratulating him upon his victory. After reading it, with evidences of much emotion, he turned to the officer who had brought it and said: "Say to General Jackson that the victory is his, and that the congratulation is due to him."

The Federal army had fallen back in disorder, by this time, toward their second line. It was about ten o'clock in the morning, and Chancellorsville was in Lee's possession.

FLANK MOVEMENT OF GENERAL SEDGWICK.

Lee hastened to bring the Southern troops into order again, and succeeded in promptly reforming his line of battle, his front extending, unbroken, along the Old Turnpike, facing the river.

His design was to press General Hooker, and reap those rich rewards of victory to which the hard fighting of the men had entitled them. Of the demoralized condition of the Federal forces there can be no doubt, and the obvious course now was to follow up their retreat and endeavor to drive them in disorder beyond the Rappahannock.

The order to advance upon the enemy was about to be given, when a messenger from Fredericksburg arrived at full gallop, and communicated intelligence which arrested the order just as it was on Lee's lips.

A considerable force of the enemy was advancing up the turnpike from Fredericksburg, to fall upon his right flank, and upon his rear in case he moved beyond Chancellorsville. The column was that of General Sedgwick. This officer, it will be remembered, had been detached to make a heavy demonstration at Fredericksburg, and was still at that point, with his troops drawn up on the southern bank, three miles below the city, on Saturday night, while Jackson was fighting. On that morning General Hooker had sent for Reynolds's corps, but, even in the absence of this force, General Sedgwick retained under him about twenty-two thousand men; and this column was now ordered to storm the heights at Fredericksburg, march up the turnpike, and attack Lee in flank.

General Sedgwick received the order at eleven o'clock on Saturday night, about the time when Jackson was carried wounded to the rear. He immediately made his preparations to obey, and at daylight moved up from below the city to storm the ridge at Marye's, and march straight upon Chancellorsville. In the first assaults he failed, suffering considerable loss from the fire of the Southern troops under General Barksdale, commanding the line at that point; but, subsequently forming an assaulting column for a straight rush at the hill, he went forward with impetuosity; drove the Southern advanced line from behind the "stone wall," which Generals Sumner and Hooker had failed in reaching, and, about eleven in the morning, stormed Marye's Hill, and killed, captured, or dispersed, the entire Southern force there. The Confederates fought hand to hand over their guns with the enemy for the possession of the crest, but their numbers were inadequate; the entire surviving force fell back over the Telegraph road southward, and General Sedgwick promptly advanced up the turnpike leading from Fredericksburg to Chancellorsville, to assail General Lee.

It was the intelligence of this threatening movement which now reached Lee, and induced him to defer further attack at the moment upon General Hooker. He determined promptly to send a force against General Sedgwick, and this resolution seems to have been based upon sound military judgment. There was little to be feared now from General Hooker, large as the force still was under that officer. He was paralyzed for the time, and would not probably venture upon any attempt to regain possession of Chancellorsville. With General Sedgwick it was different. His column was comparatively fresh, was flushed with victory, and numbered, even after his loss of one thousand, more than twenty thousand men. Compared with the entire Federal army, this force was merely a detachment, it was true, but it was a detachment numbering as many men, probably, as the effective of Lee's entire army at Chancellorsville. He had carried into that fight about thirty-four thousand men. His losses had been heavy, and the commands were much shaken. To have advanced under these circumstances upon General Hooker, without regard to General Sedgwick's twenty thousand troops, inspired by recent victory, would have resulted probably in disaster.

These comments may detract from that praise of audacity accorded to Lee in making this movement. It seems rather to have been the dictate of common-sense; to have advanced upon General Hooker would have been the audacity.

It was thus necessary to defer the final blow at the main Federal army in his front, and General Lee promptly detached a force of about five brigades to meet General Sedgwick, which, with Early's command, now in rear of the Federal column, would, it was supposed, suffice.

This body moved speedily down the turnpike to check the enemy, and encountered the head of his column about half-way, near Salem Church. General Wilcox, who had been sent by Lee to watch Banks's Ford, had already moved to bar the Federal advance. When the brigades sent by Lee joined him, the whole force formed line of battle: a brisk action ensued, continuing from about four in the afternoon until nightfall, when the fighting ceased, and General Sedgwick made no further attempt to advance on that day.

These events took place, as we have said, on Sunday afternoon, the day of the Federal defeat at Chancellorsville. On Monday morning (May 4th), the theatre of action on the southern bank of the Rappahannock presented a very remarkable complication. General Early had been driven from the ridge at Fredericksburg; but no sooner had General Sedgwick marched toward Chancellorsville, than Early returned and seized upon Marye's Heights again. He was thus in General Sedgwick's rear, and ready to prevent him from recrossing the Rappahannock at Fredericksburg. Sedgwick meanwhile was moving to assail Lee's flank and rear, and Lee was ready to attack General Hooker in front. Such was the singular entanglement of the Northern and Southern forces on Monday morning after the battle of Chancellorsville. What the result was to be the hours of that day were now to decide.

Lee resolved first, if possible, to crush General Sedgwick, when it was his design to return and make a decisive assault upon General Hooker. In accordance with this plan, he on Monday morning went in personal command of three brigades of Anderson's division, reached the vicinity of Salem Church, and proceeded to form line of battle with the whole force there. Owing to unforeseen delays, the attack was not begun until late in the afternoon, when the whole line advanced upon General Sedgwick, Lee's aim being to cut him off from the river. In this he failed, the stubborn resistance of the Federal forces enabling them to hold their ground until night. At that time, however, they seemed to waver and lose heart, whether from receiving intelligence of General Hooker's mishap, or from other causes, is not known. They were now pressed by the Southern troops, and finally gave way. General Sedgwick retreated rapidly but in good order to Banks's Ford, where a pontoon had been fortunately laid, and this enabled him to cross his men. The passage was effected under cover of darkness, the Southern cannon firing upon the retreating column; and, with this, ended the movement of General Sedgwick.

On Tuesday morning Lee returned with his men toward Chancellorsville, and during the whole day was busily engaged in preparation for a decisive attack upon General Hooker on the next morning.

When, however, the Southern sharp-shooters felt their way, at daylight, toward the Federal position, it was found that the works were entirely deserted.

General Hooker had recrossed the river, spreading pine-boughs on the pontoon bridge to muffle the sound of his artillery-wheels.

So the great advance ended.

VII.

LEE'S GENERALSHIP AND PERSONAL DEMEANOR DURING THE CAMPAIGN.

The movements of the two armies in the Chancellorsville campaign, as it is generally styled, have been so fully described in the foregoing pages, that little comment upon them is here necessary. The main feature which attracts attention, in surveying the whole series of operations, is the boldness, amounting to apparent recklessness, of Lee; and, first, the excellent generalship, and then the extraordinary tissue of military errors, of General Hooker.

Up to the 1st of May, when he emerged from the Chancellorsville thicket, every thing had succeeded with the Federal commander, and deserved to succeed. He had successfully brought over his great force, which he himself described as the "finest army on the planet," and occupied strong ground east of Chancellorsville, on the road to Fredericksburg. General Sedgwick was absent at the latter place with a strong detachment of the army, but the main body covered Banks's Ford, but twelve miles from the city, and by the afternoon of this day the whole army might have been concentrated. Then the fate of Lee would seem to have been decided. He had not only a very small army, but that army was scattered, and liable to be cut off in detail. General Sedgwick menaced his right at Fredericksburg—General Hooker was in front of his left near Chancellorsville—and to crush one of these wings before the other could come to its assistance seemed a work of no very great difficulty. General Hooker appears, however, to have distrusted his ability to effect this result, and, finding that General Lee was advancing with his main body to attack him, retired, from his strong position in the open country, to the dense thicket around Chancellorsville. That this was a grave military error there can be no doubt, as, by this retrograde movement, General Hooker not only discouraged his troops, who had been elated by his confident and inspiring general orders, but lost the great advantage of the open country, where his large force could be successfully manoeuvred.

Lee took instant advantage of this fault in his adversary, and boldly pressed the force retiring into the Wilderness, where, on the night of the 1st of May, General Hooker was shut up with his army. This unforeseen result presented the adversaries now in an entirely new light. The Federal army, which had been promised by its commander a speedy march upon Richmond in pursuit of Lee, had, instead of advancing, made a backward movement; and Lee, who it had been supposed would retreat, was now following and offering them battle.

The daring resolution of Lee, to divide his army and attack the Federal right, followed. It would seem unjust to General Hooker greatly to blame him for the success of that blow, which could not have been reasonably anticipated. In determining upon this, one of the most extraordinary movements of the war, General Lee proceeded in defiance of military rules, and was only justified in his course by the desperate character of the situation of affairs. It was impossible to make any impression upon General Hooker's front or left, owing to the elaborate defences in both quarters; it was, therefore, necessary either to retire, or attack in a different direction. As a retreat, however, upon Richmond would have surrendered to the enemy a large and fertile tract of country, it was desirable, if possible, to avoid that alternative; and the attack on the Federal right followed. The results of this were truly extraordinary. The force routed and driven back in disorder by General Jackson was but a single corps, and that corps, it is said, not a legitimate part of the old Army of the Potomac; but the disorder seems to have communicated itself to the whole army, and to have especially discouraged General Hooker. In describing the scene in question, we refrained from dwelling upon the full extent of the confusion into which the Federal forces were thrown: some sentences, taken from Northern accounts, may lead to a better understanding of the result. After Jackson's assault, a Northern historian says: "The open plain around Chancellorsville presented such a spectacle as a simoom sweeping over the desert might make. Through the dusk of nightfall a rushing whirlwind of men and artillery and wagons swept down the road, past headquarters, and on toward the fords of the Rappahannock; and it was in vain that the staff opposed their persons and drawn sabres to the panic-stricken fugitives." Another writer, an eye-witness, says the spectacle presented was that of "solid columns of infantry retreating at double-quick; a dense mass of beings flying; hundreds of cavalry-horses, left riderless at the first discharge from the rebels, dashing frantically about in all directions; scores of batteries flying from the field; battery-wagons, ambulances, horses, men, cannon, caissons, all jumbled and tumbled together in one inextricable mass—the stampede universal, the disgrace general."

After all, however, it was but one corps of the Federal army which had been thus thrown into disorder, and General Hooker had no valid grounds for distrusting his ability to defeat Lee in a more decisive action. There are many reasons for coming to the conclusion that he did from that moment distrust his powers. He had courageously hastened to the assailed point, ordering the men to "throw themselves into the breach," and receive Jackson's troops "on the bayonet;" but, after this display of soldierly resolution, General Hooker appears to have lost some of that nerve which should never desert a soldier, and on the same night sent engineers to trace out a new line of defences in his rear, to which, it seems, he already contemplated the probability of being forced to retire. Why he came to take this depressed view of the situation of affairs, it is difficult to say. One of General Sedgwick's corps reached him on this night, and his force at

Chancellorsville still amounted to between ninety and one hundred thousand men, about thrice that of Lee. No decisive trial of strength had yet taken place between the two armies; and yet the larger force was constructing defences in rear to protect them from the smaller—a circumstance not tending, it would seem, to greatly encourage the troops whose commander was thus providing for a safe retreat.

The subsequent order to General Sedgwick to march up from Fredericksburg and assail Lee's right was judicious, and really saved the army from a great disaster. Lee was about to follow up the discouraged forces of General Hooker as they fell back toward the river; and, as the Southern army was flushed with victory, the surrender of the great body might have ensued. This possible result was prevented by the flank movement of General Sedgwick, and some gratitude for assistance so important from his able lieutenant would have seemed natural and graceful in General Hooker. This view of the subject does not seem, however, to have been taken by the Federal commander. He subsequently charged the defeat of Chancellorsville upon General Sedgwick, who he declared had "failed in a prompt compliance with his orders."[1] The facts do not bear out this charge, as the reader has seen. General Sedgwick received the order toward midnight on Saturday, and, at eleven o'clock on Sunday morning, had passed over that stubborn "stone wall" which, in the battle of the preceding December, General Hooker's column had not even been able to reach; had stormed Marye's Hill, which General Hooker had described, in vindication of his own failure to carry the position, as "masonry," "a fortification," and "a mountain of rock;" and had marched thereafter so promptly as to force Lee, in his own defence, to arrest the second advance upon the Federal main body, and divert a considerable force to meet the attack on his flank.

[Footnote 1: General Hooker in Report of the Committee on the Conduct of the War, Part I., page 130. This great collection is a valuable repository of historic details, and contains the explanation of many interesting questions.]

After the repulse of General Sedgwick, and his retreat across the Rappahannock, General Hooker seems to have been completely discouraged, and hastened to put the river between himself and Lee. His losses in the battles of Saturday and Sunday had amounted to seventeen thousand one hundred and ninety-seven killed and wounded and missing, fourteen pieces of artillery, and twenty thousand stand of arms. The Confederate loss was ten thousand two hundred and eighty-one. Contrary to the ordinary course of things the assailing force had lost a less number of men than that assailed.

The foregoing reflections, which necessarily involve a criticism of General Hooker, arise naturally from a review of the events of the campaign, and seem justified by the circumstances. There can be no inducement for the present writer to underrate the military ability of the Federal commander, as that want of ability rather detracts from than adds to the merit of General Lee in defeating him. It may be said, indeed, that without these errors and shortcomings of General Hooker, Lee, humanly speaking, must have been either defeated or forced to retire upon Richmond.

After giving full weight, however, to all the advantages derived from the extraordinary Federal oversights and mistakes, General Lee's merit in this campaign was greater, perhaps, than in any other during his entire career. Had he left behind him no other record than this, it alone would have been sufficient to have conferred upon him the first glories of arms, and handed his name down to posterity as that of one of the greatest soldiers of history. It is difficult to discover a single error committed by him, in the whole series of movements, from the moment when General Sedgwick crossed at Fredericksburg, to the time of General Hooker's retreat beyond the Rappahannock. It may appear that there was unnecessary delay in permitting Tuesday to pass without a final advance upon General Hooker, in his second line of intrenchments; but, no doubt, many circumstances induced Lee to defer this attack—the fatigue of his troops, consequent upon the fighting of the four preceding days, Friday, Saturday, Sunday, and Monday; the necessity of reforming his battalions for the final blow; and the anticipation that General Hooker, who still had at his command a force of more than one hundred thousand men, would not so promptly relinquish his campaign, and retire.

With the exception of this error, if it be such, Lee had made no single false step in the whole of his movements. The campaign was round, perfect, and complete—such as a student of the art of war might pore over, and analyze as an instance of the greatest principles of military science "clothed in act." The most striking features of Lee's movements were their rapidity and audacity. It had been the fashion with some persons to speak of Lee as slow and cautious in his operations, and this criticism had not been completely silenced even in the winter of 1862, when his failure to crush General Burnside afforded his detractors another opportunity of repeating the old charge. After the Chancellorsville campaign these fault-finders were silenced—no one could be found to listen to them. The whole Southern movement completely contradicted their theory.

At the first intelligence of the advance of General Hooker's main body across the upper Rappahannock, Lee rode rapidly in that direction, and ordered his troops at the fords of the river to fall back to Chancellorsville. He then returned, and, finding that General Sedgwick had crossed at Fredericksburg, held a prompt consultation with Jackson, when it was decided at once to concentrate the main body of the army in front of General Hooker's column. At the word, Jackson moved; Lee followed. On the 1st of May, the enemy were pressed back upon Chancellorsville; on the 2d, his right was crushed, and his army thrown into confusion; on the 3d, he was driven from Chancellorsville, and, but for the flank movement of General Sedgwick, which Lee was not in sufficient force to prevent, General Hooker would, upon that same day, Sunday, have in all probability suffered a decisive defeat.

In the course of four days Lee had thus advanced, and checked, and then attacked and repulsed with heavy slaughter, an army thrice as large as his own. On the last day of April he had been nearly enveloped by a host of about one hundred and twenty thousand men. On the 3d day of May their main body was in disorderly retreat; and at daylight on the morning of the 6th there was not a Federal soldier, with the exception of the prisoners taken, on the southern bank of the Rappahannock.

During all these critical scenes, when the fate of the Confederate capital, and possibly of the Southern cause, hung suspended in the balance, General Lee preserved, as thousands of persons can testify, the most admirable serenity and composure, without that jubilant confidence displayed by General Hooker in his address to the troops, and the exclamations to his officers. Lee was equally free from gloom or any species of depression. His spirits seemed to rise under the pressure upon him, and at times he was almost gay. When one of General Jackson's aides hastened into his tent near Fredericksburg, and with great animation informed him that the enemy were crossing the river, in heavy force in his front, he seemed to be amused by that circumstance, and said, smiling: "Well, I *heard* firing, and I was beginning to think it was time some of you lazy young fellows were coming to tell me what it was all about. Say to General Jackson that he knows just as well what to do with the enemy as I do."

The commander-in-chief who could find time at such a moment to indulge in *badinage*, must have possessed excellent nerve; and this composure, mingled with a certain buoyant hopefulness, as of one sure of the event, remained with Lee throughout the whole great wrestle with General Hooker. He retained to the end his simple and quiet manner, divested of every thing like excitement. In the consultation with Jackson, on the night of the 1st of May, when the crisis was so critical, his demeanor indicated no anxiety; and when, as we have said, the news came of Jackson's wound, he said simply, "Sit down here, by me, captain, and tell me all about the fight last evening"—adding, "Ah! captain, any victory is dearly bought which deprives us of the services of General Jackson even for a short time. Don't talk about it—thank God, it is no worse!" The turns of expression here are those of a person who permits nothing to disturb his serenity, and indulges his gentler and tenderer feelings even in the hot atmosphere of a great conflict. The picture presented is surely an interesting and beautiful one. The human being who uttered the good-natured criticism at the expense of the "lazy young fellows," and who greeted the news of Jackson's misfortune with a sigh as tender as that of a woman, was the soldier who had "scized the masses of his force with the grasp of a Titan, and swung them into position as a giant might fling a mighty stone." To General Hooker's threat to crush him, he had responded by crushing General Hooker; nearly surrounded by the huge cordon of the Federal army, he had cut the cordon and emerged in safety. General Hooker with his one hundred thousand men had retreated to the north bank of the Rappahannock, and, on the south bank, Lee with his thirty thousand remained erect, threatening, and triumphant.

We have not presented in these pages the orders of Lee, on various occasions, as these papers are for the most part of an "official" character, and not of great interest to the general reader. We shall, however, occasionally present these documents, and here lay before the reader the orders of both General Hooker and General Lee, after the battle of Chancellorsville, giving precedence to the former. The order of the Federal commander was as follows:

HEADQUARTERS ARMY OF THE POTOMAC, *May* 6, 1863.

The major-general commanding tenders to this army his congratulations on its achievements of the last seven days. If it has not accomplished all that was expected, the reasons are well known to the army. It is sufficient to say, they were of a character not to be foreseen or prevented by human sagacity or resources.

In withdrawing from the south bank of the Rappahannock, before delivering a general battle to our adversaries, the army has given renewed evidence in its confidence in itself, and its fidelity to the principles it represents.

By fighting at a disadvantage, we would have been recreant to our trust, to ourselves, to our cause, and to our country. Profoundly loyal, and conscious of its strength, the Army of the Potomac will give or decline battle whenever its interests or honor may command it.

By the celerity and secrecy of our movements, our advance and passage of the river were undisputed, and on our withdrawal not a rebel dared to follow us. The events of the last week may well cause the heart of every officer and soldier of the army to swell with pride.

We have added new laurels to our former renown. We have made long marches, crossed rivers, surprised the enemy in his intrenchments, and, whenever we have fought, we have inflicted heavier blows than those we have received.

We have taken from the enemy five thousand prisoners, and fifteen colors, captured seven pieces of artillery, and placed *hors de combat* eighteen thousand of our foe's chosen troops.

We have destroyed his depots filled with vast amounts of stores, damaged his communications, captured prisoners within the fortifications of his capital, and filled his country with fear and consternation.

We have no other regret than that caused by the loss of our brave companions, and in this we are consoled by the conviction that they have fallen in the holiest cause ever submitted to the arbitration of battle.

By command of Major-General HOOKER:

S. WILLIAMS, *Assistant Adjutant-General*

General Lee's order was as follows:

HEADQUARTERS ARMY OF NORTHERN VIRGINIA,

May 7,1863.

With heart-felt gratification, the general commanding expresses to the army his sense of the heroic conduct displayed by officers and men during the arduous operations in which they have just been engaged.

Under trying vicissitudes of heat and storm you attacked the enemy, strongly intrenched in the depths of a tangled wilderness, and again on the hills of Fredericksburg, fifteen miles distant, and by the valor that has triumphed on so many fields forced him once more to seek safety beyond the Rappahannock. While this glorious victory entitles you to the praise and gratitude of the nation, we are especially called upon to return our grateful thanks to the only Giver of victory, for the signal deliverances He has wrought.

It is therefore earnestly recommended that the troops unite on Sunday next in ascribing unto the Lord of hosts the glory due unto His name.

Let us not forget, in our rejoicing, the brave soldiers who have fallen in defence of their country; and, while we mourn their loss, let us resolve to emulate their noble example.

The army and the country alike lament the absence for a time of one to whose bravery, energy, and skill, they are so much indebted for success.

The following letter from the President of the Confederate States is communicated to the army, as an expression of his appreciation of their success:

"I have received your dispatch, and reverently unite with you in giving praise to God for the success with which He has crowned our arms. In the name of the people I offer my cordial thanks, and the troops under your command, for this addition to the unprecedented series of great victories which our army has achieved. The universal rejoicing produced by this happy result will be mingled with a general regret for the good and the brave who are numbered among the killed and the wounded."

R.E. LEE, *General.*

VIII.

PERSONAL RELATIONS OF LEE AND JACKSON.

The most important incident of the great battle of Chancellorsville was the fall of Jackson. The services of this illustrious soldier had now become almost indispensable to General Lee, who spoke of him as his "right arm;" and the commander-in-chief had so long been accustomed to lean upon the strong shoulder of his lieutenant, that now, when this support was withdrawn, he seems to have felt the loss of it profoundly.

In the war, indeed, there had arisen no soldier who so powerfully drew the public eye as Jackson. In the opinion of many persons, he was a greater and abler commander than Lee himself; and, although such an opinion will not be found to stand after a full review of the characters and careers of the two leaders, there was sufficient ground for it to induce many fair and intelligent persons to adopt it. Jackson had been almost uniformly successful. He had conducted to a triumphant issue the arduous campaign of the Valley, where he was opposed in nearly every battle by a force much larger than his own; and these victories, in a quarter so important, and at a moment so critical, had come, borne on the wind of the mountain, to electrify and inspire the hearts of the people of Richmond and the entire Confederacy. Jackson's rapid march and assault on General McClellan's right on the Chickahominy had followed; he then advanced northward, defeated the vanguard of the enemy at Cedar Mountain, led the great column of Lee against the rear of General Pope, destroyed Manassas, held his ground until Lee arrived, and bore an important part in the battle which ensued. Thence he had passed to Maryland, fallen upon Harper's Ferry and captured it, returned to fight with Lee at Sharpsburg, and in that battle had borne the brunt of the enemy's main assault with an unbroken front. That the result was a drawn battle, and not a Southern defeat, was due to Lee's generalship and Jackson's fighting. The retrograde movement to the lowland followed, and Jackson was left in the Valley to embarrass McClellan's advance. In this he perfectly succeeded, and then suddenly reappeared at Fredericksburg, where he received and repulsed one of the two great assaults of the enemy. The battle of Chancellorsville followed, and Lee's statement of the part borne in this hard combat by Jackson has been given. The result was due, he said, not to his own generalship, but to the skill and energy of his lieutenant, whose congratulations he refused to receive, declaring that the victory was Jackson's.

Here had at last ended the long series of nearly unbroken victories. Jackson had become the *alter ego* of Lee, and it is not difficult to understand the sense of loss felt by the commander-in-chief. In addition to this natural sentiment, was deep regret at the death of one personally dear to him, and to whom he was himself an object of almost reverent love. The personal relations of Lee and Jackson had, from first to last, remained the same—not the slightest cloud had ever arisen to disturb the perfect union in each of admiration and affection for the other. It had never occurred to these two great soldiers to ask what their relative position was in the public eye—which was most spoken of and commended or admired. Human nature is weak at best, and the fame of Jackson, mounting to its dazzling zenith, might have disturbed a less magnanimous soul than Lee's. There is not, however, the slightest reason to believe that Lee ever gave the subject a thought. Entirely free from that vulgar species of ambition which looks with cold eyes upon the success of others, as offensive to its own *amour-propre* Lee never seems to have instituted any comparison between himself and Jackson—greeted praise of his famous lieutenant with sincere pleasure—and was the first upon every occasion, not only to express the fullest sense of Jackson's assistance, and the warmest admiration of his genius as a soldier, but to attribute to him, as after the battle of Chancellorsville, *all* the merit of every description.

It is not possible to contemplate this august affection and admiration of the two soldiers for each other, without regarding it as a greater glory to them than all their successes in arms. Lee's opinion of Jackson, and personal sentiment toward him, have been set forth in the above sentences. The sentiment of Jackson for Lee was as strong or stronger. He regarded him with mingled love and admiration. To excite such feelings in a man like Jackson, it was necessary that Lee should be not only a soldier of the first order of genius, but also a good and pious man. It was in these lights that Jackson regarded his commander, and from first to last his confidence in and admiration for him never wavered. He had defended Lee from the criticism of unskilled or ignorant persons, from the time when he assumed command of the army, in the summer of 1862. At that time some one spoke of Lee, in Jackson's presence, as "slow." The criticism aroused the indignation of the silent soldier, and he exclaimed: "General Lee is *not* 'slow.' No one knows the weight upon his heart—his great responsibilities. He is commander-in-chief, and he knows that, if an army is lost, it cannot be replaced. No! there may be some persons whose good opinion of me may make them attach some weight to my views, and, if you ever hear that said of General Lee, I beg you will contradict it in my name. I have known General Lee for five-and-twenty years. He is cautious. He ought to be. But he is *not* 'slow.' Lee is a phenomenon. He is the only man whom I would follow blindfold!"

The abrupt and energetic expressions of Jackson on this occasion indicate his profound sense of the injustice done Lee by these criticisms; and it would be difficult to imagine a stronger statement than that here made by him. It will be conceded that he himself was competent to estimate soldiership, and in Jackson's eyes Lee was "a phenomenon—the only man whom he would follow blindfold." The subsequent career of Lee seems to have strengthened and intensified this extreme admiration. What Lee advised or did was always in Jackson's eyes the very best that could be suggested or performed. He yielded his own opinions, upon every occasion, with perfect readiness and cheerfulness to those of Lee, as to the master-mind; loved him, revered him, looked up to him, and never seems to have found fault with him but upon one occasion—when he received Lee's note of congratulation after Chancellorsville. He then said: "General Lee is very kind; but he should give the glory to God."

This affection and admiration were fully returned by General Lee, who consulted Jackson upon every occasion, and confided in him as his personal friend. There was seldom any question between them of superior and subordinate—never, except when the exigency required that the decision should be made by Lee as commander-in-chief. Jackson's supreme genius, indeed, made this course natural, and no further praise is due Lee in this particular, save that of modesty and good sense; but these qualities are commendable and not universal. He committed the greatest undertakings to Jackson with the utmost confidence, certain that he would do all that could be done; and some words of his quoted above express this entire confidence. "Say to General Jackson," he replied to the young staff-officer at Fredericksburg, "that he knows just as well what to do with the enemy as I do."

Lee's personal affection was strikingly displayed after the battle of Chancellorsville, when Jackson lay painfully, but no one supposed mortally, wounded, first at Wilderness Tavern, and then at Ginney's. Prevented from visiting the wounded man, by the responsibilities of command, now all the greater from Jackson's absence, and not regarding his hurt as serious, as indeed it did not appear to be until toward the last, Lee sent him continual messages containing good wishes and inquiries after his health. The tone of these messages is very familiar and affectionate, and leaves no doubt of the character of the relations between the two men.

"Give him my affectionate regards," he said to one officer, "and tell him to make haste and get well, and come back to me as soon as he can. He has lost his left arm, but I have lost my right."

When the wound of the great soldier took a bad turn, and it began to be whispered about that the hurt might prove fatal, Lee was strongly moved, and said with deep feeling: "Surely General Jackson must recover! God will not take him from us, now that we need him so much. Surely he will be spared to us, in answer to the many prayers which are offered for him!"

He paused after uttering these words, laboring evidently under very deep and painful emotion. After remaining silent for some moments, he added: "When you return I trust you will find him better. When a suitable occasion offers, give him my love, and tell him that I wrestled in prayer for him last night, as I never prayed, I believe, for myself."

The tone of these messages is, as we have said, that of familiar affection, as from one valued friend to another. The expression, "Give him my love," is a Virginianism, which is used only when two persons are closely and firmly bound by long association and friendship. Such had been the case with Lee and Jackson, and in the annals of the war there is no other instance of a friendship so close, affectionate, and unalloyed.

Jackson died on the 10th of May, and the unexpected intelligence shocked Lee profoundly. He mourned the death of the illustrious soldier with a sorrow too deep almost to find relief in tears; and issued a general order to the troops, which was in the following words:

With deep grief the commanding general announces to the army the death of Lieutenant-General T.J. Jackson, who expired on the 10th inst., at quarter-past three P.M. The daring, skill, and energy of this great and good soldier, by the decree of an All-wise Providence, are now lost to us. But, while we mourn his death, we feel that his spirit still lives, and will inspire the whole army with his indomitable courage and unshaken confidence in God, as our hope and strength. Let his name be a watchword to his corps, who have followed him to victory on so many fields. Let his officers and soldiers emulate his invincible determination to do every thing in defence of our beloved country. R.E. LEE, *General.*

It is probable that the composition of this order cost General Lee one of the severest pangs he ever experienced.

IX.

CIRCUMSTANCES LEADING TO THE INVASION OF PENNSYLVANIA.

The defeat of General Hooker at Chancellorsville was the turning-point of the war, and for the first time there was apparently a possibility of inducing the Federal Government to relinquish its opposition to the establishment of a separate authority in the South. The idea of the formation of a Southern Confederacy, distinct from the old Union, had, up to this time, been repudiated by the authorities at Washington as a thing utterly out of the question; but the defeat of the Federal arms in the two great battles of the Rappahannock had caused the most determined opponents of separation to doubt whether the South could be coerced to return to the Union; and, what was equally or more important, the proclamations of President Lincoln, declaring the slaves of the South free, and placing the United States virtually under martial law, aroused a violent clamor from the great Democratic party of the North, who loudly asserted that all constitutional liberty was disappearing.

This combination of non-success in military affairs and usurpation by the Government emboldened the advocates of peace to speak out plainly, and utter their protest against the continuance of the struggle, which they declared had only resulted in the prostration of all the liberties of the country. Journals and periodicals, violently denunciatory of the course pursued by the Government, all at once made their appearance in New York and elsewhere. A peace convention was called to meet in Philadelphia. Mr. Vallandigham, nominee of the Democratic party for Governor of Ohio, eloquently denounced the whole policy of endeavoring to subjugate the sovereign States of the South; and Judge Curtis, of Boston, formerly Associate Judge of the Supreme Court of the United States, published a pamphlet in which the Federal President was stigmatized as a usurper and tyrant. "I do not see," wrote Judge Curtis, "that it depends upon the Executive decree whether a servile war shall be invoked to help twenty millions of the white race to assert the rightful authority of the Constitution and laws of their country over those who refuse to obey them. But I do see that this proclamation" (emancipating the Southern slaves) "asserts the power of the Executive to make such a decree! I do not perceive how it is that my neighbors and myself, residing remote from armies and their operations, and where all the laws of the land may be enforced by constitutional means, should be subjected to the possibility of arrest and imprisonment and trial before a military commission, and punishment at its discretion, for offences unknown to the law—a possibility to be converted into a fact at the mere will of the President, or of some subordinate officer, clothed by him with this power. But I do perceive that this Executive power is asserted.... It must be obvious to the meanest capacity that, if the President of the United States has an *implied* constitutional right, as Commander-in-Chief of the Army and Navy, in time of war, to disregard any one positive prohibition of the Constitution, or to exercise any one power not delegated to the United States by the Constitution, because in his judgment he may thereby 'best subdue the enemy,' he has the same right, for the same reason, to disregard each and every provision of the Constitution, and to exercise all power *needful in his opinion* to enable him 'best to subdue the enemy.' ... The time has certainly come when the people of the United States *must* understand and *must* apply those great rules of civil liberty which have been arrived at by the self-devoted efforts of thought and action of their ancestors during seven hundred years of struggle against arbitrary power."

So far had reached the thunder of Lee's guns at Chancellorsville. Their roar seemed to have awakened throughout the entire North the great party hitherto lulled to slumber by the plea of "military necessity," or paralyzed by the very extent of the Executive usurpation which they saw, but had not had heart to oppose. On all sides the advocates of peace on the basis of separation were heard raising their importunate voices; and in the North the hearts of the people began to thrill with the anticipation of a speedy termination of the bloody and exhausting struggle. The occasion was embraced by Mr. Stephens, Vice-President of the Confederate States, to propose negotiations. This able gentleman wrote from Georgia on the 12th of June to President Davis, offering to go to Washington and sound the authorities there on the subject of peace. He believed that the moment was propitious, and wished to act before further military movements were undertaken—especially before any further projects of invasion by Lee—which would tend, he thought, to silence the peace party at the North, and again arouse the war spirit. The letter of Mr. Stephens was written on the 12th of June, and President Davis responded by telegraph a few days afterward, requesting Mr. Stephens to come to Richmond. He reached that city on the 22d or 23d of June, but by that time Lee's vanguard was entering Maryland, and Gettysburg speedily followed, which terminated all hopes of peace.

The plan of moving the Southern army northward, with the view of invading the Federal territory, seems to have been the result of many circumstances. The country was elated with the two great victories of Fredericksburg and Chancellorsville, and the people were clamorous for active operations against an enemy who seemed powerless to stand the pressure of Southern steel. The army, which had been largely augmented by the return of absentees to its ranks, new levies, and the recall of Longstreet's two divisions from Suffolk, shared the general enthusiasm; and thus a very heavy pressure was brought to bear upon the authorities and on General Lee, in favor of a forward movement, which, it was supposed, would terminate in a signal victory and a treaty of peace.

Lee yielded to this view of things rather than urged it. He was not opposed to an offensive policy, and seems, indeed, to have shared the opinion of Jackson that "the Scipio Africanus policy" was the best for the South. His theory from the beginning of the war had been, that the true policy of the South was to keep the enemy as far as possible from the interior, fighting on the frontier or on Federal soil, if possible. That of the South would there thus be protected from the ravages of the enemy, and the further advantage would accrue, that the Confederate capital, Richmond, would at all times be safe from danger. This was an important consideration, as events subsequently showed. As long as the enemy were held at arm's-length, north of the Rappahannock, Richmond, with her net-work of railroads connecting with every part of the South, was safe, and the Government, undisturbed in their capital, remained a power in the eyes of the world. But, with an enemy enveloping the city, and threatening her lines of communication, the tenure of the place by the Government was uncertain. When General Grant finally thus enveloped the city, and laid hold upon the railroads, Lee's army was defeated, and the Government became fugitive, which alone would have struck a mortal blow to its prestige and authority.

It was to arrive at these results, which his sagacity discerned, that Lee always advocated such movements as would throw back the enemy, and drive him, if possible, from the soil of Virginia. Another important consideration was the question of supplies. These were at all times deficient in the Confederate armies, and it was obviously the best policy to protect as much territory, from which supplies might be drawn, as possible. More than ever before, these supplies were now needed; and when General Lee sent, in May or June, a requisition for rations to Richmond, the commissary-general is said to have endorsed upon the paper, "If General Lee wishes rations, let him seek them in Pennsylvania."

The considerations here stated were the main inducements for that great movement northward which followed the battle of Chancellorsville. The army and country were enthusiastic; the Government rather followed than led; and, throughout the month of May, Lee was busily engaged in organizing and equipping his forces for the decisive advance. Experience had now dictated many alterations and improvements in the army. It was divided into three *corps d'armée*, each consisting of three divisions, and commanded by an officer with the rank of lieutenant-general. Longstreet remained at the head of his former corps, Ewell succeeded Jackson in command of "Jackson's old corps," and A.P. Hill was assigned to a third corps made up of portions of the two others. The infantry was thus rearranged in a manner to increase greatly its efficiency, and the artillery arm was entirely reorganized. The old system of assigning one or more batteries or battalions to each division or corps was done away with, and the artillery of the army was made a distinct command, and placed under General W.N. Pendleton, a brave and energetic officer, who was thenceforward Lee's "chief of artillery." The last arm, the cavalry, was also increased in efficiency; and, on the last day of May, General Lee had the satisfaction of finding himself in command of a well-equipped and admirably-officered army of sixty-eight thousand three hundred and fifty-two bayonets, and nearly ten thousand cavalry and artillery—in all, about eighty thousand men. Never before had the Southern army had present for duty, as fighting men, so large a number, except just before the battles on the Chickahominy. There was, however, this great difference between the army then and at this time: in those first months of 1862, it was made up largely of raw troops who had never heard the discharge of a musket in their lives: while now, in May, 1863 the bulk of the army consisted of Lee's veterans, men who had followed him through the fire of Manassas, Sharpsburg, Fredericksburg, and Chancellorsville, and could be counted on to effect any thing not absolutely beyond human power. General Longstreet, conversing after the war with a gentleman of the North, declared as much. The army at that time, he said, was in a condition to undertake *any thing*.

X.
LEE'S PLANS AND OBJECTS.

The great game of chess was now about to commence, and, taking an illustration from that game, General Lee is reported to have said that he believed he would "swap queens," that is, advance and attempt to capture the city of Washington, leaving General Hooker at liberty, if he chose so to do, to seize in turn upon Richmond. What the result of so singular a manoeuvre would have been, it is impossible to say; it would certainly have proved one of the strangest incidents of a war fruitful in varied and shifting events.

Such a plan of operations, however, if ever seriously contemplated by Lee, was speedily abandoned. He nowhere makes mention of any such design in his published reports, and he probably spoke of it only in jest. His real aim in the great movement now about to commence, is stated with brevity and reserve—then absolutely necessary—but also with sufficient clearness, in his official report. The position of the enemy opposite Fredericksburg was, he says, such as to render an attack upon him injudicious. It was, therefore, desirable to manoeuvre him out of it— force him to return toward Maryland—and thus free the country of his forces. A further result was expected from this movement. The lower Shenandoah Valley was occupied by the enemy under General Milroy, who, with his headquarters at Winchester, harassed the whole region, which he ruled with a rod of iron. With the withdrawal of the Federal army under General Hooker, and before the advance of the Confederates, General Milroy would also disappear, and the fertile fields of the Valley be relieved. The whole force of the enemy would thus, says Lee, "be compelled to leave Virginia, and possibly to draw to its support troops designed to operate against other parts of the country." He adds: "In this way it was supposed that the enemy's plan of campaign for the summer would be broken up, and part of the season of active operations be consumed in the formation of new combinations and the preparations that they would require. In addition to these advantages, it was hoped that other valuable results might be attained by military success," that is to say, by a battle which Lee intended to fight when circumstances were favorable. That he expected to fight, not merely to manoeuvre the enemy from Virginia, is apparent from another sentence of the report. "It was thought," he says, "that the corresponding movements on the part of the enemy, to which those contemplated by us would probably give rise, might *offer a fair opportunity to strike a blow at the army therein, commanded by General Hooker*" the word "therein" referring to the region "north of the Potomac." In the phrase, "other valuable results which might be attained by military success," the reference is plainly to the termination of the contest by a treaty of peace, based upon the independence of the South.

These sentences, taken from the only publication ever made by Lee on the subject of the Gettysburg campaign, express guardedly, but distinctly, his designs. He aimed to draw General Hooker north of the Potomac, clear the Valley, induce the enemy to send troops in other quarters to the assistance of the main Federal army, and, when the moment came, attack General Hooker, defeat him if possible, and thus end the war. That a decisive defeat of the Federal forces at that time in Maryland or Pennsylvania, would have virtually put an end to the contest, there seems good reason to believe. Following the Southern victories of Fredericksburg and Chancellorsville, a third bloody disaster would, in all human probability, have broken the resolution of the Federal authorities. With Lee thundering at the gates of Washington or Philadelphia, and with the peace party encouraged to loud and importunate protest, it is not probable that the war would have continued. Intelligent persons in the North are said to have so declared, since the war, and the declaration seems based upon good sense.

Before passing from this necessary preface to the narrative of events, it is proper to add that, in the contemplated battle with General Hooker, when he had drawn him north of the Potomac, Lee did not intend to assume a *tactical offensive*, but to force the Federal commander, if possible, to make the attack. [Footnote: "It had not been intended to fight a general battle at such a distance from our base, unless attacked by the enemy."—*Lee's Report*] From this resolution he was afterward induced by circumstances to depart, and the result is known.

What is above written will convey to the reader a clear conception of Lee's views and intentions in undertaking his last great offensive campaign; and we now proceed to the narrative of the movements of the two armies, and the battle of Gettysburg.

XI.

THE CAVALRY-FIGHT AT FLEETWOOD.

Lee began his movement northward on the 3d day of June, just one month after the battle of Chancellorsville. From this moment to the time when his army was concentrated in the vicinity of Gettysburg, his operations were rapid and energetic, but with a cautious regard to the movements of the enemy.

Pursuing his design of manoeuvring the Federal army out of Virginia, without coming to action, Lee first sent forward one division of Longstreet's corps in the direction of Culpepper, another then followed, and, on the 4th and 5th of June, Ewell's entire corps was sent in the same direction—A.P. Hill remaining behind on the south bank of the Rappahannock, near Fredericksburg, to watch the enemy there, and bar the road to Richmond. These movements became speedily known to General Hooker, whose army lay north of the river near that point, and on the 5th he laid a pontoon just below Fredericksburg, and crossed about a corps to the south bank, opposite Hill. This threatening demonstration, however, was not suffered by Lee to arrest his own movements. Seeing that the presence of the enemy there was "intended for the purpose of observation rather than attack," and only aimed to check his operations, he continued the withdrawal of his troops, by way of Culpepper, in the direction of the Shenandoah Valley.

A brilliant pageant, succeeded by a dramatic and stirring incident, was now to prelude the march of Lee into the enemy's territory. On the 8th of June, the day of the arrival of Lee's head of column in Culpepper, a review of Stuart's cavalry took place in a field east of the court-house. The review was a picturesque affair. General Lee was present, sitting his horse, motionless, on a little knoll—the erect figure half concealed by the short cavalry-cape falling from his shoulders, and the grave face overshadowed by the broad gray hat—while above him, from a lofty pole, waved the folds of a large Confederate flag. The long column of about eight thousand cavalry was first drawn up in line, and afterward passed in front of Lee at a gallop—Stuart and his staff-officers leading the charge with sabres at tierce point, a species of military display highly attractive to the gallant and joyous young commander. The men then charged in mimic battle the guns of the "Stuart Horse-Artillery," which were posted upon an adjoining hill; and, as the column of cavalry approached, the artillerists received them with a thunderous discharge of blank ammunition, which rolled like the roar of actual battle among the surrounding hills. This sham-fight was kept up for some time, and no doubt puzzled the enemy on the opposite shore of the Rappahannock. On the next morning—either in consequence of a design formed before the review, or to ascertain what this discharge of artillery meant—two divisions of Federal cavalry, supported by two brigades of "picked infantry," were sent across the river at Kelly's and Beverley's Fords, east of the court-house, to beat up the quarters of Stuart and find what was going on in the Southern camps.

The most extensive cavalry-fight, probably, of the whole war, followed. One of Stuart's brigades, near Beverley's Ford, was nearly surprised and resolutely attacked at daylight by Buford's division, which succeeded in forcing back the brigade a short distance toward the high range called Fleetwood Hill, in the rear. From this eminence, where his headquarters were established, Stuart went to the front at a swift gallop, opened a determined fire of artillery and sharp-shooters upon the advancing enemy, and sent Hampton's division to attack them on their left. Meanwhile, however, the enemy were executing a rapid and dangerous movement against Stuart's, rear. General Gregg, commanding the second Federal cavalry division, crossed at Kelly's Ford below, passed the force left in that quarter, and came in directly on Stuart's rear, behind Fleetwood Hill. In the midst of the hard fight in front, Stuart was called now to defend his rear. He hastened to do so by falling back and meeting the enemy now charging the hill. The attack was repulsed, and the enemy's artillery charged in turn by the Southerners. This was captured and recaptured two or three times, but at last remained in the hands of Stuart.

General Gregg now swung round his right, and prepared to advance along the eastern slope of the hill. Stuart had, however, posted his artillery there, and, as the Federal line began to move, arrested it with a sudden and destructive fire of shell. At the same time a portion of Hampton's division, under the brave Georgian, General P.M.B. Young, was ordered to charge the enemy. The assault was promptly made with the sabre, unaided by carbine or pistol fire, and Young cut down or routed the force in front of him, which dispersed in disorder toward the river. The dangerous assault on the rear of Fleetwood Hill was thus repulsed, and the advance of the enemy on the left, near the river, met with the same ill success. General W.H.F. Lee, son of the commanding general, gallantly charged them in that quarter, and drove them back to the Rappahannock, receiving a severe wound, which long confined him to his bed. Hampton had followed the retreating enemy on the right, under the fire of Stuart's guns from Fleetwood Hill; and by nightfall the whole force had recrossed the Rappahannock, leaving several hundred dead and wounded upon the field. [Footnote: The Southern loss was also considerable. Colonel Williams was killed, Generals Lee and Butler severely wounded—the latter losing his foot—and General Stuart's staff had been peculiarly unfortunate. Of the small group of officers, Captain Farley was killed, Captain White wounded, and Lieutenant Goldsborough captured. The Federal force sustained a great loss in the death of the gallant Colonel Davis, of the Eighth New-York Cavalry, and other officers.]

This reconnoissance in force—the Federal numbers probably amounting to fifteen thousand—had no other result than the discovery of the fact that Lee had infantry in Culpepper. Finding that the event of the fight was critical, General Lee had moved a body of infantry in the direction of the field of action, and the gleam of the bayonets was seen by the enemy. The infantry was not, however, engaged on either side, unless the Federal infantry participated in the initial skirmish near Beverley's Ford, and General Lee's numbers and position were not discovered.

We have dwelt with some detail upon this cavalry combat, which was an animated affair, the hand-to-hand encounter of nearly twenty thousand horsemen throughout a whole day. General Stuart was censured at the time for allowing himself to be "surprised," and a ball at Culpepper Court-House, at which some of his officers were present several days before, was pointed to as the origin of this surprise. The charge was wholly unjust, Stuart not having attended the ball. Nor was there any truth in the further statement that "his headquarters were captured" in consequence of his negligence. His tents on Fleetwood Hill were all sent to the rear soon after daylight; nothing whatever was found there but a section of the horse-artillery, who fought the charging cavalry with sabres and sponge-staffs over the guns; that Fleetwood Hill was at one time in the hands of the enemy, was due not to Stuart's negligence, but to the numbers and excellent soldiership of General Gregg, who made the flank and rear attack while Stuart was breasting that in front.

These detached statements, which may seem unduly minute, are made in justice to a brave soldier, who can no longer defend himself.

XII.

THE MARCH TO GETTYSBURG.

This attempt of the enemy to penetrate his designs had not induced General Lee to interrupt the movement of his infantry toward the Shenandoah Valley. The Federal corps sent across the Rappahannock at Fredericksburg, still remained facing General Hill; and, two days after the Fleetwood fight. General Hooker moved up the river with his main body, advancing the Third Corps to a point near Beverley's Ford. But these movements were disregarded by Lee. On the same day Ewell's corps moved rapidly toward Chester Gap, passed through that defile in the mountain, pushed on by way of Front Royal, and reached Winchester on the evening of the 13th, having in three days marched seventy miles.

The position of the Southern army now exposed it to very serious danger, and at first sight seemed to indicate a deficiency of soldiership in the general commanding it. In face of an enemy whose force was at least equal to his own,[Footnote: General Hooker stated his "effective" at this time to have been diminished to eighty thousand infantry.] Lee had extended his line until it stretched over a distance of about one hundred miles. When Ewell came in sight of Winchester, Hill was still opposite Fredericksburg, and Longstreet half-way between the two in Culpepper. Between the middle and rear corps was interposed the Rapidan River, and between the middle and advanced corps the Blue Ridge Mountains. General Hooker's army was on the north bank of the Rappahannock, well in hand, and comparatively massed, and the situation of Lee's army seemed excellent for the success of a sudden blow at it.

It seems that the propriety of attacking the Southern army while thus *in transitu*, suggested itself both to General Hooker and to President Lincoln, but they differed as to the point and object of the attack. In anticipation of Lee's movement, General Hooker had written to the President, probably suggesting a counter-movement across the Rappahannock, somewhere near Fredericksburg, to threaten Richmond, and thus check Lee's advance. This, however. President Lincoln refused to sanction.

"In case you find Lee coming to the north of the Rappahannock," President Lincoln wrote to General Hooker, "I would by no means cross to the south of it. I would not take any risk of being entangled upon the river, *like an ox jumped half over a fence, and liable to be torn by dogs, front and rear, without a fair chance to gore one way or kick the other*"

Five days afterward the President wrote: "I think Lee's army, and not Richmond, is your true objective point. If he comes toward the Upper Potomac, fight him when opportunity offers. If he stays where he is, *fret him and fret him.*"

When intelligence now reached Washington that the head of Lee's column was approaching the Upper Potomac, while the rear was south of the Rappahannock, the President wrote to General Hooker: "*If the head of Lee's army is at Martinsburg, and the tail of it on the plank road* between Fredericksburg and Chancellorsville, the *animal must be very slim somewhere—could you not break him?*"

General Hooker did not seem to be able to determine upon a decisive course of action, in spite of the tempting opening presented to him by Lee. It would seem that nothing could have been plainer than the good policy of an attack upon Hill at Fredericksburg, which would certainly have checked Lee's movement by recalling Longstreet from Culpepper, and Ewell from the Valley. But this bold operation did not appear to commend itself to the Federal authorities. Instead of reënforcing the corps sent across at Fredericksburg and attacking Hill, General Hooker withdrew the corps, on the 13th, to the north bank of the river, got his forces together, and began to fall back toward Manassas, and even remained in ignorance, it seems, of all connected with his adversary's movements. Even as late as the 17th of June, his chief-of-staff, General Butterfield, wrote to one of his officers; "Try and hunt up somebody from Pennsylvania who knows something, and has a cool enough head to judge what is the actual state of affairs there with regard to the enemy. *My impression is, that Lee's movement on the Upper Potomac is a cover for a cavalry-raid on the south side of the river…. We cannot go boggling around until we know what we are going after.*"

Such was the first result of Lee's daring movement to transfer military operations to the region north of the Potomac. A Northern historian has discerned in his plan of campaign an amount of boldness which "seemed to imply a great contempt for his opponent." This is perhaps a somewhat exaggerated statement of the case. Without "boldness" a commander is but half a soldier, and it may be declared that a certain amount of that quality is absolutely essential to successful military operations. But the question is, Did Lee expose himself, by these movements of his army, to probable disaster, if his adversary—equal to the occasion—struck at his flank? A failure of the campaign of invasion would probably have resulted from such an attack either upon Hill at Fredericksburg, or upon Longstreet in Culpepper, inasmuch as Ewell's column, in that event, must have fallen back. But a *defeat* of the combined forces of Hill and Longstreet, who were within supporting distance of each other, was not an event which General Hooker could count upon with any degree of certainty. The two corps numbered nearly fifty thousand men— that is to say, two-thirds of the Southern army; General Hooker's whole force was but about eighty thousand; and it was not probable that the eighty thousand would be able to rout the fifty thousand, when at Chancellorsville less than this last number of Southerners had defeated one hundred and twenty thousand.

There seems little reason to doubt that General Lee took this view of the subject, and relied on Hill and Longstreet to unite and repulse any attack upon them, while Ewell's great "raiding column" drove forward into the heart of the enemy's territory. That the movement was bold, there can certainly be no question; that it was a reckless and hazardous operation, depending for its success, in Lee's eyes, solely on the supposed inefficiency of General Hooker, does not appear. These comments delay the narrative, but the subject is fruitful in suggestion. It may be pardoned a Southern writer if he lingers over this last great offensive movement of the Southern army. The last, it was also one of the greatest and most brilliant. The war, therefore, was to enter upon its second stage, in which the South was to simply maintain the defensive. But Lee was terminating the first stage of the contest by one of those great campaigns which project events and personages in bold relief from the broad canvas, and illumine the pages of history.

Events were now in rapid progress. Ewell's column—the sharp head of the Southern spear—reached Winchester on the 13th of June, and Rodes, who had been detached at Front Royal to drive the enemy from Berryville, reached the last-named village on the same day when the force there retreated to Winchester. On the next morning Early's division attacked the forces of Milroy at Winchester, stormed and captured their "Star Fort," on a hill near the place, and so complete was the rout of the enemy that their commander, General Milroy, had scarcely time to escape, with a handful of his men, in the direction of the Potomac.

For this disaster the unfortunate officer was harshly criticised by General Hooker, who wrote to his Government, "In my opinion, Milroy's men will fight better *under a soldier.*"

After thus clearing the country around Winchester, Ewell advanced rapidly on Martinsburg, where he took a number of prisoners and some artillery. The captures in two days had been more than four thousand prisoners and twenty-nine cannon, with four hundred horses and a large amount of stores. Ewell continued then to advance, and, entering Maryland, sent a portion of his cavalry, under General Imboden, westward, to destroy the Baltimore and Ohio Railroad, and another body, under General Jenkins, in advance, toward Chambersburg. Meanwhile, the rest of the army was moving to join him. Hill, finding that the enemy had disappeared from his front near Fredericksburg, hastened to march from that vicinity, and was sent forward by Lee, on the track of Ewell, passing in rear of Longstreet, who had remained in Culpepper. The latter was now directed by Lee to move along the eastern side of the Blue Ridge, and, by occupying Ashby's and Snicker's Gaps, protect the flank of the column in the Valley from attack—a work in which Stuart's cavalry, thrown out toward the enemy, assisted.

Such was the posture of affairs when General Hooker's chief-of-staff became so much puzzled, and described the Federal army as "boggling around," and not knowing "what they were going after." Lee's whole movement, it appears, was regarded as a feint to "cover a cavalry-raid on the south side of the river"—a strange conclusion, it would seem, in reference to a movement of such magnitude. It now became absolutely necessary that Lee's designs should be unmasked, if possible; and to effect this object Stuart's cavalry force, covering the southern flank, east of the Blue Ridge, must be driven back. This was undertaken in a deliberate manner. Three corps of cavalry, with a division of infantry and a full supply of artillery, were sent forward from the vicinity of Manassas, to drive Stuart in on all the roads leading to the mountain. A fierce struggle followed, in which Stuart, who knew the importance of his position, fought the great force opposed to him from every hill and knoll. But he was forced back steadily, in spite of a determined resistance, and at Upperville a hand-to-hand sabre-fight wound up the movement, in which the Federal cavalry was checked, when Stuart fell back toward Paris, crowned the mountain-side with his cannon, and awaited a final attack. This was not, however, made. Night approaching, the Federal force fell back toward Manassas, and on the next morning Stuart followed them, on the same road over which he had so rapidly retreated, beyond Middleburg.

Lee paid little attention to these operations on his flank east of the mountains, but proceeded steadily, in personal command of his infantry, in the direction of the Cumberland Valley. Ewell was moving rapidly toward Harrisburg, with orders to "take" that place "if he deemed his force adequate,"[1] General Jenkins, commanding cavalry, preceding the advance of his infantry. He had thus pierced the enemy's territory, and it was necessary promptly to support him. Hill and Longstreet were accordingly directed to pass the Potomac at Shepherdstown and Williamsport. The columns united at Hagerstown, and on the 27th of June entered Chambersburg.

[Footnote 1: This statement of Lee's orders is derived by the writer from Lieutenant-General Ewell.]

General Hooker had followed, crossing the Potomac, opposite Leesburg, at about the moment when Lee's rear was passing from Maryland into Pennsylvania. The direction of the Federal march was toward Frederick, from which point General Hooker could move in either one of two directions—either across the mountain toward Boonsboro, which would throw him upon Lee's communications, or northward to Westminster, or Gettysburg, which would lead to an open collision with the invading army in a pitched battle.

At this juncture of affairs, just as the Federal army was concentrating near Frederick, General Hooker, at his own request, was relieved from command. The occasion of this unexpected event seems to have been a difference of opinion between himself and General Halleck, the Federal general-in-chief, on the question whether the fortifications at Harper's Ferry should or should not be abandoned. The point at issue would appear to have been unimportant, but ill feeling seems to have arisen: General Hooker resented the action of the authorities, and requested to be relieved; his request was complied with, and his place was filled by Major-General George G. Meade.

[Illustration: Map—Sketch of the Country Around GETTYSBURG.]

General Meade, an officer of excellent soldiership, and enjoying the repute of modesty and dignity, assumed command of the Federal army, and proceeded rapidly in pursuit of Lee. The design of moving directly across the South Mountain on Lee's communications, if ever entertained by him, was abandoned. The outcry from Pennsylvania drew him perforce. Ewell, with one division, had penetrated to Carlisle; and Early, with another division, was at York; everywhere the horses, cattle, and supplies of the country, had been seized upon for the use of the troops; and General Meade was loudly called upon to go to the assistance of the people thus exposed to the terrible rebels. His movements were rapid. Assuming command on June 28th, he began to move on the 29th, and on the 30th was approaching the town of Gettysburg.[1]

[Footnote 1: The movements of the Federal commander were probably hastened by the capture, about this time at Hagerstown, of a dispatch from President Davis to General Lee. Lee, it seems, had suggested that General Beauregard should be sent to make a demonstration in the direction of Culpepper, and by thus appearing to threaten Washington, embarrass the movements of the Northern army. To this suggestion the President is said to have replied that he had no troops to make such a movement; and General Meade had thus the proof before him that Washington was in no danger. The Confederacy was thus truly unfortunate again, as in September, 1862, when a similar incident came to the relief of General McClellan.]

XIII.

LEE IN PENNSYLVANIA.

Lee, in personal command of the corps of Hill and Longstreet, had meanwhile moved on steadily in the direction of the Susquehanna, and, reaching Chambersburg on the 27th of June, "made preparations to advance upon Harrisburg."

At Chambersburg he issued an order to the troops, which should find a place in every biography of this great soldier. The course pursued by many of the Federal commanders in Virginia had been merciless and atrocious beyond words. General Pope had ravaged the counties north of the Rappahannock, especially the county of Culpepper, in a manner which reduced that smiling region wellnigh to a waste; General Milroy, with his headquarters at Winchester, had so cruelly oppressed the people of the surrounding country as to make them execrate the very mention of his name; and the excesses committed by the troops of these officers, with the knowledge and permission of their commanders, had been such, said a foreign writer, as to "cast mankind two centuries back toward barbarism."

Now, the tables were turned, and the world looked for a sudden and merciless retaliation on the part of the Southerners. Lee was in Pennsylvania, at the head of an army thirsting to revenge the accumulated wrongs against their helpless families. At a word from him the fertile territory of the North would be made to feel the iron pressure of military rule, proceeding on the theory that retaliation is a just principle to adopt toward an enemy. Fire, slaughter, and outrage, would have burst upon Pennsylvania, and the black flag, which had been virtually raised by Generals Pope and Milroy, would have flaunted now in the air at the head of the Southern army.

Instead of permitting this disgraceful oppression of non-combatants, Lee issued, at Chambersburg, the following general order to his troops:

HEADQUARTERS ARMY OF NORTHERN VIRGINIA,

CHAMBERSBURG, PA., *June* 27, 1863.

The commanding general has observed with much satisfaction the conduct of the troops on the march, and confidently anticipates results commensurate with the high spirit they have manifested. No troops could have displayed greater fortitude, or better performed the arduous marches of the past ten days. Their conduct in other respects has, with few exceptions, been in keeping with their character as soldiers, and entitles them to approbation and praise.

There have, however, been instances of forgetfulness, on the part of some, that they have in keeping the yet unsullied reputation of the army, and that the duties exacted of us by civilization and Christianity are not less obligatory in the country of the enemy than in our own.

The commanding general considers that no greater disgrace could befall the army, and, through it, our whole people, than the perpetration of the barbarous outrages on the innocent and defenceless, and the wanton destruction of private property, that have marked the course of the enemy in our own country. Such proceedings not only disgrace the perpetrators, and all connected with them, but are subversive of the discipline and efficiency of the army, and destructive of the ends of our present movements. It must be remembered that we make war only upon armed men, and that we cannot take vengeance for the wrongs our people have suffered without lowering ourselves in the eyes of all whose abhorrence has been excited by the atrocities of our enemy, without offending against Him to whom vengeance belongeth, without whose favor and support our efforts must all prove in vain.

The commanding general, therefore, earnestly exhorts the troops to abstain, with most scrupulous care, from unnecessary or wanton injury to private property; and he enjoins upon all officers to arrest and bring to summary punishment all who shall in any way offend against the orders on this subject.

R.E. LEE, *General.*

The noble maxims and truly Christian spirit of this paper will remain the undying glory of Lee. Under what had been surely a bitter provocation, he retained the calmness and forbearance of a great soul, saying to his army: "The duties exacted of us by civilization and Christianity are not less obligatory in the country of the enemy than in our own.... No greater disgrace could befall the army, and through it our whole people, than the perpetration of outrage upon the innocent and defenceless.... We make war only upon armed men, and cannot take vengeance for the wrongs our people have suffered without offending against Him to whom vengeance belongeth, without whose favor and support our efforts must all prove in vain."

Such were the utterances of Lee, resembling those we might attribute to the ideal Christian warrior; and, indeed, it was such a spirit that lay under the plain uniform of the great Virginian. What he ordered was enforced, and no one was disturbed in his person or property. Of this statement many proofs could be given. A Pennsylvania farmer said to a Northern correspondent, in reference to the Southern troops: "I must say they acted like gentlemen, and, their cause aside, I would rather have forty thousand rebels quartered on my premises than one thousand Union troops." From the journal of Colonel Freemantle, an English officer accompanying the Southern army, we take these sentences:

"In passing through Greencastle we found all the houses and windows shut up, the natives in their Sunday clothes, standing at their doors regarding the troops in a very unfriendly manner. I saw no straggling into the houses, nor were any of the inhabitants disturbed or annoyed by the soldiers. Sentries were placed at the doors of many of the best houses, to prevent any officer or soldier from getting in on any pretence.... I entered Chambersburg at 6 P.M.... Sentries were placed at the doors of all the principal houses, and the town was cleared of all but the military passing through or on duty.... No officer or soldier under the rank of a general is allowed in Chambersburg without a special order from General Lee, which he is very chary of giving, and I hear of officers of rank being refused this pass.... I went into Chambersburg again, and witnessed the singularly good behavior of the troops toward the citizens. I heard soldiers saying to one another that they did not like being in a town in which they were very naturally detested. To any one who has seen, as I have, the ravages of the Northern troops in Southern towns, this forbearance seems most commendable and surprising."

A Northern correspondent said of the course pursued by General Jenkins, in command of Ewell's cavalry: "By way of giving the devil his due, it must be said that, although there were over sixty acres of wheat and eighty acres of corn and oats in the same field, he protected it most carefully, and picketed his horses so that it could not be injured. No fences were wantonly destroyed, poultry was not disturbed, nor did he compliment our blooded cattle so much as to test the quality of their steak and roast."

Of the feeling of the troops these few words from the letter of an officer written to one of his family will convey an idea: "I felt when I first came here that I would like to revenge myself upon these people for the devastation they have brought upon our own beautiful home—that home where we could have lived so happily, and that we loved so much, from which their vandalism has driven you and my helpless little ones. But, though I had such severe wrongs and grievances to redress, and such great cause for revenge, yet, when I got among these people, I could not find it in my heart to molest them."

Such was the treatment of the people of Pennsylvania by the Southern troops in obedience to the order of the commander-in-chief. Lee in person set the example. A Southern journal made the sarcastic statement that he became irate at the robbing of cherry-trees; and, if he saw the *top rail* of a fence lying upon the ground as he rode by, would dismount and replace it with his own hands.

XIV.

CONCENTRATION AT GETTYSBURG.

This was the position of the great adversaries in the last days of June. Lee was at Chambersburg, in the Cumberland Valley, about to follow Ewell, who was approaching Harrisburg. Early had captured York; and the Federal army was concentrating rapidly on the flank of the Southern army, toward Gettysburg.

Lee had ordered the movement of Early upon York, with the object of diverting the attention of the Federal commander from his own rear, in the Cumberland Valley. The exact movements and position of General Meade were unknown to him; and this arose in large measure from the absence of Stuart's cavalry. This unfortunate incident has given rise to much comment, and Stuart has been harshly criticised for an alleged disobedience of Lee's plain orders. The question is an embarrassing one. Lee's statement is as follows: "General Stuart was left to guard the passes of the mountains" (Ashby's and other gaps in the Blue Ridge, in Virginia), "and observe the movements of the enemy, whom he was instructed to harass and impede as much as possible should he attempt to cross the Potomac. *In that event, General Stuart was directed to move into Maryland, crossing the Potomac east or west of the Blue Ridge, as in his judgment should be best, and take position on the right of our column as it advanced.*"

This order was certainly plain up to a certain point. Stuart was to harass and embarrass the movements of the enemy, in case they attempted to cross to the north bank of the Potomac. When they did cross, he also was to pass the river, either east or west of the Blue Ridge, "as in his judgment should seem best." So far the order was unmistakable. The river was to be crossed at such point as Stuart should select, either on the lower waters, or in the Valley. Lee added, however, that this movement should be made in such a manner as to enable Stuart to "take position on the right of our column as it advanced"—the meaning appearing to be that the cavalry should move *between* the two armies, in order to guard the Southern flank as it advanced into the Cumberland Valley. Circumstances arose, however, which rendered it difficult for Stuart to move on the line thus indicated with sufficient promptness to render his services valuable. The enemy crossed at Leesburg while the Southern cavalry was near Middleburg; and, from the jaded condition of his horses, Stuart feared that he would be unable, in case he crossed above, to place his column between the two armies then rapidly advancing. He accordingly took the bold resolution of passing the Potomac *below*Leesburg, designing to shape his course due northward toward Harrisburg, the objective point of the Southern army. This he did—crossing at Seneca Falls—but on the march he was delayed by many incidents. Near Rockville he stopped to capture a large train of Federal wagons; at Westminster and Hanovertown he was temporarily arrested by combats with the Federal cavalry; and, ignorant as he was of the concentration of Lee's troops upon Gettysburg, he advanced rapidly toward Carlisle, where, in the midst of an attack on that place, he was recalled by Lee.

Such were the circumstances leading to, and the incidents attending, this movement. The reader must form his own opinion of the amount of blame to be justly attached to Stuart. He always declared, and asserted in his report of these occurrences, that he had acted in exact obedience to his orders; but, on the contrary, as appears from General Lee's report, those orders were meant to prescribe a different movement. He had marched in one sense on "the right" of the Southern column "as it advanced;" but in another sense he had not done so. Victory at Gettysburg would have silenced all criticism of this difference of construction; but, unfortunately, the event was different, and the strictures directed at Stuart were natural. The absence of the cavalry unquestionably embarrassed Lee greatly; but, in his report, he is moderate and guarded, as usual, in his expressions. "The absence of cavalry," he says, "rendered it impossible to obtain accurate information" of General Meade's movements; and "the march toward Gettysburg was conducted more slowly than it would have been had the movements of the Federal army been known."

[Illustration: Map—Battle of GETTYSBURG]

To return now to the movements of Lee's infantry, after the arrival of the main body at Chambersburg. Lee was about to continue his advance in the direction of Harrisburg, when, on the night of the 29th, his scouts brought him intelligence that the Federal army was rapidly advancing, and the head of the column was near the South Mountain. A glance at the map will indicate the importance of this intelligence. General Meade would be able, without difficulty, in case the Southern army continued its march northward, to cross the South-Mountain range, and place himself directly in Lee's rear, in the Cumberland Valley. Then the Southern forces would be completely intercepted—General Meade would be master of the situation—and Lee must retreat east of the mountain or cut his way through the Federal army.

A battle was thus clearly about to be forced upon the Southern commander, and it only remained for him to so manoeuvre his army as to secure a position in which he could receive the enemy's attack with advantage. Lee accordingly put his column in motion across the mountain toward Gettysburg, and, sending couriers to Ewell and Early to return from Harrisburg and York toward the same point, made his preparations to take position and fight.

On the morning of the 1st day of July, this was then the condition of affairs. General Meade was advancing with rapidity upon the town of Gettysburg, and Lee was crossing the South Mountain, opposite Chambersburg, to meet him.

When the heads of the two columns came together in the vicinity of Gettysburg, the thunders of battle began.

XV.
THE FIRST DAY'S FIGHT AT GETTYSBURG.

The sanguinary struggle which now ensued between the Army of Northern Virginia and the Army of the Potomac continued for three days, and the character of these battles, together with their decisive results, have communicated to the events an extraordinary interest. Every fact has thus been preserved, and the incidents of the great combat, down to the most minute details, have been placed upon record. The subject is, indeed, almost embarrassed by the amount of information collected and published; and the chief difficulty for a writer, at this late day, is to select from the mass such salient events as indicate clearly the character of the conflict.

This difficulty the present writer has it in his power to evade, in great measure, by confining himself mainly to the designs and operations of General Lee. These were plain and simple. He had been forced to relinquish his march toward the Susquehanna by the dangerous position of General Meade so near his line of retreat; this rendered a battle unavoidable; and Lee was now moving to accept battle, designing, if possible, to secure such a position as would give him the advantage in the contest. Before he succeeded in effecting this object, battle was forced upon him—not by General Meade, but by simple stress of circumstances. The Federal commander had formed the same intention as that of his adversary—to accept, and not deliver, battle—and did not propose to fight near Gettysburg. He was, rather, looking backward to a strong position in the direction of Westminster, when suddenly the head of his column became engaged near Gettysburg, and this determined every thing.

A few words are necessary to convey to the reader some idea of the character of the ground. Gettysburg is a town, nestling down in a valley, with so many roads centring in the place that, if a circle were drawn around it to represent the circumference of a wheel, the roads would resemble the spokes. A short distance south of the town is a ridge of considerable height, which runs north and south, bending eastward in the vicinity of Gettysburg, and describing a curve resembling a hook. From a graveyard on this high ground it is called Cemetery Hill, or Ridge. Opposite this ridge, looking westward, is a second and lower range called Seminary Ridge. This extends also north and south, passing west of Gettysburg. Still west of Seminary Ridge are other still lower ranges, between which flows a small stream called Willoughby Run; and beyond these, distant about ten miles, rise the blue heights of the South Mountain.

Across the South Mountain, by way of the village of Cashtown, Lee, on the morning of the 1st of July, was moving steadily toward Gettysburg, when Hill, holding the front, suddenly encountered the head of the enemy's column in the vicinity of Willoughby Run. This consisted of General Buford's cavalry division, which had pushed on in advance of General Reynolds's infantry corps, the foremost infantry of the Federal army, and now, almost before it was aware of Hill's presence, became engaged with him. General Buford posted his horse-artillery to meet Hill's attack, but it soon became obvious that the Federal cavalry could not stand before the Southern infantry fire, and General Reynolds, at about ten in the morning, hastening forward, reached the field. An engagement immediately took place between the foremost infantry divisions of Hill and Reynolds. A brigade of Hill's, from Mississippi, drove back a Federal brigade, seizing upon its artillery; but, in return, Archer's brigade was nearly surrounded, and several hundred of the men captured. Almost immediately after this incident the Federal forces sustained a serious loss; General Reynolds—one of the most trusted and energetic lieutenants of General Meade—was mortally wounded while disposing his men for action, and borne from the field. The Federal troops continued, however, to fight with gallantry. Some of the men were heard exclaiming, "We have come to stay!" in reference to which, one of their officers afterward said, "And a very large portion of them never left that ground."[1]

[Footnote 1: General Doubleday: Report of Committee on the Conduct of the War, Part I., p. 307.]

Battle was now joined in earnest between the two heads of column, and on each side reënforcements were sent forward to take part in this unexpected encounter. Neither General Lee nor General Meade had expected or desired it. Both had aimed, in manoeuvring their forces, to select ground suitable for receiving instead of making an attack, and now a blind chance seemed about to bring on a battle upon ground unknown to both commanders. When the sound of the engagement was first heard by Lee, he was in the rear of his troops at the headquarters which Hill had just vacated, near Cashtown, under the South Mountain. The firing was naturally supposed by him to indicate an accidental collision with some body of the enemy's cavalry, and, when intelligence reached him that Hill was engaged with the Federal infantry, the announcement occasioned him the greatest astonishment. General Meade's presence so near him was a circumstance completely unknown to Lee, and certainly was not desired by him. But a small portion of his forces were "up." Longstreet had not yet passed the mountain, and the forces of General Ewell, although that officer had promptly fallen back, in obedience to his orders, from the Susquehanna, were not yet in a position to take part in the engagement. Under these circumstances, if the whole of General Meade's army had reached Gettysburg, directly in Lee's front, the advantage in the approaching action must be largely in favor of the Federal army, and a battle might result in a decisive Confederate defeat.

No choice, however, was now left General Lee. The head of his advancing column had come into collision with the enemy, and it was impossible to retire without a battle. Lee accordingly ordered Hill's corps to be closed up, and reënforcements to be sent forward rapidly to the point of action. He then mounted his horse and rode in the direction of the firing, guided by the sound, and the smoke which rose above the tranquil landscape.

It was a beautiful day and a beautiful season of the year. The fields were green with grass, or golden with ripening grain, over which passed a gentle breeze, raising waves upon the brilliant surface. The landscape was broken here and there by woods; in the west rose the blue range of the South Mountain; the sun was shining through showery clouds, and in the east the sky was spanned by a rainbow. This peaceful scene was now disturbed by the thundering of artillery and the rattle of musketry. The sky was darkened, here and there, by clouds of smoke rising from barns or dwelling-houses set on fire by shell; and beneath rose red tongues of flame, roaring in response to the guns.

Each side had now sent forward reinforcements to support the vanguards, and an obstinate struggle ensued, the proportions of the fight gradually increasing, until the action became a regular battle. Hill, although suffering from indisposition, which the pallor of his face indicated, met the Federal attack with his habitual resolution. He was hard pressed, however, when fortunately one of General Ewell's divisions, under Rodes, débouched from the Carlisle road, running northward from Gettysburg, and came to his assistance. Ewell had just begun to move from Carlisle toward Harrisburg—his second division, under Early, being at York—when a dispatch from Lee reached him, directing him to return, and "proceed to Gettysburg or Cashtown, as his circumstances might direct." He promptly obeyed, encamped within about eight miles of Gettysburg on the evening of the 30th, and was now moving toward Cashtown, where Johnson's division of his corps then was, when Hill sent him word that he needed his assistance. Rodes was promptly sent forward to the field of action. Early was ordered to hurry back, and Rodes soon reached the battle-field, where he formed his line on high ground, opposite the Federal right.

The appearance of this important reënforcement relieved Hill, and caused the enemy to extend his right to face Rodes. The Federal line thus resembled a crescent, the left half, fronting Hill, toward the northwest; and the right, half-fronting Rodes, toward the north—the town of Gettysburg being in rear of the curve. An obstinate attack was made by the enemy and by Rodes at nearly the same moment. The loss on both sides was heavy, but Rodes succeeded in shaking the Federal right, when Early made his appearance from the direction of York. This compelled the Federal force to still farther extend its right, to meet the new attack. The movement greatly weakened them. Rodes charged their centre with impetuosity; Early came in on their right, with Gordon's brigade in front, and under this combined attack the Federal troops gave way, and retreated in great disorder to and through Gettysburg, leaving the ground covered with their dead and wounded to the number of about five thousand, and the same number of prisoners in the hands of the Confederates.

The first collision of the two armies had thus resulted in a clear Southern victory, and it is to be regretted that this important success was not followed up by the seizure of the Cemetery Range, south of the town, which it was in the power of the Southern forces at that time to do. To whom the blame—if blame there be—of this failure, is justly chargeable, the writer of these pages is unable to state. All that he has been able to ascertain with certainty is the following: As soon as the Federal forces gave way, General Lee rode forward, and at about four o'clock in the afternoon was posted on an elevated point of Seminary Ridge, from which he could see the broken lines of the enemy rapidly retreating up the slope of Cemetery Range, in his front. The propriety of pursuit, with a view to seizing this strong position, was obvious, and General Lee sent an officer of his staff with a message to General Ewell, to the effect that "he could see the enemy flying, that they were disorganized, and that it was only necessary to push on vigorously, and the Cemetery heights were ours." [Footnote: The officer who carried the order is our authority for this statement.] Just about the moment, it would seem, when this order was dispatched—about half-past four—General Hill, who had joined Lee on the ridge, "received a message from General Ewell, requesting him (Hill) to press the enemy in front, while he performed the same operation on his right." This statement is taken from the journal of Colonel Freemantle, who was present and noted the hour. He adds: "The pressure was accordingly applied, in a mild degree, but the enemy were too strongly posted, and it was too late in the evening for a regular attack." General Ewell, an officer of great courage and energy, is said to have awaited the arrival of his third division (Johnson's) before making a decisive assault. Upon the arrival of Johnson, about sunset, General Ewell prepared to advance and seize upon the eastern terminus of the Cemetery Range, which commanded the subsequent Federal position. At this moment General Lee sent him word to "proceed with his troops to the [Confederate] right, in case he could do nothing where he was;" he proceeded to General Lee's tent thereupon to confer with him, and the result was that it was agreed to first assault the hill on the right. It was now, however, after midnight, and the attack was directed by Lee to be deferred until the next morning.

It was certainly unfortunate that the advance was not then made; but Lee, in his report, attributes no blame to any one. "The attack," he says, "was not pressed that afternoon, *the enemy's force being unknown, and it being considered advisable to await the arrival of the rest of our troops.*"

The failure to press the enemy immediately after their retreat, with the view of driving them from and occupying Cemetery Heights, is susceptible of an explanation which seems to retrieve the Southern commander and his subordinates from serious criticism. The Federal forces had been driven from the ground north and west of Gettysburg, but it was seen now that the troops thus defeated constituted only a small portion of General Meade's army, and Lee had no means of ascertaining, with any degree of certainty, that the main body was not near at hand. The fact was not improbable, and it was not known that Cemetery Hill was not then in their possession. The wooded character of the ground rendered it difficult for General Lee, even from his elevated position on Seminary Ridge, to discover whether the heights opposite were, or were not, held by a strong force. Infantry were visible there; and in the plain in front the cavalry of General Buford were drawn up, as though ready to accept battle. It was not until after the battle that it was known that the heights might have been seized upon—General Hancock, who had succeeded Reynolds, having, to defend them, but a single brigade. This fact was not known to Lee; the sun was now declining, and the advance upon Cemetery Hill was deferred until the next day.

When on the next morning, between daybreak and sunrise, General Lee, accompanied by Hill, Longstreet, and Hood, ascended to the same point on Seminary Ridge, and reconnoitred the opposite heights through his field-glass, they were seen to be occupied by heavy lines of infantry and numerous artillery. The moment had passed; the rampart in his front bristled with bayonets and cannon. General Hancock, in command of the Federal advance, had hastened back at nightfall to General Meade, who was still some distance in rear, and reported the position to be an excellent one for receiving the Southern attack. Upon this information General Meade had at once acted; by one o'clock in the morning his headquarters were established upon the ridge; and when Lee, on Seminary Hill opposite, was reconnoitring the heights, the great bulk of the Federal army was in position to receive his assault.

The adversaries were thus face to face, and a battle could not well be avoided. Lee and his troops were in high spirits and confident of victory, but every advantage of position was seen to be on the side of the enemy.

XVI.
THE TWO ARMIES IN POSITION.

The morning of the 2d of July had arrived, and the two armies were in presence of each other and ready for battle. The question was, which of the great adversaries would make the attack.

General Meade was as averse to assuming the offensive as his opponent. Lee's statement on this subject has been given, but is here repeated: "It had not been intended to fight a general battle," he wrote, "at such a distance from our base, *unless attacked by the enemy.*" General Meade said before the war committee afterward, "It was my desire to fight a defensive rather than an offensive battle," and he adds the obvious explanation, that he was "satisfied his chances of success were greater in a defensive battle than an offensive one." There was this great advantage, however, on the Federal side, that the troops were on their own soil, with their communications uninterrupted, and could wait, while General Lee was in hostile territory, a considerable distance from his base of supplies, and must, for that reason, either attack his adversary or retreat.

He decided to attack. To this decision he seems to have been impelled, in large measure, by the extraordinary spirit of his troops, whose demeanor in the subsequent struggle was said by a Federal officer to resemble that of men "drunk on champagne." General Longstreet described the army at this moment as able, from the singular afflatus which bore it up, to undertake "any thing," and this sanguine spirit was the natural result of a nearly unbroken series of victories. At Fredericksburg, Chancellorsville, and in the preliminary struggle of Gettysburg, they had driven the enemy before them in disorder, and, on the night succeeding this last victory, both officers and men spoke of the coming battle "as a certainty, and the universal feeling in the army was one of profound contempt for an enemy whom they had beaten so constantly, and under so many disadvantages."[1]

[Footnote 1: Colonel Freemantle. He was present, and speaks from observation.]

Contempt of an adversary is dangerous, and pride goes before a fall. The truth of these pithy adages was now about to be shown.

General Lee, it is said, shared the general confidence of his troops, and was carried away by it. He says in his report "Finding ourselves unexpectedly confronted by the Federal army, it became a matter of difficulty to withdraw through the mountain with our large trains; at the same time, the country was unfavorable for collecting supplies while in the presence of the enemy's main body, as he was enabled to restrain our foraging-parties by occupying the passes of the mountains with regular and local troops. A battle thus became in a measure unavoidable." But, even after the battle, when the Southern army was much weaker, it was found possible, without much difficulty, to "withdraw through the mountains" with the trains. A stronger motive than this is stated in the next sentence of General Lee's report:" *Encouraged by the successful issue of the engagement of the first day, and in view of the valuable results that would ensue from the defeat of the army of General Meade*, it was thought advisable to renew the attack." The meaning of the writer of these words is plain. The Federal troops had been defeated with little difficulty in the first day's fight; it seemed probable that a more serious conflict would have similar results; and a decisive victory promised to end the war.

General Meade, it seems, scarcely expected to be attacked. He anticipated a movement on Lee's part, over the Emmetsburg road southward. [Footnote: Testimony of General Meade before the war committee.] By giving that direction to his army, General Lee would have forced his adversary to retire from his strong position on Cemetery Hill, or come out and attack him; whether, however, it was desirable on General Lee's part to run the risk of such an attack on the Southern column *in transitu*, it is left to others better able than the present writer to determine.

This unskilled comment must pass for what it is worth. It is easy, after the event, for the smallest to criticise the greatest. Under whatever influences, General Lee determined not to retreat, either through the South Mountain or toward Emmetsburg, but marshalled his army for an attack on the position held by General Meade.

The Southern lines were drawn up on Seminary Ridge, and on the ground near Gettysburg. Longstreet's corps was posted on the right, opposite the Federal left, near the southern end of Cemetery Ridge. Next came Hill's corps, extending along the crest nearly to Gettysburg. There it was joined by Ewell's line, which, passing through the town, bent round, adapting itself to the position of the Federal right which held the high ground, curving round in the shape of a hook, at the north end of the ridge.

The Federal lines thus occupied the whole Cemetery Range—which, being higher, commanded Seminary Ridge—and consisted, counting from right to left, of the troops of Generals Howard, Hancock, Sickles, Sykes, and Sedgwick; the two latter forming a strong reserve to guard the Federal left. The position was powerful, as both flanks rested upon high ground, which gave every advantage to the assailed party; but on the Federal left an accidental error, it seems, had been committed by General Sickles. He had advanced his line to a ridge in front of the main range, which appeared to afford him a better position; but this made it necessary to retire the left wing of his corps, to cover the opening in that direction. The result was, an angle—the effect of which is to expose troops to serious danger—and this faulty disposition of the Federal left seems to have induced General Lee to direct his main attack at the point in question, with the view of breaking the Federal line, and seizing upon the main ridge in rear. "In front of General Longstreet," he says, "the enemy held a position from which, if he could be driven, it was thought that our army could be used to advantage in assailing the more elevated ground beyond." In order to coöperate in this, the main attack, Ewell was ordered at the same time to assail the Federal right toward Gettysburg, and Hill directed to threaten their centre, and, if there were an opening, make a real attack. These demonstrations against the enemy's right and centre, Lee anticipated, would prevent him from reënforcing his left. Longstreet would thus, he hoped, be "enabled to reach the west of the ridge" in rear of the Federal line; and General Meade afterward said, "If they had succeeded in occupying that, it would have prevented me from holding any of the ground which I subsequently held at the last"—that is to say, that he would have been driven from the entire Cemetery Range.

Such was the position of the two adversaries, and such the design of Lee, on the 2d of July, when the real struggle was about to begin.

XVII.

THE SECOND DAY.

Throughout the forenoon of the day about to witness one of those great passages of arms which throw so bloody a glare upon the pages of history, scarcely a sound disturbed the silence, and it was difficult to believe that nearly two hundred thousand men were watching each other across the narrow valley, ready at the word to advance and do their best to tear each other to pieces.

During all these long hours, when expectation and suspense were sufficient to try the stoutest nerves, the two commanders were marshalling their lines for the obstinate struggle which was plainly at hand. General Meade, who knew well the ability of his opponent, was seeing, in person, to every thing, and satisfying himself that his lines were in order to receive the attack. Lee was making his preparations to commence the assault, upon which, there could be little doubt, the event of the whole war depended.

From the gallantry which the Federal troops displayed in this battle, they must have been in good heart for the encounter. It is certain that the Southern army had never been in better condition for a decisive conflict. We have spoken of the extraordinary confidence of the men, in themselves and in their commander. This feeling now exhibited itself either in joyous laughter and the spirit of jesting among the troops, or in an air of utter indifference, as of men sure of the result, and giving it scarcely a thought. The swarthy gunners, still begrimed with powder from the work of the day before, lay down around the cannon in position along the crest, and passed the moments in uttering witticisms, or in slumber; and the lines of infantry, seated or lying, musket in hand, were as careless. The army was plainly ready, and would respond with alacrity to Lee's signal. Of the result, no human being in this force of more than seventy thousand men seemed to have the least doubt.

Lee was engaged during the whole morning and until past noon in maturing his preparations for the assault which he designed making against the enemy's left in front of Longstreet. All was not ready until about four in the afternoon; then he gave the word, and Longstreet suddenly opened a heavy artillery-fire on the position opposite him. At this signal the guns of Hill opened from the ridge on his left, and Ewell's artillery on the Southern left in front of Gettysburg thundered in response. Under cover of his cannon-fire, Longstreet then advanced his lines, consisting of Hood's division on the right, and McLawe's division on the left, and made a headlong assault upon the Federal forces directly in his front.

The point aimed at was the salient, formed by the projection of General Sickles's line forward to the high ground known as "The Peach Orchard." Here, as we have already said, the Federal line of battle formed an angle, with the left wing of Sickles's corps bending backward so as to cover the opening between his line and the main crest in his rear. Hood's division swung round to assail the portion of the line thus retired, and so rapid was the movement of this energetic soldier, that in a short space of time he pushed his right beyond the Federal left flank, had pierced the exposed point, and was in direct proximity to the much-coveted "crest of the ridge," upon the possession of which depended the fate of the battle. Hood was fully aware of its importance, and lost not a moment in advancing to seize it. His troops, largely composed of those famous Texas regiments which Lee had said "fought grandly and nobly," and upon whom he relied "in all tight places," responded to his ardent orders: a small run was crossed, the men rushed up the slope, and the crest was almost in their very grasp.

Success at this moment would have decided the event of the battle of Gettysburg, and in all probability that of the war. All that was needed was a single brigade upon either side—a force sufficient to seize the crest, for neither side held it—and with this brigade a rare good fortune, or rather the prompt energy of a single officer, according to Northern historians, supplied the Federal commander. Hood's line was rushing up with cheers to occupy the crest, which here takes the form of a separate peak, and is known as "Little Round Top," when General Warren, chief-engineer of the army, who was passing, saw the importance of the position, and determined, at all hazards, to defend it. He accordingly ordered the Federal signal-party, which had used the peak as a signal-station, but were hastily folding up their flags, to remain where they were, laid violent hands upon a brigade which was passing, and ordered it to occupy the crest; and, when Hood's men rushed up the rocky slope with yells of triumph, they were suddenly met by a fusillade from the newly-arrived brigade, delivered full in their faces. A violent struggle ensued for the possession of the heights. The men fought hand to hand on the summit, and the issue remained for some time doubtful. At last it was decided in favor of the Federal troops, who succeeded in driving Hood's men from the hill, the summit of which was speedily crowned with artillery, which opened a destructive fire upon the retreating Southerners. They fell back sullenly, leaving the ground strewed with their dead and wounded. Hood had been wounded, and many of his best officers had fallen. For an instant he had grasped in his strong hand the prize which would have been worth ten times the amount of blood shed; but he had been unable to retain his hold; he was falling back from the coveted crest, pursued by that roar of the enemy's cannon which seemed to rejoice in his discomfiture.

An obstinate struggle was meanwhile taking place in the vicinity of the Peach Orchard, where the left of Hood and the division of McLaws had struck the front of General Sickles, and were now pressing his line back steadily toward the ridge in his rear. In spite of resolute resistance the Federal troops at this point were pushed back to a wheat-field in the rear of the Peach Orchard, and, following up this advantage, Longstreet charged them and broke their line, which fell back in disorder toward the high ground in rear. In this attack McLaws was assisted by Hill's right division—that of Anderson. With this force Longstreet continued to press forward, and, piercing the Federal line, seemed about to inflict upon them a great disaster by seizing the commanding position occupied by the Federal left. Nothing appears to have saved them at this moment from decisive defeat but the masterly concentration of reënforcements after reënforcements at the point of danger. The heavy reserves under Generals Sykes and Sedgwick were opposite this point, and other troops were hastened forward to oppose Longstreet. This reënforcement was continuous throughout the entire afternoon. In spite of Lee's demonstrations in other quarters to direct attention, General Meade—driven by necessity—continued to move fresh troops incessantly to protect his left; and success finally came as the reward of his energy and soldiership. Longstreet found his weary troops met at every new step in advance by fresh lines, and, as night had now come, he discontinued the attack. The Federal lines had been driven considerably beyond the point which they had held before the assault, and were now east of the wheat-field, where some of the hardest fighting of the day had taken place, but, in spite of this loss of ground, they had suffered no serious disaster, and, above all, Lee had not seized upon that "crest of the ridge," which was the keystone of the position.

Thus Longstreet's attack had been neither a success nor a failure. He had not accomplished all that was expected, but he had driven back the enemy from their advanced position, and held strong ground in their front. A continuance of the assault was therefore deferred until the next day—night having now come—and General Longstreet ordered the advance to cease, and the firing to be discontinued.

During the action on the right, Hill had continued to make heavy demonstrations on the Federal centre, and Ewell had met with excellent success in the attack, directed by Lee, to be made against the enemy's right. This was posted upon the semicircular eminence, a little southeast of Gettysburg, and the Federal works were attacked by Ewell about sunset. With Early's division on his right, and Johnson's on his left, Ewell advanced across the open ground in face of a heavy artillery-fire, the men rushed up the slope, and in a brief space of time the Federal artillerists and infantry were driven from the works, which at nightfall remained in Ewell's hands.

Such had been the fate of the second struggle around Gettysburg. The moon, which rose just as the fighting terminated, threw its ghastly glare upon a field where neither side had achieved full success.

Lee had not failed, and he had not succeeded. He had aimed to drive the Federal forces from the Cemetery Range, and had not been able to effect that object; but they had been forced back upon both their right and left, and a substantial advantage seemed thus to have been gained. That the Confederate success was not complete, seems to have resulted from the failure to seize the Round-Top Hill. The crisis of the battle had undoubtedly been the moment when Hood was so near capturing this position—in reference to the importance of which we quoted General Meade's own words. It was saved to the Federal army by the presence of mind, it seems, of a single officer, and the gallantry of a single brigade. Such are the singular chances of battle, in which the smallest causes so often effect the greatest results.

General Lee, in company with General Hill, had, during the battle, occupied his former position on Seminary Ridge, near the centre of his line—quietly seated, for the greater portion of the time, upon the stump of a tree, and looking thoughtfully toward the opposite heights which Longstreet was endeavoring to storm. His demeanor was entirely calm and composed. An observer would not have concluded that he was the commander-in-chief. From time to time he raised his field-glass to his eyes, and rising said a few words to General Hill or General Long, of his staff. After this brief colloquy, he would return to his seat on the stump, and continue to direct his glass toward the wooded heights held by the enemy. A notable circumstance, and one often observed upon other occasions, was that, during the entire action, he scarcely sent an order. During the time Longstreet was engaged—from about half-past four until night—he sent but one message, and received but one report. Having given full directions to his able lieutenants, and informed them of the objects which he desired to attain, he, on this occasion as upon others, left the execution of his orders to them, relying upon their judgment and ability.

A singular incident occurred at this moment, which must have diverted Lee, temporarily, from his abstracted mood. In the midst of the most furious part of the cannonade, when the air was filled with exploding shell, a Confederate band of music, between the opposing lines, just below General Lee's position, began defiantly playing polkas and waltzes on their instruments. The incident was strange in the midst of such a hurly-burly. The bloody battle-field seemed turned into a ballroom.

With nightfall the firing sunk to silence. The moon had risen, and the pale light now lit up the faces of the dead and wounded of both sides.

Lee's first great assault had failed to secure the full results which he had anticipated from it.

XVIII.

THE LAST CHARGE AT GETTYSBURG.

The weird hours of the moonlit night succeeding the "second day at Gettysburg" witnessed a consultation between Lee and his principal officers, as to the propriety of renewing the attack on the Federal position, or falling back in the direction of the Potomac. In favor of the latter course there seemed to be many good reasons. The supplies, both of provisions and ammunition, were running short. The army, although unshaken, had lost heavily in the obstinately-disputed attack. In the event of defeat now, its situation might become perilous, and the destruction of the Army of Northern Virginia was likely to prove that of the Southern cause. On the other hand, the results of the day's fighting, if not decisive, had been highly encouraging. On both the Federal wings the Confederates had gained ground, which they still held. Longstreet's line was in advance of the Peach Orchard, held by the enemy on the morning of the second, and Ewell was still rooted firmly, it seemed, in their works near Gettysburg. These advantages were certainly considerable, and promised success to the Southern arms, if the assault were renewed. But the most weighty consideration prompting a renewal of the attack was the condition of the troops. They were undismayed and unshaken either in spirit or efficiency, and were known both to expect and to desire a resumption of the assault. Even after the subsequent charge of Pickett, which resulted so disastrously, the ragged infantry were heard exclaiming: "We've not lost confidence in the old man! This day's work won't do him no harm! Uncle Robert will get us into Washington yet!" Add to this the fact that the issue of the second day had stirred up in Lee himself all the martial ardor of his nature; and there never lived a more thorough *soldier*, when he was fully aroused, than the Virginian. All this soldiership of the man revolted at the thought of retreating and abandoning his great enterprise. He looked, on the one hand, at his brave army, ready at the word to again advance upon the enemy—at that enemy scarce able on the previous day to hold his position—and, weighing every circumstance in his comprehensive mind, which "looked before and after," Lee determined on the next morning to try a decisive assault upon the Federal troops; to storm, if possible, the Cemetery Range, and at one great blow terminate the campaign and the war.

The powerful influences which we have mentioned, coöperating, shaped the decision to which Lee had come. He would not retreat, but fight. The campaign should not be abandoned without at least one great charge upon the Federal position; and orders were now given for a renewal of the attack on the next morning. "The general plan of attack," Lee says, "was unchanged, except that one division and two brigades of Hill's corps were ordered to support Longstreet." From these words it is obvious that Lee's main aim now, as on the preceding day, was to force back the Federal left in front of Longstreet, and seize the high ground commanding the whole ridge in flank and reverse. To this end Longstreet was reënforced, and the great assault was evidently intended to take place in that quarter. But circumstances caused an alteration, as will be seen, in Lee's plans. The centre, thus weakened, was from stress of events to become the point of decisive struggle. The assaults of the previous day had been directed against the two extremities of the enemy; the assault of the third day, which would decide the fate of the battle and the campaign, was to be the furious rush of Pickett's division of Virginian troops at the enemy's centre, on Cemetery Hill.

A preliminary conflict, brought on by the Federal commander, took place early in the morning. Ewell had continued throughout the night to hold the enemy's breastworks on their right, from which he had driven them in the evening. As dawn approached now, he was about to resume the attack; and, in obedience to Lee's orders, attempt to "dislodge the enemy" from other parts of the ridge, when General Meade took the initiative, and opened upon him a furious fire of cannon, which was followed by a determined infantry charge to regain the hill. Ewell held his ground with the obstinate nerve which characterized him, and the battle raged about four hours—that is, until about eight o'clock. At that time, however, the pressure of the enemy became too heavy to stand. General Meade succeeded in driving Ewell from the hill, and the Federal lines were reëstablished on the commanding ground which they had previously occupied.

This event probably deranged, in some degree, General Lee's plans, which contemplated, as we have seen, an attack by Ewell contemporaneous with the main assault by Longstreet. Ewell was in no condition at this moment to assume the offensive again; and the pause in the fighting appears to have induced General Lee to reflect and modify his plans. Throughout the hours succeeding the morning's struggle, Lee, attended by Generals Hill and Longstreet, and their staff-officers, rode along the lines, reconnoitring the opposite heights, and the cavalcade was more than once saluted by bullets from the enemy's sharp-shooters, and an occasional shell. The result of the reconnoissance seems to have been the conclusion that the Federal left—now strengthened by breastworks, behind which powerful reserves lay waiting—was not a favorable point for attack. General Meade, no doubt, expected an assault there; and, aroused to a sense of his danger by the Confederate success of the previous day, had made every preparation to meet a renewal of the movement. The Confederate left and centre remained, but it seemed injudicious to think of attacking from Ewell's position. A concentration of the Southern force there would result in a dangerous separation of the two wings of the army; and, in the event of failure, the enemy would have no difficulty in descending and turning Lee's right flank, and thus interposing between him and the Potomac.

The centre only was left, and to this Lee now turned his attention. A determined rush, with a strong column at Cemetery Hill in his front, might wrest that point from the enemy. Then their line would be pierced; the army would follow; Lee would be rooted on this commanding ground, directly between the two Federal wings, upon which their own guns might be turned, and the defeat of General Meade must certainly follow. Such were, doubtless, the reflections of General Lee, as he rode along the Seminary Range, scanning, through his field-glass, the line of the Federal works. His decision was made, and orders were given by him to prepare the column for the assault. For the hard work at hand, Pickett's division of Virginian troops, which had just arrived and were fresh, was selected. These were to be supported by Heth's division of North Carolina troops, under General Pettigrew, who was to move on Pickett's left; and a brigade of Hill's, under General Wilcox, was to cover the right of the advancing column, and protect it from a flank attack.

The advance of the charging column was preceded by a tremendous artillery-fire, directed from Seminary Ridge at the enemy's left and centre. This began about an hour past noon, and the amount of thunder thus unloosed will be understood from the statement that Lee employed one hundred and forty-five pieces of artillery, and the enemy replied with eighty—in all *two hundred and twenty-five* guns, all discharging at the same time. For nearly two hours this frightful hurly-burly continued, the harsh roar reverberating ominously in the gorges of the hills, and thrown back, in crash after crash, from the rocky slopes of the two ridges. To describe this fire afterward, the cool soldier, General Hancock, could find no other but the word *terrific*. "Their artillery-fire," he says, "was the most terrific cannonade I ever witnessed, and the most prolonged.... It was a most terrific and appalling cannonade—one possibly hardly ever paralleled."

While this artillery-duel was in progress, the charging column was being formed on the west of Seminary Ridge, opposite the Federal centre on Cemetery Hill. Pickett drew up his line with Kemper's and Garnett's brigades in front, and Armistead's brigade in rear. The brigade under General Wilcox took position on the right, and on the left was placed the division under Pettigrew, which was to participate in the charge. The force numbered between twelve and fifteen thousand men; but, as will be seen, nearly in the beginning of the action Pickett was left alone, and thus his force of about five thousand was all that went forward to pierce the centre of the Federal army.

The opposing ridges at this point are about one mile asunder, and across this space Pickett moved at the word, his line advancing slowly, and perfectly "dressed," with its red battle-flags flying, and the sunshine darting from the gun-barrels and bayonets. The two armies were silent, concentrating their whole attention upon this slow and ominous advance of men who seemed in no haste, and resolved to allow nothing to arrest them. When the column had reached a point about midway between the opposing heights the Federal artillery suddenly opened a furious fire upon them, which inflicted considerable loss. This, however, had no effect upon the troops, who continued to advance slowly in the same excellent order, without exhibiting any desire to return the fire. It was impossible to witness this steady and well-ordered march under heavy fire without feeling admiration for the soldiership of the troops who made it. Where shell tore gaps in the ranks, the men quietly closed up, and the hostile front advanced in the same ominous silence toward the slope where the real struggle, all felt, would soon begin.

They were within a few hundred yards of the hill, when suddenly a rapid cannon-fire thundered on their right, and shell and canister from nearly fifty pieces of artillery swept the Southern line, enfilading it, and for an instant throwing the right into some disorder. This disappeared at once, however. The column closed up, and continued to advance, unmoved, toward the height. At last the moment came. The steady "common-time" step had become "quick time;" this had changed to "double-quick;" then the column rushed headlong at the enemy's breastworks on the slope of the hill. As they did so, the real thunder began. A fearful fire of musketry burst forth, and struck them in the face, and this hurricane scattered the raw troops of Pettigrew as leaves are scattered by a wind. That whole portion of the line gave way in disorder, and fled from the field, which was strewed with their dead; and, as the other supports had not kept up, the Virginians under Pickett were left alone to breast the tempest which had now burst upon them in all its fury.

They returned the fire from the breastworks in their front with a heavy volley, and then, with loud cheers, dashed at the enemy's works, which they reached, stormed, and took possession of at the point of the bayonet. Their loss, however, was frightful. Garnett was killed; Armistead fell, mortally wounded, as he leaped on the breastworks, cheering and waving his hat; Kemper was shot and disabled, and the ranks of the Virginians were thinned to a handful. The men did not, however, pause. The enemy had partially retreated, from their first line of breastworks, to a second and stronger one about sixty yards beyond, and near the crest; and here the Federal reserve, as Northern writers state, was drawn up "four deep." This line, bristling with bayonets and cannon, the Virginians now charged, in the desperate attempt to storm it with the bayonet, and pierce, in a decisive manner, the centre of the Federal army. But the work was too great for their powers. As they made their brave rush they were met by a concentrated fire full in their faces, and on both flanks at the same moment. This fire did not so much cause them to lose heart, as literally hurl them back. Before it the whole charging column seemed to melt and disappear. The bravest saw now that further fighting was useless—that the works in their front could not be stormed—and, with the frightful fire of the enemy still tearing their lines to pieces, the poor remnants of the brave division retreated from the hill. As they fell back, sullenly, like bull-dogs from whom their prey had been snatched just as it was in their grasp, the enemy pursued them with a destructive fire both of cannon and musketry, which mowed down large numbers, if large numbers, indeed, can be said to have been left. The command had been nearly annihilated. Three generals, fourteen field-officers, and three-fourths of the men, were dead, wounded, or prisoners. The Virginians had done all that could be done by soldiers. They had advanced undismayed into the focus of a fire unsurpassed, perhaps, in the annals of war; had fought bayonet to bayonet; had left the ground strewed with their dead; and the small remnant who survived were now sullenly retiring, unsubdued; and, if repulsed, not "whipped."

Such was the last great charge at Gettysburg. Lee had concentrated in it all his strength, it seemed. When it failed, the battle and the campaign failed with it.

[Illustration: Lee at Gettysburg.]

XIX.

LEE AFTER THE CHARGE.

The demeanor of General Lee at this moment, when his hopes were all reversed, and his last great blow at the enemy had failed, excited the admiration of all who witnessed it, and remains one of the greatest glories of his memory.

Seeing, from his place on Seminary Ridge, the unfortunate results of the attack, he mounted his horse and rode forward to meet and encourage the retreating troops. The air was filled with exploding shell, and the men were coming back without order. General Lee now met them, and with his staff-officers busied himself in rallying them, uttering as he did so words of hope and encouragement. Colonel Freemantle, who took particular notice of him at this moment, describes his conduct as "perfectly sublime." "Lee's countenance," he adds, "did not show signs of the slightest disappointment, care, or annoyance," but preserved the utmost placidity and cheerfulness. The hurry and confusion of the scene seemed not to move him in any manner, and he rode slowly to and fro, saying in his grave, kindly voice to the men: "All this will come right in the end. We'll talk it over afterward, but in the mean time all good men must rally. We want all good and true men just now."

Numbers of wounded passed him, some stretched on litters, which men wearing the red badge of the ambulance corps were bearing to the rear, others limping along bleeding from hurts more or less serious. To the badly wounded Lee uttered words of sympathy and kindness; to those but slightly injured, he said: "Come, bind up your wound and take a musket," adding "my friend," as was his habit.

An evidence of his composure and absence of flurry was presented by a slight incident. An officer near him was striking his horse violently for becoming frightened and unruly at the bursting of a shell, when General Lee, seeing that the horse was terrified and the punishment would do no good, said, in tones of friendly remonstrance: "Don't whip him, captain, don't whip him. I've got just such a foolish horse myself, and whipping does no good."

Meanwhile the men continued to stream back, pursued still by that triumphant roar of the enemy's artillery which swept the whole valley and slope of Seminary Ridge with shot and shell. Lee was everywhere encouraging them, and they responded by taking off their hats and cheering him—even the wounded joining in this ceremony. Although exposing himself with entire indifference to the heavy fire, he advised Colonel Freemantle, as that officer states, to shelter himself, saying: "This has been a sad day for us, colonel, a sad day. But we can't expect always to gain victories."

As he was thus riding about in the fringe of woods, General Wilcox, who, about the time of Pickett's repulse, had advanced and speedily been thrown back with loss, rode up and said, almost sobbing as he spoke, that his brigade was nearly destroyed. Lee held out his hand to him as he was speaking, and, grasping the hand of his subordinate in a friendly manner, replied with great gentleness and kindness: "Never mind, general, all this has been *my* fault. It is *I* who have lost this fight, and you must help me out of it in the best way you can."

This supreme calmness and composure in the commander-in-chief rapidly communicated itself to the troops, who soon got together again, and lay down quietly in line of battle in the fringe of woods along the crest of the ridge, where Lee placed them as they came up. In front of them the guns used in the great cannonade were still in position, and Lee was evidently making every preparation in his power for the highly probable event of an instant assault upon him in his disordered condition, by the enemy. It was obvious that the situation of affairs at the moment was such as to render such an attack highly perilous to the Southern troops—and a sudden cheering which was now heard running along the lines of the enemy on the opposite heights, seemed clearly to indicate that their forces were moving. Every preparation possible under the circumstances was made to meet the anticipated assault; the repulsed troops of Pickett, like the rest of the army, were ready and even eager for of the attack—but it did not come. The cheering was afterward ascertained to have been simply the greeting of the men to some one of their officers as he rode along the lines; and night fell without any attempt on the Federal side to improve their success.

That success was indeed sufficient, and little would have been gained, and perhaps much perilled, by a counter-attack. Lee was not defeated, but he had not succeeded. General Meade could, with propriety, refrain from an attack. The battle of Gettysburg had been a Federal victory.

Thus had ended the last great conflict of arms on Northern soil—in a decisive if not a crushing repulse of the Southern arms. The chain of events has been so closely followed in the foregoing pages, and the movements of the two armies have been described with such detail, that any further comment or illustration is unnecessary. The opposing armies had been handled with skill and energy, the men had never fought better, and the result seems to have been decided rather by an occult decree of Providence than by any other circumstance. The numbers on each side were nearly the same, or differed so slightly that, in view of past conflicts, fought with much greater odds in favor of the one side, they might be regarded as equal. The Southern army when it approached Gettysburg numbered sixty-seven thousand bayonets, and the cavalry and artillery probably made the entire force about eighty thousand. General Meade's statement is that his own force was about one hundred thousand. The Federal loss was twenty-three thousand one hundred and ninety. The Southern losses were also severe, but cannot be ascertained. They must have amounted, however, to at least as large a number, even larger, perhaps, as an attacking army always suffers more heavily than one that is attacked.

What is certain, however, is that the Southern army, if diminished in numbers and strength, was still unshaken.

XX.

LEE'S RETREAT ACROSS THE POTOMAC.

Lee commenced his retreat in the direction of the Potomac on the night of the 4th of July. That the movement did not begin earlier is the best proof of the continued efficiency of his army and his own willingness to accept battle if the enemy were inclined to offer it.

After the failure of the attack on the Federal centre, he had withdrawn Ewell from his position southeast of Gettysburg, and, forming a continuous line of battle on Seminary Ridge, awaited the anticipated assault of General Meade. What the result of such an assault would have been it is impossible to say, but the theory that an attack would have terminated in the certain rout of the Southern army has nothing whatever to support it. The *morale* of Lee's army was untouched. The men, instead of being discouraged by the tremendous conflicts of the preceding days, were irate, defiant, and ready to resume the struggle. Foreign officers, present at the time, testify fully upon this point, describing the demeanor of the troops as all that could be desired in soldiers; and General Longstreet afterward stated that, with his two divisions under Hood and McLaws, and his powerful artillery, he was confident, had the enemy attacked, of inflicting upon them a blow as heavy as that which they had inflicted upon Pickett. The testimony of General Meade himself fully corroborates these statements. When giving his evidence afterward before the war committee, he said:

"My opinion is, now, that General Lee evacuated that position, *not from the fear that he would be dislodged from it by any active operations on my part*, but that he was fearful that a force would be sent to Harper's Ferry to cut off his communications.... That was what caused him to retire."

When asked the question, "Did you discover, after the battle of Gettysburg, any symptoms of demoralization in Lee's army?" General Meade replied, "No, sir; I saw nothing of that kind."[1]

[Footnote 1: Report of Committee on Conduct of War, Part I., page 337.]

There was indeed no good reason why General Lee should feel any extreme solicitude for the safety of his army, which, after all its losses, still numbered more than fifty thousand troops; and, with that force of veteran combatants, experience told him, he could count upon holding at bay almost any force which the enemy could bring against him. At Chancellorsville, with a less number, he had nearly routed a larger army than General Meade's. If the *morale* of the men remained unbroken, he had the right to feel secure now; and we have shown that the troops were as full of fight as ever. The exclamations of the ragged infantry, overheard by Colonel Freemantle, expressed the sentiment of the whole army. Recoiling from the fatal charge on Cemetery Hill, and still followed by the terrible fire, they had heart to shout defiantly: "We've not lost confidence in the old man! This day's work won't do him no harm! Uncle Robert will get us into Washington yet—you bet he will!"

Lee's reasons for retiring toward the Potomac were unconnected with the *morale* of his army. "The difficulty of procuring supplies," he says, "rendered it impossible to continue longer where we were." What he especially needed was ammunition, his supply of which had been nearly exhausted by the three days' fighting, and it was impossible to count upon new supplies of these essential stores now that the enemy were in a condition to interrupt his communications in the direction of Harper's Ferry and Williamsport. The danger to which the army was thus exposed was soon shown not to have been overrated. General Meade promptly sent a force to occupy Harper's Ferry, and a body of his cavalry, hastening across the South Mountain, reached the Potomac near Falling Waters, where they destroyed a pontoon bridge laid there for the passage of the Southern army.

Lee accordingly resolved to retire, and, after remaining in line of battle on Seminary Ridge throughout the evening and night of the 3d and the whole of the 4th, during which time he was busy burying his dead, began to withdraw, by the Fairfield and Chambersburg roads, on the night of this latter day. The movement was deliberate, and without marks of haste, the rear-guard not leaving the vicinity of Gettysburg until the morning of the 5th. Those who looked upon the Southern army at this time can testify that the spirit of the troops was unsubdued. They had been severely checked, but there every thing had ended. Weary, covered with dust, with wounds whose bandages were soaked in blood, the men tramped on in excellent spirits, and were plainly ready to take position at the first word from Lee, and meet any attack of the enemy with a nerve as perfect as when they had advanced.

For the reasons stated by himself, General Meade did not attack. He had secured substantial victory by awaiting Lee's assault on strong ground, and was unwilling now to risk a disaster, such as he had inflicted, by attacking Lee in position. The enthusiasm of the authorities at Washington was not shared by the cool commander of the Federal army. He perfectly well understood the real strength and condition of his adversary, and seems never to have had any intention of striking at him unless a change of circumstances gave him some better prospect of success than he could see at that time.

The retrograde movement of the Southern army now began, Lee's trains retiring by way of Chambersburg, and his infantry over the Fairfield road, in the direction of Hagerstown. General Meade at first moved directly on the track of his enemy. The design of a "stern chase" was, however, speedily abandoned by the Federal commander, who changed the direction of his march and moved southward toward Frederick. When near that point he crossed the South Mountain, went toward Sharpsburg, and on the 12th of July found himself in front of the Southern army near Williamsport, where Lee had formed line of battle to receive his adversary's attack.

The deliberate character of General Meade's movements sufficiently indicates the disinclination he felt to place himself directly in his opponent's front, and thus receive the full weight of his attack. There is reason, indeed, to believe that nothing could better have suited the views of General Meade than for Lee to have passed the Potomac before his arrival—which event would have signified the entire abandonment of the campaign of invasion, leaving victory on the side of the Federal army. But the elements seemed to conspire to bring on a second struggle, despite the reluctance of both commanders. The recent rains had swollen the Potomac to such a degree as to render it unfordable, and, as the pontoon near Williamsport had been destroyed by the Federal cavalry, Lee was brought to bay on the north bank of the river, where, on the 12th, as we have said, General Meade found him in line of battle.

Lee's demeanor, at this critical moment, was perfectly undisturbed, and exhibited no traces whatever of anxiety, though he must have felt much. In his rear was a swollen river, and in his front an adversary who had been reënforced with a considerable body of troops, and now largely outnumbered him. In the event of battle and defeat, the situation of the Southern army must be perilous in the extreme. Nothing would seem to be left it, in that event, but surrender, or dispersion among the western mountains, where the detached bodies would be hunted down in detail and destroyed or captured. Confidence in himself and his men remained, however, with General Lee, and, with his line extending from near Hagerstown to a point east of Williamsport, he calmly awaited the falling of the river, resolved, doubtless, if in the mean time the enemy attacked him, to fight to the last gasp for the preservation of his army.

No attack was made by General Meade, who, arriving in front of Lee on the 12th, did no more, on that day, than feel along the Southern lines for a point to assault. On the next day he assembled a council of war, and laid the question before them, whether or not it were advisable to make an assault. The votes of the officers were almost unanimously against it, as Lee's position seemed strong and the spirit of his army defiant; and the day passed without any attempt of the Federal army to dislodge its adversary.

While General Meade was thus hesitating, Lee was acting. A portion of the pontoon destroyed by the enemy was recovered, new boats were built, and a practicable bridge was completed, near Falling Waters, by the evening of the 13th. The river had also commenced falling, and by this time was fordable near Williamsport. Toward dawn on the 14th the army commenced moving, in the midst of a violent rain-storm, across the river at both points, and Lee, sitting his horse upon the river's bank, superintended the operation, as was his habit on occasions of emergency. Loss of rest and fatigue, with that feeling of suspense unavoidable under the circumstances, had impaired the energies of even his superb physical constitution. As the bulk of the rear-guard of the army safely passed over the shaky bridge, which Lee had looked at with some anxiety as it swayed to and fro, lashed by the current, he uttered a sigh of relief, and a great weight seemed taken from his shoulders. Seeing his fatigue and exhaustion. General Stuart gave him some coffee; he drank it with avidity, and declared, as he handed back the cup, that nothing had ever refreshed him so much.

When General Meade, who is said to have resolved on an attack, in spite of the opposition of his officers, looked, on the morning of the 14th, toward the position held on the previous evening by the Southern army, he saw that the works were deserted. The Army of Northern Virginia had vanished from the hills on which it had been posted, and was at that moment crossing the Potomac. Pressing on its track toward Falling Waters, the Federal cavalry came up with the rear, and in the skirmish which ensued fell the brave Pettigrew, who had supported Pickett in the great charge at Gettysburg, where he had waved his hat in front of his men, and, in spite of a painful wound, done all in his power to rally his troops. With this exception, and a few captures resulting from accident, the army sustained no losses. The movement across the Potomac had been effected, in face of the whole Federal army, as successfully as though that army had been a hundred miles distant.[1]

[Footnote 1: Upon this point different statements were subsequently made by Generals Lee and Meade, and Lee's reply to the statements of his opponent is here given:

HEADQUARTERS ARMY NORTHERN VIRGINIA,

July 21, 1863.

General S. Cooper, Adjutant and Inspector-General C.S.A., Richmond, Va.:

GENERAL: I have seen in Northern papers what purported to be an official dispatch from General Meade, stating that he had captured a brigade of Infantry, two pieces of artillery, two caissons, and a large number of small-arms, as this army retired to the south bank of the Potomac, on the 13th and 14th inst.

This dispatch has been copied into the Richmond papers, and, as its official character may cause it to be believed, I desire to state that it is incorrect. The enemy did not capture any organized body of men on that occasion, but only stragglers, and such as were left asleep on the road, exhausted by the fatigue and exposure of one of the most inclement nights I have ever known at this season of the year. It rained without cessation, rendering the road by which our troops marched to the bridge at Falling Waters very difficult to pass, and causing so much delay that the last of the troops did not cross the river at the bridge until 1 P.M. on the 14th. While the column was thus detained on the road a number of men, worn down by fatigue, lay down in barns, and by the roadside, and though officers were sent back to arouse them, as the troops moved on, the darkness and rain prevented them from finding all, and many were in this way left behind. Two guns were left on the road. The horses that drew them became exhausted, and the officers went forward to procure others. When they returned, the rear of the column had passed the guns so far that it was deemed unsafe to send back for them, and they were thus lost. No arms, cannon, or prisoners, were taken by the enemy in battle, but only such as were left behind under the circumstances I have described. The number of stragglers thus lost I am unable to state with accuracy, but it is greatly exaggerated in the dispatch referred to.

I am, with great respect, your obedient servant,

R.E. LEE, *General.*

The solicitude here exhibited by the Southern commander, that the actual facts should be recorded, is natural, and displayed Lee's spirit of soldiership. He was unwilling that his old army should appear in the light of a routed column, retreating in disorder, with loss of men and munitions, when they lost neither.]

XXI.

ACROSS THE BLUE RIDGE AGAIN.

Lee moved his army to the old encampment on the banks of the Opequan which it had occupied after the retreat from Sharpsburg, in September, 1862, and here a few days were spent in resting.

We have, in the journal of a foreign officer, an outline of Lee's personal appearance at this time, and, as we are not diverted from these characteristic details at the moment by the narrative of great events, this account of Lee, given by the officer in question—Colonel Freemantle, of the British Army—is laid before the reader:

"General Lee is, almost without exception, the handsomest man of his age I ever saw. He is tall, broad-shouldered, very well made, well set up—a thorough soldier in appearance—and his manners are most courteous, and full of dignity. He is a perfect gentleman in every respect. I imagine no man has so few enemies, or is so universally esteemed. Throughout the South, all agree in pronouncing him as near perfection as man can be. He has none of the small vices, such as smoking, drinking, chewing, or swearing; and his bitterest enemy never accused him of any of the greater ones. He generally wears a well-worn, long gray jacket, a high black-felt hat, and blue trousers, tucked into his Wellington boots. I never saw him carry arms, and the only marks of his military rank are the three stars on his collar. He rides a handsome horse, which is extremely well governed. He himself is very neat in his dress and person, and in the most arduous marches he always looks smart and clean…. It is understood that General Lee is a religious man, though not so demonstrative in that respect as Jackson, and, unlike his late brother-in-arms, he is a member of the Church of England. His only faults, so far as I can learn, arise from his excessive amiability."

This personal description is entirely correct, except that the word "jacket" conveys a somewhat erroneous idea of Lee's undress uniform coat, and his hat was generally gray. Otherwise, the sketch is exactly accurate, and is here presented as the unprejudiced description and estimate of a foreign gentleman, who had no inducement, such as might be attributed to a Southern writer, to overcolor his portrait. Such, in personal appearance, was the leader of the Southern army—a plain soldier, in a plain dress, without arms, with slight indications of rank, courteous, full of dignity, a "perfect gentleman," and with no fault save an "excessive amiability." The figure is attractive to the eye—it excited the admiration of a foreign officer, and remains in many memories now, when the sound of battle is hushed, and the great leader, in turn, has finished his life-battle and lain down in peace.

The movements of the two armies were soon resumed, and we shall briefly follow those movements, which led the adversaries back to the Rappahannock.

Lee appears to have conceived the design, after crossing the Potomac at Williamsport, to pass the Shenandoah River and the Blue Ridge, and thus place himself in the path of General Meade if he crossed east of the mountain, or threaten Washington. This appears from his own statement. "Owing," he says, "to the swollen condition of *the Shenandoah River, the plan of operations which had been contemplated when we recrossed the Potomac could not be put in execution*". The points fixed upon by Lee for passing the mountain were probably Snicker's and Ashby's Gaps, opposite Berryville and Millwood. The rains had, however, made the river, in these places, unfordable. On the 17th and 18th days of July, less than a week after Lee's crossing at Williamsport, General Meade passed the Potomac above Leesburg, and Lee moved his army in the direction of Chester Gap, near Front Royal, toward Culpepper.

The new movements were almost identically the same as the old, when General McClellan advanced, in November, 1862, and the adoption of the same plans by General Meade involves a high compliment to his predecessor. He acted with even more energy. As Lee's head of column was defiling toward Chester Gap, beyond Front Royal, General Meade struck at it through Manassas Gap, directly on its flank, and an action followed which promised at one time to become serious. The enemy was, however, repulsed, and the Southern column continued its way across the mountain. The rest of the army followed, and descended into Culpepper, from which position, when Longstreet was detached to the west, Lee retired, taking post behind the Rapidan.

General Meade thereupon followed, and occupied Culpepper, his advance being about half-way between Culpepper Court-House and the river.

Such was the position of the two armies in the first days of October, when Lee, weary, it seemed, of inactivity, set out to flank and fight his adversary.

PART VII.

LAST CAMPAIGNS OF THE YEAR 1863.

I.

THE CAVALRY OF LEE'S ARMY.

In a work of the present description, the writer has a choice between two courses. He may either record the events of the war in all quarters of the country, as bearing more or less upon his narrative, or may confine himself to the life of the individual who is the immediate subject of his volume. Of these two courses, the writer prefers the latter for many reasons. To present a narrative of military transactions in all portions of the South would expand this volume to undue proportions; and there is the further objection that these occurrences are familiar to all. It might be necessary, in writing for persons ignorant of the events of the great conflict, to omit nothing; but this ignorance does, not probably exist in the case of the readers of these pages; and the writer will continue, as heretofore, to confine himself to the main subject, only noting incidentally such prominent events in other quarters as affected Lee's movements.

One such event was the fall of Vicksburg, which post surrendered at the same moment with the defeat at Gettysburg, rendering thereafter impossible all movements of invasion; and another was the advance of General Rosecrans toward Atlanta, which resulted, in the month of September, in a Southern victory at Chickamauga.

The immediate effect of the Federal demonstration toward Chattanooga had been to detach Longstreet's corps from General Lee's army, for service under General Bragg. General Meade's force is said to have also been somewhat lessened by detachments sent to enforce the draft in New York; and these circumstances had, in the first days of October, reduced both armies in Virginia to a less force than they had numbered in the past campaign. General Meade, however, presented a bold front to his adversary, and, with his headquarters near Culpepper Court-House, kept close watch upon Lee, whose army lay along the south bank of the Rapidan.

For some weeks no military movements took place, and an occasional cavalry skirmish between the troopers of the two armies was all which broke the monotony of the autumn days. This inactivity, however, was now about to terminate. Lee had resolved to attempt a flank movement around General Meade's right, with the view of bringing him to battle; and a brief campaign ensued, which, if indecisive, and reflecting little glory upon the infantry, was fruitful in romantic incidents and highly creditable to the cavalry of the Southern army.

In following the movements, and describing the operations of the main body of the army—the infantry—we have necessarily been compelled to pass over, to a great extent, the services of the cavalry in the past campaign. These had, nevertheless, been great—no arm of the service had exhibited greater efficiency; and, but for the fact that in all armies the brunt of battle falls upon the foot-soldiers, it might be added that the services of the cavalry had been as important as those of the infantry. Stuart was now in command of a force varying from five to eight thousand sabres, and among his troopers were some of the best fighting-men of the South. The cavalry had always been the favorite arm with the Southern youth; it had drawn to itself, as privates in the ranks, thousands of young men of collegiate education, great wealth, and the highest social position; and this force was officered, in Virginia, by such resolute commanders as Wade Hampton, Fitz Lee, William H.F. Lee, Rosser, Jones, Wickham, Young, Munford, and many others. Under these leaders, and assisted by the hard-fighting "Stuart Horse-Artillery" under Pelham and his successors, the cavalry had borne their full share in the hard marches and combats of the army. On the Chickahominy; in the march to Manassas, and the battles in Maryland; in the operations on the Rappahannock, and the incessant fighting of the campaign to Gettysburg, Stuart and his troopers had vindicated their claim to the first honors of arms; and, if these services were not duly estimated by the infantry of the army, the fact was mainly attributable to the circumstance that the fighting of the cavalry had been done at a distance upon the outposts, far more than in the pitched battles, where, in modern times, from the improved and destructive character of artillery, playing havoc with horses, the cavalry arm can achieve little, and is not risked. The actual losses in Stuart's command left, however, no doubt of the obstinate soldiership of officers and men. Since the opening of the year he had lost General Hampton, cut down in a hand-to-hand sabre-fight at Gettysburg; General W.H.F. Lee, shot in the fight at Fleetwood; Colonels Frank Hampton and Williams, killed in the same action; Colonel Butler, torn by a shell; Major Pelham, Chief of Artillery, killed while leading a charge; [Footnote: In this enumeration the writer mentions only such names as occur at the moment to his memory. A careful examination of the records of the cavalry would probably furnish the names of ten times as many, equally brave and unfortunate.] about six officers of his personal staff either killed, wounded, or captured; and in the Gettysburg campaign he had lost nearly one-third of his entire command. Of its value to the army, the infantry might have their doubts, but General Lee had none. Stuart and his horsemen had been the eyes and ears of the Army of Northern Virginia; had fought incessantly as well as observed the enemy; and Lee never committed the injustice of undervaluing this indispensable arm, which, if his official commendation of its operations under Stuart is to be believed, was only second in importance in his estimation to the infantry itself.

The army continued, nevertheless, to amuse itself at the expense of the cavalry, and either asserted or intimated, on every favorable occasion, that the *real fighting* was done by themselves. This flattering assumption might be natural under the circumstances, but it was now about to be shown to be wholly unfounded. A campaign was at hand in which the cavalry were to turn the tables upon their jocose critics, and silence them; where the infantry were doomed to failure in nearly all which they attempted, and the troopers were to do the greater part of the fighting and achieve the only successes.

To the narrative of this brief and romantic episode of the war we now proceed. General Lee's aim was to pass around the right flank of his adversary, and bring him to battle; and, although the promptness of General Meade's movements defeated the last-named object nearly completely, the manoeuvres of the two armies form a highly-interesting study. The eminent soldiers commanding the forces played a veritable game of chess with each other. There was little hard fighting, but more scientific manoeuvring than is generally displayed in a campaign. The brains of Lee and Meade, rather than the two armies, were matched against each other; and the conflict of ideas proved more interesting than the actual fighting.

II.

LEE FLANKS GENERAL MEADE.

In prosecution of the plan determined upon, General Lee, on the morning of the 9th of October, crossed the Rapidan at the fords above Orange Court-House, with the corps of Ewell and A.P. Hill, and directed his march toward Madison Court-House.

Stuart moved with Hampton's cavalry division on the right of the advancing column— General Fitz Lee having been left with his division to guard the front on the Rapidan—and General Imboden, commanding west of the Blue Ridge, was ordered by Lee to "advance down the Valley, and guard the gaps of the mountains on our left."

We have said that Lee's design was to bring General Meade to battle. It is proper to state this distinctly, as some writers have attributed to him in the campaign, as his real object, the design of manoeuvring his adversary out of Culpepper, and pushing him back to the Federal frontier. His own words are perfectly plain. He set out "with the design," he declares, "of *bringing on an engagement with the Federal army*"—that is to say, of *fighting* General Meade, not simply forcing him to fall back. His opponent, it seems, was not averse to accepting battle; indeed, from expressions attributed to him, he appears to have ardently desired it, in case he could secure an advantageous position for receiving the Southern attack. It is desirable that this readiness in both commanders to fight should be kept in view. The fact adds largely to the interest of this brief "campaign of manoeuvres," in which the army, falling back, like that advancing, sought battle.

To proceed to the narrative, which will deal in large measure with the operations of the cavalry—that arm of the service, as we have said, having borne the chief share of the fighting, and achieved the only successes. Stuart moved out on the right of the infantry, which marched directly toward Madison Court-House, and near the village of James City, directly west of Culpepper Court-House, drove in the cavalry and infantry outposts of General Kilpatrick on the main body beyond the village. Continuous skirmishing ensued throughout the rest of the day— Stuart's object being to occupy the enemy, and divert attention from the infantry movement in his rear. In this he seems to have fully succeeded. Lee passed Madison Court-House, and moving, as he says, "by circuitous and concealed roads," reached the vicinity of Griffinsburg, on what is called the Sperryville Road, northwest of Culpepper Court-House. A glance at the map will show the relative positions of the two armies at this moment. General Meade lay around Culpepper Court-House, with his advance about half-way between that place and the Rapidan, and Lee had attained a position which gave him fair hopes of intercepting his adversary's retreat. That retreat must be over the line of the Orange and Alexandria Railroad; but from Griffinsburg to Manassas was no farther than from Culpepper Court-House to the same point. If the Federal army fell back, as Lee anticipated, it would be a question of speed between the retreating and pursuing columns; and, as the narrative will show, the race was close—a few hours lost making the difference between success and failure in Lee's movement.

On the morning of the 10th while the infantry were still near Griffinsburg, General Stuart moved promptly down upon Culpepper Court-House, driving the enemy from their large camps near Stonehouse Mountain. These were elaborately provided with luxuries of every description, and there were many indications of the fact that the troops had expected to winter there. No serious fighting occurred. A regiment of infantry was charged and dispersed by the Jefferson Company of Captain Baylor, and Stuart then proceeded rapidly to Culpepper Court-House, where the Federal cavalry, forming the rear-guard of the army, awaited him.

General Meade was already moving in the direction of the Rappahannock. The presence of the Southern army near Griffinsburg had become known to him; he was at no loss to understand Lee's object; and, leaving his cavalry to cover his rear, he moved toward the river. As Stuart attacked the Federal horse posted on the hills east of the village, the roar of cannon on his right, steadily drawing nearer, indicated that General Fitz Lee was forcing the enemy in that direction to fall back. Stuart was now in high spirits, and indulged in hearty laughter, although the enemy's shells were bursting around him.

"Ride back to General Lee," he said to an officer of his staff, "and tell him we are forcing the enemy back on the Rappahannock, and I think I hear Fitz Lee's guns toward the Rapidan."

The officer obeyed, and found General Lee at his headquarters, which consisted of one or two tents, with a battle-flag set up in front, on the highway, near Griffinsburg. He was conversing with General Ewell, and the contrast between the two soldiers was striking. Ewell was thin, cadaverous, and supported himself upon a crutch, for he had not yet recovered from the wound received at Manassas. General Lee, on the contrary, was erect, ruddy, robust, and exhibited indications of health and vigor in every detail of his person. When Stuart's message was delivered to him, he bowed with that grave courtesy which he exhibited alike toward the highest and the lowest soldier in his army, and said: "Thank you. Tell General Stuart to continue to press them back toward the river."

He then smiled, and added, with that accent of sedate humor which at times characterized him: "But tell him, too, to spare his horses—to spare his horses. It is not necessary to send so many messages."

He turned as he spoke to General Ewell, and, pointing to the officer who had come from Stuart, and another who had arrived just before him, said, with lurking humor: "I think these two young gentlemen make *eight* messengers sent me by General Stuart!"

He then said to Ewell: "You may as well move on with your troops, I suppose, general;" and soon afterward the infantry began to advance.

Stuart was meanwhile engaged in an obstinate combat with the Federal cavalry near Brandy, in the immediate vicinity of Fleetwood Hill, the scene of the great fight in June. The stand made by the enemy was resolute, but the arrival of General Fitz Lee decided the event. That officer had crossed the Rapidan and driven General Buford before him. The result now was that, while Stuart was pressing the enemy in his front, General Buford came down on Stuart's rear, and Fitz Lee on the rear of Buford. The scene which ensued was a grand commingling of the tragic and serio-comic. Every thing was mingled in wild confusion, but the day remained with the Southern cavalry, who, at nightfall, had pressed their opponents back toward the river, which the Federal army crossed that night, blowing up the railroad bridge behind them.

Such was the first act of the bustling drama. At the approach of Lee, General Meade had vanished from Culpepper, and so well arranged was the whole movement, in spite of its rapidity, that scarce an empty box was left behind. Lee's aim to bring his adversary to battle south of the Rappahannock had thus failed; but the attempt was renewed by a continuation of the flanking movement toward Warrenton Springs, "with the design," Lee says, "of reaching the Orange and Alexandria Railroad, north of the river, and interrupting the retreat of the enemy." Unfortunately, however, for this project, which required of all things rapidity of movement, it was found necessary to remain nearly all day on the 11th near Culpepper Court-House, to supply the army with provisions. It was not until the 12th that the army again moved. Stuart preceded it, and after a brisk skirmish drove the enemy from Warrenton Springs—advancing in person in front of his column as it charged through the river and up the hill beyond, where a considerable body of Federal marksmen were put to flight. The cavalry then pressed on toward Warrenton, and the infantry, who had witnessed their prowess and cheered them heartily, followed on the same road. The race between Lee and General Meade was in full progress.

It was destined to become complicated, and an error committed by General Meade came very near exposing him to serious danger. It appears that, after retreating across the Rappahannock, the Federal commander began to entertain doubt whether the movement had not been hasty, and would not justly subject him to the charge of yielding to sudden panic. Influenced apparently by this sentiment, he now ordered three corps of the Federal army, with a division of cavalry, back to Culpepper; and this, the main body, accordingly crossed back, leaving but one corps north of the river. Such was now the very peculiar situation of the two armies. General Lee was moving steadily in the direction of Warrenton to cut off his adversary from Manassas, and that adversary was moving back into Culpepper to hunt up Lee there. The comedy of errors was soon terminated, but not so soon as it otherwise would have been but for a *ruse de guerre* played by Generals Rosser and Young. General Rosser had been left by Stuart near Brandy, with about two hundred horsemen and one gun; and, when the three infantry corps and the cavalry division of General Meade moved forward from the river, they encountered this obstacle. Insignificant as was his force. General Rosser so manoeuvred it as to produce the impression that it was considerable; and, though forced, of course, to fall back, he did so fighting at every step. Assistance reached him just at dusk in the shape of a brigade of cavalry, from above the court-house under General Young, the same officer whose charge at the Fleetwood fight had had so important a bearing upon the result there. Young now formed line with his men dismounted, and, advancing with a confident air, opened fire upon the Federal army. The darkness proved friendly, and, taking advantage of it, General Young kindled fires along a front of more than a mile, ordered his band to play, and must have caused the enemy to doubt whether Lee was not still in large force near Culpepper Court-House. They accordingly went into camp to await the return of daylight, when at midnight a fast-riding courier came with orders from General Meade.

These orders were urgent, and directed the Federal troops to recross the river with all haste. General Lee, it was now ascertained, had left an insignificant force in Culpepper, and, with nearly his whole army, was moving rapidly toward Warrenton to cut off his adversary.

III.

A RACE BETWEEN TWO ARMIES.

The game of hide-and-seek—to change the figure—was now in full progress, and nothing more dramatic could be conceived of than the relative positions of the two armies.

At midnight, on Monday, October 12th, Lee's army was near Warrenton Springs, ready to advance in the morning upon Warrenton, while three of the four corps under General Meade were half-way between the Rappahannock and Culpepper Court-House, expecting battle there. Thus a choice of two courses was presented to the Federal commander: to order back his main force, and rapidly retreat toward Manassas, or move the Fourth Corps to support it, and place his whole army directly in Lee's rear. The occasion demanded instant decision. Every hour now counted. But, unfortunately for General Meade, he was still in the dark as to the actual amount of Lee's force in Culpepper. The movement toward Warrenton might be a mere *ruse*. The great master of the art of war to whom he was opposed might have laid this trap for him—have counted upon his falling into the snare—and, while a portion of the Southern force was engaged in Culpepper, might design an attack with the rest upon the Federal right flank or rear. In fact, the situation of affairs was so anomalous and puzzling that Lee might design almost any thing, and succeed in crushing his adversary.

The real state of the case was, that Lee designed nothing of this description, having had no intimation whatever of General Meade's new movement back toward Culpepper. He was advancing toward Warrenton, under the impression that his adversary was retreating, and aimed to come up with him somewhere near that place and bring him to battle. Upon this theory his opponent now acted by promptly ordering back his three corps to the north bank of the Rappahannock. They began to march soon after midnight; recrossed the river near the railroad; and on the morning of the 13th hastened forward by rapid marches to pass the dangerous point near Warrenton, toward which Lee was also moving with his infantry.

In this race every advantage seemed to be on the side of Lee. The three Federal corps had fully twice as far to march as the Southern forces. Lee was concentrating near Warrenton, while they were far in the rear; and, if the Confederates moved with only half the rapidity of their adversaries, they were certain to intercept them, and compel them either to surrender or cut their way through.

These comments—tedious, perhaps—are necessary to the comprehension of the singular "situation." We proceed now with the narrative. Stuart had pushed on past Warrenton with his cavalry, toward the Orange Railroad, when, on the night of the 13th, he met with one of those adventures which were thickly strewed throughout his romantic career. He was near Auburn, just at nightfall, when, as his rear-guard closed up, information reached him from that quarter that the Federal army was passing directly in his rear. Nearly at the same moment intelligence arrived that another column of the enemy, consisting, like the first, of infantry, cavalry, and artillery, was moving across his front.

Stuart was now in an actual trap, and his situation was perilous in the extreme. He was enclosed between two moving walls of enemies, and, if discovered, his fate seemed sealed. But one course was left him: to preserve, if possible, complete silence in his command; to lie *perdu* in the wood, and await the occurrence of some fortunate event to extricate him from his highly-embarrassing situation. He accordingly issued stringent orders to the men that no noise of any description should be made, and not a word be uttered; and there was little necessity to repeat this command. The troopers remained silent and motionless in the saddle throughout the night, ready at any instant to move at the order; and thus passed the long hours of darkness—the Southern horsemen as silent as phantoms; the Federal columns passing rapidly, with the roll of artillery-wheels, the tramp of cavalry-horses, and the shuffling sound of feet, on both sides of the command—the column moving in rear of Stuart being distant but two or three hundred yards.

This romantic incident was destined to terminate fortunately for Stuart, who, having dispatched scouts to steal through the Federal column, and announce his situation to General Lee, prepared to seize upon the first opportunity to release his command from its imminent peril. The opportunity came at dawn. The Federal rear, under General Caldwell, had bivouacked near, and had just kindled fires to cook their breakfast, when, from the valley beneath the hill on which the troops had halted, Stuart opened suddenly upon them with his Horse-Artillery, and, as he says in his report, knocked over coffee-pots and other utensils at the moment when the men least expected it. He then advanced his sharp-shooters and directed a rapid fire upon the disordered troops; and, under cover of this fire, wheeled to the left and emerged safely toward Warrenton. The army greeted him with cheers, and he was himself in the highest spirits. He had certainly good reason for this joy, for he had just grazed destruction.

As Stuart's artillery opened, the sound was taken up toward Warrenton, where Ewell, in obedience to Lee's orders, had attacked the Federal column. Nothing resulted, however, from this assault: General Meade had concentrated his army, and was hastening toward Manassas. All now depended again upon the celerity of Lee's movements in pursuit. He had lost many hours at Warrenton, where "another halt was made," he says, "to supply the troops with provisions." Thus, on the morning of the 14th he was as far from intercepting General Meade as before; and all now depended upon the movements of Hill, who, while Ewell moved toward Greenwich, had been sent by way of New Baltimore to come in on the Federal line of retreat at Bristoe Station, near Manassas. In spite, however, of his excellent soldiership and habitual promptness, Hill did not arrive in time. He made the détour prescribed by Lee, passed New Baltimore, and hastened on toward Bristoe, where, on approaching that point, he found only the rear-guard of the Federal army—the whole force, with this exception, having crossed Broad Run, and hastened on toward Manassas. Hill's arrival had thus been tardy: it would have been fortunate for him if he had not arrived at all. Seeing the Federal column under General Warren hastening along the railroad to pass Broad Run, he ordered a prompt attack, and Cooke's brigade led the charge. The result was unfortunate for the Confederates. General Warren, seeing his peril, had promptly disposed his line behind the railroad embankment at the spot, where, protected by this impromptu breastwork, the men rested their guns upon the iron rails and poured a destructive fire upon the Southerners rushing down the open slope in front. By this fire General Cooke was severely wounded and fell, and his brigade lost a considerable part of its numbers. Before a new attack could be made, General Warren hastily withdrew, carrying off with him in triumph a number of prisoners, and five pieces of artillery, captured on the banks of the run. Before his retreat could be again interrupted, he was safe on the opposite side of the stream, and lost no time in hurrying forward to join the main body, which was retreating on Centreville.

General Meade had thus completely foiled his adversary. Lee had set out with the intention of bringing the Federal commander to battle; had not succeeded in doing so, owing to the rapidity of his retreat; had come up only with his rear-guard, under circumstances which seemed to seal the fate of that detached force, and the small rear-guard had repulsed him completely, capturing prisoners and artillery from him, and retiring in triumph. Such had been the issue of the campaign; all the success had been on the side of General Meade. He is said to have declared that "it was like pulling out his eye-teeth not to have had a fight;" but something resembling *bona-fide* fighting had occurred on the banks of Broad Run, and the victory was clearly on the side of the Federal troops.

To turn to General Lee, it would be an interesting question to discuss whether he really desired to *intercept* General Meade, if there were any data upon which to base a decision. The writer hazards the observation that it seems doubtful whether this was Lee's intention. He had a high opinion of General Meade, and is said to have declared of that commander, that he "gave him" (Lee) "as much trouble as any of them." Lee was thus opposed to a soldier whose ability he respected, and it appears doubtful whether he desired to move so rapidly as to expose his own communications to interruption by his adversary. This view seems to derive support from the apparently unnecessary delays at Culpepper Court-House and Warrenton. There was certainly no good reason why, under ordinary circumstances, an army so accustomed to rapid marches as the Army of Northern Virginia should not have been able to reach Warrenton from the neighborhood of Culpepper Court-House in less than *four days*. "We were *compelled* to halt," Lee writes of the delay at Culpepper; but of that at Warrenton he simply says, "Another halt was made." Whether these views have, or have not foundation, the reader must judge. We shall aim, in a few pages, to conclude our account of this interesting campaign.

IV.

THE FIGHT AT BUCKLAND.

Lee rode forward to the field upon which General Hill had sustained his bloody repulse, and Hill—depressed and mortified at the mishap—endeavored to explain the *contretemps* and vindicate himself from censure. Lee is said to have listened in silence, as they rode among the dead bodies, and to have at length replied, gravely and sadly: "Well, well, general, bury these poor men, and let us say no more about it."

He had issued orders that the troops should cease the pursuit, and riding on the next morning, with General Stuart, to the summit of a hill overlooking Broad Run, dismounted, and held a brief conversation with the commander of his cavalry, looking intently, as he spoke, in the direction of Manassas. His demeanor was that of a person who is far from pleased with the course of events, and the word *glum* best describes his expression. The safe retreat of General Meade, with the heavy blow struck by him in retiring, was indeed enough to account for this ill-humor. The campaign was altogether a failure, since General Meade's position at Centreville was unassailable; and, if he were only driven therefrom, he had but to retire to the defences at Washington. Lee accordingly gave Stuart directions to follow up the enemy in the direction of Centreville, and, ordering the Orange and Alexandria Railroad to be torn up back to the Rappahannock, put his infantry in motion, and marched back toward Culpepper.

We shall now briefly follow the movements of the cavalry. Stuart advanced to Manassas, following up the Federal rear, and hastening their retreat across Bull Run beyond. He then left Fitz Lee's division near Manassas in the Federal front, and moving, with Hampton's division, to the left toward Groveton, passed the Little Catharpin, proceeded thence through the beautiful autumn forest toward Frying Pan, and there found and attacked, with his command dismounted and acting as sharp-shooters, the Second Corps of the Federal army. This sudden appearance of Southern troops on the flank of Centreville, is said to have caused great excitement there, as it was not known that the force was not General Lee's army. The fact was soon apparent, however, that it was merely a cavalry attack. The Federal infantry advanced, whereupon Stuart retired; and the adventurous Southern horsemen moved back in the direction of Warrenton.

They were not to rejoin Lee's army, however, before a final conflict with the Federal cavalry; and the circumstances of this conflict were as dramatic and picturesque as the *ruse de guerre* of Young in Culpepper, and the midnight adventure of Stuart near Auburn. The bold assault on the Second Corps seemed to have excited the ire of the Federal commander, and he promptly sent forward a considerable body of his cavalry, under General Kilpatrick, to pursue Stuart, and if possible come up with and defeat him.

Stuart was near the village of Buckland, on the road to Warrenton, when intelligence of the approach of the Federal cavalry reached him. The movement which followed was suggested by General Fitz Lee. He proposed that Stuart should retire toward Warrenton with Hampton's division, while he, with his own division, remained on the enemy's left flank. Then, at a given signal, Stuart was to face about; he, General Fitz Lee, would attack them in flank; when their rout would probably ensue. This plan was carried out to the letter. General Kilpatrick, who seems to have been confident of his ability to drive Stuart before him, pressed forward on the Warrenton road, closely following up his adversary, when the sudden boom of artillery from General Fitz Lee gave the signal. Stuart wheeled at the signal, and made a headlong charge upon his pursuers. Fitz Lee came in at the same moment and attacked them in flank; and the result was that General Kilpatrick's entire command was routed, and retreated in confusion, Stuart pursuing, as he wrote, "from within three miles of Warrenton to Buckland, the horses at full speed the whole distance." So terminated an incident afterward known among the troopers of Stuart by the jocose title of "The Buckland Races," and the Southern cavalry retired without further molestation behind the Rappahannock.

The coöperation of General Imboden in the campaign should not be passed over. That officer, whose special duty had been to guard the gaps in the Blue Ridge, advanced from Berryville to Charlestown, attacked the Federal garrison at the latter place, drove them in disorder toward Harper's Ferry, and carried back with him four or five hundred prisoners. The enemy followed him closely, and he was forced to fight them off at every step. He succeeded, however, in returning in safety, having performed more than the duty expected of him.

Lee was now behind the Rappahannock, and it remained to be seen what course General Meade would pursue—whether he would remain near Centreville, or strive to regain his lost ground.

All doubt was soon terminated by the approach of the Federal army, which, marching from Centreville on October 19th, and repairing the railroad as it advanced, reached the Rappahannock on the 7th of November. Lee's army at this time was in camp toward Culpepper Court-House, with advanced forces in front of Kelly's Ford and the railroad bridge. General Meade acted with vigor. On his arrival he promptly sent a force across at Kelly's Ford; the Southern troops occupying the rifle-pits there were driven off, with the loss of many prisoners; and an attack near the railroad bridge had still more unfortunate results for General Lee. A portion of Early's division had been posted in the abandoned Federal works, on the north bank at this point, and these were now attacked, and, after a fierce resistance, completely routed. Nearly the whole command was captured—the remnant barely escaping—and, the way having thus been cleared, General Meade threw his army across into Culpepper.

General Lee retired before him with a heavy heart and a deep melancholy, which, in spite of his great control over himself, was visible in his countenance. The infantry-fighting of the campaign had begun, and ended in disaster for him. In the thirty days he had lost at least two thousand men, and was back again in his old camps, having achieved absolutely nothing.

V.

THE ADVANCE TO MINE RUN.

November of the bloody year 1863 had come; and it seemed not unreasonable to anticipate that a twelvemonth, marked by such incessant fighting at Chancellorsville, Fredericksburg, Salem Church, Winchester, Gettysburg, Front Royal, Bristoe, and along the Rappahannock, would now terminate in peace, permitting the combatants on both sides, worn out by their arduous work, to go into winter-quarters, and recuperate their energies for the operations of the ensuing spring.

But General Meade had otherwise determined. He had resolved to try a last advance, in spite of the inclement weather; and Lee's anticipations of a season of rest and refreshment for his troops, undisturbed by hostile demonstrations on the part of the enemy, were destined speedily to be disappointed. The Southern army had gone regularly into winter-quarters, south of the Rapidan, and the men were felicitating themselves upon the prospect of an uninterrupted season of leisure and enjoyment in their rude cabins, built in sheltered nooks, or under their breadths of canvas raised upon logs, and fitted with rough but comfortable chimneys, built of notched pine-saplings, when suddenly intelligence was brought by scouts that the Federal army was in motion. The fact reversed all their hopes of rest, and song, and laughter, by the good log-fires. The musket was taken from its place on the rude walls, the cartridge-box assumed, and the army was once more ready for battle—as gay, hopeful, and resolved, as in the first days of spring.

General Meade had, indeed, resolved that the year should not end without another blow at his adversary, and the brief campaign, known as the "Advance to Mine Run," followed. It was the least favorable of all seasons for active operations; but the Federal commander is vindicated from the charge of bad soldiership by two circumstances which very properly had great weight with him. The first was, the extreme impatience of the Northern authorities and people at the small results of the bloody fighting of the year. Gettysburg had seemed to them a complete defeat of Lee, since he had retreated thereafter without loss of time to Virginia; and yet three months afterward the defeated commander had advanced upon and forced back his victorious adversary. That such should be the result of the year's campaigning seemed absurd to the North. A clamorous appeal was made to the authorities to order another advance; and this general sentiment is said to have been shared by General Meade, who had declared himself bitterly disappointed at missing a battle with Lee in October. A stronger argument in favor of active operations lay in the situation, at the moment, of the Southern army. Lee, anticipating no further fighting during the remainder of the year, opposed the enemy on the Rapidan with only one of his two corps—that of Ewell; while the other—that of Hill—was thrown back, in detached divisions, at various points on the Orange and the Virginia Central Railroads, for the purpose of subsistence during the winter. This fact, becoming known to General Meade, dictated, it is said, his plan of operations. An advance seemed to promise, from the position of the Southern forces, a decisive success. Ewell's right extended no farther than Morton's Ford, on the Rapidan, and thus the various fords down to Chancellorsville were open. If General Meade could cross suddenly, and by a rapid march interpose between Ewell and the scattered divisions of Hill far in rear, it appeared not unreasonable to conclude that Lee's army would be completely disrupted, and that the two corps, one after another, might be crushed by the Federal army.

This plan, which is given on the authority of Northern writers, exhibited good soldiership, and, if Lee were to be caught unawares, promised to succeed. Without further comment we shall now proceed to the narrative of this brief movement, which, indecisive as it was in its results, was not uninteresting, and may prove as attractive to the military student as other operations more imposing and accompanied by bloodier fighting.

General Meade began to move toward the Rapidan on November 26th, and every exertion was made by him to advance with such secrecy and rapidity as to give him the advantage of a surprise. In this, however, he was disappointed. No sooner had his orders been issued, and the correspondent movements begun, than the accomplished scouts of Stuart hurried across the Rapidan with the intelligence. Stuart, whose headquarters were in a hollow of the hills near Orange, and not far from General Lee's, promptly communicated in person to the commander-in-chief this important information, and Lee dispatched immediately an order to General A.P. Hill, in rear, to march at once and form a junction with Ewell in the vicinity of Verdierville. The latter officer was directed to retire from his advanced position upon the Rapidan, which exposed him to an attack on his right flank and rear, and to fall back and take post behind the small stream called Mine Run.

In following with a critical eye the operations of General Lee, the military student must be struck particularly by one circumstance, that in all his movements he seemed to proceed less according to the nice technicalities of the art of war, than in accordance with the dictates of a broad and comprehensive good sense. It may be said that, in choosing position, he always chose the right and never the wrong one; and the choice of Mine Run now as a defensive line was a proof of this. The run is a small water-course which, rising south of the great highway between Orange and Chancellorsville, flows due northward amid woods and between hills to the Rapidan, into which it empties itself a few miles above Germanna, General Meade's main place of crossing. This stream is the natural defence of the right flank of an army posted between Orange and the Rapidan. It is also the natural and obvious line upon which to receive the attack of a force marching from below toward Gordonsville. Behind Mine Run, therefore, just east of the little village of Verdierville, General Lee directed his two corps to concentrate; and at the word, the men, lounging but now carelessly in winter-quarters, sprung to arms, "fell in," and with burnished muskets took up the line of march.

We have spoken of the promptness with which the movement was made, and it may almost be said that General Meade had scarcely broken up his camps north of the Rapidan, when Lee was in motion to go and meet him. On the night of the 26th, Stuart, whose cavalry was posted opposite the lower fords, pushed forward in person, and bivouacked under some pines just below Verdierville; and before daylight General Lee was also in the saddle, and at sunrise had reached the same point. The night had been severely cold, for winter had set in in earnest; but General Lee, always robust and careless of weather, walked down, without wrapping, and wearing only his plain gray uniform, to Stuart's *impromptu* headquarters under the pines, where, beside a great fire, and without other covering than his army-blanket, the commander of the cavalry had slept since midnight.

As Lee approached, Stuart came forward, and Lee said, admiringly, "What a hardy soldier!"

They consulted, Stuart walking back with General Lee, and receiving his orders. He then promptly mounted, and hastened to the front, where, taking command of his cavalry, he formed it in front of the advancing enemy, and with artillery and dismounted sharp-shooters, offered every possible impediment to their advance.

General Meade made the passage of the Rapidan without difficulty; and, as his expedition was unencumbered with wagons, advanced rapidly. The only serious obstruction to his march was made by Johnson's division of Ewell's corps, which had been thrown out beyond the run, toward the river. Upon this force the Federal Third Corps, under General French, suddenly blundered, by taking the wrong road, it is said, and an active engagement followed, which resulted in favor of the Southerners. The verdict of Lee's troops afterward was, that the enemy fought badly; but General French probably desired nothing better than to shake off this hornets'-nest into which he had stumbled, and to reach, in the time prescribed by General Meade, the point of Federal concentration near Robertson's Tavern.

Toward that point the Northern forces now converged from the various crossings of the river; and Stuart continued to reconnoitre and feel them along the entire front, fighting obstinately, and falling back only when compelled to do so. Every step was thus contested with sharp-shooters and the Horse-Artillery, from far below to above New-Hope Church. The Federal infantry, however, continued steadily to press forward, forcing back the cavalry, and on the 27th General Meade was in face of Mine Run.

Lee was ready. Hill had promptly marched, and his corps was coming into position on the right of Ewell. Receiving intelligence of the enemy's movement only upon the preceding day, Lee had seemed to move the divisions of Hill, far back toward Charlottesville, as by the wave of his hand. The army was concentrated; the line of defence occupied; and General Meade's attempt to surprise his adversary, by interposing between his widely-separated wings, had resulted in decisive failure. If he fought now, the battle must be one of army against army; and, what was worst of all, it was Lee who held all the advantages of position.

We have spoken of Mine Run: it is a strong defensive position, on its right bank and on its left. Flowing generally between hills, and with densely-wooded banks, it is difficult to cross from either side in face of an opposing force; and it was Lee's good fortune to occupy the attitude of the party to be assailed. He seemed to feel that he had nothing to fear, and was in excellent spirits, as were the men; an eye-witness describes them as "gay, lively, laughing, magnificent." In front of his left wing he had already erected works; his centre and right were as yet undefended, but the task of strengthening the line at these points was rapidly prosecuted. Lee superintended in person the establishment of his order of battle, and it was plain to those who saw him thus engaged that the department of military engineering was a favorite one with him. Riding along the western bank of the water-course, a large part of which was densely clothed in oak, chestnut, and hickory, he selected, with the quick eye of the trained engineer, the best position for his line—promptly moved it when it had been established on bad ground—pointed out the positions for artillery; and, as he thus rode slowly along, the works which he had directed seemed to spring up behind him as though by magic. As the troops of Hill came up and halted in the wood, the men seized axes, attacked the large trees, which soon fell in every direction, and the heavy logs were dragged without loss of time to the prescribed line, where they were piled upon each other in double walls, which were filled in rapidly with earth; and thus, in an inconceivably short space of time the men had defences breast-high which would turn a cannon-shot. In front, for some distance, too, the timber had been felled and an *abatis* thus formed. A few hours after the arrival of the troops on the line marked out by Lee, they were rooted behind excellent breastworks, with forest, stream, and *abatis* in front, to delay the assailing force under the fire of small-arms and cannon.

This account of the movements of the army, and the preparations made to receive General Meade's attack, may appear of undue length and minuteness of detail, in view of the fact that no battle ensued. But the volume before the reader is not so much a history of the battles of Virginia, which have often been described, as an attempt to delineate the military and personal character of General Lee, which displayed itself often more strikingly in indecisive events than in those whose results attract the attention of the world. It was the vigorous brain, indeed, of the great soldier, that made events indecisive—warding off, by military acumen and ability, the disaster with which he was threatened. At Mine Run, Lee's quick eye for position, and masterly handling of his forces, completely checkmated an adversary who had advanced to deliver decisive battle. With felled trees, breastworks, and a crawling stream, Lee reversed all the calculations of the commander of the Federal army.

From the 27th of November to the night of the 1st of December, General Meade moved to and fro in front of the formidable works of his adversary, feeling them with skirmishers and artillery, and essaying vainly to find some joint in the armor through which to pierce. There was none. Lee had inaugurated that great system of breastworks which afterward did him such good service in his long campaign with General Grant. A feature of the military art unknown to Jomini had thus its birth in the woods of America; and this fact, if there were naught else of interest in the campaign, would communicate to the Mine-Run affair the utmost interest.

General Meade, it seems, was bitterly opposed to foregoing an attack. In spite of the powerful position of his adversary, he ordered an assault, it is said; but this did not take place, in consequence, it would appear, of the reluctance of General Warren to charge the Confederate right. This seemed so strong that the men considered it hopeless. When the order was communicated to them, each one wrote his name on a scrap of paper and pinned it to his breast, that his corpse might be recognized, and, if possible, conveyed to his friends. This was ominous of failure: General Warren suspended the attack; and General Meade, it is said, acquiesced in his decision. He declared, it is related, that he could carry the position *with a loss of thirty thousand men*; but, as that idea was frightful, there seemed nothing to do but retreat.

Lee seemed to realize the embarrassment of his adversary, and was in excellent heart throughout the whole affair. Riding to and fro along his line among his "merry men"—and they had never appeared in finer spirits, or with greater confidence in their commander—he addressed encouraging words to them, exposed himself with entire indifference to the shelling, and seemed perfectly confident of the result. It was on this occasion that, finding a party of his ragged soldiers devoutly kneeling in one of the little glades behind the breastworks, and holding a praying-meeting in the midst of bursting shells, he dismounted, took off his hat, and remained silently and devoutly listening until the earnest prayer was concluded. A great revival was then going on in the army, and thousands were becoming professors of religion. The fact may seem strange to those who have regarded Lee as only a West-Pointer and soldier, looking, like all soldiers, to military success; but the religious enthusiasm of his men in this autumn of 1863 probably gave him greater joy than any successes achieved over his Federal adversary. Those who saw him on the lines at Mine Run will remember the composed satisfaction of his countenance. An eye-witness recalls his mild face, as he rode along, accompanied by "Hill, in his drooping hat, simple and cordial; Early, laughing; Ewell, pale and haggard, but with a smile *de bon coeur*" [Footnote: Journal of a staff-officer.] He was thus attended, sitting his horse upon a hill near the left of his line, when a staff officer rode up and informed him that the enemy were making a heavy demonstration against his extreme right.

"Infantry or cavalry?" he asked, with great calmness.

"Infantry, I think, general, from the appearance of the guns. General Wilcox thinks so, and has sent a regiment of sharp-shooters to meet them."

"Who commands the regiment?" asked General Lee; and it was to introduce this question that this trifle has been mentioned. Lee knew his army man by man almost, and could judge of the probable result of the movement here announced to him by the name of the officer in command.

Finding that General Meade would not probably venture to assail him. Lee determined, on the night of December 1st, to attack his adversary on the next morning. His mildness on this night yielded to soldierly ardor, and he exclaimed:

"They must be attacked! they must be attacked!"

His plan is said to have contemplated a movement of his right wing against the Federal left flank, for which the ground afforded great advantages. All was ready for such a movement, and the orders are said to have been issued, when, as the dawn broke over the hills, the Federal camps were seen to be deserted. General Meade had abandoned his campaign, and was in full retreat toward the Rapidan.

The army immediately moved in pursuit, with Lee leading the column. The disappearance of the enemy was an astounding event to them, and they could scarcely realize it. An entertaining illustration of this fact is found in the journal of a staff-officer, who was sent with an order to General Hampton. "In looking for him," says the writer, "I got far to our right, and in a hollow of the woods found a grand guard of the Eleventh Cavalry, with pickets and videttes out, gravely sitting their horses, and watching the wood-roads for the advance of an enemy who was then retreating across Ely's Ford!" Stuart was pressing their rear with his cavalry, while the infantry were steadily advancing. But the pursuit was vain. General Meade had disappeared like a phantom, and was beyond pursuit, to the extreme regret and disappointment of General Lee, who halted his troops, in great discouragement, at Parker's Store.

"Tell General Stuart," he said, with an air of deep melancholy, to an officer whom he saw passing, "that I had received his dispatch when he turned into the Brock Road, and have halted my infantry here, not wishing to march them unnecessarily."

Even at that early hour all chance of effective pursuit was lost. General Meade, without wagons, and not even with the weight of the rations brought over, which the men had consumed, had moved with the rapidity of cavalry, and was already crossing the river far below. He was afterward asked by a gentleman of Culpepper whether in crossing the Rapidan he designed a real advance.

"Certainly," he is reported by the gentleman in question to have replied, "I meant to go to Richmond if I could, but Lee's position was so strong that to storm it would have cost me thirty thousand men. I could not remain without a battle—the weather was so cold that my sentinels froze to death on post."

The pursuit was speedily abandoned by General Lee as entirely impracticable, and the men were marched back between the burning woods, set on fire by the Federal campfires. The spectacle was imposing—the numerous fires, burning outward in the carpet of thick leaves, formed picturesque rings of flame resembling brilliant necklaces; and, as the flames reached the tall trees, wrapped to the summit in dry vines, these would blaze aloft like gigantic torches—true "torches of war"—let fall by the Federal commander in his hasty retrograde.

Twenty-four hours afterward the larger part of General Lee's army were back in their winter-quarters. In less than a week the Mine-Run campaign had begun and ended. The movement of General Meade might have been compared to that of the King of France and his forty thousand men in the song; but the campaign was not ill devised, was rather the dictate of sound military judgment. All that defeated it was the extreme promptness of Lee, the excellent choice of position, and the beginning of that great system of impromptu breastworks which afterward became so powerful an engine against General Grant.

VI.

LEE IN THE AUTUMN AND WINTER OF 1863.

General Lee's headquarters remained, throughout the autumn and winter of 1863, in a wood on the southern slope of the spur called Clarke's Mountain, a few miles east of Orange Court-House.

Here his tents had been pitched, in a cleared space amid pines and cedars; and the ingenuity of the "couriers," as messengers and orderlies were called in the Southern army, had fashioned alleys and walks leading to the various tents, the tent of the commanding general occupying the centre. Of the gentlemen of General Lee's staff we have not considered it necessary to speak; but it may here be said that it was composed of officers of great efficiency and of the most courteous manners, from Colonel Taylor, the indefatigable adjutant-general, to the youngest and least prominent member of the friendly group. Among these able assistants of the commander-in-chief were Colonel Marshall, of Maryland, a gentleman of distinguished intellect; Colonel Peyton, who had entered the battle of Manassas as a private in the ranks, but, on the evening of that day, for courage and efficiency, occupied the place of a commissioned officer on Beauregard's staff; and others whose names were comparatively unknown to the army, but whose part in the conduct of affairs, under direction of Lee, was most important.

With the gentlemen of his staff General Lee lived on terms of the most kindly regard. He was a strict disciplinarian, and abhorred the theory that a commissioned officer, from considerations of rank, should hold himself above the private soldiers; but there was certainly no fault of this description to be found at army headquarters, and the general and his staff worked together in harmonious coöperation. The respect felt for him by gentlemen who saw him at all hours, and under none of the guise of ceremony, was probably greater than that experienced by the community who looked upon him from a distance. That distant perspective, hiding little weaknesses, and revealing only the great proportions of a human being, is said to be essential generally to the heroic sublime. No man, it has been said, can be great to those always near him; but in the case of General Lee this was far from being the fact. He seemed greater and nobler, day by day, as he was better and more intimately known; and upon this point we shall quote the words of the brave John B. Gordon, one of his most trusted lieutenants:

"It has been my fortune in life," says General Gordon, "from circumstances, to have come in contact with some whom the world pronounced great—some of the earth's celebrated and distinguished; but I declare it here to-day, that of any mortal man whom it has ever been my privilege to approach, he was the greatest; and I assert here, that, *grand as might be your conception of the man before, he arose in incomparable majesty on more familiar acquaintance.* This can be affirmed of few men who have ever lived or died, and of no other man whom it has ever been my fortune to approach. Like Niagara, the more you gazed, the more its grandeur grew upon you, the more its majesty expanded and filled your spirit with a full satisfaction that left a perfect delight without the slightest feeling of oppression. Grandly majestic and dignified in all his deportment, he was genial as the sunlight of this beautiful day; and not a ray of that cordial social intercourse but brought warmth to the heart as it did light to the understanding."

Upon this point, General Breckinridge, too, bears his testimony: "During the last year of that unfortunate struggle," he says, "it was my good fortune to spend a great deal of time with him. I was almost constantly by his side, and it was during the two months immediately preceding the fall of Richmond that I came to know and fully understand the true nobility of his character. In all those long vigils, he was considerate and kind, gentle, firm, and self-poised. I can give no better idea of the impression it made upon me, than to say it inspired me with an ardent love of the man and a profound veneration of his character. It was so massive and noble, so grand in its proportions, that all men must admire its heroism and gallantry, yet so gentle and tender that a woman might adopt and claim it as her own."

We beg the reader to observe that in these two tributes to the worth of the great soldier, his distinguished associates dwell with peculiar emphasis upon the charms of private intercourse with him, and bear their testimony to the fact that to know him better was to love and admire him more and more. The fact is easily explained. There was in this human being's character naught that was insincere, assumed, or pretentious. It was a great and massive soul—as gentle, too, and tender, as a woman's or a child's—that lay beneath the reserved exterior, and made the soldier more beloved as its qualities were better known. Other men reveal their weaknesses on nearer acquaintance—Lee only revealed his greatness; and he was more and more loved and admired.

The justice of these comments will be recognized by all who had personal intercourse with the illustrious soldier; and, in this autumn and winter of 1863, his army, lying around him along the Rapidan, began to form that more intimate acquaintance which uniformly resulted in profound admiration for the man. In the great campaigns of the two past years the gray soldier had shared their hardships, and never relaxed his fatherly care for all their wants; he had led them in battle, exposing his own person with entire indifference; had never exposed *them* when it was possible to avoid it; and on every occasion had demanded, often with disagreeable persistence from the civil authorities, that the wants of his veterans should be supplied if all else was neglected. These facts were now known to the troops, and made Lee immensely popular. From the highest officers to the humblest private soldiers he was universally respected and beloved. The whole army seemed to feel that, in the plainly-clad soldier, sleeping, like themselves, under canvas, in the woods of Orange, they had a guiding and protecting head, ever studious of their well-being, jealous of their hard-earned fame, and ready, both as friend and commander, to represent them and claim their due.

We have spoken of the great revival of religion which at this time took place in the army. The touching spectacle was presented of bearded veterans, who had charged in a score of combats, kneeling devoutly under the rustic roofs of evergreens, built for religious gatherings, and praying to the God of battles who had so long protected them. A commander-in-chief of the old European school might have ridiculed these emotional assemblages, or, at best, passed them without notice, as freaks in which he disdained to take part. Lee, on the contrary, greeted the religious enthusiasm of his troops with undisguised pleasure. He went among them, conversed with the chaplains, assisted the good work by every means in his power; and no ordained minister of the Gospel could have exhibited a simpler, sincerer, or more heartfelt delight than himself at the general extension of religious feeling throughout the army. We have related how, in talking with army-chaplains, his cheeks flushed and his eyes filled with tears at the good tidings. He begged them to pray for him too, as no less needing their pious intercession; and in making the request he was, as always, simple and sincere. Unaccustomed to exhibit his feelings upon this, the profoundest and most sacred of subjects, he was yet penetrated to his inmost soul by a sense of his own weakness and dependence on divine support; and, indeed, it may be questioned whether any other element of the great soldier's character was so deep-seated and controlling as his spirit of love to God. It took, in the eyes of the world, the form of a love of duty; but with Lee the word duty was but another name for the will of the Almighty; and to discover and perform this was, first and last, the sole aim of his life.

We elaborate this point before passing to the last great campaign of the war, since, to understand Lee in those last days, it is absolutely necessary to keep in view this utter subjection of the man's heart to the sense of an overruling Providence—that Providence which "shapes our ends, rough-hew them how we will." We shall be called upon to delineate the soldier meeting adverse circumstances and disaster at every turn with an imperial calmness and a resolution that never shook; and, up to a certain point, this noble composure may be attributed to the stubborn courage of the man's nature. There came in due time, however, a moment of trial when military courage simply was of no avail—when that human being never lived, who, looking to earthly support alone, would not have lost heart and given up the contest. Lee did not, in this hour of conclusive trial, either lose heart or give up the struggle; and the world, not understanding the phenomenon, gazed at him with wonder. Few were aware of the true explanation of his utter serenity when all things were crumbling around him, and when he knew that they were crumbling. The stout heart of the soldier who will not yield to fate was in his breast; but he had a still stronger sentiment than manly courage to support him—the consciousness that he was doing his duty, and that God watched over him, and would make all things work together for good to those who loved Him.

As yet that last great wrestle of the opposing armies lay in the future. The veterans of the Army of Northern Virginia defended the line of the Rapidan, and the gray commander-in-chief, in his tent on Clarke's Mountain, serenely awaited the further movements of the enemy. During the long months of winter he was busily engaged, as usual, in official correspondence, in looking to the welfare of his men, and in preparations for the coming campaign. He often rode among the camps, and the familiar figure in the well-known hat, cape, and gray uniform, mounted upon the powerful iron-gray—the famous "Traveller," who survived to bear his master after the war—was everywhere greeted by the ragged veterans with cheers and marks of the highest respect and regard. At times his rides were extended to the banks of the Rapidan, and, in passing, he would stop at the headquarters of General Stuart, or other officers. On these occasions he had always some good-humored speech for all, not overlooking the youngest officer; but he shone in the most amiable light, perhaps, in conversing with some old private soldier, gray-haired like himself. At such moments the general's countenance was a pleasant spectacle. A kindly smile lit up the clear eyes, and moved the lips half-concealed by the grizzled mustache. The *bonhomie* of this smile was irresistible, and the aged private soldier, in his poor, tattered fighting-jacket, was made to feel by it that his commander-in-chief regarded him as a friend and comrade.

We dwell at too great length, perhaps, upon these slight personal traits of the soldier, but all relating to such a human being is interesting, and worthy of record. To the writer, indeed, this is the most attractive phase of his subject. The analysis and description of campaigns and battles is an unattractive task to him; but the personal delineation of a good and great man, even in his lesser and more familiar traits, is a pleasing relief—a portion of his subject upon which he delights to linger. What the writer here tries to draw, he looked upon with his own eyes, the figure of a great, calm soldier, with kindly sweetness and dignity, but, above all, a charming sincerity and simplicity in every movement, accent, and expression. Entirely free from the trappings of high command, and with nothing to distinguish him from any other soldier save the well-worn stars on the collar of his uniform-coat, the commander-in-chief was recognizable at the very first glance, and no less the simple and kindly gentleman. His old soldiers remember him as he appeared on many battle-fields, and will describe his martial seat in the saddle as he advanced with the advancing lines. But they will speak of him with even greater pleasure as he appeared in the winters of 1862 and 1863, on the Rappahannock and the Rapidan—a gray and simple soldier, riding among them and smiling kindly as his eyes fell upon their tattered uniforms and familiar faces.

PART VIII.

LEE'S LAST CAMPAIGNS AND LAST DAYS.

I.

GENERAL GRANT CROSSES THE RAPIDAN.

In the first days of May, 1864, began the immense campaign which was to terminate only with the fall of the Confederacy.

For this, which was regarded as the decisive trial of strength, the Federal authorities had made elaborate preparations. New levies were raised by draft to fill up the ranks of the depleted forces; great masses of war material were accumulated at the central depots at Washington, and the Government summoned from the West an officer of high reputation to conduct hostilities on what was more plainly than ever before seen to be the theatre of decisive conflict—Virginia. The officer in question was General Ulysses S. Grant, who had received the repute of eminent military ability by his operations in the West; he was now commissioned lieutenant-general, and President Lincoln assigned him to the command of "all the armies of the United States," at that time estimated to number one million men.

General Grant promptly accepted the trust confided to him, and, relinquishing to Major-General Sherman the command of the Western forces, proceeded to Culpepper and assumed personal command of the Army of the Potomac, although nominally that army remained under command of General Meade. The spring campaign was preceded, in February, by two movements of the Federal forces: one the advance of General B.F. Butler up the Peninsula to the Chickahominy, where for a few hours he threatened Richmond, only to retire hastily when opposed by a few local troops; the other the expedition of General Kilpatrick with a body of cavalry, from the Rapidan toward Richmond, with the view of releasing the Federal prisoners there. This failed completely, like the expedition up the Peninsula. General Kilpatrick, after threatening the city, rapidly retreated, and a portion of his command, under Colonel Dahlgren, was pursued, and a large portion killed, including their commander. It is to be hoped, for the honor of human nature, that Colonel Dahlgren's designs were different from those which are attributed to him on what seems unassailable proof. Papers found upon his body contained minute directions for releasing the prisoners and giving up the city to them, and for putting to death the Confederate President and his Cabinet.

To return to the more important events on the Rapidan. General Grant assumed the direction of the Army of the Potomac under most favorable auspices. Other commanders—especially General McClellan—had labored under painful disadvantages, from the absence of coöperation and good feeling on the part of the authorities. The new leader entered upon the great struggle under very different circumstances. Personally and politically acceptable to the Government, he received their hearty coöperation: all power was placed in his hands; he was enabled to concentrate in Virginia the best troops, in large numbers; and the character of this force seemed to promise him assured victory. General McClellan and others had commanded troops comparatively raw, and were opposed by Confederate armies in the full flush of anticipated success. General Grant had now under him an army of veterans, and the enemy he was opposed to had, month by month, lost strength. Under these circumstances it seemed that he ought to succeed in crushing his adversary.

The Federal army present and ready for duty May 1, 1864, numbered one hundred and forty-one thousand one hundred and sixty-six men. That of General Lee numbered fifty-two thousand six hundred and twenty-six. Colonel Taylor, adjutant-general of the Army, states the strictly effective at a little less, viz.:

Ewell 13,000
Hill 17,000
Longstreet 10,000
    Infantry 40,000
Cavalry and artillery 10,000
    Total 50,000

The two statements do not materially differ, and require no discussion. The force at Lee's command was a little over one-third of General Grant's; and, if it be true that the latter commander continued to receive reënforcements between the 1st and 4th days of May, when he crossed the Rapidan, Lee's force was probably less than one-third of his adversary's.

Longstreet, it will be seen, had been brought back from the West, but the Confederates labored under an even more serious disadvantage than want of sufficient force. Lee's army, small as it was, was wretchedly supplied. Half the men were in rags, and, worse still, were but one-fourth fed. Against this suicidal policy, in reference to an army upon which depended the fate of the South, General Lee had protested in vain. Whether from fault in the authorities or from circumstances over which they could exercise no control, adequate supplies of food did not reach the army; and, when it marched to meet the enemy, in the first days of May, the men were gaunt, half-fed, and in no condition to enter upon so arduous a campaign. There was naught to be done, however, but to fight on to the end. Upon the Army of Northern Virginia, depleted by casualties, and unprovided with the commonest necessaries, depended the fate of the struggle. Generals Grant and Lee fully realized that fact; and the Federal commander had the acumen to perceive that the conflict was to be long and determined. He indulged no anticipations of an early or easy success. His plan, as stated in his official report, was "to *hammer continuously* against the armed force of the enemy and his resources, until *by mere attrition*, if by nothing else, there should be nothing left of him but an equal submission with the loyal section of our common country to the Constitution and the laws." The frightful cost in blood of this policy of hammering continuously and thus wearing away his adversary's strength by mere attrition, did or did not occur to General Grant. In either case he is not justly to be blamed.

It was the only policy which promised to result in Federal success. Pitched battles had been tried for nearly three years, and in victory or in defeat the Southern army seemed equally unshaken and dangerous. This fact was now felt and acknowledged even by its enemies. "Lee's army," said a Northern writer, referring to it at this time, "is an army of veterans: it is an instrument sharpened to a perfect edge. You turn its flanks—well, its flanks are made to be turned. This effects little or nothing. All that we reckon as gained, therefore, is the loss of life inflicted on the enemy." With an army thus trained in many combats, and hardened against misfortune, defeat in one or a dozen battles decided nothing. General Grant seems to have understood this, and to have resolutely adopted the programme of "attrition"—coldly estimating that, even if he lost ten men to General Lee's one, he could better endure that loss, and could afford it, if thereby he "crushed the rebellion."

The military theory of the Federal commander having thus been set forth in his own words, it remains to notice his programme for the approaching campaign. He had hesitated between two plans—"one to cross the Rapidan below Lee, moving by his right flank; the other above, moving by his left." The last was abandoned from the difficulty of keeping open communication with any base of supplies, and the latter adopted. General Grant determined to "fight Lee between Culpepper and Richmond, if he would stand;" to advance straight upon the city and invest it from the north and west, thereby cutting its communications in three directions; and then, crossing the James River above the city, form a junction with the left of Major-General Butler, who, moving with about thirty thousand men from Fortress Monroe, at the moment when the Army of the Potomac crossed the Rapidan, was to occupy City Point, advance thence up the south side of James River, and reach a position where the two armies might thus unite.

It is proper to keep in view this programme of General Grant. Lee completely reversed it by promptly moving in front of his adversary at every step which he took in advance; and it will be seen that the Federal commander was finally compelled to adopt a plan which does not seem to have entered his mind, save as a *dernier ressort*, at the beginning of the campaign.

On the morning of the 4th of May, General Grant commenced crossing the Rapidan at Germanna and other fords above Chancellorsville, and by the morning of the 5th his army was over. It appears from his report that he had not anticipated so easy a passage of the stream, and greatly felicitated himself upon effecting it so successfully. "This I regarded," he says, "as a great success, and it removed from my mind the most serious apprehension I had entertained, that of crossing the river in the face of an active, large, well-appointed, and ably-commanded army." Lee had made no movement to dispute the passage of the stream, from the fact, perhaps, that his army was *not* either "large" or "well-appointed." He preferred to await the appearance of his adversary, and direct an assault on the flank of his column as it passed across his front. From a speech attributed to General Meade, it would seem to have been the impression in the Federal army that Lee designed falling back to a defensive position somewhere near the South Anna. His movements were, however, very different. Instead of retiring before General Grant in the direction of Richmond, he moved with his three corps toward the Wilderness, to offer battle.

[Illustration: Routes of Lee & Grant, May and June 1864.]

The head of the column consisted of Ewell's corps, which had retained its position on the Rapidan, forming the right of Lee's line. General A.P. Hill, who had been stationed higher up, near Liberty Mills, followed; and Longstreet, who lay near Gordonsville, brought up the rear. These dispositions dictated, as will be seen, the positions of the three commands in the ensuing struggle. Ewell advanced in front down the Old Turnpike, that one of the two great highways here running east and west which is nearest the Rapidan; Hill came on over the Orange Plank-road, a little south of the turnpike, and thus formed on Ewell's right; and Longstreet, following, came in on the right of Hill.

General Grant had plunged with his army into the dense and melancholy thicket which had been the scene of General Hooker's discomfiture. His army, followed by its great train of four thousand wagons, indicating the important nature of the movement, had reached Wilderness Tavern and that Brock Road over which Jackson advanced in his secret flank-march against the Federal right in May, 1863. In May of 1864, now, another Federal army had penetrated, the sombre and depressing shadows of the interminable thickets of the Wilderness, and a more determined struggle than the first was to mark with its bloody hand this historic territory.

II.

THE FIRST COLLISION IN THE WILDERNESS.

To understand the singular combat which now ensued, it is necessary to keep in view the fact that nothing more surprised General Grant than the sudden appearance of his adversary face to face with him in the Wilderness.

It had not been supposed, either by the lieutenant-general or his corps-commanders, that Lee, with his small army, would have recourse to a proceeding so audacious. It was anticipated, indeed, that, somewhere on the road to Richmond, Lee would make a stand and fight, in a carefully-selected position which would enable him to risk collision with his great adversary; but that Lee himself would bring on this collision by making an open attack, unassisted by position of any sort, was the last thing which seems to have occurred to his adversary.

Such, however, as has been said, was the design, from the first, of the Southern commander, and he moved with his accustomed celerity and energy. As soon as General Grant broke up his camps north of the Rapidan, Lee was apprised of the fact, and ordered his three corps to concentrate in the direction of Chancellorsville. Those who were present in the Southern army at this time will bear record to the soldierly promptness of officers and men. On the evening of the 3d of May the camps were the scenes of noise, merriment, and parade: the bands played; the woods were alive; nothing disturbed the scene of general enjoyment of winter-quarters. On the morning of the 4th all this was changed. The camps were deserted; no sound was anywhere heard; the troops were twenty miles away, fully armed and ready for battle. General Lee was in the saddle, and his presence seemed to push forward his column. Ewell, marching with celerity, bivouacked that night directly in face of the enemy; and it was the suddenly-discovered presence of the troops of this commander which arrested General Grant, advancing steadily in the direction of Spottsylvania Court-House.

He must have inwardly chafed at a circumstance so unexpected and embarrassing. It had been no part of his plan to fight in the thickets of the Wilderness, and yet an adversary of but one-third his own strength was about to reverse his whole programme, and dictate the terms of the first battles of the campaign. There was nothing to do, however, but to fight, and General Grant hastened to form order of battle for that purpose, with General Sedgwick commanding his right, Generals Warren and Burnside his centre, and General Hancock his left, near the Brock Road. The line thus formed extended from northwest to southeast, and, as the right wing was in advance with respect to Lee, that circumstance occasioned the first collision.

This occurred about mid-day on the 5th of May, and was brought on by General Warren, who attacked the head of Swell's column, on the Old Turnpike. An obstinate engagement ensued, and the division which received the assault was forced back. It quickly, however, reformed, and being reënforced advanced in turn against General Warren, and, after a hard fight, he was driven back with a loss of three thousand men and two pieces of artillery.

This first collision of the armies on the Confederate left was followed almost immediately by a bloody struggle on the centre. This was held by A.P. Hill, who had marched down the Plank-road, and was near the important point of junction of that road with the Brock Road, when he was suddenly attacked by the enemy. The struggle which ensued was long and determined. General Lee wrote: "The assaults were repeated and desperate, but every one was repulsed." When night fell, Hill had not been driven back, but had not advanced; and the two armies rested on their arms, awaiting the return of light to continue the battle.

III.

THE BATTLE OF THE 6TH OF MAY.

The morning of the 6th of May came, and, with the first light of dawn, the adversaries, as by a common understanding, advanced at the same moment to attack each other.

The battle which followed is wellnigh indescribable, and may be said, in general terms, to have been naught but the blind and desperate clutch of two great bodies of men, who could scarcely see each other when they were but a few feet apart, and who fired at random, rather by sound than sight. A Southern writer, describing the country and the strange combat, says: "The country was sombre—a land of thicket, undergrowth, jungle, ooze, where men could not see each other twenty yards off, and assaults had to be made by the compass. The fights there were not even as easy as night attacks in open country, for at night you can travel by the stars. Death came unseen; regiments stumbled on each other, and sent swift destruction into each other's ranks, guided by the crackling of the bushes. It was not war—military manoeuvring: science had as little to do with it as sight. Two wild animals were hunting each other; when they heard each other's steps, they sprung and grappled. The conqueror advanced, or went elsewhere. The dead were lost from all eyes in the thicket. The curious spectacle was here presented of officers advancing to the charge, in the jungle, *compass in hand*, attacking, not by sight, but by the bearing of the needle. In this mournful and desolate thicket did the great campaign of 1864 begin. Here, in blind wrestle as at midnight, did two hundred thousand men in blue and gray clutch each other—bloodiest and weirdest of encounters. War had had nothing like it. The genius of destruction, tired apparently of the old commonplace killing, had invented the 'unseen death.' At five in the morning, the opponents closed in, breast to breast, in the thicket. Each had thrown up here and there slight, temporary breastworks of saplings and dirt; beyond this, they were unprotected. The question now was, which would succeed in driving his adversary from these defences, almost within a few yards of each other, and from behind which crackled the musketry. Never was sight more curious. On the low line of these works, dimly seen in the thicket, rested the muzzles spouting flame; from the depths rose cheers; charges were made and repulsed, the lines scarcely seeing each other; men fell and writhed, and died unseen—their bodies lost in the bushes, their death-groans drowned in the steady, continuous, never-ceasing crash."

These sentences convey a not incorrect idea of the general character of this remarkable engagement, which had no precedent in the war. We shall now proceed to speak of General Lee's plans and objects, and to indicate where they failed or succeeded. The commanders of both armies labored under great embarrassments. General Grant's was the singular character of the country, with which he was wholly unacquainted; and General Lee's, the delay in the arrival of Longstreet. Owing to the distance of the camps of the last-named officer, he had not, at dawn, reached the field of battle. As his presence was indispensable to a general assault, this delay in his appearance threatened to result in unfortunate consequences, as it was nearly certain that General Grant would make an early and resolute attack. Under these circumstances, Lee resolved to commence the action, and did so, counting, doubtless, on his ability, with the thirty thousand men at his command, to at least maintain his ground. His plan seems to have been to make a heavy demonstration against the Federal right, and, when Longstreet arrived, throw the weight of his whole centre and right against the Federal left, with the view of seizing the Brock Road, running southward, and forcing back the enemy's left wing into the thickets around Chancellorsville. This brilliant conception, which, if carried out, would have arrested General Grant in the beginning of his campaign, was very near meeting with success. The attack on the Federal right, under General Sedgwick, commenced at dawn, and the fighting on both sides was obstinate. It continued with indecisive results throughout the morning, gradually involving the Federal centre; but, nearly at the moment when it began, a still more obstinate conflict was inaugurated between General Hancock, holding the Federal left, and Hill, who opposed him on the Plank-road. The battle raged in this quarter with great fury for some time, but, attacked in front and flank at once by his able opponent, Hill was forced back steadily, and at last, in some disorder, a considerable distance from the ground which had witnessed the commencement of the action. At this point, however, he was fortunately met by Longstreet. That commander rapidly brought his troops into line, met the advancing enemy, attacked them with great fury, and, after a bloody contest, in which General Wadsworth was killed, drove them back to their original position on the Brock Road.

It now seemed nearly certain that Lee's plan of seizing upon this important highway would succeed. General Hancock had been forced back with heavy loss, Longstreet was pressing on, and, as he afterward said, he "thought he had another Bull Run on them," when a singular casualty defeated all. General Longstreet, who had ridden in front of his advancing line, turned to ride back, when he was mistaken by his own men for a Federal cavalryman, fired upon, and disabled by a musket-ball. This threw all into disorder, and the advance was discontinued. General Lee, as soon as he was apprised of the accident, hastened to take personal command of the corps, and, as soon as order was restored, directed the line to press forward. The most bloody and determined struggle of the day ensued. The thicket filled the valleys, and, as at Chancellorsville, a new horror was added to the horror of battle. A fire broke out in the thicket, and soon wrapped the adversaries in flame and smoke. They fought on, however, amid the crackling flames. Lee continued to press forward; the Federal breastworks along a portion of their front were carried, and a part of General Hancock's line was driven from the field. The struggle had, however, been decisive of no important results, and, from the lateness of the hour when it terminated, it could not be followed up. On the left Lee had also met with marked but equally indecisive success. General Gordon had attacked the Federal right, driven the force at that point in disorder from their works, and but for the darkness this success might have been followed up and turned into a complete defeat of that wing of the enemy. It was only discovered on the next morning what important successes Gordon had effected with a single brigade; and there is reason to believe that with a larger force this able soldier might have achieved results of a decisive character.[1]

[Footnote 1: General Early, in his "Memoir of the Last Year of the War for Independence," bears his testimony to the important character of the blow struck by General Gordon. He says: "At light, on the morning of the 7th, an advance was made, which disclosed the fact that the enemy had given up his line of works in front of my whole line and a good portion of Johnson's. Between the lines a large number of his dead had been left, and at his breastworks a large number of muskets and knapsacks had been abandoned, and there was every indication of great confusion. It was not till then that we understood the full extent of the success attending the movement of the evening before." General Gordon had proposed making the attack on the *morning* of the 6th, but was overruled.]

Such had been the character and results of the first conflicts between the two armies in the thickets of the Wilderness. As we have already said, the collision there was neither expected nor desired by General Grant, who, unlike General Hooker, in May of the preceding year, seems fully to have understood the unfavorable nature of the region for manoeuvring a large army. His adversary had, however, forced him to accept battle, leaving him no choice, and the result of the actions of the 5th and 6th had been such as to determine the Federal commander to emerge as soon as possible from the tangled underwood which hampered all his movements. On the 7th he accordingly made no movement to attack Lee, and on the night of that day marched rapidly in the direction of Hanover Junction, following the road by Todd's Tavern toward Spottsylvania Court-House.

For this determination to avoid further fighting in the Wilderness, General Grant gives a singular explanation. "On the morning of the 7th," he says, "reconnoissance showed that the enemy *had fallen behind his intrenched lines*, with pickets to the front, covering a part of the battle-field. From this it was evident that the two-days' fighting had satisfied him of his inability to further maintain the contest in the open field, *notwithstanding his advantage of position*, and that he would wait an attack behind his works." The "intrenched lines" and "advantage of position" of Lee, were both imaginary. No lines of intrenchment had been made, and the ground was not more favorable on General Lee's side than on General Grant's. Both armies had erected impromptu breastworks of felled trees and earth, as continued to be their habit throughout the campaign, and the flat country gave no special advantage to either. The forward movement of General Grant is susceptible of much easier explanation. The result of the two-days' fighting had very far from pleased him; he desired to avoid further conflict in so difficult a country, and, taking advantage of the quiescence of Lee, and the hours of darkness, he moved with his army toward the more open country.

IV.

THE 12TH OF MAY.

Throughout the entire day succeeding this first great conflict, General Lee remained quiet, watching for some movement of his adversary. His success in the preliminary struggle had been gratifying, considering the great disproportion of numbers, but he indulged no expectation of a retrograde movement across the Rapidan, on the part of General Grant. He expected him rather to advance, and anxiously awaited some development of this intention. There were no indications of such a design up to the night of the 7th, but at that time, to use the words of a confidential member of Lee's staff, "he all at once seemed to conceive the idea that his enemy was preparing to forsake his position, and move toward Hanover Junction *via* the Spottsylvania Court-House, and, believing this, he at once detailed Anderson's division with orders to proceed rapidly toward the court-house."

General Anderson commenced his march about nine o'clock at night, when the Federal column was already upon its way. A race now began for the coveted position, and General Stuart, with his dismounted sharp-shooters behind improvised breastworks, harassed and impeded the Federal advance, at every step, throughout the night. This greatly delayed their march, and their head of column did not reach the vicinity of Spottsylvania Court-House until past sunrise. General Warren, leading the Federal advance, then hurried forward, followed by General Hancock, when suddenly he found himself in front of breastworks, and was received with a fire of musketry. Lee had succeeded in interposing himself between General Grant and Richmond. On the same evening the bulk of the two armies were facing each other on the line of the Po.

By the rapidity of his movements General Lee had thus completely defeated his adversary's design to seize on the important point, Spottsylvania Court-House. General Grant, apparently conceiving some explanation of this untoward event to be necessary, writes: "The enemy, having become aware of our movement, and *having the shorter line*, was enabled to reach there first." The statement that General Lee had the shorter of the two lines to march over is a mistake. The armies moved over parallel roads until beyond Todd's Tavern, after which the distance to the south bank of the Po was greater by Lee's route than General Grant's. The map will sufficiently indicate this. Two other circumstances defeated General Grant's attempt to reach the point first—the extreme rapidity of the march of the Confederate advance force, and the excellent fighting of Stuart's dismounted men, who harassed and delayed General Warren, leading the Federal advance throughout the entire night.

An additional fact should be mentioned, bearing upon this point, and upon General Lee's designs. "General Lee's orders to me," says General Early, who, from the sickness of A.P. Hill, had been assigned to the command of the corps, "were to *move by Todd's Tavern along the Brock Road*, to Spottsylvania Court-House, as soon as our front was clear of the enemy." From this order it would appear either that General Lee regarded the Brock Road, over which General Grant moved, as the "shorter line," or that he intended the movement of Early on the enemy's rear to operate as a check upon them, while he went forward to their front with his main body.

These comments may seem tedious to the general reader, but all that illustrates the military designs, or defends the good soldiership of Lee, is worthy of record.

We proceed now to the narrative. In the Wilderness General Grant had found a dangerous enemy ready to strike at his flank. He now saw in his front the same active and wary adversary, prepared to bar the direct road to Richmond. General Lee had taken up his position on the south bank of one of the four tributaries of the Mattapony. These four streams are known as the Mat, Ta, Po, and Nye Rivers, and bear the same relation to the main stream that the fingers of the open hand do to the wrist. General Lee was behind the Po, which is next to the Nye, the northernmost of these water-courses. Both were difficult to cross, and their banks heavily wooded. It was now to be seen whether, either by a front attack or a turning movement, General Grant could oust his adversary, and whether General Lee would stand on the defensive or attack.

All day, during the 9th, the two armies were constructing breastworks along their entire fronts, and these works, from the Rapidan to the banks of the Chickahominy, remain yet in existence. On the evening of this day a Federal force was thrown across the Po, on the Confederate left, but soon withdrawn; and on the 10th a similar movement took place near the same point, which resulted in a brief but bloody conflict, during which the woods took fire, and many of the assaulting troops perished miserably in the flames. The force was then recalled, and, during that night and the succeeding day, nothing of importance occurred, although heavy skirmishing and an artillery-fire took place along the lines.

On the morning of the 12th, at the first dawn of day, General Grant made a more important and dangerous assault than any yet undertaken in the campaign. This was directed at a salient on General Lee's right centre, occupied by Johnson's division of Ewell's corps, and was one of the bloodiest and most terrible incidents of the war. For this assault General Grant is said to have selected his best troops. These advanced in a heavy charging column, through the half darkness of dawn, passed silently over the Confederate skirmishers, scarcely firing a shot, and, just as the first streak of daylight touched the eastern woods, burst upon the salient, which they stormed at the point of the bayonet. In consequence of the suddenness of the assault and the absence of artillery—against whose removal General Johnston is stated to have protested, and which arrived too late—the Federal forces carried all before them, and gained possession of the works, in spite of a stubborn and bloody resistance.

Such was the excellent success of the Federal movement, and the Southern line seemed to be hopelessly disrupted. Nearly the whole of Johnson's division were taken prisoners—the number amounting to about three thousand—and eighteen pieces of artillery fell into the hands of the assaulting column.

The position of affairs was now exceedingly critical; and, unless General Lee could reform his line at the point, it seemed that nothing was left him but an abandonment of his whole position. The Federal army had broken his line; was pouring into the opening; and, to prevent him from concentrating at the point to regain possession of the works, heavy attacks were begun by the enemy on his right and left wings. It is probable that at no time during the war was the Southern army in greater danger of a bloody and decisive disaster.

At this critical moment General Lee acted with the nerve and coolness of a soldier whom no adverse event can shake. Those who saw him will testify to the stern courage of his expression; the glance of the eye, which indicated a great nature, aroused to the depth of its powerful organization. Line of battle was promptly formed a short distance in rear of the salient then in the enemy's possession, and a fierce charge was made by the Southerners, under the eye of Lee, to regain it. It was on this occasion that, on fire with the ardor of battle, which so seldom mastered him, Lee went forward in front of his line, and, taking his station beside the colors of one of his Virginian regiments, took off his hat, and, turning to the men, pointed toward the enemy. A storm of cheers greeted the general, as he sat his gray war-horse, in front of the men— his head bare, his eyes flashing, and his cheeks flushed with the fighting-blood of the soldier. General Gordon, however, spurred to his side and seized his rein.

"General Lee!" he exclaimed, "this is no place for you. Go to the rear. These are Virginians and Georgians, sir—men who have never failed!—Men, you will not fail now!" he cried, rising in his stirrups and addressing the troops.

"No, no!" was the reply of the men; and from the whole line burst the shout, "Lee to the rear! Lee to the rear!"

Instead of being needed, it was obvious that his presence was an embarrassment, as the men seemed determined not to charge unless he retired. He accordingly did so, and the line advanced to the attack, led by General Gordon and other officers of approved ability and courage. The charge which followed was resolute, and the word ferocious best describes the struggle which followed. It continued throughout the entire day, Lee making not less than five distinct assaults in heavy force to recover the works. The fight involved the troops on both flanks, and was desperate and unyielding. The opposing flags were at times within only a few yards of each other, and so incessant and concentrated was the fire of musketry, that a tree of about eighteen inches in diameter was cut down by bullets, and is still preserved, it is said, in the city of Washington, as a memorial of this bloody struggle.

[Illustration: The Wilderness. "Lee to the Rear"]

The fighting only ceased several hours after dark. Lee had not regained his advanced line of works, but he was firmly rooted in an interior and straighter line, from which the Federal troops had found it impossible to dislodge him. This result of the stubborn action was essentially a success, as General Grant's aim in the operation had been to break asunder his adversary's army—in which he very nearly succeeded.

At midnight all was again silent. The ground near the salient was strewed with dead bodies. The loss of the three thousand men and eighteen guns of Johnson had been followed by a bloody retaliation, the Federal commander having lost more than eight thousand men.

V.
FROM SPOTTSYLVANIA TO THE CHICKAHOMINY.

After the bloody action of the 12th of May, General Grant remained quiet for many days, "awaiting," he says, "the arrival of reënforcements from Washington." The number of these fresh troops is not known to the present writer. General Lee had no reinforcements to expect, and continued to confront his adversary with his small army, which must have been reduced by the heavy fighting to less than forty thousand men, while that of General Grant numbered probably about one hundred and forty thousand.

Finding that his opponent was not disposed to renew hostilities. General Lee, on the 19th of May, sent General Ewell to turn his right flank; but this movement resulted in nothing, save the discovery by General Ewell that the Federal army was moving. This intelligence was dispatched to General Lee on the evening of the 21st, and reached him at Souther's House, on the banks of the Po, where he was calmly reconnoitring the position of the enemy.

As soon as he read the note of General Ewell, he mounted his horse, saying, in his grave voice, to his staff, "Come, gentlemen;" and orders were sent to the army to prepare to move. The troops began their march on the same night, in the direction of Hanover Junction, which they reached on the evening of the 22d. When, on May 23d, General Grant reached the banks of the North Anna, he found Lee stationed on the south bank, ready to oppose his crossing.

The failure of General Grant to reach and seize upon the important point of Hanover Junction before the arrival of Lee, decided the fate of the plan of campaign originally devised by him. If the reader will glance at the map of Virginia, this fact will become apparent. Hanover Junction is the point where the Virginia Central and Richmond and Fredericksburg Railroads cross each other, and is situated in the angle of the North Anna and South Anna Rivers, which unite a short distance below to form the Pamunkey. Once in possession of this point, General Grant would have had easy communication with the excellent base of supplies at Aquia Creek; would have cut the Virginia Central Railroad; and a direct march southward would have enabled him to invest Richmond from the north and northwest, in accordance with his original plan. Lee had, however, reached the point first, and from that moment, unless the Southern force were driven from its position, the entire plan of campaign must necessarily be changed.

The great error of General Grant in this arduous campaign would seem to have been the feebleness of the attack which he here made upon Lee. The position of the Southern army was not formidable, and on his arrival they had had no time to erect defences. The river is not difficult of crossing, and the ground on the south bank gives no decided advantage to a force occupying it. In spite of these facts—which it is proper to say General Grant denies, however— nothing was effected, and but little attempted. A few words will sum up the operations of the armies during the two or three days. Reaching the river, General Grant threw a column across some miles up the stream, at a point known as Jericho Ford, where a brief but obstinate encounter ensued between Generals Hill and Warren, and this was followed by the capture of an old redoubt defending the Chesterfield bridge, near the railroad crossing, opposite Lee's right, which enabled another column to pass the stream at that point. These two successful passages of the river on Lee's left and right seemed to indicate a fixed intention on the part of his adversary to press both the Southern flanks, and bring on a decisive engagement; and, to coöperate in this plan, a third column was now thrown over opposite Lee's centre.

These movements were, however, promptly met. Lee retired his two wings, but struck suddenly with his centre at the force attempting to cross there; and then active operations on both sides ceased. In spite of having passed the river with the bulk of his army, and formed line of battle, General Grant resolved not to attack. His explanation of this is that Lee's position was found "stronger than either of his previous ones."

Such was the result of the able disposition of the Southern force at this important point. General Grant found his whole programme reversed, and, on the night of the 26th, silently withdrew and hastened down the north bank of the Pamunkey toward Hanovertown preceded by the cavalry of General Sheridan.

That officer had been detached from the army as it approached Spottsylvania Court-House, to make a rapid march toward Richmond, and destroy the Confederate communications. In this he partially succeeded, but, attempting to ride into Richmond, was repulsed with considerable loss. The only important result, indeed, of the expedition, was the death of General Stuart. This distinguished commander of General Lee's cavalry had been directed to pursue General Sheridan; had done so, with his customary promptness, and intercepted his column near Richmond, at a spot known as the Yellow Tavern; and here, in a stubborn engagement, in which Stuart strove to supply his want of troops by the fury of his attack, the great chief of cavalry was mortally wounded, and expired soon afterward. His fall was a grievous blow to General Lee's heart, as well as to the Southern cause. Endowed by nature with a courage which shrunk from nothing; active, energetic, of immense physical stamina, which enabled him to endure any amount of fatigue; devoted, heart and soul, to the cause in which he fought, and looking up to the commander of the army with childlike love and admiration, Stuart could be ill spared at this critical moment, and General Lee was plunged into the deepest melancholy at the intelligence of his death. When it reached him he retired from those around him, and remained for some time communing with his own heart and memory. When one of his staff entered, and spoke of Stuart, General Lee said, in a low voice, "I can scarcely think of him without weeping."

The command of the cavalry devolved upon General Hampton, and it was fought throughout the succeeding campaign with the nerve and efficiency of a great soldier; but Stuart had, as it were, formed and moulded it with his own hands; he was the first great commander of horse in the war; and it was hard for his successors, however great their genius, to compete with his memory. His name will thus remain that of the greatest and most prominent cavalry-officer of the war.

Crossing the Pamunkey at Hanovertown, after a rapid night-march, General Grant sent out a force toward Hanover Court-House to cut off Lee's retreat or discover his position. This resulted in nothing, since General Lee had not moved in that direction. He had, as soon as the movement of General Grant was discovered, put his lines in motion, directed his march across the country on the direct route to Cold Harbor, and, halting behind the Tottapotomoi, had formed his line there, to check the progress of his adversary on the main road from Hanovertown toward Richmond. For the third time, thus, General Grant had found his adversary in his path; and no generalship, or rapidity in the movement of his column, seemed sufficient to secure to him the advantages of a surprise. On each occasion the march of the Federal army had taken place in the night; from the Wilderness on the night of May 7th; from Spottsylvania on the night of May 21st; and from near the North Anna on the night of May 26th. Lee had imitated these movements of his opponent, interposing on each occasion, at the critical moment, in his path, and inviting battle. This last statement may be regarded as too strongly expressed, as it seems the opinion of Northern writers that Lee, in these movements, aimed only to maintain a strict defensive, and, by means of breastworks, simply keep his adversary at arm's length. This is an entire mistake. Confident of the efficiency of his army, small as it was, he was always desirous to bring on a decisive action, under favorable circumstances. General Early bears his testimony to the truth of this statement. "I happen to know," says this officer, "that General Lee had always the greatest anxiety to strike at Grant in the open field." During the whole movement from the Wilderness to Cold Harbor, the Confederate commander was in excellent spirits. When at Hanover Junction he spoke of the situation almost jocosely, and said to the venerable Dr. Gwathmey, speaking of General Grant, "If I can get one more pull at him, I will defeat him."

This expression does not seem to indicate any depression or want of confidence in his ability to meet General Grant in an open pitched battle. It may, however, be asked why, if such were his desire, he did not come out from behind his breastworks and fight. The reply is, that General Grant invariably defended his lines by breastworks as powerful as—in many cases much more powerful than—his adversary's. The opposing mounds of earth and trees along the routes of the two armies remain to prove the truth of what is here stated. At Cold Harbor, especially, the Federal works are veritable forts. In face of them, the theory that General Grant uniformly acted upon the offensive, without fear of offensive operations in turn on the part of Lee, will be found untenable. Nor is this statement made with the view of representing General Grant as over-cautious, or of detracting from his merit as a commander. It was, on the contrary, highly honorable to him, that, opposed to an adversary of such ability, he should have neglected nothing.

Reaching the Tottapotomoi, General Grant found his opponent in a strong position behind that sluggish water-course, prepared to dispute the road to Richmond; and it now became necessary to force the passage in his front, or, by another flank march, move still farther to the left, and endeavor to cross the Chickahominy somewhere in the vicinity of Cold Harbor. This last operation was determined upon by General Grant, and, sending his cavalry toward Cold Harbor, he moved rapidly in the same direction with his infantry. This movement was discovered at once by Lee; he sent Longstreet's corps forward, and, when the Federal army arrived, the Southern forces were drawn up in their front, between them and Richmond, thus barring, for the fourth time in the campaign, the road to the capital.

During these movements, nearly continuous fighting had taken place between the opposing columns, which clung to each other, as it were, each shaping its march more or less by that of the other. At last they had reached the ground upon which the obstinate struggle of June, 1862, had taken place, and it now became necessary for General Grant either to form some new plan of campaign, or, by throwing his whole army, in one great mass, against his adversary, break through all obstacles, cross the Chickahominy, and seize upon Richmond. This was now resolved upon.

Heavy fighting took place on June 2d, near Bethesda Church and at other points, while the armies were coming into position; but this was felt to be but the preface to the greater struggle which General Lee now clearly divined. It came without loss of time. On the morning of the 3d of June, soon after daylight, General Grant threw his whole army straightforward against Lee's front—all along his line. The conflict which followed was one of those bloody grapples, rather than battles, which, discarding all manoeuvring or brain-work in the commanders, depend the result upon the brute strength of the forces engaged. The action did not last half an hour, and, in that time, the Federal loss was thirteen thousand men. When General Lee sent a messenger to A.P. Hill, asking the result of the assault on his part of the line, Hill took the officer with him in front of his works, and, pointing to the dead bodies which were literally lying upon each other, said: "Tell General Lee it is the same all along my front."

The Federal army had, indeed, sustained a blow so heavy, that even the constant mind and fixed resolution of General Grant and the Federal authorities seem to have been shaken. The war seemed hopeless to many persons in the North after the frightful bloodshed of this thirty minutes at Cold Harbor, of which fact there is sufficient proof. "So gloomy," says a Northern historian,[1] "was the military outlook after the action on the Chickahominy, and to such a degree, by consequence, had the moral spring of the public mind become relaxed, that there was at this time great danger of a collapse of the war. The history of this conflict, truthfully written, will show this. The archives of the State Department, when one day made public, will show how deeply the Government was affected by the want of military success, and to what resolutions the Executive had in consequence come. Had not success elsewhere come to brighten the horizon, it would have been difficult to have raised new forces to recruit the Army of the Potomac, which, shaken in its structure, its valor quenched in blood, and thousands of its ablest officers killed and wounded, was the Army of the Potomac no more."

[Footnote 1: Mr. Swinton, in his able and candid "Campaigns of the Army of the Potomac."]

The campaign of one month—from May 4th to June 4th—had cost the Federal commander sixty thousand men and three thousand officers—numbers which are given on the authority of Federal historians—while the loss of Lee did not exceed eighteen thousand. The result would seem an unfavorable comment upon the choice of the route across the country from Culpepper instead of that by the James. General McClellan, two years before, had reached Cold Harbor with trifling losses. To attain the same point had cost General Grant a frightful number of lives. Nor could it be said that he had any important successes to offset this loss. He had not defeated his adversary in any of the battle-fields of the campaign; nor did it seem that he had stricken him any serious blow. The Army of Northern Virginia, not reënforced until it reached Hanover Junction, and then only by about nine thousand men under Generals Breckinridge and Pickett, had held its ground against the large force opposed to it; had repulsed every assault; and, in a final trial of strength with a force largely its superior, had inflicted upon the enemy, in about an hour, a loss of thirteen thousand men.

These facts, highly honorable to Lee and his troops, are the plainest and most compendious comment we can make upon the campaign. The whole movement of General Grant across Virginia is, indeed, now conceded even by his admirers to have been unfortunate. It failed to accomplish the end expected from it—the investment of Richmond on the north and west—and the lives of about sixty thousand men were, it would seem, unnecessarily lost, to reach a position which might have been attained with losses comparatively trifling, and without the unfortunate prestige of defeat.

VI.

FIRST BATTLES AT PETERSBURG.

General Lee remained facing his adversary in his lines at Cold Harbor, for many days after the bloody struggle of the 3d of June, confident of his ability to repulse any new attack, and completely barring the way to Richmond. The Federal campaign, it was now seen, was at an end on that line, and it was obvious that General Grant must adopt some other plan, in spite of his determination expressed in the beginning of the campaign, to "fight it out on that line if it took all the summer." The summer was but begun, and further fighting on that line was hopeless. Under these circumstances the Federal commander resolved to give up the attempt to assail Richmond from the north or east, and by a rapid movement to Petersburg, seize upon that place, cut the Confederate railroads leading southward, and thus compel an evacuation of the capital.

[Illustration: Map of Petersburg and Environs.]

It would be interesting to inquire what the course of General Lee would have been in the event of the success of this plan, and how the war would have resulted. It would seem that, under such circumstances, his only resource would have been to retire with his army in the direction of Lynchburg, where his communications would have remained open with the south and west. If driven from that point, the fastnesses of the Alleghanies were at hand; and, contemplating afterward the possibility of being forced to take refuge there, he said: "With my army in the mountains of Virginia, I could carry on this war for twenty years longer." That spectacle was lost to the world—Lee and his army fighting from mountain fastness to mountain fastness—and the annals of war are not illustrated by a chapter so strange. That Lee was confident of his ability to carry on such a struggle successfully is certain; and Washington had conceived the same idea in the old Revolution, when he said that if he were driven from the seaboard he would take refuge in West Augusta, and thereby prolong the war interminably.

To return from these speculations to the narrative of events. General Grant remained in front of Lee until the 12th of June, when, moving again by his left flank, he crossed the Chickahominy, proceeded in the direction of City Point, at which place the Appomattox and James Rivers mingle their waters, and, crossing the James on pontoons, hastened forward in order to seize upon Petersburg. This important undertaking had been strangely neglected by Major-General Butler, who, in obedience to General Grant's orders, had sailed from Fortress Monroe on the 4th of May, reached Bermuda Hundred, the peninsula opposite City Point, made by a remarkable bend in James River, and proceeded to intrench himself. It was in his power on his arrival to have seized upon Petersburg, but this he failed to do at that time, and the appearance of a force under General Beauregard, from the south, soon induced him to give his entire attention to his own safety. An attack by Beauregard had been promptly made, which nearly resulted in General Butler's destruction. He succeeded, however, in retiring behind his works across the neck of the Peninsula, in which he now found himself completely shut up; and so powerless was his situation, with his large force of thirty thousand men, that General Grant wrote, "His army was as completely shut off ... as if it had been in a bottle strongly corked."

The attempt of General Grant to seize upon Petersburg by a surprise failed. His forces were not able to reach the vicinity of the place until the 15th, when they were bravely opposed behind impromptu works by a body of local troops, who fought like regular soldiers, and succeeded in holding the works until night ended the contest.

When morning came long lines were seen defiling into the breastworks, and the familiar battle-flags of the Army of Northern Virginia rose above the long line of bayonets giving assurance that the possession of Petersburg would be obstinately disputed.

General Lee had moved with his accustomed celerity, and, as usual, without that loss of time which results from doubt of an adversary's intentions. If General Grant retired without another battle on the Chickahominy, it was obvious to Lee that he must design one of two things: either to advance upon Richmond from the direction of Charles City, or attempt a campaign against the capital from the south of James River. Lee seems at once to have satisfied himself that the latter was the design. An inconsiderable force was sent to feel the enemy near the White-Oak Swamp; he was encountered there in some force, but, satisfied that this was a feint to mislead him, General Lee proceeded to cross the James River above Drury's Bluff, near "Wilton," and concentrate his army at Petersburg. On the 16th he was in face of his adversary there. General Grant had adopted the plan of campaign which Lee expected him to adopt. General McClellan had not been permitted in 1862 to carry out the same plan; it was now undertaken by General Grant, who sustained better relations toward the Government, and the result would seem to indicate that General McClellan was, after all, a soldier of sound views.

As soon as General Lee reached Petersburg, he began promptly to draw a regular line of earthworks around the city, to the east and south, for its defence. It was obvious that General Grant would lose no time in striking at him, in order to take advantage of the slight character of the defences already existing; and this anticipation was speedily realized. General Lee had scarcely gotten his forces in position on the 16th when he was furiously attacked, and such was the weight of this assault that Lee was forced from his advanced position, east of the city, behind his second line of works, by this time well forward in process of construction. Against this new line General Grant threw heavy forces, in attack after attack, on the 17th and 18th, losing, it is said, more than four thousand men, but effecting nothing. On the 21st General Lee was called upon to meet a more formidable assault than any of the preceding ones—this time more to his right, in the vicinity of the Weldon Railroad, which runs southward from Petersburg. A heavy line was advanced in that quarter by the enemy; but, observing that an interval had been left between two of their corps, General Lee threw forward a column under General Hill, cut the Federal lines, and repulsed their attack, bearing off nearly three thousand prisoners.

On the same night an important cavalry expedition, consisting of the divisions of General Wilson and Kautz, numbering about six thousand horse, was sent westward to cut the Weldon, Southside, and Danville Railroads, which connected the Southern army with the South and West. This raid resulted in apparently great but really unimportant injury to the Confederate communications against which it was directed. The Federal cavalry tore up large portions of the tracks of all three railroads, burning the wood-work, and laying waste the country around; but the further results of the expedition were unfavorable. They were pursued and harassed by a small body of cavalry under General W. H.F. Lee, and, on their return in the direction of Reams's Station, were met near Sapponey Church by a force of fifteen hundred cavalry under General Hampton. That energetic officer at once attacked; the fighting continued furiously throughout the entire night, and at dawn the Federal horse retreated in confusion. Their misfortunes were not, however, ended. Near Reams's, at which point they attempted to cross the Weldon Railroad, they were met by General Fitz Lee's horsemen and about two hundred infantry under General Mahone, and this force completed their discomfiture. After a brief attempt to force their way through the unforeseen obstacle, they broke in disorder, leaving behind them twelve pieces of artillery, and more than a thousand prisoners, and, with foaming and exhausted horses, regained the Federal lines.

Such was the result of an expedition from which General Grant probably expected much. The damage done to Lee's communications was inconsiderable, and did not repay the Federal commander for the losses sustained. The railroads were soon repaired and in working order again; and the Federal cavalry was for the time rendered unfit for further operations.

It was now the end of June, and every attempt made by General Grant to force Lee's lines had proved unsuccessful. It was apparent that surprise of the able commander of the Confederate army was hopeless. His works were growing stronger every day, and nothing was left to his great adversary but to lay regular siege to the long line of fortifications; to draw lines for the protection of his own front from attack; and, by gradually extending his left, reach out toward the Weldon and Southside Railroads.

To obtain possession of these roads was from this time General Grant's great object; and all his movements were shaped by that paramount consideration.

VII.

THE SIEGE OF RICHMOND BEGUN.

The first days of July, 1864, witnessed, at Petersburg, the commencement of a series of military manoeuvres, for which few, if any, precedents existed in all the annals of war. An army of forty or fifty thousand men, intrenched along a line extending finally over a distance of nearly forty miles, was defending, against a force of about thrice its numbers, a capital more than twenty miles in its rear; and, from July of one year to April of the next, there never was a moment when, to have broken through this line, would not have terminated the war, and resulted in the destruction of the Confederacy.

A few words in reference to the topography of the country and the situation will show this. Petersburg is twenty-two miles south of Richmond, and is connected with the South and West by the Weldon and Southside Railroads, which latter road crosses the Danville Railroad, the main line of communication between the capital and the Gulf States. With the enemy once holding these roads and those north of the city, as they were preparing to do, the capital would be isolated, and the Confederate Government must evacuate Virginia. In that event the Army of Northern Virginia had also nothing left to it but retreat. Virginia must be abandoned; the Federal authority would be extended over the oldest and one of the largest and most important members of the Confederacy; and, under circumstances so adverse, it might well be a question whether, disheartened as they would be by the loss of so powerful an ally, the other States of the Confederacy would have sufficient resolution to continue the contest.

These considerations are said to have been fully weighed by General Lee, whose far-reaching military sagacity divined the exact situation of affairs, and the probable results of a conflict so unequal as that which General Grant now forced upon him. We have noticed, on a preceding page, his opinions upon this subject, expressed to a confidential friend as far back as 1862. He then declared that the true line of assault upon Richmond was that now adopted by General Grant. As long as the capital was assailed from the north or the east, he might hope with some reason, by hard fighting, to repulse the assault, and hold Richmond. But, with an enemy at Petersburg, threatening with a large force the Southern railroads, it was obviously only a question of time when Richmond, and consequently Virginia, must be abandoned.

General Lee, we repeat, fully realized the facts here stated, when his adversary, giving up all other lines, crossed James River to Petersburg. Lee is said, we know not with what truth, to have coolly recommended an evacuation of Richmond. But this met with no favor. A powerful party, including both the friends and enemies of the Executive, spoke of the movement as a "pernicious idea." If recommended by Lee, it was speedily abandoned, and all the energies of the Government were concentrated upon the difficult task of holding the enemy at arm's length south of the Appomattox and in Charles City.

In a few weeks after the appearance of the adversaries opposite each other at Petersburg, the lines of leaguer and defence were drawn, and the long struggle began. General Grant had crossed a force into Charles City, on the north bank of James River, and thus menaced Richmond with an assault from that quarter. His line extended thence across the neck of the Peninsula of Bermuda Hundred, and east and south of Petersburg, where, day by day, it gradually reached westward, approaching nearer and nearer to the railroads feeding the Southern army and capital. Lee's line conformed itself to that of his adversary. In addition to the works east and southeast of Richmond, an exterior chain of defences had been drawn, facing the hostile force near Deep Bottom; and the river at Drury's Bluff, a fortification of some strength, had been guarded, by sunken obstructions, against the approach of the Federal gunboats. The Southern lines then continued, facing those of the enemy north of the Appomattox, and, crossing that stream, extended around the city of Petersburg, gradually moving westward in conformity with the works of General Grant. A glance at the accompanying diagram will clearly indicate the positions and relations to each other of the Federal and Confederate works. These will show that the real struggle was anticipated, by both commanders, west of Petersburg; and, as the days wore on, it was more and more apparent that somewhere in the vicinity of Dinwiddie Court-House the last great wrestle of the opposing armies must take place.

To that conclusive trial of strength we shall advance with as few interruptions as possible. The operations of the two armies at Petersburg do not possess, for the general reader, that dramatic interest which is found in battles such as those of Chancellorsville and Gettysburg, deciding for the time the fates of great campaigns. At Petersburg the fighting seemed to decide little, and the bloody collisions had no names. The day of pitched battles, indeed, seemed past. It was one long battle, day and night, week after week, and month after month—during the heat of summer, the sad hours of autumn, and the cold days and nights of winter. It was, in fact, the siege of Richmond which General Grant had undertaken, and the fighting consisted less of battles, in the ordinary acceptation of that word, than of attempts to break through the lines of his adversary—now north of James River, now east of Petersburg, now at some point in the long chain of redans which guarded the approaches to the coveted Southside Railroad, which, once in possession of the Federal commander, would give him victory.

Of this long, obstinate, and bloody struggle we shall describe only those prominent incidents which rose above the rest with a species of dramatic splendor. For the full narrative the reader must have recourse to military histories aiming to chronicle the operations of each corps, division, and brigade in the two armies—a minuteness of detail beyond our scope, and probably not desired by those who will peruse these pages.

VIII.
LEE THREATENS WASHINGTON.

The month of July began and went upon its way, with incessant fighting all along the Confederate front, both north of James River and south of the Appomattox. General Grant was thus engaged in the persistent effort to, at some point, break through his opponent's works, when intelligence suddenly reached him, by telegraph from Washington, that a strong Confederate column had advanced down the Shenandoah Valley, crossed the Potomac, and was rapidly moving eastward in the direction of the Federal capital.

This portentous incident was the result of a plan of great boldness devised by General Lee, from which he expected much. A few words will explain this plan.

A portion of General Grant's plan of campaign had been an advance up the Valley, and another from Western Virginia, toward the Lynchburg and Tennessee Railroad—the two columns to coöperate with the main army by cutting the Confederate communications. The column in Western Virginia effected little, but that in the Valley, under General Hunter, hastened forward, almost unopposed, from the small numbers of the Southern force, and early in June threatened Lynchburg. The news reached Lee at Cold Harbor soon after his battle there with General Grant, and he promptly detached General Early, at the head of about eight thousand men, with orders to "move to the Valley through Swift-Run Gap, or Brown's Gap, attack Hunter, and then cross the Potomac and threaten Washington." [Footnote: This statement of his orders was derived from Lieutenant-General Early.]

General Early, an officer of great energy and intrepidity, moved without loss of time, and an engagement ensued between him and General Hunter near Lynchburg. The battle was soon decided. General Hunter, who had more cruelly oppressed the inhabitants of the Valley than even General Milroy, was completely defeated, driven in disordered flight toward the Ohio, and Early hastened down the Valley, and thence into Maryland, with the view of threatening Washington, as he had been ordered to do by Lee. His march was exceedingly rapid, and he found the road unobstructed until he reached the Monocacy near Frederick City, where he was opposed by a force under General Wallace. This force he attacked, and soon drove from the field; he then pressed forward, and on the 11th of July came in sight of Washington.

It was the intelligence of this advance of a Confederate force into Maryland, and toward the capital, which came to startle General Grant while he was hotly engaged with Lee at Petersburg. The Washington authorities seem to have been completely unnerved, and to have regarded the capture of the city as nearly inevitable. General Grant, however, stood firm, and did not permit the terror of the civil authorities to affect him. He sent forward to Washington two army corps, and these arrived just in time. If it had been in the power of General Early to capture Washington—which seems questionable—the opportunity was lost. He found himself compelled to retire across the Potomac again to avoid an attack in his rear; and this he effected without loss, taking up, in accordance with orders from Lee, a position in the Valley, where he remained for some months a standing threat to the enemy.

Such was the famous march of General Early to Washington; and there seems at present little reason to doubt that the Federal capital had a narrow escape from capture by the Confederates. What the result of so singular an event would have been, it is difficult to say; but it is certain that it would have put an end to General Grant's entire campaign at Petersburg. Then—but speculations of this character are simply loss of time. The city was not captured; the war went upon its way, and was destined to terminate by pure exhaustion of one of the combatants, unaffected by *coups de main* in any part of the theatre of conflict.

We have briefly spoken of the engagement between Generals Early and Hunter, near Lynchburg, and the abrupt retreat of the latter to the western mountains and thence toward the Ohio. It may interest the reader to know General Lee's views on the subject of this retreat, which, it seems, were drawn from him by a letter addressed to him by General Hunter:

"As soon after the war as mail communications were opened," writes the gentleman of high character from whom we derive this incident, "General David Hunter wrote to General Lee, begging that he would answer him frankly on two points:"

'I. His (Hunter's) campaign in 1864 was undertaken on information received by General Halleck that General Lee was about to detach forty thousand picked troops to send to Georgia. Did not his (Hunter's) move prevent this?

'II. When he found it necessary to retreat from Lynchburg, did he not take the most feasible route?'

General Lee wrote a very courteous reply, in which he said:

'I. General Halleck was misinformed. I had *no troops to spare*, and forty thousand would have taken nearly my whole army.

'II. I am not advised as to the motives which induced you to adopt your line of retreat, and am not, perhaps, competent to judge of the question; *but I certainly expected you to retreat by way* of the Shenandoah Valley.'

"General Hunter," adds our correspondent, "never published this letter, but I heard General Lee tell of it one day with evident pleasure."

Lee's opinion of the military abilities of both Generals Hunter and Sheridan was indeed far from flattering. He regarded those two commanders—especially General Sheridan—as enjoying reputations solely conferred upon them by the exhaustion of the resources of the Confederacy, and not warranted by any military efficiency in themselves.

IX.

THE MINE EXPLOSION.

The end of the month of July was now approaching, and every attempt made by General Grant to break through Lee's lines had resulted in failure. At every point which he assailed, an armed force, sufficient to repulse his most vigorous attacks, seemed to spring from the earth; and no movement of the Federal forces, however sudden and rapid, had been able to take the Confederate commander unawares. The campaign was apparently settling down into stubborn fighting, day and night, in which the object of General Grant was to carry out his programme of attrition. Such was the feeling in both armies when, at dawn on the 30th of July, a loud explosion, heard for thirty miles, took place on the lines near Petersburg, and a vast column of smoke, shooting upward to a great height, seemed to indicate the blowing up of an extensive magazine.

Instead of a magazine, it was a mine which had thus been exploded; and the incident was not the least singular of a campaign unlike any which had preceded it.

The plan of forming a breach in the Southern works, by exploding a mine beneath them, is said by Northern writers to have originated with a subordinate officer of the Federal army, who, observing the close proximity of the opposing works near Petersburg, conceived it feasible to construct a subterranean gallery, reaching beneath those of General Lee. The undertaking was begun, the earth being carried off in cracker-boxes; and such was the steady persistence of the workmen that a gallery five hundred feet long, with lateral openings beneath the Confederate works, was soon finished; and in these lateral recesses was placed a large amount of powder.

All was now ready, and the question was how to utilize the explosion. General Grant decided to follow it by a sudden charge through the breach, seize a crest in rear, and thus interpose a force directly in the centre of Lee's line. A singular discussion, however, arose, and caused some embarrassment. Should the assaulting column consist of white or negro troops? This question was decided, General Grant afterward declared, by "pulling straws or tossing coppers"—the white troops were the fortunate or unfortunate ones—and on the morning of July 30th the mine was exploded. The effect was frightful, and the incident will long be remembered by those present and escaping unharmed. The small Southern force and artillery immediately above the mine were hurled into the air. An opening, one hundred and fifty feet long, sixty feet wide, and thirty feet deep, suddenly appeared, where a moment before had extended the Confederate earthworks; and the Federal division, selected for the charge, rushed forward to pierce the opening.

The result did not justify the sanguine expectations which seem to have been excited in the breasts of the Federal officers. A Southern writer thus describes what ensued:

"The 'white division' charged, reached the crater, stumbled over the *débris*, were suddenly met by a merciless fire of artillery, enfilading them right and left, and of infantry fusillading them in front; faltered, hesitated, were badly led, lost heart, gave up the plan of seizing the crest in rear, huddled into the crater, man on top of man, company mingled with company; and upon this disordered, unstrung, quivering mass of human beings, white and black—for the black troops had followed—was poured a hurricane of shot, shell, canister, musketry, which made the hideous crater a slaughter-pen, horrible and frightful beyond the power of words. All order was lost; all idea of charging the crest abandoned. Lee's infantry was seen concentrating for the carnival of death; his artillery was massing to destroy the remnants of the charging divisions; those who deserted the crater, to scramble over the *débris* and run back, were shot down; then all that was left to the shuddering mass of blacks and whites in the pit was to shrink lower, evade the horrible *mitraille*, and wait for a charge of their friends to rescue them or surrender."

These sentences sufficiently describe the painful scene which followed the explosion of the mine. The charging column was unable to advance in face of the very heavy fire directed upon them by the Southern infantry and artillery; and the effect of this fire was so appalling that General Mahone, commanding at the spot, is said to have ordered it to cease, adding that the spectacle made him sick. The Federal forces finally succeeded in making their way back, with a loss of about four thousand prisoners; and General Lee, whose losses had been small, reëstablished his line without interruption.

Before passing from this incident, a singular circumstance connected with it is deserving of mention. This was the declaration of the Congressional Committee, which in due time investigated the whole affair.

The conclusion of the committee was not flattering to the veteran Army of the Potomac. The report declared that "the first and great cause of disaster was the employment of white instead of black troops to make the charge."

X.

END OF THE CAMPAIGN OF 1864.

Throughout the months of August and September, Lee continued to be attacked at various points along his entire front, but succeeded in repulsing every assault. General Grant's design may be said, in general terms, to have been a steady extension of his left toward the Confederate communications west of Petersburg, while taking the chances, by attacks north of James River, to break through in that quarter and seize upon Richmond. It is probable that his hopes of effecting the last-mentioned object were small; but operations in that direction promised the more probable result of causing Lee to weaken his right, and thus uncover the Southside Railroad.

An indecisive attack on the north of James River was followed, toward the end of August, by a heavy advance, to seize upon the Weldon Railroad near Petersburg. In this General Grant succeeded, an event clearly foreseen by Lee, who had long before informed the authorities that he could not hold this road. General Grant followed up this success by sending heavy forces to seize Reams's Station, on the same road, farther south, and afterward to destroy it to Hicksford— which, however, effected less favorable results, Lee meeting and defeating both forces after obstinate engagements, in which the Federal troops lost heavily, and were compelled to retreat.

These varying successes did not, however, materially affect the general result. The Federal left gradually reached farther and farther westward, until finally it had passed the Vaughan, Squirrel Level, and other roads, running south-westward from Petersburg, and in October was established on the left bank of Hatcher's Run, which unites with Gravelly Run to form the Rowanty. It was now obvious that a further extension of the Federal left would probably enable General Grant to seize upon the Southside Railroad. An energetic attempt was speedily made by him to effect this important object, to which it is said he attached great importance from its anticipated bearing on the approaching presidential election.

On the 27th of October a heavy column was thrown across Hatcher's Run, in the vicinity of Burgess's Mill, on the Boydton Road, and an obstinate attack was made on Lee's lines there with the view of breaking through to the Southside Road. In this, however, General Grant did not succeed. His column was met in front and flank by Generals Hampton—who here lost his brave son, Preston—and W.H.F. Lee, with dismounted sharp-shooters; infantry was hastened to the threatened point by General Lee, and, after an obstinate struggle, the Federal force was driven back. General Lee reporting that General Mahone charged and "broke three lines of battle."[1]

[Footnote 1: *Dispatch of Lee, October* 28, 1864.—It was the habit of General Lee, throughout the last campaign of the war, to send to Richmond, from time to time, brief dispatches announcing whatever occurred along the lines; and these, in the absence of official reports of these occurrences on the Confederate side, are valuable records of the progress of affairs. These brief summaries are reliable from the absence of all exaggeration, but cannot be depended upon by the historian, for a very singular reason, namely, that almost invariably the Confederate successes are understated. On the present occasion, the Federal loss in prisoners near Burgess's Mill and east of Richmond—where General Grant had attacked at the same time to effect a diversion—are put down by General Lee at eight hundred, whereas thirteen hundred and sixty-five were received at Richmond.

Lee's dispatch of October 28th is here given, as a specimen of these brief military reports.

HEADQUARTERS ARMY NORTHERN VIRGINIA,
October 28, 1864.
Hon. Secretary of War.

General Hill reports that the attack of General Heth upon the enemy on the Boydton Plank-road, mentioned in my dispatch last evening, was made by three brigades under General Mahone in front, and General Hampton in the rear. Mahone captured four hundred prisoners, three stand of colors, and six pieces of artillery. The latter could not be brought off, the enemy having possession of the bridge.

In the attack subsequently made by the enemy General Mahone broke three lines of battle, and during the night the enemy retreated from the Boydton Road, leaving his wounded and more than two hundred and fifty dead on the field.

About nine o'clock P.M. a small force assaulted and took possession of our works on the Baxter Road, in front of Petersburg, but were soon driven out.

On the Williamsburg Road General Field captured upward of four hundred prisoners and seven stand of colors. The enemy left a number of dead in front of our works, and to-day retreated to his former position.

R.E. Lee]

With this repulse of the Federal forces terminated active operations of importance for the year; and but one other attempt was made, during the winter, to gain ground on the left. This took place early in February, and resulted in failure like the former—the Confederates losing, however, the brave General John Pegram.

The presidential election at the North had been decided in favor of Mr. Lincoln—General McClellan and Mr. Pendleton, the supposed advocates of peace, suffering defeat. The significance of this fact was unmistakable. It was now seen that unless the Confederates fought their way to independence, there was no hope of a favorable termination of the war, and this conclusion was courageously faced by General Lee. The outlook for the coming year was far from encouraging; the resources of the Confederacy were steadily being reduced; her coasts were blockaded; her armies were diminishing; discouragement seemed slowly to be invading every heart—but, in the midst of this general foreboding, the commander of the Army of Northern Virginia retained an august composure; and, conversing with one of the Southern Senators, said, "For myself, I intend to die sword in hand."

That his sense of duty did not afterward permit him to do so, was perhaps one of the bitterest pangs of his whole life.

XI.
LEE IN THE WINTER OF 1864-'65.

Before entering upon the narrative of the last and decisive campaign of the war, we shall speak of the personal demeanor of General Lee at this time, and endeavor to account for a circumstance which astonished many persons—his surprising equanimity, and even cheerfulness, under the pressure of cares sufficient, it would seem, to crush the most powerful organization.

He had established his headquarters a mile or two west of Petersburg, on the Cox Road, nearly opposite his centre, and here he seemed to await whatever the future would bring with a tranquillity which was a source of surprise and admiration to all who were thrown in contact with him. Many persons will bear their testimony to this extraordinary composure. His countenance seldom, if ever, exhibited the least traces of anxiety, but was firm, hopeful, and encouraged those around him in the belief that he was still confident of success. That he did not, however, look forward with any thing like hope to such success, we have endeavored already to show. From the first, he seems to have regarded his situation, unless his army were largely reënforced, as almost desperate; those reënforcements did not come; and yet, as he saw his numbers day by day decreasing, and General Grant's increasing a still larger ratio, he retained his courage, confronting the misfortunes closing in upon him with unmoved composure, and at no time seemed to lose his "heart of hope."

Of this phenomenon the explanation has been sought in the constitutional courage of the individual, and that instinctive rebound against fate which takes place in great organizations. This explanation, doubtless, is not without a certain amount of truth; but an attentive consideration of the principles which guided this eminent soldier throughout his career, will show that his equanimity, at a moment so trying, was due to another and more controlling sentiment. This sentiment was his devotion to Duty—"the sublimest word in our language." Throughout his entire life he had sought to discover and perform his duty, without regard to consequences. That had been with him the great question in April, 1861, when the war broke out: he had decided in his own mind what he ought to do, and had not hesitated.

From that time forward he continued to do what Duty commanded without a murmur. In the obscure campaign of Western Virginia—in the unnoted work of fortifying the Southern coast—in the great campaigns which he had subsequently fought—and everywhere, his consciousness of having performed his duty to the best of his knowledge and ability sustained him. It sustained him, above all, at Gettysburg, where he had done his best, giving him strength to take upon himself the responsibility of that disaster; and, now, in these last dark days at Petersburg, it must have been the sense of having done his whole duty, and expended upon the cause every energy of his being, which enabled him to meet the approaching catastrophe with a calmness which seemed to those around him almost sublime.

If this be not the explanation of the composure of General Lee, throughout the last great struggle with the Federal Army, the writer of these pages is at a loss to account for it. The phenomenon was plain to all eyes, and crowned the soldier with a glory greater than that which he had derived from his most decisive military successes. Great and unmoved in the dark hour as in the bright, he seemed to have determined to perform his duty to the last, and to shape his conduct, under whatever pressure of disaster, upon the two maxims, "Do your duty," and "Human virtue should be equal to human calamity."

There is little reason to doubt that General Lee saw this "calamity" coming, for the effort to reënforce his small army with fresh levies seemed hopeless. The reasons for this unfortunate state of things must be sought elsewhere. The unfortunate fact will be stated, without comment, that, while the Federal army was regularly and largely reënforced, so that its numbers at no time fell below one hundred and fifty thousand men. Lee's entire force at Petersburg at no time reached sixty thousand, and in the spring of 1865, when he still continued to hold his long line of defences, numbered scarcely half of sixty thousand. This was the primary cause of the failure of the struggle. General Grant's immense hammer continued to beat upon his adversary, wearing away his strength day by day. No new troops arrived to take the places of those who had fallen; and General Lee saw, drawing closer and closer, the inevitable hour when, driven from his works, or with the Federal army upon his communications, he must cut his way southward or surrender.

A last circumstance in reference to General Lee's position at this time should be stated; the fact that, from the autumn of 1864 to the end in the spring of 1865, he was felt by the country and the army to be the sole hope of the Confederacy. To him alone now all men looked as the *deus ex machinâ* to extricate them from the dangers surrounding them. This sentiment needed no expression in words. It was seen in the faces and the very tones of voice of all. Old men visited him, and begged him with faltering voices not to expose himself, for, if he were killed, all would be lost. The troops followed him with their eyes, or their cheers, whenever he appeared, feeling a singular sense of confidence from the presence of the gray-haired soldier in his plain uniform, and assured that, as long as Lee led them, the cause was safe. All classes of the people thus regarded the fate of the Confederacy as resting, not partially, but solely, upon the shoulders of Lee; and, although he was not entitled by his rank in the service to direct operations in other quarters than Virginia, there was a very general desire that the whole conduct of the war everywhere should be intrusted to his hands. This was done, as will be seen, toward the spring of 1865, but it was too late.

These notices of General Lee individually are necessary to a clear comprehension of the concluding incidents of the great conflict. It is doubtful if, in any other struggle of history, the hopes of a people were more entirely wrapped up in a single individual. All criticisms of the eminent soldier had long since been silenced, and it may, indeed, be said that something like a superstitious confidence in his fortunes had become widely disseminated. It was the general sentiment, even when Lee himself saw the end surely approaching, that all was safe while he remained in command of the army. This hallucination must have greatly pained him, for no one ever saw more clearly, or was less blinded by irrational confidence. Lee fully understood and represented to the civil authorities—with whom his relations were perfectly friendly and cordial—that if his lines were broken at any point, the fate of the campaign was sealed. Feeling this truth, of which his military sagacity left him in no doubt, he had to bear the further weight of that general confidence which he did not share. He did not complain, however, or in any manner indicate the desperate straits to which he had come. He called for fresh troops to supply his losses; when they did not arrive he continued to oppose his powerful adversary with the remnant still at his command. These were now more like old comrades than mere private soldiers under his orders. What was left of the army was its best material. The fires of battle had tested the metal, and that which emerged from the furnace was gold free from alloy. The men remaining with Lee were those whom no peril of the cause in which they were fighting could dishearten or prompt to desert or even temporarily absent themselves from the Southern standard; and this *corps d' élite* was devoted wholly to their commander. For this devotion they certainly had valid reason. Never had leader exhibited a more systematic, unfailing, and almost tender care of his troops. Lee seemed to feel that these veterans in their ragged jackets, with their gaunt faces, were personal friends of his own, who were entitled to his most affectionate exertions for their welfare. His calls on the civil authorities in their behalf were unceasing. The burden of these demands was that, unless his men's wants were attended to, the Southern cause was lost; and it plainly revolted his sense of the fitness of things that men upon whom depended the fate of the South should be shoeless, in tatters, and forced to subsist on a quarter of a pound of rancid bacon and a little corn bread, when thousands remaining out of the army, and dodging the enrolling-officers, were well clothed and fed, and never heard the whistle of a bullet. The men understood this care for them, and returned the affectionate solicitude of their commander in full. He was now their ideal of a leader, and all that he did was perfect in their eyes. All awe of him had long since left them—they understood what treasures of kindness and simplicity lay under the grave exterior. The tattered privates approached the commander-in-chief without embarrassment, and his reception of them was such as to make them love him more than ever. Had we space we might dwell upon this marked respect and attention paid by General Lee to his private soldiers. He seemed to think them more worthy of marks of regard than his highest officers. And there was never the least air of condescension in him when thrown with them, but a perfect simplicity, kindness, and unaffected sympathy, which went to their hearts. This was almost a natural gift with Lee, and arose from the genuine goodness of his heart. His feeling toward his soldiers is shown in an incident which occurred at this time, and was thus related in one of the Richmond journals: "A gentleman who was in the train from this city to Petersburg, a very cold morning not long ago, tells us his attention was attracted by the efforts of a young soldier, with his arm in a sling, to get his overcoat on. His teeth, as well as his sound arm, were brought into use to effect the object; but, in the midst of his efforts, an officer rose from his seat, advanced to him, and very carefully and tenderly assisted him, drawing the coat gently over his wounded arm, and buttoning it up comfortably; then, with a few kind and pleasant words, returning to his seat. Now the officer in question was not clad in gorgeous uniform, with a brilliant wreath upon his collar, and a multitude of gilt lines upon the sleeves, resembling the famous labyrinth of Crete, but he was clad in a simple suit of gray, distinguished from the garb of a civilian only by the three stars which every Confederate colonel in the service, by the regulations, is entitled to wear. And yet he was no other than our chief, General Robert E. Lee, who is not braver than he is good and modest."

To terminate this brief sketch of General Lee, personally, in the winter of 1864. He looked much older than at the beginning of the war, but by no means less hardy or robust. On the contrary, the arduous campaigns through which he had passed seemed to have hardened him—developing to the highest degree the native strength of his physical organization. His cheeks were ruddy, and his eye had that clear light which indicates the presence of the calm, self-poised will. But his hair had grown gray, like his beard and mustache, which were worn short and well-trimmed. His dress, as always, was a plain and serviceable gray uniform, with no indications of rank save the stars on the collar. Cavalry-boots reached nearly to his knees, and he seldom wore any weapon. A broad-brimmed gray-felt hat rested low upon the forehead; and the movements of this soldierly figure were as firm, measured, and imposing, as ever. It was impossible to discern in General Lee any evidences of impaired strength, or any trace of the wearing hardships through which he had passed. He seemed made of iron, and would remain in his saddle all day, and then at his desk half the night, without apparently feeling any fatigue. He was still almost an anchorite in his personal habits, and lived so poorly that it is said he was compelled to borrow a small piece of meat when unexpected visitors dined with him.

Such, in brief outline, was the individual upon whose shoulders, in the last months of 1864 and the early part of 1865, rested the Southern Confederacy.

XII.

THE SITUATION AT THE BEGINNING OF 1865.

In approaching the narrative of the last tragic scenes of the Confederate struggle, the writer of these pages experiences emotions of sadness which will probably be shared by not a few even of those readers whose sympathies, from the nature of things, were on the side of the North. To doubt this would be painful, and would indicate a contempt for human nature. Not only in the eyes of his friends and followers, but even in the eyes of his bitterest enemies, Lee must surely have appeared great and noble. Right or wrong in the struggle, he believed that he was performing his duty; and the brave army at his back, which had fought so heroically, were inspired by the same sentiment, and risked all on the issue.

This great soldier was now about to suffer the cruellest pang which the spite of Fate can inflict, and his army to be disbanded, to return in poverty and defeat to their homes. That spectacle was surely tragic, and appealed to the hardest heart; and if any rejoiced in such misery he must have been unsusceptible of the sentiment of admiration for heroism in misfortune.

The last and decisive struggle between the two armies at Petersburg began in March, 1865. But events of great importance in many quarters had preceded this final conflict, the result of which had been to break down all the outer defences of the Confederacy, leaving only the inner citadel still intact. The events in question are so familiar to those who will peruse these pages, that a passing reference to them is all that is necessary. Affairs in the Valley of Virginia, from autumn to spring, had steadily proceeded from bad to worse. In September, General Sheridan, with a force of about forty-five thousand, had assailed General Early near Winchester, with a force of about eight or nine thousand muskets, and succeeded in driving him up the Valley beyond Strasburg, whence, attacked a second time, he had retreated toward Staunton. This was followed, in October, by another battle at Cedar Run, where Early attacked and nearly crushed General Sheridan, but eventually was again repulsed, and forced a second time to retreat up the Valley to Waynesboro', where, in February, his little remnant was assailed by overwhelming numbers and dispersed. General Sheridan, who had effected this inglorious but important success, then proceeded to the Lowlands, joined General Grant's army, and was ready, with his large force of horse, to take part in the coming battles.

A more important success had attended the Federal arms in the West. General Johnston, who had been restored to command there at the solicitation of Lee, had found his force insufficient to oppose General Sherman's large army; the Confederates had accordingly retreated; and General Sherman, almost unresisted, from the exhaustion of his adversary, marched across the country to Savannah, which fell an easy prize, and thence advanced to Goldsborough, in North Carolina, where he directly threatened Lee's line of retreat from Virginia.

Such was the condition of affairs in the months of February and March, 1865. In the former month, commissioners from the Confederate Government had met President Lincoln in Hampton Roads, but no terms of peace could be agreed upon; the issue was still left to be decided by arms, and every advantage was upon the Federal side. General Lee, who had just been appointed "General-in-Chief"—having thus imposed upon him the mockery of a rank no longer of any value—saw the armies of the enemy closing in upon him, and did not deceive himself with the empty hope that he could longer hold his lines at Petersburg. The country, oppressed as it was, and laboring under a sentiment akin to despair, still retained in almost undiminished measure its superstitious confidence in him; but he himself saw clearly the desperate character of the situation. General Grant was in his front with a force of about one hundred and fifty thousand men, and General Sherman was about to enter Virginia with an army of about the same numbers. Lee's force at Petersburg was a little over thirty thousand men—that of Johnston was not so great, and was detained by Sherman. Under these circumstances, it was obviously only a question of time when the Army of Northern Virginia would be overwhelmed. In February, 1865, these facts were perfectly apparent to General Lee: but one course was left to him—to retreat from Virginia; and he promptly began that movement in the latter part of the month, ordering his trains to Amelia Court-House, and directing pontoons to be got ready at Roanoke River. His aim was simple—to unite his army with that of General Johnston, and retreat into the Gulf States. In the mountains of Virginia he could carry on the war, he had said, for twenty years; in the fertile regions of the South he might expect to prolong hostilities, or at least make favorable terms of peace—which would be better than to remain in Virginia until he was completely surrounded, and an unconditional submission would alone be left him.

It will probably remain a subject of regret to military students, that Lee was not permitted to carry out this retreat into the Gulf States. The movement was arrested after a consultation with the civil authorities at Richmond. Upon what grounds a course so obviously necessary was opposed, the present writer is unable to declare. Whatever the considerations, Lee yielded his judgment; the movement suddenly stopped; and the Army of Northern Virginia—if a skeleton can be called such—remained to await its fate.

The condition of the army in which "companies" scarce existed, "regiments" were counted by tens, and "divisions" by hundreds only, need not here be elaborately dwelt upon. It was indeed the phantom of an army, and the gaunt faces were almost ghostly. Shoeless, in rags, with just sufficient coarse food to sustain life, but never enough to keep at arm's-length the gnawing fiend Hunger, Lee's old veterans remained firm, scattered like a thin skirmish-line along forty miles of works; while opposite them lay an enemy in the highest state of efficiency, and numbering nearly five men to their one. That the soldiers of the army retained their nerve under circumstances so discouraging is surely an honorable fact, and will make their names glorious in history. They remained unshaken and fought undismayed to the last, although their courage was subjected to trials of the most exhausting character. Day and night, for month after month, the incessant fire of the Federal forces had continued, and every engine of human destruction had been put in play to wear away their strength. They fought all through the cheerless days of winter, and, when they lay down in the cold trenches at night, the shell of the Federal mortars rained down upon them, bursting, and mortally wounding them. All day long the fire of muskets and cannon—then, from sunset to dawn, the curving fire of the roaring mortars, and the steady, never-ceasing crack of the sharp-shooters along the front. Snow, or blinding sleet, or freezing rains, might be falling, but the fire went on—it seemed destined to go on to all eternity.

In March, 1865 however, the end was approaching, and General Lee must have felt that all was lost. His last hope had been the retreat southward in the month of February. That hope had been taken from him; the result was at hand; and his private correspondence, if he intrusted to paper his views of the situation, will probably show that from that moment he gave up all anticipation of success, and prepared to do his simple duty as a soldier, leaving the issue of affairs to Providence. Whatever may have been his emotions, they were not reflected in his countenance. The same august composure which had accompanied him in his previous campaigns remained with him still, and cheered the fainting hearts around him. To the 2d of April, and even up to the end, this remarkable calmness continued nearly unchanged, and we can offer no explanation of a circumstance so astonishing, save that which we have already given in a preceding chapter.

XIII.

LEE ATTACKS THE FEDERAL CENTRE.

General Lee became aware, as the end of March drew near, that preparations were being made in the Federal army for some important movement. What that movement would be, there was little reason to doubt. The Federal lines had been extended gradually toward the Southside Railroad; and it was obvious now that General Grant had in view a last and decisive advance in that quarter, which should place him on his opponent's communications, and completely intercept his retreat southward.

The catastrophe which General Lee had plainly foreseen for many months now stared him in the face, and, unless he had recourse to some expedient as desperate as the situation, the end of the struggle must soon come. The sole course left to him was retreat, but this now seemed difficult, if not impossible. General Grant had a powerful force not far from the main roads over which Lee must move; and, unless a diversion of some description were made, it seemed barely possible that the Southern army could extricate itself. This diversion General Lee now proceeded to make; and although we have no authority to state that his object was to follow up the blow, if it were successful, by an evacuation of his lines at Petersburg, it is difficult to conceive what other design he could have had in risking an operation so critical. He had resolved to throw a column against the Federal centre east of Petersburg, with the view to break through there and seize the commanding ground in rear of the line. He would thus be rooted in the middle of General Grant's army, and the Federal left would probably be recalled, leaving the way open if he designed to retreat. If he designed, however, to fight a last pitched battle which should decide all, he would be able to do so, in case the Federal works were broken, to greater advantage than under any other circumstances.

The point fixed upon was Fort Steadman, near the south bank of the Appomattox, where the opposing works were scarcely two hundred yards from each other. The ground in front was covered with *abatis*, and otherwise obstructed, but it was hoped that the assaulting column would be able to pass over the distance undiscovered. In that event a sudden rush would probably carry the works—a large part of the army would follow—the hill beyond would be occupied—and General Grant would be compelled to concentrate his army at the point, for his own protection.

On the morning of March 25th, before dawn, the column was ready. It consisted of three or four thousand men under General Gordon, but an additional force was held in reserve to follow up the attack if it succeeded. Just as dawn appeared, Gordon put his column in motion. It advanced silently over the intervening space, made a rush for the Federal works, mounted them, drove from them in great confusion the force occupying them, and a loud cheer proved that the column of Gordon had done its work. But this auspicious beginning was the only success achieved by the Confederates. For reasons unknown to the present writer, the force directed by Lee to be held in readiness, and to move at once to Gordon's support, did not go forward; the brave commander and his men were left to breast the whole weight of the Federal onslaught which ensued; and disaster followed the first great success. The forts to the right and left of Fort Steadman suddenly opened their thunders, and something like a repetition of the scene succeeding the mine explosion ensued. A considerable portion of the assaulting column was unable to get back, and fell into the enemy's hands; their works were quickly reoccupied; and Lee saw that his last hope had failed. Nothing was left to him now but such courageous resistance as it was in his power to make, and he prepared, with the worn weapon which he still held in his firm grasp, to oppose as he best could the immense "hammer"—to use General Grant's own illustration—which was plainly about to be raised to strike.

XIV.

THE SOUTHERN LINES BROKEN.

The hour of the final struggle now rapidly drew near. On the 29th of March, General Lee discovered that a large portion of the Federal army was moving steadily in the direction of his works beyond Burgen Mill, and there could be no doubt what this movement signified. General Grant was plainly about to make a decisive attack on the Confederate right, on the White-Oak Road; and, if that attack succeeded, Lee was lost.

Had not General Lee and his men become accustomed to retain their coolness under almost any circumstances of trial, the prospect now before them must have filled them with despair. The bulk of the Federal army was obviously about to be thrown against the Confederate right, and it was no secret in the little body of Southerners that Lee would be able to send thither only a painfully inadequate force, unless his extensive works were left in charge of a mere line of skirmishers. This could not be thought of; the struggle on the right must be a desperate one, and the Southern troops must depend upon hard fighting rather than numbers if they hoped to repulse the attack of the enemy.

Such was the situation of affairs, and neither the Confederate commander nor his men shrunk in the hour of trial. Leaving Longstreet to confront the enemy north of the James, and Gordon in command of Ewell's corps—if it could be called such—in front of Petersburg, Lee moved with nearly the whole remainder of his small force westward, beyond Hatcher's Run, to meet the anticipated attack. The force thus moved to the right to receive General Grant's great assault consisted of about fifteen thousand infantry, and about two thousand cavalry under General Fitz Lee, who, in consequence of the departure of Hampton to North Carolina, now commanded the cavalry of the army. This force, however, was cavalry only in name; and General Lee, speaking afterward of General Sheridan, said that his victories were won "when we had no horses for our cavalry, and no men to ride the few broken-down steeds that we could muster."

With this force, amounting in all to about seventeen thousand men, Lee proceeded to take position behind the works extending along the White-Oak Road, in the direction of Five Forks, an important *carrefour* beyond his extreme right. The number of men left north of James River and in front of Petersburg was a little under twenty thousand. As General Grant had at his command a force about four times as great as his adversary's, it seemed scarcely possible that Lee would be able to offer serious resistance.

It soon became evident, however, that, in spite of this great disproportion of force, General Lee had determined to fight to the last. To attribute this determination to despair and recklessness, would be doing injustice to the great soldier. It was still possible that he might be able to repulse the assault upon his right, and, by disabling the Federal force there, open his line of retreat. To this hope he no doubt clung, and the fighting-blood of his race was now thoroughly aroused. At Chancellorsville and elsewhere the odds had been nearly as great, and a glance at his gaunt veterans showed him that they might still be depended upon for a struggle as obstinate as any in the past history of the war.

The event certainly vindicated the justice of this latter view, and we shall briefly trace the occurrences of the next three or four days which terminated the long conflict at Petersburg.

General Grant's assaulting force was not in position near the Boydton Road, beyond Hatcher's Run, until March 31st, when, before he could attack, Lee suddenly advanced and made a furious onslaught on the Federal front. Before this attack, the divisions first encountered gave way in confusion, and it seemed that the Confederate commander, at a single blow, was about to extricate himself from his embarrassing situation. The force opposed to him, however, was too great, and he found himself unable to encounter it in the open field. He therefore fell back to his works, and the fighting ceased, only to be renewed, however, at Five Forks. This had been seized by the cavalry of General Sheridan, and, as the point was one of importance, Lee detached a small body of infantry to drive away the Federal horse. This was done without difficulty, and the Confederate infantry then advanced toward Dinwiddie Court-House; but late at night it was withdrawn, and the day's fighting ended.

On the next day, the 1st of April, a more determined struggle ensued, for the possession of Five Forks, where Lee had stationed the small remnants of the divisions of Pickett and Johnson. These made a brave resistance, but were wholly unable to stand before the force brought against them. They maintained their ground as long as possible, but were finally broken to pieces and scattered in confusion, the whole right of the Confederate line and the Southside Road falling into the hands of the enemy.

[Illustration: Lee at Petersburg]

140

This was virtually the end of the contest, but General Grant, it would appear, deemed it inexpedient to venture any thing. So thinly manned were the lines in front of Petersburg, in the absence of Longstreet north of James River, and the troops sent beyond Hatcher's Run, that on the 1st of April the Federal commander might have broken through the works at almost any point. He elected to wait, however, until the following day, thereby running the risk of awaking to find that Lee had retreated.

At dawn on the 2d the long struggle ended. The Federal forces advanced all along the Confederate front, made a furious attack, and, breaking through in front of the city, carried all before them. The forts, especially Fort Gregg, made a gallant resistance. This work was defended by the two hundred and fifty men of Harris's Mississippi Brigade, and these fought until their numbers were reduced to thirty, killing or wounding five hundred of the assailants. The fort was taken at last, and the Federal lines advanced toward the city. In this attack fell the eminent soldier General A.P. Hill, whose record had been so illustrious, and whose fortune it was to thus terminate his life while the Southern flag still floated.

XV.
LEE EVACUATES PETERSBURG.

Any further resistance upon the part of General Lee seemed now impossible, and nothing appeared to be left him but to surrender his army. This course he does not seem, however, to have contemplated. It was still possible that he might be able to maintain his position on an inner line near the city until night; and, if he could do so, the friendly hours of darkness might enable him to make good his retreat to the north bank of the Appomattox, and shape his course toward North Carolina, where General Johnston awaited him. If the movements of the Federal forces, however, were so prompt as to defeat his march in that direction, he might still be able to reach Lynchburg, beyond which point the defiles of the Alleghanies promised him protection against the utmost efforts of his enemy. Of his ability to reach North Carolina, following the line of the Danville Railroad, Lee, however, seems to have had no doubt. The Federal army would not probably be able to concentrate in sufficient force in his path to bar his progress if his march were rapid; if detached bodies only opposed him on his line of retreat, there was little doubt that the Army of Northern Virginia, reduced as it was, would be able to cut its way through them.

This preface is necessary to an intelligent comprehension of Lee's movements on the unfortunate 2d of April when his lines were broken. This occurrence took place, as we have said, about sunrise, and, an hour or two afterward, the Federal forces pressed forward all along the line, surging toward the suburbs of Petersburg. We have mentioned the position of General Lee's headquarters, about a mile and a half west of the city, on the Cox Road, nearly opposite the tall Federal observatory. Standing on the lawn, in front of his headquarters, General Lee now saw, approaching rapidly, a heavy column of Federal infantry, with the obvious design of charging a battery which had opened fire upon them from a hill to the right. The spectacle was picturesque and striking. Across the extensive fields houses set on fire by shell were sending aloft huge clouds of smoke and tongues of flame; at every instant was seen the quick glare of the Federal artillery, firing from every knoll, and in front came on the charging column, moving at a double quick, with burnished gun-barrels and bayonets flashing in the April sunshine.

General Lee watched with attention, but with perfect composure, this determined advance of the enemy; and, although he must have realized that his army was on the verge of destruction, it was impossible to discern in his features any evidences of emotion. He was in full uniform, and had buckled on his dress-sword, which he seldom wore—having, on this morning declared, it is said, that if he were compelled to surrender he would do so in full harness. Of his calmness at this trying moment the writer is able to bear his personal testimony. Chancing to hear a question addressed to a member of his staff, General Lee turned with great courtesy, raised his gray hat in response to the writer's salute, and gave him the desired information in a voice entirely measured and composed. It was impossible to regard a calmness so striking without strong sentiments of admiration, and Lee's appearance and bearing at this moment will always remain vividly impressed upon the writer's memory.

The Federal column was soon in dangerous proximity to the battery on the hill, and it was obliged to retire at a gallop to escape capture. An attempt was made to hold the ground near the headquarters, but a close musketry-fire from the enemy rendered this also impossible—the artillery was withdrawn—and General Lee, mounting his iron-gray, slowly rode back, accompanied by a number of officers, toward his inner line. He still remained entirely composed, and only said to one of his staff, in his habitual tone: "This is a bad business, colonel."

"Well, colonel," he said afterward to another officer, "it has happened as I told them it would at Richmond. The line has been stretched until it has broken."

The Federal column was now pressing forward along the Cox Road toward Petersburg, and General Lee continued to ride slowly back in the direction of the city. He was probably recognized by officers of the Federal artillery, or his *cortége* drew their fire. The group was furiously shelled, and one of the shells burst a few feet in rear of him, killing the horse of an officer near him, cutting the bridle-reins of others, and tearing up the ground in his immediate vicinity. This incident seemed to arouse in General Lee his fighting-blood. He turned his head over his right shoulder, his cheeks became flushed, and a sudden flash of the eye showed with what reluctance he retired before the fire directed upon him. No other course was left him, however, and he continued to ride slowly toward his inner line—a low earthwork in the suburbs of the city—where a small force was drawn up, ardent, hopeful, defiant, and saluting the shell, now bursting above them, with cheers and laughter. It was plain that the fighting-spirit of the ragged troops remained unbroken; and the shout of welcome with which they received Lee indicated their unwavering confidence in him, despite the untoward condition of affairs.

Arrangements were speedily made to hold the inner line, if possible, until night. To General Gordon had been intrusted the important duty of defending the lines east of the city, and General Longstreet had been directed to vacate the works north of James River, and march at once to the lines of Petersburg. This officer made his appearance, with his small force, at an early hour of the day; and, except that the Federal army continued firing all along the front, no other active operations took place. To those present on the Confederate side this fact appeared strange. As the force beyond Hatcher's Run had been completely defeated and dispersed, General Lee's numbers for the defence of Petersburg on this day did not amount to much, if any, more than fifteen thousand men. General Grant's force was probably one hundred and fifty thousand, of whom about one hundred thousand might, it would appear, have been concentrated in an hour or two directly in front of the city. That, with this large force at his disposal, the Federal commander did not at once attack, and so end all on that day, surprised the Confederate troops, and still continues to surprise the writer.

Night came at last, and General Lee began his retreat. He had sent, early in the morning, a dispatch to the civil authorities, at Richmond, informing them of the fact that his lines had been broken, and that he would that night retreat from Petersburg. Orders had also been sent to all the forces holding the lines north of James River to move at once and join him, and, just at nightfall, the army at Petersburg began crossing the Appomattox. This movement was effected without interruption from the enemy; and the army, turning into what is called the Hickory Road, leading up the north bank of the river, moved on steadily through the half light. Its march was superintended by Lee in person. He had stationed himself at the mouth of the Hickory Road, and, standing with the bridle of his horse in his hand, gave his orders. His bearing still remained entirely composed, and his voice had lost none of its grave strength of intonation. When the rear was well closed up, Lee mounted his horse, rode on slowly with his men; and, in the midst of the glare and thunder of the exploding magazines at Petersburg, the small remnant of the Army of Northern Virginia, amounting to about fifteen thousand men, went on its way through the darkness.

XVI.

THE RETREAT AND SURRENDER.

On the morning of the 3d of April, General Lee, after allowing his column a brief period of rest, continued his march up the north bank of the Appomattox.

The aspect of affairs at this time was threatening, and there seemed little ground to hope that the small force would be able to make good its retreat to North Carolina. General Grant had a short and direct route to the Danville Railroad—a considerable portion of his army was already as far west as Dinwiddie Court-House—and it was obvious that he had only to use ordinary diligence to completely cut General Lee off in the vicinity of Burkesville Junction. A glance at the map will indicate the advantages possessed by the Federal commander. He could move over the chord, while Lee was compelled to follow the arc of the circle. Unless good fortune assisted Lee and ill fortune impeded his opponent, the event seemed certain; and it will be seen that these conditions were completely reversed.

Under the circumstances here stated, it appeared reasonable to expect in Lee and his army some depression of spirits. The fact was strikingly the reverse. The army was in excellent spirits, probably from the highly-agreeable contrast of the budding April woods with the squalid trenches, and the long-unfelt joy of an unfettered march through the fields of spring. General Lee shared this hopeful feeling in a very remarkable degree. His expression was animated and buoyant, his seat in the saddle erect and commanding, and he seemed to look forward to assured success in the critical movement which he had undertaken.

"I have got my army safe out of its breastworks," he said, on the morning of this day, "and, in order to follow me, the enemy must abandon his lines, and can derive no further benefit from his railroads or James River."

The design of the Confederate commander has been already stated, but an important condition upon which he depended for success has not been mentioned. This was a supply of food for his army. The troops, during the whole winter, had lived, from day to day, on quarter-rations, doled out to them with a sparing hand; and, in moving now from Petersburg, Lee saw that he must look to supplies somewhere upon his line of retreat. These he had directed to be brought from the south and deposited at Amelia Court-House; and the expectation of finding at that point full subsistence for his men, had doubtless a great effect in buoying up his spirits. An evil chance, however, reversed all the hopes based on this anticipation. From fault or misapprehension, the train loaded with supplies proceeded to Richmond without depositing the rations at Amelia Court-House; there was no time to obtain other subsistence, and when, after unforeseen delay, in consequence of high water in the Appomattox, Lee, at the head of his half-starved soldiers, reached Amelia Court-House, it was only to find that there was nothing there for the support of his army, and to realize that a successful retreat, under the circumstances, was wellnigh hopeless.

Those who accompanied the Southern army on this arduous march will recall the dismayed expression of the emaciated faces at this unlooked-for calamity; and no face wore a heavier shadow than that of General Lee. The failure of the supply of rations completely paralyzed him. He had intended, and was confident of his ability, to cut his way through the enemy; but an army cannot march and fight without food. It was now necessary to halt and send out foraging parties into the impoverished region around. Meanwhile General Grant, with his great force, was rapidly moving to bar his adversary's further advance; the want of a few thousand pounds of bread and meat had virtually terminated the war.

An anxious and haggard expression came to General Lee's face when he was informed of this great misfortune; and, at once abandoning his design of cutting his way through to North Carolina, he turned westward, and shaped his march toward Lynchburg. This movement began on the night of the 5th of April, and it would seem that General Grant had had it in his power to arrest it by an attack on Lee at Amelia Court-House. General Sheridan was in the immediate vicinity, with a force of about eighteen thousand well-mounted cavalry, and, although it was not probable that this command could effect any thing against Lee's army of about the same number of infantry, it might still have delayed him by constructing breastworks in his way, and thus giving the Federal infantry time to come up and attack.

[Illustration: LEE AT THE SURRENDER.]

The opportunity of crushing his adversary at Amelia Court-House was thus allowed to pass, and General Grant now pressed forward his infantry, to bring Lee to bay, if possible, before he reached Lynchburg. From this moment began the struggle between the adversaries which was to continue, day and night, without intermission, for the next four days. The phenomenon was here presented of an army, reduced to less than twenty thousand men, holding at arm's-length an enemy numbering about one hundred and fifty thousand, and very nearly defeating every effort of the larger force to arrest their march. It would not interest the reader, probably, to follow in minute detail the circumstances of this melancholy retreat. From the importance of the transactions, and the natural attention directed to them, both North and South, they are doubtless familiar to all who will read these pages. We shall only speak of one or two incidents of the retreat, wherein General Lee appeared prominent personally, leaving to the imagination of the reader the remainder of the long and tragic struggle whose result decided the fate of the Confederacy.

General Grant doubtless saw now that every thing depended upon the celerity of his movements, and, sending in advance his large body of cavalry, he hastened forward as rapidly as possible with his infantry, bent on interposing, if possible, a heavy force in his adversary's front. Lee's movements were equally rapid. He seemed speedily to have regained his old calmness, after the trying disappointment at Amelia Court-House; and those who shared his counsels at this time can testify that the idea of surrender scarcely entered his mind for a moment—or, if it did so, was speedily banished. Under the pressure of circumstances so adverse that they seemed calculated to break down the most stubborn resolution, General Lee did not falter; and throughout the disheartening scenes of the retreat, from the moment when he left Amelia Court-House to the hour when his little column was drawing near Appomattox, still continued to believe that the situation was not desperate, and that he would be able to force his way through to Lynchburg.

On the evening of the 6th, when the army was near Farmville, a sudden attack was made by the Federal cavalry on the trains of the army moving on a parallel road; and the small force of infantry guarding them was broken and scattered. This occurrence took place while General Lee was confronting a body of Federal infantry near Sailor's Creek; and, taking a small brigade, he immediately repaired to the scene of danger. The spectacle which followed was a very striking and imposing one, and is thus described by one who witnessed it: "The scene was one of gloomy picturesqueness and tragic interest. On a plateau raised above the forest from which they had emerged, were the disorganized troops of Ewell and Anderson, gathered in groups, un-officered, and uttering tumultuous exclamations of rage and defiance. Rising above the weary groups which had thrown themselves upon the ground, were the grim barrels of cannon, in battery, ready to fire, as soon as the enemy appeared. In front of all was the still line of battle, just placed by Lee, and waiting calmly. General Lee had rushed his infantry over, just at sunset, leading it in person, his face animated, and his eye brilliant with the soldier's spirit of fight, but his bearing unflurried as before. An artist desiring to paint his picture, ought to have seen the old cavalier at this moment, sweeping on upon his large iron-gray, whose mane and tail floated in the wind; carrying his field-glass half-raised in his right hand; with head erect, gestures animated, and in the whole face and form the expression of the hunter close upon his game. The line once interposed, he rode in the twilight among the disordered groups above mentioned, and the sight of him aroused a tumult. Fierce cries resounded on all sides, and, with hands clinched violently and raised aloft, the men called on him to lead them against the enemy. 'It's General Lee!' 'Uncle Robert!' 'Where's the man who won't follow Uncle Robert?' I heard on all sides—the swarthy faces full of dirt and courage, lit up every instant by the glare of the burning wagons. Altogether, the scene was indescribable."

On the 7th the army pressed on beyond Farmville, still harassed as it advanced by the Federal infantry and cavalry; but, in some of these encounters, the pursuing force met with what was probably a very unexpected discomfiture. General Fitz Lee, bringing up the rear of the army with his force of about fifteen hundred cavalry on broken-down horses, succeeded not only in repulsing the attacks of the large and excellently-mounted force under General Sheridan, but achieved over them highly-honorable successes. One such incident took place on the 7th, when General Gregg attacked with about six thousand horse, but was met, defeated, and captured by General Fitz Lee, to the great satisfaction of General Lee, who said to his son, General W.H.F. Lee:

"Keep your command together and in good spirits, general—don't let them think of surrender—I will get you out of this."

On the 8th and 9th, however, this hope seemed unwarranted by the circumstances, and the commander-in-chief appeared to be almost the only human being who remained sanguine of the result. The hardships of the retreat, arising chiefly from want of food, began to seriously impair the resolution of the troops, and the scenes through which they advanced were not calculated to raise their spirits. "These scenes," declares one who witnessed them, "were of a nature which can be apprehended only by men who are thoroughly familiar with the harrowing details of war. Behind and on either flank, a ubiquitous and increasingly adventurous enemy— every mud-hole and every rise in the road choked with blazing wagons—the air filled with the deafening reports of ammunition exploding, and shells bursting when touched by the flames, dense columns of smoke ascending to heaven from the burning and exploding vehicles, exhausted men, worn-out mules and horses, lying down side by side—gaunt Famine glaring hopelessly from sunken, lack-lustre eyes—dead mules, dead horses, dead men everywhere— death many times welcomed as God's messenger in disguise—who can wonder if many hearts, tried in the fiery furnace of four unparalleled years, and never hitherto found wanting, should have quailed in presence of starvation, fatigue, sleeplessness, misery, unintermitted for five or six days, and culminating in hopelessness?" It cannot, however, be said with truth, that any considerable portion of the Southern forces were greatly demoralized, to use the military phrase, as the fighting of the last two days, when the suffering of the retreat culminated, will show. The men were almost entirely without food, and were glad to find a little corn to eat; but those who were not physically unable longer to carry their muskets—and the number of these latter was large—still marched and fought with soldierly cheerfulness and resolution.

General Lee's spirits do not seem at any time to have flagged, and up to a late period of the retreat he had not seriously contemplated surrender. The necessity for this painful course came home to his corps commanders first, and they requested General Pendleton, the efficient chief of artillery of the army, to inform General Lee that in their opinion further struggle was hopeless. General Pendleton informed General Lee of this opinion of his officers, and it seemed to communicate something like a shock to him.

"Surrender!" he exclaimed with a flash of the eye, "I have too many good fighting-men for that!"

Nevertheless, the necessity of seriously contemplating this result was soon forced upon him. Since the morning of the 7th, a correspondence had taken place between himself and General Grant; and, as these notes are interesting, we here present those which were exchanged up to the night of the 8th:

April 7, 1865.

General R.E. Lee, commanding C.S.A.:

GENERAL: The result of the last week must convince you of the hopelessness of further resistance on the part of the Army of Northern Virginia in this struggle. I feel that it is so, and regard it as my duty to shift from myself the responsibility of any further effusion of blood, by asking of you the surrender of that portion of the Confederate Southern Army known as the Army of Northern Virginia.

Very respectfully,

Your obedient servant,

U.S. GRANT,

Lieutenant-General commanding Armies of the United States.

April 7, 1865.

GENERAL: I have received your note of this day. Though not entirely of the opinion you express of the hopelessness of further resistance on the part of the Army of Northern Virginia, I reciprocate your desire to avoid useless effusion of blood, and therefore, before considering your proposition, ask the terms you will offer on condition of its surrender.

R.E. LEE, *General.*

To LIEUTENANT-GENERAL U.S. GRANT,

Commanding Armies of the United States.

April 8, 1865.

To General R.E. Lee, commanding C.S.A.:

GENERAL: Your note of last evening, in reply to mine of the same date, asking the conditions on which I will accept the surrender of the Army of Northern Virginia is just received.

In reply, I would say, that peace being my first desire, there is but one condition that I insist upon, viz.:

That the men surrendered shall be disqualified for taking up arms again against the Government of the United States until properly exchanged.

I will meet you, or designate officers to meet any officers you may name for the same purpose, at any point agreeable to you, for the purpose of arranging definitely the terms upon which the surrender of the Army of Northern Virginia will he received.

Very respectfully,

Your obedient servant,

U.S. GRANT, *Lieutenant-General, commanding Armies of the United States.*

April 8, 1865.

GENERAL: I received, at a late hour, your note of to-day, in answer to mine of yesterday.

I did not intend to propose the surrender of the Army of Northern Virginia, but to ask the terms of your proposition. To be frank, I do not think the emergency has arisen to call for the surrender.

But as the restoration of peace should be the sole object of all, I desire to know whether your proposals would tend to that end.

I cannot, therefore, meet you with a view to surrender the Army of Northern Virginia; but so far as your proposition may affect the Confederate States forces under my command and tend to the restoration of peace, I should be pleased to meet you at 10 A.M. to-morrow, on the old stage-road to Richmond, between the picket-lines of the two armies. Very respectfully,

Your obedient servant,

R.E. LEE, *General C.S.A.*

To LIEUTENANT-GENERAL GRANT,

Commanding Armies of the United States.

[Illustration: Last Council of War.]

No reply was received to this last communication from General Lee, on the evening of the 8th, and that night there was held, around a bivouac-fire in the woods, the last council of war of the Army of Northern Virginia. The scene was a very picturesque one. The red glare from the bivouac-fire lit up the group, and brought out the details of each figure. None were present but General Lee and Generals Longstreet, Gordon, and Fitz Lee, all corps commanders. Generals Gordon and Fitz Lee half reclined upon an army-blanket near the fire; Longstreet sat upon a log, smoking; and General Lee stood by the fire, holding in his hand the correspondence which had passed between himself and General Grant. The question what course it was advisable to pursue, was then presented, in a few calm words, by General Lee to his corps commanders, and an informal conversation ensued. It was finally agreed that the army should advance, on the next morning, beyond Appomattox Court-House, and, if only General Sheridan's cavalry were found in front, brush that force from its path, and proceed on its way to Lynchburg. If, however, the Federal infantry was discovered in large force beyond the Court-House, the attempt to break through was to be abandoned, and a flag dispatched to General Grant requested an interview for the arrangement of the terms of a capitulation of the Southern army.

With a heavy heart, General Lee acquiesced in this plan of proceeding, and soon afterward the council of war terminated—the corps commanders saluting the commander-in-chief, who returned their bows with grave courtesy, and separating to return to their own bivouacs.

In spite, however, of the discouraging and almost desperate condition of affairs, General Lee seems still to have clung to the hope that he might be able to cut his way through the force in his front. He woke from brief slumber beside his bivouac-fire at about three o'clock in the morning, and calling an officer of his staff, Colonel Venable, sent him to General Gordon, commanding the front, to ascertain his opinion, at that moment, of the probable result of an attack upon the enemy. General Gordon's reply was, "Tell General Lee that my old corps is reduced to a frazzle, and, unless I am supported by Longstreet heavily, I do not think we can do any thing more."

General Lee received this announcement with an expression of great feeling, and after a moment's silence said: "There is nothing left but to go to General Grant, and I would rather die a thousand deaths!"

His staff-officers had now gathered around him, and one of them said: "What will history say of our surrendering if there is any possibility of escape? Posterity will not understand it." To these words, General Lee replied: "Yes, yes, they will not understand our situation; but that is not the question. The question is, whether it is *right*; and, if it is right, I take the responsibility."

His expression of buoyant hopefulness had now changed to one of deep melancholy, and it was evident to those around him that the thought of surrender was worse to him than the bitterness of death. For the first time his courage seemed to give way, and he was nearly unmanned. Turning to an officer standing near him, he said, his deep voice filled with hopeless sadness: "How easily I could get rid of this, and be at rest! I have only to ride along the line and all will be over!"

He was silent for a short time after uttering these words, and then added, with a heavy sigh: "But it is our duty to live. What will become of the women and children of the South, if we are not here to protect them?"

The moment had now come when the fate of the retreat was to be decided. To General Gordon, who had proved himself, in the last operations of the war, a soldier of the first ability, had been intrusted the command of the advance force; and this was now moved forward against the enemy beyond Appomattox Court-House. Gordon attacked with his infantry, supported by Fitz Lee's cavalry, and the artillery battalion of Colonel Carter, and such was the impetuosity of his advance that he drove the Federal forces nearly a mile. But at that point he found himself in face of a body of infantry, stated afterward, by Federal officers, to number about eighty thousand. As his own force was less than five thousand muskets, he found it impossible to advance farther; and the Federal lines were already pressing forward to attack him, in overwhelming force, when the movement suddenly ceased. Seeing the hopelessness of further resistance. General Lee had sent a flag to General Grant, requesting an interview looking to the arrangement, if possible, of terms of surrender; and to this end the forward movement of the Federal forces was ordered to be discontinued.

The two armies then remained facing each other during the interview between the two commanders, which took place in a farm-house in Appomattox Court-House. General Lee was accompanied only by Colonel Marshall, of his staff, and on the Federal side only a few officers were present. General Grant's demeanor was courteous, and that of General Lee unmarked by emotion of any description. The hardships of the retreat had somewhat impaired his strength, and his countenance exhibited traces of fatigue; but no other change had taken place in his appearance. He was erect, calm, courteous, and confined his observations strictly to the disagreeable business before him. The interview was brief; and, seated at a plain table, the two commanders wrote and exchanged the accompanying papers:

APPOMATTOX COURT-HOUSE, *April* 9, 1865.

General R.E. Lee, commanding C.S.A.:

In accordance with the substance of my letter to you of the 8th inst., I propose to receive the surrender of the Army of Northern Virginia on the following terms, to wit:

Rolls of all the officers and men to be made in duplicate, one copy to be given to an officer designated by me, the other to be retained by such officers as you may designate.

The officers to give their individual parole not to take arms against the Government of the United States until properly exchanged; and each company or regimental commander to sign a like parole for the men of their commands.

The arms, artillery, and public property, to be parked and stacked, and turned over to the officers appointed by me to receive them. This will not embrace the side-arms of the officers, nor their private horses or baggage.

This done, each officer and man will be allowed to return to their homes, not to be disturbed by United States authority so long as they observe their parole and the laws in force where they may reside.

Very respectfully,

U.S. GRANT, *Lieutenant-General.*

HEADQUARTERS ARMY OF NORTHERN VIRGINIA,

April 9,1865.

Lieut.-General U.S. Grant, commanding U.S.A.:

GENERAL: I have received your letter of this date, containing the terms of surrender of the Army of Northern Virginia, as proposed by you. As they are substantially the same as those expressed in your letter of the 8th inst., they are accepted. I will proceed to designate the proper officers to carry the stipulations into effect.

Very respectfully, your obedient servant,

R.E. LEE, *General.*

The two generals then bowed to each other, and, leaving the house, General Lee mounted his gray, and rode back to his headquarters.

The scene as he passed through the army was affecting. The men gathered round him, wrung his hand, and in broken words called upon God to help him. This pathetic reception by his old soldiers profoundly affected Lee. The tears came to his eyes, and, looking at the men with a glance of proud feeling, he said, in suppressed tones, which trembled slightly: "We have fought through the war together. I have done the best I could for you. My heart is too full to say more!"

These few words seemed to be all he could utter. He rode on, and, reaching his headquarters in the woods, disappeared in his tent, whither we shall not follow him.

On the next day the Army of Northern Virginia, numbering about twenty-six thousand men, of whom but seven thousand eight hundred carried muskets, was formally surrendered, and the Confederate War was a thing of the past.

XVII.

LEE RETURNS TO RICHMOND.

General Lee, on the day following the capitulation of his army, issued an address to his old soldiers, which they received and read with very deep emotion. The address was in these words:

HEADQUARTERS ARMY NORTHERN VIRGINIA,

April 10, 1865.

After four years of arduous service, marked by unsurpassed courage and fortitude, the Army of Northern Virginia has been compelled to yield to overwhelming numbers and resources.

I need not tell the survivors of so many hard-fought battles, who have remained steadfast to the last, that I have consented to this result from no distrust of them; but, feeling that valor and devotion could accomplish nothing that could compensate for the loss that would have attended the continuation of the contest, I have determined to avoid the useless sacrifice of those whose past services have endeared them to their countrymen.

By the terms of agreement, officers and men can return to their homes and remain there until exchanged.

You will take with you the satisfaction that proceeds from the consciousness of duty faithfully performed; and I earnestly pray that a merciful God will extend to you His blessing and protection.

With an unceasing admiration of your constancy and devotion to your country, and a grateful remembrance of your kind and generous consideration of myself, I bid you an affectionate farewell.

R.E. LEE, *General.*

The painful arrangements connected with the capitulation were on this day concluded; and General Lee prepared to set out on his return to Richmond—like his men, a "paroled prisoner of the Army of Northern Virginia." The parting between him and his soldiers was pathetic. He exchanged with all near him a close pressure of the hand, uttered a few simple words of farewell, and, mounting his iron-gray, "Traveller," who had passed through all the fighting of the campaign unharmed, rode slowly in the direction of Richmond. He was escorted by a detachment of Federal cavalry, preceded only by a guidon; and the party, including the officers who accompanied him, consisted of about twenty-five horsemen. The *cortége* was followed by several wagons carrying the private effects of himself and his companions, and by the well-known old black open vehicle which he had occasionally used during the campaigns of the preceding year, when indisposition prevented him from mounting his horse. In this vehicle it had been his custom to carry stores for the wounded—it had never been used for articles contributing to his personal convenience.

General Lee's demeanor on his way to Richmond was entirely composed, and his thoughts seemed much more occupied by the unfortunate condition of the poor people, at whose houses he stopped, than by his own situation. When he found that all along his route the impoverished people had cooked provisions in readiness for him, and were looking anxiously for him, with every indication of love and admiration, he said to one of his officers: "These good people are kind—too kind. Their hearts are as full as when we began our first campaigns in 1861. They do too much—more than they are able to do—for us."

His soldierly habits remained unchanged, and he seemed unwilling to indulge in any luxuries or comforts which could not be shared by the gentlemen accompanying him At a house which he reached just as night came, a poor woman had prepared an excellent bed for him, but, with a courteous shake of the head, he spread his blanket, and slept upon the floor. Stopping on the next day at the house of his brother, Charles Carter Lee, in Powhatan, he spent the evening in conversation; but, when bedtime came, left the house, in spite of the fact that it had begun to rain, and, crossing the road into the woods, took up his quarters for the night on the hard planks of his old black vehicle. On the route he exhibited great solicitude about a small quantity of oats which he had brought with him, in one of the wagons, for his old companion, "Traveller," mentioning it more than once, and appearing anxious lest it should be lost or used by some one.

[Illustration: LEE'S ENTRY INTO RICHMOND AFTER THE SURRENDER.]

The party came in sight of Richmond at last, and, two or three miles from the city, General Lee rode ahead of his escort, accompanied only by a few officers, and, crossing the pontoon bridge below the ruins of Mayo's bridge, which had been destroyed when the Confederate forces retreated, entered the capital. The spectacle which met his eyes at this moment must have been exceedingly painful. In the great conflagration which had taken place on the morning of the 3d of April, a large portion of the city had been burned; and, as General Lee rode up Main Street, formerly so handsome and attractive, he saw on either hand only masses of blackened ruins. As he rode slowly through the opening between these masses of *débris*, he was recognized by the few persons who were on the street, and instantly the intelligence of his presence spread through the city. The inhabitants hastened from their houses and flocked to welcome him, saluting him with cheers and the waving of hats and handkerchiefs. He seemed desirous, however, of avoiding this ovation, and, returning the greeting by simply raising his hat, rode on and reached his house on Franklin Street, where, respecting his desire for privacy under circumstances so painful, his admirers did not intrude upon him.

We have presented this brief narrative of the incidents attending General Lee's return to his home after the surrender, to show with what simplicity and good sense he accepted his trying situation. A small amount of diplomacy—sending forward one of his officers to announce his intended arrival; stopping for a few moments as he ascended Main Street; making an address to the citizens who first recognized him, and thus affording time for a crowd to assemble—these proceedings on the part of General Lee would have resulted in an ovation such as a vanquished commander never before received at the hands of any people. Nothing, however, was less desired by General Lee than this tumultuous reception. The native modesty of the man not only shrunk from such an ovation; he avoided it for another reason—the pretext it would probably afford to the Federal authorities to proceed to harsh measures against the unfortunate persons who took part in it. In accordance with these sentiments, General Lee had not announced his coming, had not stopped as he rode through the city; and now, shutting himself up in his house, signified his desire to avoid a public reception, and to be left in privacy.

This policy he is well known to have pursued from that time to the end of his life. He uniformly declined, with great courtesy, but firmly, invitations to attend public gatherings of any description, where his presence might arouse passions or occasion discussions connected with the great contest in which he had been the leader of the South. A mind less firm and noble would doubtless have yielded to this great temptation. It is sweet to the soldier, who has been overwhelmed and has yielded up his sword, to feel that the love and admiration of a people still follow him; and to have the consolation of receiving public evidences of this unchanged devotion. That this love of the Southern people for Lee deeply touched him, there can be no doubt; but it did not blind him to his duty as the representative individual of the South. Feeling that nothing was now left the Southern people but an honest acceptance of the situation, and a cessation, as far as possible, of all rancor toward the North, he refused to encourage sentiments of hostility between the two sections, and did all in his power to restore amicable feeling. "I am very glad to learn," he said in a note to the present writer, "that your life of General Jackson is of the character you describe. I think all topics or questions calculated to excite angry discussion or hostile feelings should be avoided." These few words convey a distinct idea of General Lee's views and feelings. He had fought to the best of his ability for Southern independence of the North; the South had failed in the struggle, and it was now, in his opinion, the duty of every good citizen to frankly acquiesce in the result, and endeavor to avoid all that kept open the bleeding wounds of the country.

His military career had placed him, in the estimation of the first men of his time, among the greatest soldiers of history; but the dignity and moderation of the course pursued by him, from the end of the war to the time of his death, will probably remain, in the opinion of both his friends and enemies, the noblest illustration of the character of the man.

XVIII.

GENERAL LEE AFTER THE WAR.

In the concluding pages of this volume we shall not be called upon to narrate either military or political events. With the surrender at Appomattox Court-House the Confederate War ended—no attempt was made by General Johnston or other commanders to prolong it—in that great whirlpool all hopes of further resistance disappeared.

We have, therefore, now no task before us but to follow General Lee into private life, and present a few details of his latter years, and his death. These notices will be brief, but will not, we hope, be devoid of interest. The soldier who had so long led the Confederate armies was to enter in his latter days upon a new field of labor; and, if in this field he won no new glories, he at least displayed the loftiest virtues, and exhibited that rare combination of greatness and gentleness which makes up a character altogether lovely.

Adhering to the resolution, formed in 1861, never again to draw his sword except in defence of Virginia, General Lee, after the surrender, sought for some occupation, feeling the necessity, doubtless, of in some manner employing his energies. He is said to have had offered to him, but to have courteously declined, estates in England and Ireland; and to have also declined the place of commercial agent of the South in New York, which would have proved exceedingly lucrative. In the summer of 1865, however, he accepted an offer more congenial to his feelings— that of the presidency of Washington College at Lexington—and in the autumn of that year entered upon his duties, which he continued to perform with great energy and success to the day of his death. Of the excellent judgment and great administrative capacity which he displayed in this new field of labor, we have never heard any question. It was the name and example, however, of Lee which proved so valuable, drawing to the college more than five hundred students from all portions of the South, and some even from the North.

Upon the subject of General Lee's life at Washington College, a more important authority than that of the present writer will soon speak. In the "Memorial Volume," whose publication will probably precede or immediately follow the appearance of this work, full details will, no doubt, be presented of this interesting period. The subject possesses rare interest, and the facts presented will, beyond all question, serve to bring out new beauties in a character already regarded with extraordinary love and admiration by men of all parties and opinions. To the volume in question we refer the reader who desires the full-length portrait of one concerning whom too much cannot be written.

During the period extending between the end of the war and General Lee's death, he appeared in public but two or three times—once at Washington, as a "witness" before a Congressional committee, styled "The Reconstruction Committee," to inquire into the condition of things in the South; again, as a witness on the proposed trial of President Davis; and perhaps on one or two additional occasions not of great interest or importance. His testimony was not taken on the trial of the President, which was deferred and finally abandoned; but he was subjected before the Washington committee to a long and searching examination, in which it is difficult to decide whether his own calmness, good sense, and outspoken frankness, or the bad taste of some of the questions prepounded to him, were the more remarkable. As the testimony of General Lee, upon this occasion, presents a full exposition of his views upon many of the most important points connected with the condition of the South, and the "reconstruction" policy, a portion of the newspaper report of his evidence is here given, as both calculated to interest the reader, and to illustrate the subject.

The examination of General Lee took place in March, 1866, and the following is the main portion of it:

General ROBERT E. LEE, sworn and examined by Mr. Howard:

Question. Where is your present residence?

Answer. Lexington, Va.

Q. How long have you resided in Lexington?

A. Since the 1st of October last—nearly five months.

THE FEELING IN VIRGINIA.

Q. Are you acquainted with the state of feeling among what we call secessionists in Virginia, at present, toward the Government of the United States?

A. I do not know that I am; I have been living very retired, and have had but little communication with politicians; I know nothing more than from my own observation, and from such facts as have come to my knowledge.

Q. From your observation, what is your opinion as to the loyalty toward the Government of the United States among the secession portion of the people of that State at this time?

A. So far as has come to my knowledge, I do not know of a single person who either feels or contemplates any resistance to the Government of the United States, or indeed any opposition to it; no word has reached me to either purpose.

Q. From what you have observed among them, is it your opinion that they are friendly toward the Government of the United States, and that they will coöperate to sustain and uphold the Government for the future?

A. I believe that they entirely acquiesce in the Government of the United States, and, so far as I have heard any one express an opinion, they are for coöperating with President Johnson in his policy.

Q. In his policy in regard to what?

A. His policy in regard to the restoration of the whole country; I have heard persons with whom I have conversed express great confidence in the wisdom of his policy of restoration, and they seem to look forward to it as a hope of restoration.

Q. How do they feel in regard to that portion of the people of the United States who have been forward and zealous in the prosecution of the war against the rebellion?

A. Well, I don't know as I have heard anybody express any opinion in regard to it; as I said before, I have not had much communication with politicians in the country, if there are any; every one seems to be engaged in his own affairs, and endeavoring to restore the civil government of the State; I have heard no expression of a sentiment toward any particular portion of the country.

Q. How do the secessionists feel in regard to the payment of the debt of the United States contracted in the prosecution of the war?

A. I have never heard anyone speak on the subject; I suppose they must expect to pay the taxes levied by the Government; I have heard them speak in reference to the payment of taxes, and of their efforts to raise money to pay taxes, which, I suppose, are for their share of the debt; I have never heard any one speak in opposition to the payment of taxes, or of resistance to their payment; their whole effort has been to try and raise the money for the payment of the taxes.

THE DEBT.

Q. From your knowledge of the state of public feeling in Virginia, is it your opinion that the people would, if the question were left to them, repudiate and reject that debt?

A. I never heard any one speak on that subject; but, from my knowledge of the people, I believe that they would be in favor of the payment of all just debts.

Q. Do they, in your opinion, regard that as a just debt?

A. I do not know what their opinion is on the subject of that particular debt; I have never heard any opinion expressed contrary to it; indeed, as I said in the beginning, I have had very little discussion or intercourse with the people; I believe the people will pay the debts they are called upon to pay; I say that from my knowledge of the people generally.

Q. Would they pay that debt, or their portion of it, with as much alacrity as people ordinarily pay their taxes to their Government?

A. I do not know that they would make any distinction between the two. The taxes laid by the Government, so far as I know, they are prepared to pay to the best of their ability. I never heard them make any distinction.

Q. What is the feeling of that portion of the people of Virginia in regard to the payment of the so-called Confederate debt?

A. I believe, so far as my opinion goes—I have no facts to go upon, but merely base my opinion on the knowledge I have of the people—that they would be willing to pay the Confederate debt, too.

Q. You think they would?

A. I think they would, if they had the power and ability to do so. I have never heard any one in the State, with whom I have conversed, speak of repudiating any debt.

Q. I suppose the Confederate debt is almost entirely valueless, even in the market in Virginia?

A. Entirely so, as far as I know. I believe the people generally look upon it as lost entirely. I never heard any question on the subject.

Q. Do you recollect the terms of the Confederate bonds—when they were made payable?

A. I think I have a general recollection that they were made payable six months after a declaration of peace.

Q. Six months after the ratification of a treaty of peace between the United States and the Confederate Government?

A. I think they ran that way.

Q. So that the bonds are not due yet by their terms?

A. I suppose, unless it is considered that there is a peace now, they are not due.

THE FREEDMEN.

Q. How do the people of Virginia, secessionists more particularly, feel toward the freedmen?

A. Every one with whom I associate expresses the kindest feelings toward the freedmen. They wish to see them get on in the world, and particularly to take up some occupation for a living, and to turn their hands to some work. I know that efforts have been made among the farmers near where I live to induce them to engage for the year at regular wages.

Q. Do you think there is a willingness on the part of their old masters to give them fair living wages for their labor?

A. I believe it is so; the farmers generally prefer those servants who have been living with them before; I have heard them express their preferences for the men whom they knew, who had lived with them before, and their wish to get them to return to work.

Q. Are you aware of the existence of any combination among the "whites" to keep down the wages of the "blacks?"

A. I am not; I have heard that in several counties the land-owners have met in order to establish a uniform rate of wages, but I never heard, nor do I know of any combination to keep down wages or establish any rule which they did not think fair; the means of paying wages in Virginia are very limited now, and there is a difference of opinion as to how much each person is able to pay.

Q. How do they feel in regard to the education of the blacks? Is there a general willingness to have them educated?

A. Where I am, and have been, the people have exhibited a willingness that the blacks should be educated, and they express an opinion that it would be better for the blacks and better for the whites.

Q. General, you are very competent to judge of the capacity of black men for acquiring knowledge—I want your opinion on that capacity as compared with the capacity of white men?

A. I do not know that I am particularly qualified to speak on that subject, as you seem to intimate, but I do not think that the black man is as capable of acquiring knowledge as the white man. There are some more apt than others. I have known some to acquire knowledge and skill in their trade or profession. I have had servants of my own who learned to read and write very well.

Q. Do they show a capacity to obtain knowledge of mathematics and the exact sciences?

A. I have no knowledge on that subject; I am merely acquainted with those who have learned the common rudiments of education.

Q. General, are you aware of the existence among the blacks of Virginia, anywhere within the limits of the State, of combinations, having in view the disturbance of the peace, or any improper or unlawful acts?

A. I am not; I have seen no evidence of it, and have heard of none; wherever I have been they have been quiet and orderly; not disposed to work; or, rather, not disposed to any continuous engagement to work, but just very short jobs to provide them with the immediate means of subsistence.

Q. Has the colored race generally as great love of money and property as the white race possesses?

A. I do not think it has; the blacks with whom I am acquainted look more to the present time than to the future.

Q. Does that absence of a lust of money and property arise more from the nature of the negro than from his former servile condition?

A. Well, it may be in some measure attributed to his former condition; they are an amiable, social race; they like their ease and comfort, and I think look more to their present than to their future condition.

IN CASE OF WAR, WOULD VIRGINIA JOIN OUR ENEMIES?

Q. In the event of a war between the United States and any foreign power, such as England or France, if there should be held out to the secession portion of the people of Virginia, or the other recently rebel States, a fair prospect of gaining their independence and shaking off the Government of the United States, is it or is it not your opinion that they would avail themselves of that opportunity?

A. I cannot answer with any certainty on that point; I do not know how far they might be actuated by their feelings; I have nothing whatever to base an opinion upon; so far as I know, they contemplate nothing of the kind now; what may happen in the future I cannot say.

Q. Do you not frequently hear, in your intercourse with secessionists in Virginia, expressions of a hope that such a war may break out?

A. I cannot say that I have heard it; on the contrary, I have heard persons—I do not know whether you could call them secessionists or not, I mean those people in Virginia with whom I associate—express the hope that the country may not be led into a war.

Q. In such an event, do you not think that that class of people whom I call secessionists would join the common enemy?

A. It is possible; it depends upon the feeling of the individual.

Q. If it is a fair question—you may answer or not, as you choose—what, in such an event, might be your choice?

A. I have no disposition now to do it, and I never have had.

Q. And you cannot foresee that such would be your inclination in such an event?

A. No; I can only judge from the past; I do not know what circumstances it may produce; I cannot pretend to foresee events; so far as I know the feeling of the people of Virginia, they wish for peace.

Q. During the civil war, was it not contemplated by the Government of the Confederacy to form an alliance with some foreign nation if possible?

A. I believe it was their wish to do so if they could; it was their wish to have the Confederate Government recognized as an independent government; I have no doubt that if it could have made favorable treaties it would have done so, but I know nothing of the policy of the government; I had no hand or part in it; I merely express my own opinion.

Q. The question I am about to put to you, you may answer or not, as you choose. Did you take an oath of fidelity, or allegiance, to the Confederate Government?

A. I do not recollect having done so, but it is possible that when I was commissioned I did; I do not recollect whether it was required; if it was required, I took it, or if it had been required I would have taken it; but I do not recollect whether it was or not.

Q. (By Mr. Blow.) In reference to the effect of President Johnson's policy, if it were adopted, would there be any thing like a return of the old feeling? I ask that because you used the expression "acquiescing in the result."

A. I believe it would take time for the feelings of the people to be of that cordial nature to the Government they were formerly.

Q. Do you think that their preference for that policy arises from a desire to have peace and good feeling in the country, or from the probability of their regaining political power?

PRESIDENT JOHNSON'S POLICY.

A. So far as I know the desire of the people of the South, it is for restoration of their civil government, and they look upon the policy of President Johnson as the one which would most clearly and most surely reëstablish it.

CONDITION OF THE POORER CLASSES.

Q. Do you see any change among the poorer classes in Virginia, in reference to industry? Are they as much, or more, interested in developing their material interests than they were?

A. I have not observed any change; every one now has to attend to his business for his support.

Q. The poorer classes are generally hard at work, are they?

A. So far as I know, they are; I know nothing to the contrary.

Q. Is there any difference in their relations to the colored people? Is their prejudice increased or diminished?

A. I have noticed no change; so far as I do know the feelings of all the people of Virginia, they are kind to the colored people; I have never heard any blame attributed to them as to the present condition of things, or any responsibility.

Q. There are very few colored laborers employed, I suppose?

A. Those who own farms have employed, more or less, one or two colored laborers; some are so poor that they have to work themselves.

Q. Can capitalists and workingmen from the North go into any portion of Virginia with which you are familiar and go to work among the people?

A. I do not know of any thing to prevent them. Their peace and pleasure there would depend very much on their conduct. If they confined themselves to their own business and did not interfere to provoke controversies with their neighbors, I do not believe they would be molested.

Q. There is no desire to keep out capital?

A. Not that I know of. On the contrary, they are very anxious to get capital into the State.

Q. You see nothing of a disposition to prevent such a thing?

A. I have seen nothing, and do not know of any thing, as I said before; the manner in which they would be received would depend entirely upon the individuals themselves; they might make themselves obnoxious, as you can understand.

Q. (By Mr. Howard.) Is there not a general dislike of Northern men among secessionists?

A. I suppose they would prefer not to associate with them; I do not know that they would select them as associates.

Q. Do they avoid and ostracize them socially?

A. They might avoid them; they would not select them as associates unless there was some reason; I do not know that they would associate with them unless they became acquainted; I think it probable they would not admit them into their social circles.

THE POSITION OF THE COLORED RACE.

Q. (By Mr. Blow.) What is the position of the colored men in Virginia with reference to persons they work for? Do you think they would prefer to work for Northern or Southern men?

A. I think it very probable they would prefer the Northern man, although I have no facts to go upon.

Q. That having been stated very frequently in reference to the cotton States, does it result from a bad treatment on the part of the resident population, or from the idea that they will be more fairly treated by the new-comers? What is your observation in that respect in regard to Virginia?

A. I have no means of forming an opinion; I do not know any case in Virginia; I know of numbers of the blacks engaging with their old masters, and I know of many to prefer to go off and look for new homes; whether it is from any dislike of their former masters, or from any desire to change, or they feel more free and independent, I don't know.

THE MATERIAL INTERESTS OF VIRGINIA.

Q. What is your opinion in regard to the material interests of Virginia; do you think they will be equal to what they were before the rebellion under the changed aspect of affairs?

A. It will take a long time for them to reach their former standard; I think that after some years they will reach it, and I hope exceed it; but it cannot be immediately, in my opinion.

Q. It will take a number of years?

A. It will take a number of years, I think.

Q. On the whole, the condition of things in Virginia is hopeful both in regard to its material interests and the future peace of the country?

A. I have heard great hopes expressed, and there is great cheerfulness and willingness to labor.

Q. Suppose this policy of President Johnson should be all you anticipate, and that you should also realize all that you expect in the improvement of the material interests, do you think that the result of that will be the gradual restoration of the old feeling?

A. That will be the natural result, I think; and I see no other way in which that result can be brought about.

Q. There is a fear in the public mind that the friends of the policy in the South adopt it because they see in it the means of repairing the political position which they lost in the recent contest. Do you think that that is the main idea with them, or that they merely look to it, as you say, as the best means of restoring civil government and the peace and prosperity of their respective States?

A. As to the first point you make, I do not know that I ever heard any person speak upon it; I never heard the points separated; I have heard them speak generally as to the effect of the policy of President Johnson; the feeling is, so far as I know now, that there is not that equality extended to the Southern States which is enjoyed by the North.

Q. You do not feel down there that, while you accept the result, we are as generous as we ought to be under the circumstances?

A. They think that the North can afford to be generous.

Q. That is the feeling down there?

A. Yes; and they think it is the best policy; those who reflect upon the subject and are able to judge.

Q. I understand it to be your opinion that generosity and liberality toward the entire South would be the surest means of regaining their good opinion?

A. Yes, and the speediest.

Q. (By Mr. Howard.) I understand you to say generally that you had no apprehension of any combination among the leading secessionists to renew the war, or any thing of the kind?

A. I have no reason in the world to think so.

Q. Have you heard that subject talked over among any of the politicians?

A. No, sir; I have not; I have not heard that matter even suggested.

Q. Let me put another hypothetical state of things. Suppose the executive government of the United States should be held by a President who, like Mr. Buchanan, rejected the right of coercion, so called, and suppose a Congress should exist here entertaining the same political opinions, thus presenting to the once rebel States the opportunity to again secede from the Union, would they, or not, in your opinion, avail themselves of that opportunity, or some of them?

A. I suppose it would depend: upon the circumstances existing at the time; if their feelings should remain embittered, and their affections alienated from the rest of the States, I think it very probable they might do so, provided they thought it was to their interests.

Q. Do you not think that at the present time there is a deep-seated feeling of dislike toward the Government of the United States on the part of the secessionists?

A. I do not know that there is any deep-seated dislike; I think it is probable there may be some animosity still existing among the people of the South.

Q. Is there not a deep-seated feeling of disappointment and chagrin at the result of the war?

A. I think that at the time they were disappointed at the result of the war.

Q. Do you mean to be understood as saying that there is not a condition of discontent against the Government of the United States among the secessionists generally?

A. I know none.

Q. Are you prepared to say that they respect the Government of the United States, and the loyal people of the United States, so much at the present time as to perform their duties as citizens of the United States, and of the States, faithfully and well?

A. I believe that they will perform all the duties that they are required to perform; I think that is the general feeling so far as I know.

Q. Do you think it would be practicable to convict a man in Virginia of treason for having taken part in this rebellion against the Government by a Virginian jury without packing it with direct reference to a verdict of guilty?

A. On that point I have no knowledge, and I do not know what they would consider treason against the United States—if you refer to past acts.

Mr. Howard: Yes, sir.

Witness: I have no knowledge what their views on that subject in the past are.

Q. You understand my question. Suppose a jury was impanelled in your own neighborhood, taken by lot, would it be possible to convict, for instance, Jefferson Davis, for having levied war upon the United States, and thus having committed the crime of treason?

A. I think it is very probable that they would not consider he had committed treason.

THEIR VIEWS OF TREASON.

Q. Suppose the jury should be clearly and plainly instructed by the Court that such an act of war upon the part of Mr. Davis or any other leading man constituted the crime of treason under the Constitution of the United States, would the jury be likely to heed that instruction, and, if the facts were plainly in proof before them, convict the offender?

A. I do not know, sir, what they would do on that question.

Q. They do not generally suppose that it was treason against the United States, do they?

A. I do not think that they so consider it.

Q. In what light would they view it? What would be their excuse or justification? How would they escape, in their own mind? I refer to the past—I am referring to the past and the feelings they would have?

A. So far as I know, they look upon the action of the State in withdrawing itself from the Government of the United States as carrying the individuals of the State along with it; that the State was responsible for the act, not the individuals, and that the ordinance of secession, so called, or those acts of the State which recognized a condition of war between the State and the General Government stood as their justification for their bearing arms against the Government of the United States; yes, sir, I think they would consider the act of the State as legitimate; that they were merely using the reserved rights, which they had a right to do.

Q. State, if you please—and if you are disinclined to answer the question you need not do so—what your own personal views on that question are?

154

A. That was my view; that the act of Virginia in withdrawing herself from the United States carried me along as a citizen of Virginia, and that her laws and her acts were binding on me.

Q. And that you felt to be your justification in taking the course you did?

A. Yes, sir.

Q. I have been told, general, that you have remarked to some of your friends, in conversation, that you were rather wheedled or cheated into that course by politicians?

A. I do not recollect ever making any such remark; I do not think I ever made it.

Q. If there be any other matter about which you wish to speak on this occasion, do so, freely.

A. Only in reference to that last question you put to me. I may have said and may have believed that the positions of the two sections which they held to each other was brought about by the politicians of the country; that the great masses of the people, if they understood the real question, would have avoided it; but not that I had been individually wheedled by the politicians.

Q. That is probably the origin of the whole thing.

A. I may have said that, but I do not even recollect that; but I did believe at the time that it was an unnecessary condition of affairs, and might have been avoided if forbearance and wisdom had been practised on both sides.

Q. You say that you do not recollect having sworn allegiance and fidelity to the Confederate Government?

A. I do not recollect it, nor do I know it was ever required. I was regularly commissioned in the army of the Confederate States, but I do not really recollect that that oath was required. If it was required, I have no doubt I took it; or, if it had been required, I would have taken it.

Q. Is there any other matter which you desire to state to the committee?

A. No, sir; I am ready to answer any question which you think proper to put to me.

NEGRO CITIZENSHIP.

Q. How would an amendment to the Constitution be received by the secessionists, or by the people at large, allowing the colored people, or certain classes of them, to exercise the right of voting at elections?

A. I think, so far as I can form an opinion, in such an event they would object.

Q. They would object to such an amendment?

A. Yes, sir.

Q. Suppose an amendment should nevertheless be adopted, conferring on the blacks the right of suffrage, would that, in your opinion, lead to scenes of violence or breaches of the peace between the two races in Virginia?

A. I think it would excite unfriendly feelings between the two races; I cannot pretend to say to what extent it would go, but that would be the result.

Q. Are you acquainted with the proposed amendment now pending in the Senate of the United States?

A. No, sir, I am not; I scarcely ever read a paper. [The substance of the proposed amendment was here explained to the witness by Mr. Conkling.] So far as I can see, I do not think that the State of Virginia would object to it.

Q. Would she consent, under any circumstances, to allow the black people to vote, even if she were to gain a large number of representatives in Congress?

A. That would depend upon her interests; if she had the right of determining that, I do not see why she would object; if it were to her interest to admit these people to vote, that might overrule any other objection that she had to it.

Q. What, in your opinion, would be the practical result? Do you think that Virginia would consent to allow the negro to vote?

A. I think that at present she would accept the smaller representation; I do not know what the future may develop; if it should be plain to her that these persons will vote properly and understandingly, she might admit them to vote.

Q. (By Mr. Blow.) Do you not think it would turn a good deal, in the cotton States, upon the value of the labor of the black people? Upon the amount which they produce?

A. In a good many States in the South, and in a good many counties in Virginia, if the black people were allowed to vote, it would, I think, exclude proper representation—that is, proper, intelligent people would not be elected, and, rather than suffer that injury, they would not let them vote at all.

Q. Do you not think that the question as to whether any Southern State would allow the colored people the right of suffrage in order to increase representation would depend a good deal on the amount which the colored people might contribute to the wealth of the State, in order to secure two things—first, the larger representation, and, second, the influence desired from those persons voting?

A. I think they would determine the question more in reference to their opinion as to the manner in which those votes would be exercised, whether they consider those people qualified to vote; my own opinion is, that at this time they cannot vote intelligently, and that giving them the right of suffrage would open the door to a good deal of demagogism, and lead to embarrassments in various ways; what the future may prove, how intelligent they may become, with what eyes they may look upon the interests of the State in which they may reside, I cannot say more than you can.

The above extract presents the main portion of General Lee's testimony, and is certainly an admirable exposition of the clear good sense and frankness of the individual. Once or twice there is obviously an under-current of dry satire, as in his replies upon the subject of the Confederate bonds. When asked whether he remembered at what time these bonds were made payable, he replied that his "general recollection was, that they were made payable six months after a declaration of peace." The correction was at once made by his interrogator in the words "six months after *the ratification of a treaty of peace*" etc. "I think they ran that way," replied General Lee. "So that," retorted his interrogator, "the bonds are not yet due by their terms?" General Lee's reply was, "I suppose, *unless it is considered that there is a peace now, they are not due.*"

This seems to have put an abrupt termination to the examination on that point. To the question whether he had taken an oath of allegiance to the Confederate Government, he replied: "I do not recollect having done so, but it is possible that when I was commissioned I did; I do not recollect whether it was required; if it was required, I took it, or if it had been required, I would have taken it."

If this reply of General Lee be attentively weighed by the reader, some conception may be formed of the bitter pang which he must have experienced in sending in, as he did, to the Federal Government, his application for pardon. The fact cannot be concealed that this proceeding on the part of General Lee was a subject of deep regret to the Southern people; but there can be no question that his motive was disinterested and noble, and that he presented, in so doing, the most remarkable evidence of the true greatness of his character. He had no personal advantage to expect from a pardon; cared absolutely nothing whether he were "pardoned" or not; and to one so proud, and so thoroughly convinced of the justice of the cause in which he had fought, to appear as a supplicant must have been inexpressibly painful. He, nevertheless, took this mortifying step—actuated entirely by that sense of duty which remained with him to the last, overmastering every other sentiment of his nature. He seems in this, as in many other things, to have felt the immense import of his example. The old soldiers of his army, and thousands of civilians, were obliged to apply for amnesty, or remain under civic disability. Brave men, with families depending upon them, had been driven to this painful course, and General Lee seems to have felt that duty to his old comrades demanded that he, too, should swallow this bitter draught, and share their humiliation as he had shared their dangers and their glory. If this be not the explanation of the motives controlling General Lee's action, the writer is unable to account for the course which he pursued. That it is the sole explanation, the writer no more doubts than he doubts the fact of his own existence.

XIX.
GENERAL LEE'S LAST YEARS AND DEATH.

For about five years—from the latter part of 1865 nearly to the end of 1870—General Lee continued to concentrate his entire attention and all his energies upon his duties as President of Washington College, to which his great name, and the desire of Southern parents to have their sons educated under a guide so illustrious, attracted, as we have said, more than five hundred students. The sedentary nature of these occupations was a painful trial to one so long accustomed to lead a life of activity; but it was not in the character of the individual to allow personal considerations to interfere with the performance of his duty; and the laborious supervision of the education of this large number of young gentlemen continued, day after day, and year after year, to occupy his mind and his time, to the exclusion, wellnigh, of every other thought. His personal popularity with the students was very great, and it is unnecessary to add that their respect for him was unbounded. By the citizens of Lexington, and especially the graver and more pious portion, he was regarded with a love and admiration greater than any felt for him during the progress of his military career.

This was attributable, doubtless, to the franker and clearer exhibition by General Lee, in his latter years, of that extraordinary gentleness and sweetness, culminating in devoted Christian piety, which—concealed from all eyes, in some degree, during the war—now plainly revealed themselves, and were evidently the broad foundation and controlling influences of his whole life and character. To speak first of his gentleness and moderation in all his views and utterances. Of these eminent virtues—eminent and striking, above all, in a defeated soldier with so much to embitter him—General Lee presented a very remarkable illustration. The result of the war seemed to have left his great soul calm, resigned, and untroubled by the least rancor. While others, not more devoted to the South, permitted passion and sectional animosity to master them, and dictate acts and expressions full of bitterness toward the North, General Lee refrained systematically from every thing of that description; and by simple force of greatness, one would have said, rose above all prejudices and hatreds of the hour, counselling, and giving in his own person to all who approached him the example of moderation and Christian charity. He aimed to keep alive the old Southern traditions of honor and virtue; but not that sectional hatred which could produce only evil. To a lady who had lost her husband in the war, and, on bringing her two sons to the college, indulged in expressions of great bitterness toward the North, General Lee said, gently: "Madam, do not train up your children in hostility to the Government of the United States. Remember that we are one country now. Dismiss from your mind all sectional feeling, and bring them up to be Americans."

A still more suggestive exhibition of his freedom from rancor was presented in an interview which is thus described:

"One day last autumn the writer saw General Lee standing at his gate, talking pleasantly to an humbly-clad man, who seemed very much pleased at the cordial courtesy of the great chieftain, and turned off, evidently delighted, as we came up. After exchanging salutations, the general said, pointing to the retreating form, 'That is one of our old soldiers, who is in necessitous circumstances.' I took it for granted that it was some veteran Confederate, when the noble-hearted chieftain quietly added, 'He fought on the other side, but we must not think of that.' I afterward ascertained—not from General Lee, for he never alluded to his charities—that he had not only spoken kindly to this 'old soldier' who had 'fought on the other side,' but had sent him on his way rejoicing in a liberal contribution to his necessities."

Of the extent of this Christian moderation another proof was given by the soldier, at a moment when he might not unreasonably have been supposed to labor under emotions of the extremest bitterness. Soon after his return to Richmond, in April, 1865, when the *immedicabile vulnus* of surrender was still open and bleeding, a gentleman was requested by the Federal commander in the city to communicate to General Lee the fact that he was about to be indicted in the United States courts for treason.[1] In acquitting himself of his commission, the gentleman expressed sentiments of violent indignation at such a proceeding. But these feelings General Lee did not seem to share. The threat of arraigning him as a traitor produced no other effect upon him than to bring a smile to his lips; and, taking the hand of his friend, as the latter rose to go, he said, in his mildest tones: "We must forgive our enemies. I can truly say that not a day has passed since the war began that I have not prayed for them."

[Footnote 1: This was afterward done by one of the Federal judges, but resulted in nothing.]

The incidents here related define the views and feelings of General Lee as accurately as they could be set forth in a whole volume. The defeated commander, who could open his poor purse to "one of *our*old soldiers who *fought on the other side*," and pray daily during the bitterest of conflicts for his enemies, must surely have trained his spirit to the perfection of Christian charity.

Of the strength and controlling character of General Lee's religious convictions we have more than once spoken in preceding pages of this volume. These now seemed to exert a more marked influence over his life, and indeed to shape every action and utterance of the man. During the war he had exhibited much greater reserve upon this the most important of all subjects which can engage the attention of a human being; and, although he had been from an early period, we believe, a communicant of the Protestant Episcopal Church, he seldom discussed religious questions, or spoke of his own feelings, presenting in this a marked contrast, as we have said, to his illustrious associate General Jackson.

Even during the war, however, as the reader has seen in our notices of his character at the end of 1863, General Lee's piety revealed itself in conversations with his chaplains and other good men; and was not concealed from the troops, as on the occasion of the prayer-meeting in the midst of the fighting at Mine Run. On another occasion, when reviewing his army near Winchester, he was seen to raise his hat to a chaplain with the words, "I salute the Church of God;" and again, near Petersburg, was observed kneeling in prayer, a short distance from the road, as his troops marched by. Still another incident of the period—that of the war—will be recorded here in the words of the Rev. J. William Jones, who relates it:

"Not long before the evacuation of Petersburg, the writer was one day distributing tracts along the trenches, when he perceived a brilliant cavalcade approaching. General Lee—accompanied by General John B. Gordon, General A.P. Hill, and other general officers, with their staffs—was inspecting our lines and reconnoitring those of the enemy. The keen eye of

Gordon recognized, and his cordial grasp detained, the humble tract-distributor, as he warmly inquired about his work. General Lee at once reined in his horse and joined in the conversation, the rest of the party gathered around, and the humble colporteur thus became the centre of a group of whose notice the highest princes of earth might well be proud. General Lee asked if we ever had calls for prayer-books, and said that if we would call at his headquarters he would give us some for distribution—'that some friend in Richmond had given him a new prayer-book, and, upon his saying that he would give his old one, that he had used ever since the Mexican War, to some soldier, the friend had offered him a dozen new books for the old one, and he had, of course, accepted so good an offer, and now had twelve instead of one to give away.' We called at the appointed hour. The general had gone out on some important matter, but (even amid his pressing duties) had left the prayer-books with a member of his staff, with instructions concerning them. He had written on the fly-leaf of each, 'Presented by R.E. Lee,' and we are sure that those of the gallant men to whom they were given who survive the war will now cherish them as precious legacies, and hand them down as heirlooms in their families."

These incidents unmistakably indicate that General Lee concealed, under the natural reserve of his character, an earnest religious belief and trust in God and our Saviour. Nor was this a new sentiment with him. After his death a well-worn pocket Bible was found in his chamber, in which was written, "R.E. Lee, Lieutenant-Colonel, U.S. Army." It was plain, from this, that, even during the days of his earlier manhood, in Mexico and on the Western prairies, he had read his Bible, and striven to conform his life to its teachings.

With the retirement of the great soldier, however, from the cares of command which necessarily interfered in a large degree with pious exercises and meditations, the religious phase of his character became more clearly defined, assuming far more prominent and striking proportions. The sufferings of the Southern people doubtless had a powerful effect upon him, and, feeling the powerlessness of man, he must have turned to God for comfort. But this inquiry is too profound for the present writer. He shrinks from the attempt to sound the depths of this truly great soul, with the view of discovering the influences which moulded it into an almost ideal perfection. General Lee was, fortunately for the world, surrounded in his latter days by good and intelligent men, fully competent to present a complete exposition of his views and feelings—and to these the arduous undertaking is left. Our easier task is to place upon record such incidents as we have gathered, bearing upon the religious phase of the illustrious soldier's character.

His earnest piety cannot be better displayed than in the anxiety which he felt for the conversion of his students, Conversing with the Rev. Dr. Kirkpatrick, of the Presbyterian Church, on the subject of the religious welfare of those intrusted to his charge, "he was so overcome by emotion," says Dr. Kirkpatrick, "that he could not utter the words which were on his tongue." His utterance was choked, but recovering himself, with his eyes overflowing with tears, his lips quivering with emotion, and both hands raised, he exclaimed: "Oh! doctor, if I could only know that all the young men in the college were good Christians, I should have nothing more to desire."

When another minister, the Rev. Mr. Jones, delivered an earnest address at the "Concert of Prayer for Colleges," urging that all Christians should pray for the aid of the Holy Spirit in changing the hearts of the students, General Lee, after the meeting, approached the minister and said with great warmth: "I wish, sir, to thank you for your address. It was just what we needed. Our great want is a revival, which shall bring these young men to Christ."

One morning, while the venerable Dr. White was passing General Lee's house, on his way to chapel, the general joined him, and they entered into conversation upon religious subjects. General Lee said little, but, just as they reached the college, stopped and remarked with great earnestness, his eyes filling with tears as he spoke: "I shall be disappointed, sir, I shall fail in the leading object that brought me here, unless the young men all become real Christians; and I wish you and others of your sacred profession to de all you can to accomplish this result."

When a great revival of religious feeling took place at the Virginia Military Institute, in 1868, General Lee said to the clergyman of his church with deep feeling: "That is the best news I have heard since I have been in Lexington. Would that we could have such a revival in all our colleges!"

Although a member of the Protestant Episcopal Church, and preferring that communion, General Lee seems to have been completely exempt from sectarian feeling, and to have aimed first and last to be a true Christian, loving God and his neighbor, and not busying himself about theological dogmas. When he was asked once whether he believed in the Apostolic succession, he replied that he had never thought of it, and aimed only to become a "real Christian." His catholic views were shown by the letters of invitation, which he addressed, at the commencement of each session of the college, to ministers of all religious denominations at Lexington, to conduct, in turn, the religious exercises at the college chapel; and his charities, which were large for a person of his limited means, were given to all alike. These charities he seems to have regarded as a binding duty, and were so private that only those receiving them knew any thing of them. It only came to be known accidentally that in 1870 he gave one hundred dollars for the education of the orphans of Southern soldiers, one hundred dollars to the Young Men's Christian Association, and regularly made other donations, amounting in all to considerable sums. Nearly his last act was a liberal contribution to an important object connected with his church.

We shall conclude these anecdotes, illustrating General Lee's religious character, with one for which we are indebted to the kindness of a reverend clergyman, of Lexington, who knew General Lee intimately in his latter years, and enjoyed his confidence. The incident will present in an agreeable light the great soldier's simplicity and love for children, and no less his catholic feelings in reference to sects in the Christian Church:

"I will give you just another incident," writes the reverend gentleman, "illustrating General Lee's love for children, and their freedom with him. When I first came to Lexington, my boy Carter (just four years old then) used to go with me to chapel service when it was my turn to officiate. The general would tell him that he must always sit by him; and it was a scene for a painter, to see the great chieftain reverentially listening to the truths of God's word, and the little boy nestling close to him. One Sunday our Sunday-school superintendent told the children that they must bring in some new scholars, and that they must bring old people as well as the young, since none were too old or too wise to learn God's word. The next Sabbath Carter was with me at the chapel, from which he was to go with me to the Sunday-school. At the close of the service, I noticed that Carter was talking very earnestly with General Lee, who seemed very much amused, and, on calling him to come with me, he said, with childish simplicity: 'Father, I am trying to get General Lee to go to the Sunday-school and *be my scholar*.' 'But,' said I, 'if the general goes to any school, he will go to his own.' 'Which is his own, father?' 'The Episcopal,' I replied. Heaving a deep sigh, and with a look of disappointment, the little fellow said: 'I am very sorry he is '*Piscopal*. I wish he was a Baptist, so he could go to *our* Sunday-school, and be my scholar.' The general seemed very much amused and interested as he replied, 'Ah! Carter, we must all try and be *good Christians*—that is the most important thing.' 'He knew all the children in town,' adds Mr. Jones, 'and their grief at his death was very touching.'"

This incident may appear singular to those who have been accustomed to regard General Lee as a cold, reserved, and even stern human being—a statue, beneath whose chill surface no heart ever throbbed. But, instead of a marble heart, there lay, under the gray uniform of the soldier, one of warm flesh and blood—tender, impressible, susceptible to the quick touches of all gentle and sweet emotion, and filling, as it were, with quiet happiness, at the sight of children and the sound of their voices. This impressibility has even been made the subject of criticism. A foreign writer declares that the soldier's character exhibited a "feminine" softness, unfitting him for the conduct of affairs of moment. What the Confederacy wanted, intimates the writer in question, was a rough dictator, with little regard for nice questions of law—one to lay the rough hand of the born master on the helm, and force the crew, from the highest to the lowest, to obey his will. That will probably remain a question. General Lee's *will* was strong enough to break down all obstacles but those erected by rightful authority; that with this masculine strength he united an exquisite gentleness, is equally beyond question. A noble action flushed his cheek with an emotion that the reader may, if he will, call "feminine." A tale of suffering brought a sudden moisture to his eyes; and a loving message from one of his poor old soldiers was seen one day to melt him to tears.

This poor and incomplete attempt to indicate some of the less-known traits of the illustrious commander-in-chief of the Southern armies will now be brought to a conclusion; we approach the sorrowful moment when, surrounded by his weeping family,[1] he tranquilly passed away.

[Footnote 1: General Lee had three sons and four daughters, all of whom are living except one of the latter, Miss Anne Lee, who died in North Carolina during the war. The sons were General G.W. Custis Lee, aide-de-camp to President Davis—subsequently commander of infantry in the field, and now president of Washington and Lee College, an officer of such ability and of character so eminent that President Davis regarded him as a fit successor of his illustrious father in command of the Army of Northern Virginia—General W.H.F. Lee, a prominent and able commander of cavalry, and Captain Robert E. Lee, an efficient member of the cavalry-staff. These gentlemen bore their full share in the perils and hardships of the war, from its commencement to the surrender at Appomattox.]

On the 28th of September, 1870, after laborious attention to his duties during the early part of the day, General Lee attended, in the afternoon, a meeting of the Vestry of Grace Church, of which he was a member. Over this meeting he presided, and it was afterward remembered that his last public act was to contribute the sum of fifty-five dollars to some good object, the requisite amount to effect which was thus made up. After the meeting, General Lee returned to his home, and, when tea was served, took his place at the table to say grace, as was his habit, as it had been in camp throughout the war. His lips opened, but no sound issued from them, and he sank back in his chair, from which he was carried to bed.

The painful intelligence immediately became known throughout Lexington, and the utmost grief and consternation were visible upon every face. It was hoped, at first, that the attack would not prove serious, and that General Lee would soon be able to resume his duties. But this hope was soon dissipated. The skilful physicians who hastened to his bedside pronounced his malady congestion of the brain, and, from the appearance of the patient, who lay in a species of coma, the attack was evidently of the most alarming character. The most discouraging phase of the case was, that, physically, General Lee was—if we may so say—in perfect health. His superb physique, although not perhaps as vigorous and robust as during the war, exhibited no indication whatever of disease. His health appeared perfect, and twenty years more of life might have been predicted for him from simple reference to his appearance.

The malady was more deeply seated, however, than any bodily disease; the cerebral congestion was but a symptom of the mental malady which was killing its victim. From the testimony of the able physicians who watched the great soldier, day and night, throughout his illness, and are thus best competent to speak upon the subject, there seems no doubt that General Lee's condition was the result of mental depression produced by the sufferings of the Southern people. Every mail, it is said, had brought him the most piteous appeals for assistance, from old soldiers whose families were in want of bread; and the woes of these poor people had a prostrating effect upon him. A year or two before, his health had been seriously impaired by this brooding depression, and he had visited North Carolina, the White Sulphur Springs, and other places, to divert his mind. In this he failed. The shadow went with him, and the result was, at last, the alarming attack from which he never rallied. During the two weeks of his illness he scarcely spoke, and evidently regarded his condition as hopeless. When one of his physicians said to him, "General, you must make haste and get well; *Traveller* has been standing so long in his stable that he needs exercise." General Lee shook his head slowly, to indicate that he would never again mount his favorite horse.

He remained in this state, with few alterations in his condition, until Wednesday; October 12th, when, about nine in the morning, in the midst of his family, the great soldier tranquilly expired.

Of the universal grief of the Southern people when the intelligence was transmitted by telegraph to all parts of the country, it is not necessary that we should speak. The death of Lee seemed to make all hearts stand still; and the tolling of bells, flags at half-mast, and public meetings of citizens, wearing mourning, marked, in every portion of the South, the sense of a great public calamity. It is not an exaggeration to say that, in ten thousand Southern homes, tears came to the eyes not only of women, but of bearded men, and that the words, "Lee is dead!" fell like a funeral-knell upon every heart.

When the intelligence reached Richmond, the Legislature passed resolutions expressive of the general sorrow, and requesting that the remains of General Lee might be interred in Holywood Cemetery—Mr. Walker, the Governor, expressing in a special message his participation in the grief of the people of Virginia and the South. The family of General Lee, however, preferred that his remains should rest at the scene of his last labors, and beneath the chapel of Washington College they were accordingly interred. The ceremony was imposing, and will long be remembered.

On the morning of the 13th, the body was borne to the college chapel. In front moved a guard of honor, composed of old Confederate soldiers; behind these came the clergy; then the hearse; in rear of which was led the dead soldier's favorite war-horse "Traveller," his equipments wreathed with crape. The trustees and faculty of the college, the cadets of the Military Institute, and a large number of citizens followed—and the procession moved slowly from the northeastern gate of the president's house to the college chapel, above which, draped in mourning, and at half-mast, floated the flag of Virginia—the only one displayed during this or any other portion of the funeral ceremonies.

On the platform of the chapel the body lay in state throughout this and the succeeding day. The coffin was covered with evergreens and flowers, and the face of the dead was uncovered that all might look for the last time on the pale features of the illustrious soldier. The body was dressed in a simple suit of black, and the appearance of the face was perfectly natural. Great crowds visited the chapel, passing solemnly in front of the coffin—the silence interrupted only by sobs.

Throughout the 14th the body continued to be in state, and to be visited by thousands. On the 15th a great funeral procession preceded the commission of it to its last resting place. At an early hour the crowd began to assemble in the vicinity of the college, which was draped in mourning. This great concourse was composed of men, women, and children, all wearing crape, and the little children seemed as much penetrated by the general distress as the elders. The bells of the churches began to toll; and at ten o'clock the students of the college, and officers and soldiers of the Confederate army—numbering together nearly one thousand persons—formed in front of the chapel. Between the two bodies stood the hearse, and the gray horse of the soldier, both draped in mourning.

The procession then began to move, to the strains of martial music. The military escort, together with the staff-officers of General Lee, moved in front; the faculty and students followed behind the hearse; and in rear came a committee of the Legislative dignitaries of the Commonwealth, and a great multitude of citizens from all portions of the State. The procession continued its way toward the Institute, where the cadets made the military salute as the hearse passed in front of them, and the sudden thunder of artillery awoke the echoes from the hills. The cadets then joined the procession, which was more than a mile in length; and, heralded by the fire of artillery every few minutes, it moved back to the college chapel, where the last services were performed.

General Lee had requested, it is said, that no funeral oration should be pronounced above his remains, and the Rev. William N. Pendleton simply read the beautiful burial-service of the Episcopal Church. The coffin, still covered with evergreens and flowers, was then lowered to its resting-place beneath the chapel, amid the sobs and tears of the great assembly; and all that was mortal of the illustrious soldier disappeared from the world's eyes.

What thus disappeared was little. What remained was much—the memory of the virtues and the glory of the greatest of Virginians.

APPENDIX.

We here present to the reader a more detailed account of the ceremonies attending the burial of General Lee, and a selection from the countless addresses delivered in various portions of the country when his death was announced. To notice the honors paid to his memory in every city, town, and village of the South, would fill a volume, and be wholly unnecessary. It is equally unnecessary to speak of the great meetings at Richmond, Baltimore, and elsewhere, resulting in the formation of the "Lee Memorial Association" for the erection of a monument to the dead commander.

The addresses here presented are placed on record rather for their biographical interest, than to do honor to the dead. Of him it may justly be said that he needs no record of his virtues and his glory. His illustrious memory is fresh to-day, and will be fresh throughout all coming generations, in every heart.

I.

THE FUNERAL OF GENERAL LEE.

The morning of the obsequies of General Lee broke bright and cheerful over the sorrowful town of Lexington. Toward noon the sun poured down with all the genial warmth of Indian summer, and after mid-day it was hot, though not uncomfortably so. The same solemnity of yesterday reigned supreme, with the difference, that people came thronging into town, making a mournful scene of bustle. The gloomy faces, the comparative silence, the badges and emblems of mourning that everywhere met the eye, and the noiseless, strict decorum which was observed, told how universal and deep were the love and veneration of the people for the illustrious dead. Every one uniformly and religiously wore the emblematic crape, even to the women and children, who were crowding to the college chapel with wreaths of flowers fringed with mourning. All sorrowfully and religiously paid their last tributes of respect and affection to the great dead, and none there were who did not feel a just pride in the sad offices.

AT THE COLLEGE GROUNDS.

Immediately in front of the chapel the scene was peculiarly sad. All around the buildings were gloomily draped in mourning, and the students strolled listlessly over the grounds, awaiting the formation of the funeral procession. Ladies thronged about the chapel with tearful eyes, children wept outright, every face wore a saddened expression, while the solemn tolling of the church-bells rendered the scene still more one of grandeur and gloom. The bells of the churches joined in the mournful requiem.

THE FUNERAL PROCESSION.

At ten o'clock precisely, in accordance with the programme agreed upon, the students, numbering four hundred, formed in front and to the right of the chapel. To the left an escort of honor, numbering some three hundred ex-officers and soldiers, was formed, at the head of which, near the southwestern entrance to the grounds, was the Institute band. Between these two bodies—the soldiers and students—stood the hearse and the gray war-steed of the dead hero, both draped in mourning. The marshals of the procession, twenty-one in number, wore spotless white sashes, tied at the waist and shoulders with crape, and carrying *bâtons* also enveloped in the same emblematic material.

Shortly after ten, at a signal from the chief marshal, the solemn *cortége* moved off to the music of a mournful dirge. General Bradley Johnson headed the escort of officers and soldiers, with Colonel Charles T. Venable and Colonel Walters H. Taylor, both former assistant adjutant-generals on the staff of the lamented dead. The physicians of General Lee and the Faculty of the college fell in immediately behind the hearse, the students following. Slowly and solemnly the procession moved from the college grounds down Washington Street to Jefferson Street, up Jefferson Street to Franklin Hall, thence to Main Street, where they were joined by a committee of the Legislature, dignitaries of the State, and the citizens generally. Moving still onward, this grand funeral pageant, which had now assumed gigantic proportions, extending nearly a mile in length, soon reached the northeastern extremity of the town, when it took the road to the Virginia Military Institute.

AT THE MILITARY INSTITUTE.

Here the scene was highly impressive and imposing. In front of the Institute the battalion of cadets, three hundred in number, were drawn up in line, wearing their full gray uniform, with badges of mourning, and having on all their equipments and side-arms, but without their muskets. Spectators thronged the entire line of the procession, gazing sadly as it wended its way, and the sites around the Institute were crowded. As the *cortége* entered the Institute grounds a salute of artillery thundered its arrival, and reverberated it far across the distant hills and valleys of Virginia, awakening echoes which have been hushed since Lee manfully gave up the struggle of the "lost cause" at Appomattox. Winding along the indicated route toward the grounds of Washington College, the procession slowly moved past the Institute, and when the war-horse and hearse of the dead chieftain came in front of the battalion of cadets, they uncovered their heads as a salute of reverence and respect, which was promptly followed by the spectators. When this was concluded, the visitors and Faculty of the Institute joined the procession, and the battalion of cadets filed into the line in order, and with the greatest precision.

ORDER OF THE PROCESSION.

The following was the order of the procession when it was completed:

Music.

Escort of Honor, consisting of Officers and Soldiers of the Confederate
Army.

Chaplain and other Clergy.

Hearse and Pall-bearers.

General Lee's Horse.

The Attending Physicians.

Trustees and Faculty of Washington College.

Dignitaries of the State of Virginia.

Visitors and Faculty of the Virginia Military Institute.

Other Representative Bodies and Distinguished Visitors.

Alumni of Washington College.

Citizens.

Cadets Virginia Military Institute.

Students of Washington College as Guard of Honor

AT THE CHAPEL.

After the first salute, a gun was fired every three minutes. Moving still to the sound of martial music, in honor of the dead, the procession reëntered the grounds of Washington College by the northeastern gate, and was halted in front of the chapel. Then followed an imposing ceremony. The cadets of the Institute were detached from the line, and marched in double file into the chapel up one of the aisles, past the remains of the illustrious dead, which lay in state on the rostrum, and down the other aisle out of the church. The students of Washington College followed next, passing with bowed heads before the mortal remains of him they revered and loved so much and well as their president and friend. The side-aisles and galleries were crowded with ladies, Emblems of mourning met the eye on all sides, and feminine affection had hung funeral garlands of flowers upon all the pillars and walls. The central pews were filled with the escort of honor, composed of former Confederate soldiers from this and adjoining counties, while the spacious platform was crowded with the trustees, faculties, clergy, Legislative Committee, and distinguished visitors. Within and without the consecrated hall the scene was alike imposing. The blue mountains of Virginia, towering in the near horizon; the lovely village of Lexington, sleeping in the calm, unruffled air, and the softened autumn sunlight; the vast assemblage, mute and sorrowful; the tolling bells, and pealing cannon, and solemn words of funeral service, combined to render the scene one never to be forgotten.

The sons of General Lee—W.H.F. Lee, G.W.C. Lee, and Robert E. Lee—with their sisters, Misses Agnes and Mildred Lee, and the nephews of the dead, Fitzhugh, Henry C., and Robert C. Lee, entered the church with bowed heads, and silently took seats in front of the rostrum.

THE FUNERAL SERVICES AND INTERMENT.

Then followed the impressive funeral services of the Episcopal Church for the dead, amid a silence and solemnity that were imposing and sublimely grand. There was no funeral oration, in compliance with the expressed wish of the distinguished dead; and at the conclusion of the services in the chapel the vast congregation went out and mingled with the crowd without, who were unable to gain admission. The coffin was then carried by the pall-bearers to the library-room, in the basement of the chapel, where it was lowered into the vault prepared for its reception. The funeral services were concluded in the open air by prayer, and the singing of General Lee's favorite hymn, commencing with the well-known line—

"How firm a foundation, ye saint of the Lord,
Is laid for your faith in His excellent Word!"

and thus closed the funeral obsequies of Robert Edward Lee, to whom may be fitly applied the grand poetic epitaph:

"Ne'er to the mansions where the mighty rest,
Since their foundations, came a nobler guest;
Nor e'er was to the bowers of bliss conveyed
A purer saint or a more welcome shade."

II.

TRIBUTES TO GENERAL LEE.

In the deep emotion with which the death of General Lee has filled all classes of our people—says the *Southern Magazine*, from whose pages this interesting summary is taken—we have thought that a selection of the most eloquent or otherwise interesting addresses delivered at the various memorial meetings may not be unacceptable.

LOUISVILLE, KY.

On October 15th nearly the whole city was draped in mourning, and business was suspended. A funeral service was held at St. Paul's Church. In the evening an immense meeting assembled at Weissiger Hall, and, after an opening address by Mayor Baxter, the following resolutions were adopted:

"*Resolved*, That, in the death of Robert E. Lee, the American people, without regard to States or sections, or antecedents, or opinions, lose a great and good man, a distinguished and useful citizen, renowned not less in arms than in the arts of peace; and that the cause of public instruction and popular culture is deprived of a representative whose influence and example will be felt by the youth of our country for long ages after the passions in the midst of which he was engaged, but which he did not share, have passed into history, and the peace and fraternity of the American Republic are cemented and restored by the broadest and purest American sentiment."

"*Resolved*, That a copy of these resolutions be forwarded to the family of General Lee, to the Trustees of Washington College, and to the Governor and General Assembly of Virginia."

ADDRESS OF GENERAL BRECKINRIDGE.

"*Mr. President, Ladies, and Gentlemen*: In the humble part which it falls to me to take in these interesting ceremonies, if for any cause it has been supposed that I am to deliver a lengthy address, I am not responsible for the origination of that supposition. I came here to-night simply to mingle my grief with yours at the loss of one of our most distinguished citizens, and, indeed, I feel more like silence than like words. I am awe-stricken in the presence of this vast assemblage, and my mind goes back to the past. It is preoccupied by memories coming in prominent review of the frequent and ever-varying vicissitudes which have characterized the last ten years. I find myself in the presence of a vast assemblage of the people of this great and growing city, who meet together, without distinction of party, and presided over by your chief officer, for the purpose of expressing respect to the memory of the man who was the leader of the Confederate armies in the late war between the States. It is in itself the omen of reunion. I am not surprised at the spectacle presented here. Throughout the entire South one universal cry of grief has broken forth at the death of General Lee, and in a very large portion of the North manly and noble tributes have been paid to his memory.

"My words shall be brief but plain. Why is it that at the South we see this universal, spontaneous demonstration? First, because most of the people mourn the loss of a leader and a friend, but beyond that I must say they seem to enter an unconscious protest against the ascription either to him or them of treason or personal dishonor. It may be an unconscious protest against the employment by a portion of the public press of those epithets which have ceased to be used in social intercourse. It is an invitation on their part to the people of the North and South, East and West, if there be any remaining rancor in their bosoms, to bury it in the grave forever. I will not recall the past. I will not enter upon any considerations of the cause of that great struggle. This demonstration we see around us gives the plainest evidence that there is no disposition to indulge in useless repinings at the results of that great struggle. It is for the pen of the historian to declare the cause, progress, and probable consequences of it. In regard to those who followed General Lee, who gloried in his successes and shared his misfortunes, I have but this to say: the world watched the contest in which they were engaged, and yet gives testimony to their gallantry,

"The magnanimity with which they accepted the results of their defeat, the obedience they have yielded to the laws of the Federal Government, give an exhibition so rare that they are ennobled by their calm yet noble submission. For the rest their escutcheon is unstained. The conquerors themselves, for their own glory, must confess that they were brave. Neither, my friends, do I come here to-night to speak of the military career of General Lee. I need not speak of it this evening. I believe that this is universally recognized, not only in the United States, but in Europe; it has made the circuit of the world. I come but to utter my tribute to him as a man and as a citizen. As a man he will be remembered in history as a man of the epoch. How little need I to speak of his character after listening to the thrilling delineation of it which we had this morning! We all know that he was great, noble, and self-poised. He was just and moderate, but was, perhaps, misunderstood by those who were not personally acquainted with him. He was supposed to be just, but cold. Far from it. He had a warm, affectionate heart. During the last year of that unfortunate struggle it was my good fortune to spend a great deal of time with him. I was almost constantly by his side, and it was during the two months immediately preceding the fall of Richmond that I came to know and fully understand the true nobility of his character. In all those long vigils he was considerate and kind, gentle, firm, and self-poised. I can give no better idea of the impression it made upon me than to say it inspired me with an ardent love of the man and a profound veneration of his character. It was so massive and noble, so grand in its proportions, that all men must admire its heroism and gallantry, yet so gentle and tender that a woman might adopt and claim it as her own. If the spirit which animates the assembly before me to-night shall become general and permeate the whole country, then may we say the wounds of the late war are truly healed. We ask for him only what we give to others. Among the more eminent of the departed Federal generals who were distinguished for their gallantry, their nobility of character, and their patriotism, may be mentioned Thomas and McPherson. What Confederate is there who would refuse to raise his cap as their funeral-train went by or hesitate to drop a flower upon their graves? Why? Because they were men of courage, honor, and nobility; because they were true to their convictions of right, and soldiers whose hands were unstained by cruelty or pillage.

"Those of us who were so fortunate as to know him, and who have appeared before this assemblage, composed of all shades of opinion, claim for him your veneration, because he was pure and noble, and it is because of this that we see the cities and towns of the South in mourning. This has been the expression throughout the whole South, without distinction of party, and also of a large portion of the North. Is not this why these tributes have been paid to his memory? Is it not because his piety was humble and sincere? Because he accorded in victory; because he filled his position with admirable dignity; because he taught his prostrate comrades how to suffer and be strong? In a word, because he was one of the noblest products of this hemisphere, a fit object to sit in the niche which he created in the Temple of Fame.

"But he failed. The result is in the future. It may be for better or for worse. We hope for the better. But this is not the test for his greatness and goodness. Success often gilds the shallow man, but it is disaster alone that reveals the qualities of true greatness. Was his life a failure? Is only that man successful who erects a material monument of greatness by the enforcement of his ideas? Is not that man successful also, who, by his valor, moderation, and courage, with all their associate virtues, presents to the world such a specimen of true manhood as his children and children's children will be proud to imitate? In this sense he was not a failure.

"Pardon me for having detained you so long. I know there are here and there those who will reach out and attempt to pluck from his name the glory which surrounds it, and strike with malignant fury at the honors awarded to him; yet history will declare that the remains which repose in the vault beneath the little chapel in the lovely Virginia Valley are not only those of a valorous soldier, but those of a great and good American."

General John W. Finnell next addressed the audience briefly, and was followed by.
GENERAL WILLIAM PRESTON.

"*Mr. Chairman, Ladies, and Gentlemen*: I feel that it would be very difficult for me to add any eulogy to those which are contained in the resolutions of the committee, or a more merited tribute of praise than those which have already fallen from the lips of the gentlemen who have preceded me. Yet, on an occasion like this, I am willing to come forward and add a word to testify my appreciation of the great virtues and admirable character of one that commands, not only our admiration, but that of the entire country. Not alone of the entire country, but his character has excited more admiration in Europe than among ourselves. In coming ages his name will be marked with lustre, and will be one of the richest treasures of the future. I speak of one just gone down to death; ripe in all the noble attributes of manhood, and illustrious by deeds the most remarkable in character that have occurred in the history of America since its discovery. It is now some two-and-twenty years since I first made the acquaintance of General Lee. He was then in the prime of manhood, in Mexico, and I first saw him as the chief-engineer of General Scott in the Valley of Mexico. I see around me two old comrades who then saw General Lee. He was a man of remarkable personal beauty and great grace of body. He had a finished form, delicate hands, graceful in person, while here and there a gray hair streaked with silver the dark locks with which Nature had clothed his noble brow. There were discerning minds that appreciated his genius, and saw in him the coming Captain of America. His commander and his comrades appreciated his ability. To a club which was then organized he belonged, together with General McClellan, General Albert Sydney Johnston, General Beauregard, and a host of others. They recognized in Lee a master-spirit..

"He was never violent; he never wrangled. He was averse to quarrelling, and not a single difficulty marked his career; but all acknowledged his justness and wonderful evenness of mind. Rare intelligence, combined with these qualities, served to make him a fit representative of his great prototype, General Washington. He had been accomplished by every finish that a military education could bestow.

"I remember when General Lee was appointed lieutenant-colonel, at the same time that Sydney Johnston was appointed colonel, and General Scott thought that Lee should have been colonel. I was talking with General Scott on the subject long before the late struggle between the North and South took place, and he then said that Lee was the greatest living soldier in America. He did not object to the other commission, but he thought Lee should have been first promoted. Finally, he said to me with emphasis, which you will pardon me for relating, 'I tell you that, if I were on my death-bed to-morrow, and the President of the United States should tell me that a great battle was to be fought for the liberty or slavery of the country, and asked my judgment as to the ability of a commander, I would say with my dying breath, let it be Robert E. Lee.' Ah! great soldier that he was, princely general that he was, he has fulfilled his mission, and borne it so that no invidious tongue can level the shafts of calumny at the great character which he has left behind him.

"But, ladies and gentlemen, it was not in this that the matchless attributes of his character were found. You have assembled here, not so much to do honor to General Lee, but to testify your appreciation of the worth of the principles governing his character; and if the minds of this assemblage were explored, you would find there was a gentleness and a grace in his character which had won your love and brought forth testimonials of universal admiration. Take but a single instance. At the battle of Gettysburg, after the attack on the cemetery, when his troops were repulsed and beaten, the men threw up their muskets and said, 'General, we have failed, and it is our fault.' 'No, my men,' said he, knowing the style of fighting of General Stonewall Jackson, 'you have done well; 'tis my fault; I am to blame, and no one but me.' What man is there that would not have gone to renewed death for such a leader? So, when we examine his whole character, it is in his private life that you find his true greatness—the Christian simplicity of his character and his great veneration for truth and nobility, the grand elements of his greatness. What man could have laid down his sword at the feet of a victorious general with greater dignity than did he at Appomattox Court-House? He laid down his sword with grace and dignity, and secured for his soldiers the best terms that fortune would permit. In that he shows marked greatness seldom shown by great captains.

"After the battle of Sedan, the wild cries of the citizens of Paris went out for the blood of the emperor; but at Appomattox, veneration and love only met the eyes of the troops who looked upon their commander. I will not trespass upon your time much farther. When I last saw him the raven hair had turned white. In a small village church his reverent head was bowed in prayer. The humblest step was that of Robert E. Lee, as he entered the portals of the temple erected to God. In broken responses he answered to the services of the Church. Noble, sincere, and humble in his religion, he showed forth his true character in laying aside his sword to educate the youth of his country. Never did he appear more noble than at that time. He is now gone, and rests in peace, and has crossed that mysterious stream that Stonewall Jackson saw with inspired eyes when he asked that he might be permitted to take his troops across the river and forever rest beneath the shadows of the trees."

After a few remarks from Hon. D.Y. Lyttle, the meeting adjourned.

165

AUGUSTA, GA.

A meeting was held at Augusta, on October 18th, at the City Hall. The preamble and resolutions adopted were as follows:

"*Whereas*, This day, throughout all this Southern land, sorrow, many-tongued, is ascending to heaven for the death of Robert E. Lee, and communities everywhere are honoring themselves in striving to do honor to that great name; and we, the people of Augusta, who were not laggards in upholding his glorious banner while it floated to the breeze, would swell the general lamentation of his departure:

therefore be it

"*Resolved*, That no people in the tide of time has been bereaved as we are bereaved; for no other people has had such a man to lose. Greece, rich in heroes; Rome, prolific mother of great citizens, so that the name of Roman is the synonyme of all that is noblest in citizenship—had no man coming up to the full measure of this great departed. On scores of battle-fields, consummate commander; everywhere, bravest soldier; in failure, sublimest hero; in disbanding his army, most pathetic of writers; in persecution, most patient of power's victims; in private life, purest of men—he was such that all Christendom, with one consent, named him GREAT. We, recalling that so also mankind have styled Alexander, Caesar, Frederick, and Napoleon, and beholding in the Confederate leader qualities higher and better than theirs, find that language poor indeed which only enables us to call him 'great'—him standing among the great of all ages preëminent.

"*Resolved*, That our admiration of the man is not the partial judgment of his adherents only; but so clear stand his greatness and his goodness, that even the bitterest of foes has not ventured to asperse him. While the air has been filled with calumnies and revilings of his cause, none have been aimed at him. If there are spirits so base that they cannot discover and reverence his greatness and his goodness, they have at least shrunk from encountering the certain indignation of mankind. This day—disfranchised by stupid power as he was; branded, as he was, in the perverted vocabulary of usurpers as rebel and traitor—his death has even in distant lands moved more tongues and stirred more hearts than the siege of a mighty city and the triumphs of a great king.

"*Resolved*, That, while he died far too soon for his country, he had lived long enough for his fame. This was complete, and the future could unfold nothing to add to it. In this age of startling changes, imagination might have pictured him, even in the years which he yet lacked of the allotted period of human life, once more at the head of devoted armies and the conqueror of glorious fields; but none could have been more glorious than those he had already won. Wrong, too, might again have triumphed over Right, and he have borne defeat with sublimest resignation; but this he had already done at Appomattox. Unrelenting hate to his lost cause might have again consigned him to the walks of private life, and he have become an exemplar of all the virtues of a private station; but this he had already been in the shades of Lexington. The contingencies of the future could only have revealed him greatest soldier, sublimest hero, best of men; and he was already all of these. The years to come were barren of any thing which could add to his perfect name and fame. He had nothing to lose; but, alas! we, his people, every thing by his departure from this world, which was unworthy of him, to that other where the good and the pure of all ages will welcome him. Thither follow him the undying love of every true Southern man and woman, and the admiration of all the world."

ADDRESS OF GENERAL A.R. WRIGHT.

"*Mr. Chairman*: I rise simply to move the adoption of the resolutions which have just been read to the meeting by Major Cumming. You have heard, and the people here assembled have heard, these resolutions. They are truthful, eloquent, and expressive. Although announced as a speaker on this sad occasion, I had determined to forego any such attempt; but an allusion, a passing reference to one of the sublime virtues of the illustrious dead, made in the resolutions which have just been read in your hearing, has induced me to add a word or two. Your resolutions speak of General Lee's patience under the persecutions of power. It was this virtue which ennobled the character, as it was one of the most prominent traits in the life, of him for whose death a whole nation, grief-stricken, mourns, and to pay a tribute to the memory of whom this multitude has assembled here this morning. While General Lee was all, and more than has been said of him—the great general, the true Christian, and the valiant soldier—there was another character in which he appeared more conspicuously than in any of the rest—the quiet dignity with which he encountered defeat, and the patience with which he met the persecution of malignant power. We may search the pages of all history, both sacred and profane, and there seems to be but one character who possessed in so large a degree this remarkable trait. Take General Lee's whole life and examine it; observe his skill and courage as a soldier, his patriotism and his fidelity to principle, the purity of his private life, and then remember the disasters which he faced and the persecutions to which he was subjected, and it would seem that *no one* ever endured so much—not even David, the sweet singer of Israel. Job has been handed down to posterity by the pages of sacred history as the embodiment of patience, as the man who, overwhelmed with the most numerous and bitter afflictions, never lost his fortitude, and who endured every fresh trial with uncomplaining resignation; but it seems to me that even Job displayed not the patience of our own loved hero; for, while Job suffered much, he endured less than General Lee. Job was compelled to lose his children, his friends, and his property, but he was never required to give up country; General Lee was, and, with more than the persecutions of Job, he stands revealed to the world the truest and the most sublime hero whom the ages have produced. To a patriot like Lee the loss of country was the greatest evil which could be experienced, and it was this last blow which has caused us to assemble here to-day to mourn his departure. He lost friends and kindred and property in the struggle, and yet, according to the news which the telegraph brought us this morning, it was the loss of his cause which finally sundered the heart-strings of the hero, and drew him from earth to heaven. Yes, the weight of this great sorrow which first fell upon him under the fatal apple-tree at Appomattox, has dwelt with him, growing heavier and more unendurable with each succeeding year, from that time until last Wednesday morn when the soul of Lee passed away.

"As I said before, Mr. Chairman, I only rose to move the adoption of the resolutions; and if I have said more than I ought to have said, it is because I knew the illustrious dead, because I loved him, and because I mourn his loss."

ADDRESS OF JUDGE HILLIARD.

"It is proper that the people should pay a public tribute to the memory of a great man when he dies. Not a ruler, not one who merely holds a great public position, but a great man, one who has served his day and generation. It cannot benefit the dead, but it is eminently profitable to the living. The consciousness than when we cease to live our memory will be cherished, is a noble incentive to live well. This great popular demonstration is due to General Lee's life and character. It is not ordered by the Government—the Government ignored him; but is rendered as a spontaneous tribute to the memory of an illustrious man—good, true, and great. He held no place in the Government, and since the war has had no military rank; but he was a true man. After all, that is the noblest tribute you can pay to any man, to say of him he was a true man.

"General Lee's character was eminently American. In Europe they have their ideas, their standards of merit, their rewards for great exploits. They cover one with decorations; they give him a great place in the government; they make him a marshal. Wellington began his career with humble rank. He was young Wellesley; he rose to be the Duke of Wellington. In our country we have no such rewards for great deeds. One must enjoy the patronage of the Government, or he must take the fortunes of private life.

"General Lee was educated at the great Military Academy, West Point. He entered the army; was promoted from time to time for brilliant services; in Mexico fought gallantly under the flag of the United States; and was still advancing in his military career in 1861, when Virginia became involved in the great contest that then grew up between the States. Virginia was his mother; she called him to her side to defend her, and, resigning his commission in the Army of the United States, not for a moment looking for advancement there, not counting the cost, not offering his sword to the service of power, nor yet laying it down at the feet of the Government—he unsheathed it and took his stand in defence of the great principles asserted by Virginia in the Revolution, when she contended with Great Britain the right of every people to choose their own form of government. Lost or won, to him the cause was always the same—it was the cause of constitutional liberty. He stood by it to the last. What must have been the convictions of a man like General Lee, when, mounted on the same horse that had borne him in battle, upon which he was seated when the lines of battle formed by his own heroic men wavered, and he seized the standard to lead the charge; but his soldiers rushed to him, and laying their hands on his bridle, said, 'General, we cannot fire a gun unless you retire?' What must have been his emotions as he rode, through his own lines at Appomattox, to the commander of the opposing army, and tendered him his sword? Search the annals of history, ancient and modern; consult the lives of heroes; study the examples of greatness recorded in Greece leading the way on the triumphs of popular liberty, or in Rome in the best days of her imperial rule; take statesmen, generals, or men of patient thought who outwatched the stars in exploring knowledge, and I declare to you that I do not find anywhere a sublimer sentiment than General Lee uttered when he said, 'Human virtue ought to be equal to human calamity.' It will live forever.

"General Lee died at the right time. His sun did not go down in the strife of battle, in the midst of the thunder of cannon, dimmed by the lurid smoke of war. He survived all this: lived with so much dignity; silent, yet thoughtful; unseduced by the offers of gain or of advancement however tempting; disdaining to enter into contests for small objects, until the broad disk went down behind the Virginia hills, shedding its departing lustre not only upon this country but upon

167

the whole world. His memory is as much respected in England as it is here; and at the North as well as at the South true hearts honor it.

"There is one thing I wish to say before I take my seat. General Lee's fame ought to rest on the true base. He did not draw his sword to perpetuate human slavery, whatever may have been his opinions in regard to it; he did not seek to overthrow the Government of the United States. He drew it in defence of constitutional liberty. That cause is not dead, but will live forever. The result of the war established the authority of the United States; the Union will stand—let it stand forever. The flag floats over the whole country from the Atlantic to the Pacific; let it increase in lustre, and let the power of the Government grow; still the cause for which General Lee struck is not a lost cause. It is conceded that these States must continue united under a common government. We do not wish to sunder it, nor to disturb it. But the great principle that underlies the Government of the United States—the principle that the people have a right to choose their own form of government, and to have their liberties protected by the provisions of the Constitution—is an indestructible principle. You cannot destroy it. Like Milton's angels, it is immortal; you may wound, but you cannot kill it. It is like the volcanic fires that flame in the depths of the earth; it will yet upheave the ocean and the land, and flame up to heaven.

"Young Emmett said, 'Let no man write my epitaph until my country is free, and takes her place among the nations of the earth.' But you may write General Lee's epitaph now. The principle for which he fought will survive him. His evening was in perfect harmony with his life. He had time to think, to recall the past, to prepare for the future. An offer, originating in Georgia, and I believe in this very city, was made to him to place an immense sum of money at his disposal if he would consent to reside in the city of New York and represent Southern commerce. Millions would have flowed to him. But he declined. He said: 'No; I am grateful, but I have a self-imposed task which I must accomplish. I have led the young men of the South in battle; I have seen many of them fall under my standard. I shall devote my life now to training young men to do their duty in life.' And he did. It was beautiful to see him in that glorious valley where Lexington stands, the lofty mountains throwing their protecting shadows over its quiet home. General Lee's fame is not bounded by the limits of the South, nor by the continent. I rejoice that the South gave him birth; I rejoice that the South will hold his ashes. But his fame belongs to the human race. Washington, too, was born in the South and sleeps in the South. But his great fame is not to be appropriated by this country; it is the inheritance of mankind. We place the name of Lee by that of Washington. They both belong to the world."

NEW ORLEANS.

A meeting was held in the St. Charles Theatre, as the largest building in the city. The Hon. W.M. Burwell delivered an eloquent address, of which we regret that we have been able to obtain no report. The meeting was then addressed by the

HON. THOMAS J. SEMMES.

"Robert E. Lee is dead. The Potomac, overlooked by the home of the hero, once dividing contending peoples, but now no longer a boundary, conveys to the ocean a nation's tears. South of the Potomac is mourning; profound grief pervades every heart, lamentation is heard from every hearth, for Lee sleeps among the slain whose memory is so dear to us. In the language of Moina:

'They were slain for us,
And their blood flowed out in a rain for us,
Red, rich, and pure, on the plain for us;
And years may go,
But our tears shall flow
O'er the dead who have died in vain for us.'

"North of the Potomac not only sympathizes with its widowed sister, but, with respectful homage, the brave and generous, clustering around the corpse of the great Virginian, with one accord exclaim:

'This earth that bears thee dead,
Bears not alive so stout a gentleman.'

"Sympathetic nations, to whom our lamentations have been transmitted on the wings of lightning, will with pious jealousy envy our grief, because Robert E. Lee was an American. Seven cities claimed the honor of having given birth to the great pagan poet; but all Christian nations, while revering America as the mother of Robert E. Lee, will claim for the nineteenth century the honor of his birth. There was but one Lee, the great Christian captain, and his fame justly belongs to Christendom. The nineteenth century has attacked every thing—it has attacked God, the soul, reason, morals, society, the distinction between good and evil. Christianity is vindicated by the virtues of Lee. He is the most brilliant and cogent argument in favor of a system illustrated by such a man; he is the type of the reign of law in the moral order—that reign of law which the philosophic Duke of Argyll has so recently and so ably discussed as pervading the natural as well as the supernatural world. One of the chief characteristics of the Christian is duty. Throughout a checkered life the conscientious performance of duty seems to have been the mainspring of the actions of General Lee. In his relations of father, son, husband, soldier, citizen, duty shines conspicuous in all his acts. His agency as he advanced to more elevated stations attracts more attention, and surrounds him with a brighter halo of glory; but he is unchanged; from first to last it is Robert E. Lee.

"The most momentous act of his life was the selection of sides at the commencement of the political troubles which immediately preceded the recent conflict. High in military rank, caressed by General Scott, courted by those possessed of influence and authority, no politician, happy in his domestic relations, and in the enjoyment of competent fortune, consisting in the main of property situated on the borders of Virginia—nevertheless impelled by a sense of duty, as he himself testified before a Congressional committee since the war, General Lee determined to risk all and unite his fortunes with those of his native State, whose ordinances as one of her citizens he considered himself bound to obey.

"Having joined the Confederate army, he complained not that he was assigned to the obscure duty of constructing coast-defences for South Carolina and Georgia, nor that he was subsequently relegated to unambitious commands in Western Virginia. The accidental circumstance that General Joseph E. Johnston was wounded at the battle of Seven Pines in May, 1862, placed Lee in command of the Army of Northern Virginia. As commander of that army he achieved world-wide reputation, without giving occasion during a period of three years to any complaint on the part of officers, men, or citizens, or enemies, that he had been guilty of any act, illegal, oppressive, unjust, or inhuman in its character. This is the highest tribute possible to the wisdom and virtue of General Lee; for, as a general rule, law was degraded; officers, whether justly or unjustly, were constantly the subject of complaint and discord, and jealousy prevailed in camp and in the Senate-chamber. There was a fraction of our people represented by an unavailing minority in Congress, who either felt, or professed to feel, a jealousy whose theory was just, but whose application, at such a time, was unsound. They wished to give as little power as possible because they dreaded a military despotism, and thus desired to send our armies forth with half a shield and broken swords to protect the government from its enemies, lest, if the bucklers were entire and the swords perfect, they might be tempted, in the heyday of victory, to smite their employers. But this want of confidence never manifested itself toward General Lee, whose conduct satisfied the most suspicious that his ambition was not of glory but of the performance of duty. The army always felt this: the fact that he sacrificed no masses of human beings in desperate charges that he might gather laurels from the spot enriched by their gore. A year or more before he was appointed commander-in-chief of all the Confederate forces, a bill passed Congress creating that office. It failed to become a law, the President having withheld his approval. Lee made no complaints; his friends solicited no votes to counteract the veto. When a bill for the same purpose was passed at a subsequent period, it was whispered about that he could not accept the position. To a committee of Virginians who had called on him to ascertain the truth, his reply was, that he felt bound to accept any post the duties of which his country believed him competent to perform. After the battle of Gettysburg he tendered his resignation to President Davis, because he was apprehensive his failure, the responsibility for which he did not pretend to throw on his troops or officers, would produce distrust of his abilities and destroy his usefulness. I am informed the President, in a beautiful and touching letter, declined to listen to such a proposition. During the whole period of the war he steadily declined all presents, and when, on one occasion, a gentleman sent him several dozen of wine, he turned it over to the hospitals in Richmond, saying the wounded and sick needed it more than he. He was extremely simple and unostentatious in his habits, and shared with his soldiers their privations as well as their dangers. Toward the close of the war, meat was very scarce within the Confederate lines in the neighborhood of the contending armies. An aide of the President, having occasion to visit General Lee en official business in the field, was invited to dinner. The meal spread on the table consisted of corn-bread and a small piece of bacon buried in a large dish of greens. The quick-eyed aide discovered that none of the company, which was composed of the general's personal staff, partook of the meat, though requested to do so in the most urbane manner by the general, who presided; he, therefore, also declined, and noticed that the meat was carried off untouched. After the meal was over, he inquired of one of the officers present what was the reason for this extraordinary conduct. His reply was, 'We had borrowed the meat for the occasion, and promised to return it.'

"Duty alone induced this great soldier to submit to such privation, for the slightest intimation given to friends in Richmond would have filled his tent with all the luxuries that blockade-runners and speculators had introduced for the favored few able to purchase.

"This performance of duty was accompanied by no harsh manner or cynical expressions; for the man whose soul is ennobled by true heroism, possesses a heart as tender as it is firm. His calmness under the most trying circumstances, and his uniform sweetness of manner, were almost poetical. They manifested 'the most sustained tenderness of soul that ever caressed the chords of a lyre.' In council he was temperate and patient, and his words fell softly and evenly as snow-flakes, like the sentences that fell from the lips of Ulysses.

"On the termination of the war, his conduct until his death has challenged the admiration of friends and foes; he honestly acquiesced in the inevitable result of the struggle; no discontent, sourness, or complaint, has marred his tranquil life at Washington College, where death found him at his post of duty, engaged in fitting the young men of his country, by proper discipline and education, for the performance of the varied duties of life. It is somewhat singular that both Lee and his great lieutenant, Jackson, should in their last moments have referred to Hill. It is reported that General Lee said, 'Let my tent be struck; send for Hill;' while the lamented Jackson in his delirium cried out, 'Let A.P. Hill prepare for action; march the infantry rapidly to the front. Let us cross over the river and rest under the shade of the trees.' Both heroes died with commands for military movements on their lips; both the noblest specimens of the Christian soldier produced by any country or any age; both now rest under the shade of the trees of heaven."

REV. DR. PALMER

Then spoke as follows:

"*Ladies and Gentlemen*: I should have been better pleased had I been permitted to sit a simple listener to the eloquent tribute paid to the immortal chieftain who now reposes in death, by the speaker who has just taken his seat. The nature of my calling so far separates me from public life that I am scarcely competent for the office of alluding to the elements which naturally gather around his career. When informed that other artists would draw the picture of the warrior and the hero, I yielded a cheerful compliance, in the belief that nothing was left but to describe the Christian and the man. You are entirely familiar with the early life of him over whose grave you this night shed tears; with his grave and sedate boyhood giving promise of the reserved force of mature manhood; with his academic career at West Point, where he received the highest honors of a class brilliant with such names as General Joseph E. Johnston; his seizure of the highest honors of a long apprenticeship in that institution, and his abrupt ascension in the Mexican War from obscurity to fame—all are too firmly stamped in the minds of his admirers to require even an allusion. You are too familiar to need a repetition from my lips of that great mental and spiritual struggle passed, not one night, but many, when, abandoning the service in which he had gathered so much of honor and reputation, he determined to lay his heart upon the altar of his native State, and swear to live or die in her defence.

"It would be a somewhat singular subject of speculation to discover how it is that national character so often remarkably expresses itself in single individuals who are born as representatives of a class. It is wonderful, for it has been the remark of ages, how the great are born in clusters; sometimes, indeed, one star shining with solitary splendor in the firmament above, but generally gathered in grand constellations, filling the sky with glory. What is that combination of influences, partly physical, partly intellectual, but somewhat more moral, which should make a particular country productive of men great over all others on earth and to all ages of time? Ancient Greece, with her indented coast, inviting to maritime adventures, from her earliest period was the mother of heroes in war, of poets in song, of sculptors and artists, and stands up after the lapse of centuries the educator of mankind, living in the grandeur of her works and in the immortal productions of minds which modern civilization with all its cultivation and refinement and science never surpassed and scarcely equalled. And why in the three hundred years of American history it should be given to the Old Dominion to be the grand mother, not only of States, but of the men by whom States and empires are formed, it might be curious were it possible for us to inquire. Unquestionably, Mr. President, there is in this problem the element of race; for he is blind to all the truths of history, to all the revelations of the past, who does not recognize a select race as we recognize a select individual of a race, to make all history; but pretermitting all speculation of that sort, when Virginia unfolds the scroll of her immortal sons—not because illustrious men did not precede him gathering in constellations and clusters, but because the name shines out through those constellations and clusters in all its peerless grandeur—we read the name of George Washington. And then, Mr. President, after the interval of three-quarters of a century, when your jealous eye has ranged down the record and traced the names that history will never let die, you come to the name—the only name in all the annals of history that can be named in the perilous connection—of Robert E. Lee, the second Washington. Well may old Virginia be proud of her twin sons! born almost a century apart, but shining like those binary stars which open their glory and shed their splendor on the darkness of the world.

170

"Sir, it is not an artifice of rhetoric which suggests this parallel between two great names in American history; for the suggestion springs spontaneously to every mind, and men scarcely speak of Lee without thinking of a mysterious connection that binds the two together. They were alike in the presage of their early history—the history of their boyhood. Both earnest, grave, studious; both alike in that peculiar purity which belongs only to a noble boy, and which makes him a brave and noble man, filling the page of a history spotless until closed in death; alike in that commanding presence which seems to be the signature of Heaven sometimes placed on a great soul when to that soul is given a fit dwelling-place; alike in that noble carriage and commanding dignity, exercising a mesmeric influence and a hidden power which could not be repressed, upon all who came within its charm; alike in the remarkable combination and symmetry of their intellectual attributes, all brought up to the same equal level, no faculty of the mind overlapping any other—all so equal, so well developed, the judgment, the reason, the memory, the fancy, that you are almost disposed to deny them greatness, because no single attribute of the mind was projected upon itself, just as objects appear sometimes smaller to the eye from the exact symmetry and beauty of their proportions; alike, above all, in that soul-greatness, that Christian virtue to which so beautiful a tribute has been rendered by my friend whose high privilege it was to be a compeer and comrade with the immortal dead, although in another department and sphere; and yet alike, Mr. President, in their external fortune, so strangely dissimilar—the one the representative and the agent of a stupendous revolution which it pleased Heaven to bless and give birth to one of the mightiest nations on the globe; the other the representative and agent of a similar revolution, upon which it pleased high Heaven to throw the darkness of its frown; so that, bearing upon his generous heart the weight of this crushed cause, he was at length overwhelmed; and the nation whom he led in battle gathers with spontaneity of grief over all this land which is ploughed with graves and reddened with blood, and the tears of a widowed nation in her bereavement are shed over his honored grave.

"But these crude suggestions, which fall almost impromptu from my lips, suggest that which I desire to offer before this audience to-night. I accept Robert E. Lee as the true type of the American man and the Southern gentleman. A brilliant English writer has well remarked, with a touch of sound philosophy, that when a nation has rushed upon its fate, the whole force of the national life will sometimes shoot up in one grand character, like the aloe which blooms at the end of a hundred years, shooting up in one single spike of glory, and then expires. And wherever philosophy, refinement, and culture, have gone upon the globe, it is possible to place the finger upon individual men who are the exemplars of a nation's character, those typical forms under which others less noble, less expanded, have manifested themselves. That gentle, that perfect moderation, that self-command which enabled him to be so self-possessed amid the most trying difficulties of his public career, a refinement almost such as that which marks the character of the purest woman, were blended in him with that massive strength, that mighty endurance, that consistency and power which gave him and the people whom he led such momentum under the disadvantages of the struggle through which he passed. Born from the general level of American society, blood of a noble ancestry flowed in his veins, and he was a type of the race from which he sprang. Such was the grandeur and urbaneness of his manner, the dignity and majesty of his carriage, that his only peer in social life could be found in courts and among those educated amid the refinements of courts and thrones. In that regard there was something beautiful and appropriate that he should become, in the later years of his life, the educator of the young. Sir, it is a cause for mourning before high Heaven to-night that he was not spared thirty years to educate a generation for the time that is to come; for, as in the days when the red banner streamed over the land, the South sent her sons to fight under his flag and beneath the wave of his sword, these sons have been sent again to sit at his feet when he was the disciple of the Muses and the teacher of philosophy. Oh, that he might have brought his more than regal character, his majestic fame, all his intellectual and moral endowments, to the task of fitting those that should come in the crisis of the future to take the mantle that had fallen from his shoulders and bear it to the generations that are unborn!

"General Lee I accept as the representative of his people, and of the temper with which this whole Southland entered into that gigantic, that prolonged, and that disastrous struggle which has closed, but closed as to us in grief. Sir, they wrong us who say that the South was ever impatient to rupture the bonds of the American Union. The war of 1776, which, sir, has no more yet a written history than has the war of 1861 to 1865, tells us that it was this Southland that wrought the Revolution of 1776. We were the heirs of all the glory of that immortal struggle. It was purchased with our blood, with the blood of our fathers which yet flows in these veins, and which we desire to transmit, pure and consecrated, to the sons that are born to our loins. The traditions of the past sixty years were a portion of our heritage, and it never was easy for any great heart and reflective mind even to seem to part with that heritage to enter upon the perilous effort of establishing a new nationality.

"Mr. President, it was my privilege once to be thrilled in a short speech, uttered by one of the noblest names clustering upon the roll of South Carolina; for, sir, South Carolina was Virginia's sister, and South Carolina stood by Virginia in the old struggle, as Virginia stood by South Carolina in the new, and the little State, small as Greece, barren in resources but great only in the grandeur of the men, in their gigantic proportions, whom she, like Virginia, was permitted to produce—I heard, sir, one of South Carolina's noblest sons speak once thus: 'I walked through the Tower of London, that grand repository where are gathered the memorials of England's martial prowess; and when the guide, in the pride of his English heart, pointed to the spoils of war collected through centuries of the past,' said this speaker, lifting himself upon tiptoe that he might reach to his greatest height, 'I said, "You cannot point to one single trophy from my people, or my country, though England engaged in two disastrous wars with her."' Sir, this was the sentiment. We loved every inch of American soil, and loved every part of that canvas [pointing to the Stars and Stripes above him], which, as a symbol of power and authority, floated from the spires and from the mast-head of our vessels; and it was after the anguish of a woman in birth that this land, that now lies in her sorrow and ruin, took upon herself that great peril; but it is all emblematized in the regret experienced by him whose praises are upon our lips, and who, like the English Nelson, recognized duty engraved in letters of light as the only ensign he could follow, and who, tearing away from all the associations of his early life, and, abandoning the reputation gained in the old service, made up his mind to embark in the new, and, with that modesty and that firmness belonging only to the truly great, expressed his willingness to live and die in the position assigned to him.

"And I accept this noble chieftain equally as the representative of this Southland in the spirit of his retirement from struggle. It could not escape any speaker upon this platform to allude to the dignity of that retirement; how, from the moment he surrendered he withdrew from observation, holding aloof from all political complications, and devoting his entire energies to the great work he had undertaken to discharge. In this he represents—an the true attitude of the South since the close of the war attitude of quiet submission to the conquering power and of obedience to all exactions; but without resiling from those great principles which were embalmed in the struggle, and which, as the convictions of a lifetime, no honest mind could release.

"All over this land of ours there are men like Lee—not as great, not as symmetrical in the development of character, not as grand in the proportions which they have reached, but who, like him, are sleeping upon memories that are holy as death, and who, amid all reproach, appeal to the future, and to the tribunal of History, when she shall render her final verdict in reference to the struggle closed, for the vindication of the people embarked in that struggle. We are silent, resigned, obedient, and thoughtful, sleeping upon solemn memories, Mr. President; but, as said by the poet-preacher in the Good Book, 'I sleep, but my heart waketh,' looking upon the future that is to come, and powerless in every thing except to pray to Almighty God, who rules the destinies of nations, that those who have the power may at least have the grace given them to preserve the constitutional principles which we have endeavored to maintain. And, sir, were it my privilege to speak in the hearing of the entire nation, I would utter with the profoundest emphasis this pregnant truth: that no people ever traversed those moral ideas which underlie its character, its constitution, its institutions, and its laws, that did not in the end perish in disaster, in shame, and in dishonor. Whatever be the glory, the material civilization, of which such a nation may boast, it still holds true that the truth is immortal, and that ideas rule the world.

"And now I have but a single word to say, and that is, that the grave of this noble hero is bedewed with the most tender and sacred tears ever shed upon a human tomb. I was thinking in my study this afternoon, striving to strike out something I might utter on this platform, and this parallel between the first Washington and the second occurred to me. I asked my own heart the question, 'Would you not accept the fame and the glory and the career of Robert E. Lee just as soon as accept the glory and career of the immortal man who was his predecessor?' Sir, there is a pathos in fallen fortunes which stirs the sensibilities, and touches the very fountain of human feeling. I am not sure that at this moment Napoleon, the enforced guest of the Prussian king, is not grander than when he ascended the throne of France. There is a grandeur in misfortune when that misfortune is borne by a noble heart, with the strength of will to endure, and endure without complaining or breaking. Perhaps I slip easily into this train of remarks, for it is my peculiar office to speak of that chastening with which a gracious Providence visits men on this earth, and by which He prepares them for heaven hereafter; and what is true of individuals in a state of adversity, is true of nations when clothed in sorrow. Sir, the men in these galleries that once wore the gray are here to-night that they may bend the knee in reverence at the grave of him whose voice and hand they obeyed amid the storms of battle: the young widow, who but as yesterday leaned upon the arm of her soldier-husband, but now clasps wildly to her breast the young child that never beheld its father's face, comes here to shed her tears over this grave to-night; and the aged matron, with the tears streaming from her eyes as she recalls her unforgotten dead, lying on the plains of Gettysburg, or on the heights of Fredericksburg, now, to-night, joins in our dirge over him who was that son's chieftain and counsellor and friend. A whole nation has risen up in the spontaneity of its grief to render the tribute of its love. Sir, there is a unity in the grapes when they grow together in the clusters upon the vine, and holding the bunch in your hand you speak of it as one; but there is another unity when you throw these grapes into the wine-press, and the feet of those that bruise these grapes trample them almost profanely beneath their feet together in the communion of pure wine; and such is the union and communion of hearts that have been fused by tribulation and sorrow, and that meet together in the true feeling of an honest grief to express the homage of their affection, as well as to render a tribute of praise to him upon whose face we shall never look until on that immortal day when we shall behold it transfigured before the throne of God."

The meeting then adopted the following preamble and resolutions:

"*Whereas*, Like orphans at the grave of a parent untimely snatched away, our hearts have lingered and brooded, with a grief that no cunning of speech could interpret, over the thought that Robert Edward Lee exists no more, in bodily life, in sensible form, in visible presence, for our love and veneration, for our edification and guidance, for our comfort and solace; and—

"*Whereas*, We have invoked all mute funeral emblems to aid us with their utmost eloquence of woe, and we cannot content ourselves with contemplating, from the depth and the gloom of our bereavement, the exalted and radiant virtues of the dead:

"*Resolved*, That we, the people of New Orleans, have come together under one common impulse to render united homage to the memory which holds mastery in our minds, whether we turn with bitter regard to the past, or with prayerful and chastened aspirations to the future.

"*Resolved*, That as Louisianians, as Southerners, as Americans, we proudly claim our share in the fame of Lee as an inheritance rightfully belonging to us, and endowed with which we shall piously cherish, though all calamities should rain upon us, true poverty—the poverty indeed that abases and starves the spirit can never approach us with its noisome breath and withering look.

"*Resolved*, That it is infinitely more bitter to have to mourn the loss of our Lee, than not to have learned to prize him as the noblest gift which could have been allotted to a people and an epoch; a grand man, rounded to the symmetry of equal moral and intellectual powers, graces, and accomplishments; a man whose masterly and heroic energy left nothing undone in defending a just cause while there was a possibility of striking for it a rational and hopeful blow, and whose sublime resignation when the last blow was struck in vain, and when human virtue was challenged to match itself with the consummation of human adversity, taught wiser, more convincing, more reassuring, more soul-sustaining lessons than were to be found in all the philosophies of all books.

"*Resolved*, That worthily to show our veneration for this majestic and beautiful character, we must revolve it habitually in our thoughts, and try to appropriate it to the purification and elevation of our lives, and so educate our children that they shall, if possible, grow up into its likeness.

"*Resolved*, That while it is honorable for a people to deeply lament the death of such a man, it would be glorious for a generation to mould itself after his model; for it would be a generation fraught with all high manly qualities, tempered with all gentle and Christian virtues; for truth, love, goodness, health, strength, would be with it, and consequently victory, liberty, majesty, and beauty.

"*Resolved*, That we would hail the erection of the proposed monument as well adapted to the purpose of preserving this admirable and most precious memory as a vital and beneficent influence for all time to come, and we will therefore cordially aid in promoting the Lee Monument which has just been inaugurated."

ATLANTA, GA.

A crowded meeting assembled in this city on October 15th. After an impressive prayer from the Rev. Dr. Brantly, the meeting was addressed by

GENERAL JOHN B. GORDON.

"*My Friends*: We have met to weep, to mingle our tears, and give vent to our bursting hearts. The sorrowing South, already clad in mourners' weeds, bows her head afresh to-day in a heart-stricken orphanage; and if I could have been permitted to indulge the sensibilities of my heart, I would have fled this most honorable task, and in solitude and silence have wept the loss of the great and good man whose death we so deplore. I loved General Lee; for it was my proud privilege to know him well. I loved him with a profound and all-filial love, with a sincere and unfaded affection. I say I would have retired from this flattering task which your kindness has imposed, but remembering that his words, his deeds, his great example, has taught us that duty was the most commanding obligation, I yield this morning to your wishes.

"We have met to honor General Lee, to honor him dead whom we loved while living. Honor General Lee! How utterly vain, what a mockery of language do these words seem! Honor Lee! Why, my countrymen, his deeds have honored him! The very trump of Fame itself is proud to honor him! Europe and the civilized world have united to honor him supremely, and History itself has caught the echo and made it immortal. Honor Lee! Why, sir, as the sad news of his death is with the speed of thought communicated to the world, it will carry a pang even to the hearts of marshals and of monarchs; and I can easily fancy that, amid the din and clash and carnage of war, the cannon itself, in mute pause at the whispering news, will briefly cease its roar around the walls of Paris. The task is not without pain, while yet his manly frame lies stretched upon his bier, to attempt to analyze the elements that made him truly great. It has been my fortune in life from circumstances to have come in contact with some whom the world pronounced great—some of the earth's celebrated and distinguished; but I declare it here to-day that, of any mortal man whom it has ever been my privilege to approach, he was the greatest; and I assert here that, grand as might be your conceptions of the man before, he arose in incomparable majesty on more familiar acquaintance. This can be affirmed of few men who have ever lived or died, and of no other man whom it has ever been my fortune to approach. Like Niagara, the more you gazed the more his grandeur grew upon you, the more his majesty expanded and filled your spirit with a full satisfaction that left a perfect delight without the slightest feeling of oppression. Grandly majestic and dignified in all his deportment, he was genial as the sunlight of this beautiful day, and not a ray of that cordial, social intercourse but brought warmth to the heart as it did light to the understanding.

"But as one of the great captains will General Lee first pass review and inspection before the criticism of history. We will not compare him with Washington. The mind will halt instinctively at the comparison of two such men, so equally and gloriously great. But with modest, yet calm and unflinching confidence we place him by the side of the Marlboroughs and Wellingtons who take high niches in the pantheon of immortality. Let us dwell for a moment, my friends, on this thought. Marlborough never met defeat, it is true. Victory marked every step of his triumphant march; but when, where, and whom did Marlborough fight? The ambitious and vain but able Louis XIV. But he had already exhausted the resources of his kingdom before Marlborough stepped upon the stage. The great marshals Turenne and Condé were no more, and Luxembourg the beloved had vanished from the scene. Marlborough, preëminently great as he certainly was, nevertheless led the combined forces of England and of Holland, in the freshness of their strength and the fulness of their financial ability, against prostrate France, with a treasury depleted, a people worn out, discouraged, and dejected. But let us turn to another comparison. The great Von Moltke, who now rides upon the whirlwind and commands the storm of Prussian invasion, has recently declared that General Lee, in all respects, was fully the equal of Wellington, and you may the better appreciate this admission when you remember that Wellington was the benefactor of Prussia, and probably Von Moltke's special idol. But let us examine the arguments ourselves. France was already prostrate when Wellington met Napoleon. That great emperor had seemed to make war upon the very elements themselves, to have contended with Nature, and to have almost defeated Providence itself. The enemies of the North, more savage than Goth or Vandal, mounting the swift gales of a Russian winter, had carried death, desolation, and ruin, to the very gates of Paris. Wellington fought at Waterloo a bleeding and broken nation—a nation electrified, it is true, to almost superhuman energy by the genius of Napoleon, but a nation prostrate and bleeding nevertheless. Compare this, my friends, the condition of France and the condition of the United States, in the freshness of her strength, in the luxuriance of her resources, in the lustihood of her gigantic youth. Tell me whether to place the chaplet of military superiority with him, or with Marlborough, or Wellington? Even the greatest of captains, in his Italian campaigns, flashing fame in lightning splendor over the world, even Bonaparte met and crushed in battle but three or four (I think) Austrian armies; while our Lee, with one army badly equipped, in time incredibly short, met and hurled back in broken and shattered fragments five of the greatest prepared and most magnificently appointed invasions. Yea, more! He discrowned, in rapid succession, one after another of the United States' most, accomplished and admirable commanders.

"Lee was never really defeated. Lee could not be defeated! Overpowered, foiled in his efforts, he might be; but never defeated until the props which supported him gave way. Never, until the platform sank beneath him, did any enemy ever dare pursue. On that melancholy occasion, the downfall of the Confederacy, no Leipsic, no Waterloo, no Sedan, can ever be recorded.

"General Lee is known to the world as a military man; but it is easy to divine from his history how mindful of all just authority, how observant of all constitutional restriction, would have been his career as a civilian. When, near the conclusion of the war, darkness was thickening about the falling fortunes of the Confederacy, when its very life was in the sword of Lee, it was my proud privilege to know with a special admiration the modest demeanor, the manly decorum, respectful homage, which marked all his dealings with the constituted authorities of his country. Clothed with all power, he hid its very symbol behind a genial modesty, and refused ever to exert it save in obedience to law. And even in his triumphant entry into the territory of the enemy, so regardful was he of civilized warfare, that the observance of his general orders as to private property and private rights left the line of his march marked and marred by no devastated fields, charred ruins, or desolated homes. But it is in his private character, or rather I should say his personal emotion and virtue, which his countrymen will most delight to consider and dwell upon. His magnanimity, transcending all historic precedent, seemed to form a new chapter in the book of humanity. Witness that letter to Jackson, after his wounds at Chancellorsville, in which he said: 'I am praying for you with more fervor than I have ever prayed for myself;' and that other, more disinterested and pathetic: 'I could, for the good of my country, wish that the wounds which you have received had been inflicted upon my own body;' or that of the latter message, saying to General Jackson that 'his wounds were not so severe as mine, for he loses but his left arm, while I, in my loss, lose my right;' or that other expression of unequalled magnanimity which enabled him to ascribe the glory of their joint victory to the sole credit of the dying hero. Did I say unequalled? Yes, that was an avowal of unequalled magnanimity, until it met its parallel in his own grander self-negation in assuming the sole responsibility for the defeat at Gettysburg. Ay, my countrymen, Alexander had his Arbela, Caesar his Pharsalia, Napoleon his Austerlitz; but it was reserved for Lee to grow grander and more illustrious in defeat than even in victory—grander, because in defeat he showed a spirit greater than in the heroism of battles or all the achievements of war, a spirit which crowns him with a chaplet grander far than ever mighty conqueror wore.

"I turn me now to that last closing scene at Appomattox, and I will draw thence a picture of that man as he laid aside the sword, the unrivalled soldier, to become the most exemplary of citizens.

"I can never forget the deferential homage paid this great citizen by even the Federal soldiers, as with uncovered heads they contemplated in mute admiration this now captive hero as he rode through their ranks. Impressed forever, daguerreotyped on my heart is that last parting scene with that handful of heroes still crowding around him. Few indeed were the words then spoken, but the quivering lip and the tearful eye told of the love they bore him, in symphonies more eloquent than any language can describe. Can I ever forget? No, never can I forget the words which fell from his lips as I rode beside him amid the defeated, dejected, and weeping soldiery, when, turning to me, he said, 'I could wish that I was numbered among the fallen in the last battle;' but oh! as he thought of the loss of the cause—of the many dead scattered over so many fields, who, sleeping neglected, with no governmental arms to gather up their remains—sleeping neglected, isolated, and alone, beneath the weeping stars, with naught but their soldiers' blankets about them!—oh! as these emotions swept over his great soul, he felt that he would have laid him down to rest in the same grave where lay buried the common hope of his people. But Providence willed it otherwise. He rests now forever, my countrymen, his spirit in the bosom of that Father whom he so faithfully served, his body beside the river whose banks are forever memorable, and whose waters are vocal with the glories of his triumphs. No sound shall ever wake him to martial glory again; no more shall he lead his invincible lines to victory; no more shall we gaze upon him and draw from his quiet demeanor lessons of life. But oh! it is a sweet consolation to us, my countrymen, who loved him, that no more shall his bright spirit be bowed down to earth with the burdens of the people's wrongs. It is sweet consolation to us that his last victory, through faith in his crucified Redeemer, is the most transcendently glorious of all his triumphs. At this very hour, while we mourn here, kind friends are consigning the last that remains of our hero to his quiet sleeping-place, surrounded by the mountains of his native State—mountains the autumnal glory of whose magnificent forests to-day seem but habiliments of mourning. In the Valley, the pearly dew-drops seem but tears of sadness upon the grasses and flowers. Let him rest! And now as he has gone from us, and as we regard him in all the aspects of his career and character and attainments as a great captain, ranking among the first of any age; as a patriot, whose sacrificing devotion to his country ranks him with Washington; as a Christian, like Havelock, recognizing his duty to his God above every other earthly consideration, with a native modesty that refused to appropriate the glory of his own, and which surrounds now his entire character and career with a halo of unfading light; with an integrity of life and a sacred regard for truth which no man dare assail; with a fidelity to principle which no misfortune could shake—he must ever stand peerless among men in the estimation of Christendom, this representative son of the South, Robert E. Lee, of Virginia."

RICHMOND, VA.

A meeting was held on November 3d, presided over by Mr. Jefferson Davis. Mr. Davis delivered an address, of which we regret that we have received no complete copy. We give it as reported in the Richmond *Dispatch*.

REMARKS OF PRESIDENT DAVIS.

As Mr. Davis arose to walk to the stand, every person in the house stood, and there followed such a storm of applause as seemed to shake the very foundations of the building, while cheer upon cheer was echoed from the throats of veterans saluting one whom they delighted to honor.

Mr. Davis spoke at length, and with his accustomed thrilling, moving eloquence. We shall not attempt, at the late hour at which we write, to give a full report of his address.

He addressed his hearers as "Soldiers and sailors of the Confederacy, comrades and friends: Assembled on this sad occasion, with hearts oppressed with the grief that follows the loss of him who was our leader on many a bloody battle-field, a pleasing though melancholy spectacle is presented. Hitherto, and in all times, men have been honored when successful; but here is the case of one who amid disaster went down to his grave, and those who were his companions in misfortune have assembled to honor his memory. It is as much an honor to you who give as to him who receives; for, above the vulgar test of merit, you show yourselves competent to discriminate between him who enjoys and him who deserves success.

"Robert E. Lee was my associate and friend in the Military Academy, and we were friends until the hour of his death. We were associates and friends when he was a soldier and I a Congressman; and associates and friends when he led the armies of the Confederacy and I presided in its cabinet. We passed through many sad scenes together, but I cannot remember that there was ever aught but perfect harmony between us. If ever there was difference of opinion, it was dissipated by discussion, and harmony was the result. I repeat, *we never disagreed*; and I may add that I never in my life saw in him the slightest tendency to self-seeking. It was not his to make a record, it was not his to shift blame to other shoulders; but it was his, with an eye fixed upon the welfare of his country, never faltering, to follow the line of duty to the end. His was the heart that braved every difficulty; his was the mind that wrought victory out of defeat.

"He has been charged with 'want of dash.' I wish to say that I never knew Lee to falter to attempt any thing ever man could dare. An attempt has also been made to throw a cloud upon his character because he left the Army of the United States to join in the struggle for the liberty of his State. Without trenching at all upon politics, I deem it my duty to say one word in reference to this charge. Virginian born, descended from a family illustrious in Virginia's annals, given by Virginia to the service of the United States, he represented her in the Military Academy at West Point. He was not educated by the Federal Government, but by Virginia; for she paid her full share for the support of that institution, and was entitled to demand in return the services of her sons. Entering the Army of the United States, he represented Virginia there also, and nobly. On many a hard-fought field Lee was conspicuous, battling for his native State as much as for the Union. He came from Mexico crowned with honors, covered by brevets, and recognized, young as he was, as one of the ablest of his country's soldiers. And, to prove that he was estimated then as such, let me tell you that when Lee was a captain of engineers stationed in Baltimore, the Cuban Junta in New York selected him to be their leader in the struggle for the independence of their native country. They were anxious to secure his services, and offered him every temptation that ambition could desire. He thought the matter over, and, I remember, came to Washington to consult me as to what he should do; and when I began to discuss the complications which might arise from his acceptance of the trust, he gently rebuked me, saying that this was not the line upon which he wished my advice: the simple question was, 'Whether it was right or not?' He had been educated by the United States, and felt wrong to accept a place in the army of a foreign power. Such was his extreme delicacy, such was the nice sense of honor of the gallant gentleman whose death we deplore. But when Virginia withdrew, the State to whom he owed his first and last allegiance, the same nice sense of honor led him to draw his sword and throw it in the scale for good or for evil. Pardon me for this brief defence of my illustrious friend.

"When Virginia joined the Confederacy, Robert Lee, the highest officer in the little army of Virginia, came to Richmond; and, not pausing to inquire what would be his rank in the service of the Confederacy, went to Western Virginia under the belief that he was still an officer of the State. He came back, carrying the heavy weight of defeat, and unappreciated by the people whom he served, for they could not know, as I knew, that if his plans and orders had been carried out the result would have been victory rather than retreat. You did not know, for I would not have known it had he not breathed it in my ear only at my earnest request, and begging that nothing be

176

said about it. The clamor which then arose followed him when he went to South Carolina, so that it became necessary on his going to South Carolina to write a letter to the Governor of that State, telling him what manner of man he was. Yet, through all this, with a magnanimity rarely equalled, he stood in silence without defending himself or allowing others to defend him, for he was unwilling to offend any one who was wearing a sword and striking blows for the Confederacy."

Mr. Davis then spoke of the straits to which the Confederacy was reduced, and of the danger to which her capital was exposed, just after the battle of Seven Pines, and told how General Lee had conceived and executed the desperate plan to turn their flank and rear, which, after seven days of bloody battle, was crowned with the protection of Richmond, while the enemy was driven far from the city.

The speaker referred also to the circumstances attending General Lee's crossing the Potomac on the march into Pennsylvania. He (Mr. Davis) assumed the responsibility of that movement. The enemy had long been concentrating his force, and it was evident that if he continued his steady progress the Confederacy would be overwhelmed. Our only hope was to drive him to the defence of his own capital, we being enabled in the mean time to reënforce our shattered army. How well General Lee carried out that dangerous experiment need not be told. Richmond was relieved, the Confederacy was relieved, and time was obtained, if other things had favored, to reënforce the army.

"But," said Mr. Davis, "I shall not attempt to review the military career of our fallen chieftain. Of the man, how shall I speak? He was my friend, and in that word is included all that I could say of any man. His moral qualities rose to the height of his genius. Self-denying; always intent upon the one idea of duty; self-controlled to an extent that many thought him cold, his feelings were really warm, and his heart melted freely at the sight of a wounded soldier, or the story of the sufferings of the widow and orphan. During the war he was ever conscious of the inequality of the means at his control; but it was never his to complain or to utter a doubt; it was always his to do. When, in the last campaign, he was beleaguered at Petersburg, and painfully aware of the straits to which we were reduced, he said: 'With my army in the mountains of Virginia, I could carry on this war for twenty years longer.' His men exhausted, and his supplies failing, he was unable to carry out his plans. An untoward event caused him to anticipate the movement, and the Army of Northern Virginia was overwhelmed. But, in the surrender, he anticipated conditions that have not been fulfilled; he expected his army to be respected, and his paroled soldiers to be allowed the enjoyments of life and property. Whether these conditions have been fulfilled, let others say.

"Here he now sleeps in the land he loved so well; and that land is not Virginia only, for they do injustice to Lee who believe he fought only for Virginia. He was ready to go anywhere, on any service, for the good of his country; and his heart was as broad as the fifteen States struggling for the principles that our forefathers fought for in the Revolution of 1776. He is sleeping in the same soil with the thousands who fought under the same flag, but first offered up their lives. Here, the living are assembled to honor his memory, and there the skeleton sentinels keep watch over his grave. This citizen, this soldier, this great general, this true patriot, left behind him the crowning glory of a true Christian. His Christianity ennobled him in life, and affords us grounds for the belief that he is happy beyond the grave.

"But, while we mourn the loss of the great and the true, drop we also tears of sympathy with her who was his helpmeet—the noble woman who, while her husband was in the field leading the army of the Confederacy, though an invalid herself, passed the time in knitting socks for the marching soldiers! A woman fit to be the mother of heroes; and heroes are descended from her. Mourning with her, we can only offer the consolation of a Christian. Our loss is not his; but he now enjoys the rewards of a life well spent, and a never-wavering trust in a risen Saviour. This day we unite our words of sorrow with those of the good and great throughout Christendom, for his fame is gone over the water; his deeds will be remembered, and when the monument we build shall have crumbled into dust, his virtues will still live, a high model for the imitation of generations yet unborn."

We have given but a faint idea of the eloquent thoughts and chaste oratory of the speaker. His words were heard with profound attention, and received with frequent applause.

MEMORIAL RESOLUTIONS.

Colonel C.S. Venable then presented the following report of the Committee on Resolutions:

"*Whereas*, It is a high and holy duty, as well as a noble privilege, to perpetuate the honors of those who have displayed eminent virtues and performed great achievements, that they may serve as incentives and examples to the latest generation of their countrymen, and attest the reverential admiration and affectionate regard of their compatriots; and—

"*Whereas*, This duty and privilege devolve on all who love and admire General Robert E. Lee throughout this country and the world, and in an especial manner upon those who followed him in the field, or who fought in the same cause, who shared in his glories, partook of his trials, and were united with him in the same sorrows and adversity, who were devoted to him in war by the baptism of fire and blood, and bound to him in peace by the still higher homage due to the rare and grand exhibition of a character pure and lofty and gentle and true, under all changes of fortune, and serene amid the greatest disasters:

therefore, be it

"*Resolved*, That we favor an association to erect a monument at Richmond to the memory of Robert E. Lee, as an enduring testimonial of our love and respect, and devotion to his fame.

"*Resolved*, That, while donations will be gladly received from all who recognize in the excellences of General Lee's character an honor and an encouragement to our common humanity, and an abiding hope that coming generations may be found to imitate his virtues, it is desirable that every Confederate soldier and sailor should make some contribution, however small, to the proposed monument.

"*Resolved*, That, for the purpose of securing efficiency and dispatch in the erection of the monument, an executive committee of seventy-five, with a president, secretary, treasurer, auditor, etc., be appointed, to invite and collect subscriptions, to procure designs for said monument, to select the best, to provide for the organization of central executive committees in other States, which may serve as mediums of communication between the executive committee of the Association and the local associations of these States.

"*Resolved*, That we respectfully invite the ladies of the Hollywood Association to lend us their assistance and coöperation in the collection of subscriptions.

"*Resolved*, That we cordially approve of the local monument now proposed to be erected by other associations at Atlanta, and at Lexington, his last home, whose people were so closely united with him in the last sad years of his life.

"*Resolved*, That, while we cordially thank the Governor and Legislature of Virginia, for the steps they have taken to do honor to the memory of General Lee, yet in deference to the wishes of his loved and venerated widow, with whom we mourn, we will not discuss the question of the most fitting resting-place for his ever-glorious remains, but will content ourselves with expressing the earnest desire and hope that at some future proper time they will be committed to the charge of this Association."

Generals John S. Preston, John B. Gordon, Henry A. Wise, and William Henry Preston, and Colonels Robert E. Withers and Charles Marshall, delivered eloquent and appropriate speeches, and argued that Richmond is the proper place for the final interment of the remains of General Lee.

The resolutions were adopted, and the meeting adjourned.

COLUMBIA, S.C.

At a meeting in this city the following remarks were made by—

GENERAL WADE HAMPTON.

"*Fellow-Citizens*: We are called together to-day by an announcement which will cause profound sorrow throughout the civilized world, and which comes to us bearing the additional grief of a personal and private bereavement. The foremost man in all the world is no more; and, as that news is carried by the speed of lightning through every town, village, and hamlet of this land which he loved so well, and among those people who loved and honored and venerated him so profoundly, every true heart in the stricken South will feel that the country has lost its pride and glory, and that the citizens of that country have lost a father. I dare not venture to speak of him as I feel. Nor do we come to eulogize him. Not only wherever the English language is spoken, but wherever civilization extends, the sorrow—a part at least of the sorrow—we feel will be felt, and more eloquent tongues than mine will tell the fame and recount the virtues of Robert E. Lee. We need not come to praise him. We come only to express our sympathy, our grief, our bereavement. We come not to mourn him, for we know that it is well with him. We come only to extend our sympathy to those who are bereaved.

"Now that he is fallen, I may mention what I have never spoken of before, to show you not only what were the feelings that actuated him in the duty to which his beloved countrymen called him, but what noble sentiments inspired him when he saw the cause for which he had been fighting so long about to perish. Just before the surrender, after a night devoted to the most arduous duties, as one of his staff came in to see him in the morning, he found him worn and weary and disheartened, and the general said to him, 'How easily I could get rid of this and be at rest! I have only to ride along the line, and all will be over. But,' said he—and there spoke the Christian patriot—'it is our duty to *live*, for what will become of the women and children of the South if we are not here to protect them?' That same spirit of duty which had actuated him

178

through all the perils and all the hardships of that unequalled conflict which he had waged so heroically, that same high spirit of duty told him that he must live to show that he was great— greater, if that were possible, in peace than in war; live to teach the people whom he had before led to victory how to bear defeat; live to show what a great and good man can accomplish; live to set an example to his people for all time; live to bear, if nothing else, his share of the sorrows, and the afflictions, and the troubles, which had come upon his people. He is now at rest; and surely we of the South can say of him, as we say of his great exemplar, the 'Father of his Country,' that 'he was first in war, first in peace, and first in the hearts of his countrymen.'"

BALTIMORE.

At a meeting of the officers and soldiers who served under General Lee, held in this city on October 15th, a number of addresses were made, which we are compelled to somewhat condense. That of Colonel Marshall, General Lee's chief of staff, was as follows:

COLONEL CHARLES MARSHALL.

"In presenting the resolutions of the committee, I cannot refrain from expressing the feelings inspired by the memories that crowd upon my mind when I reflect that these resolutions are intended to express what General Lee's surviving soldiers feel toward General Lee. The committee are fully aware of their inability to do justice to the sentiments that inspire the hearts of those for whom they speak. How can we portray in words the gratitude, the pride, the veneration, the anguish, that now fill the hearts of those who shared his victories and his reverses, his triumphs and his defeats? How can we tell the world what we can only feel ourselves? How can we give expression to the crowding memories called forth by the sad event we are met to deplore?

"We recall him as he appeared in the hour of victory, grand, imposing, awe-inspiring, yet self-forgetful and humble. We recall the great scenes of his triumph, when we hailed him victor on many a bloody field, and when above the paeans of victory we listened with reverence to his voice as he ascribed 'all glory to the Lord of hosts, from whom all glories are.' We remember that grand magnanimity that never stooped to pluck those meaner things that grew nearest the earth upon the tree of victory, but which, with eyes turned toward the stars, and hands raised toward heaven, gathered the golden fruits of mercy, pity, and holy charity, that ripen on its topmost boughs beneath the approving smile of the great God of battles. We remember the sublime self-abnegation of Chancellorsville, when, in the midst of his victorious legions, who, with the light of battle yet on their faces, hailed him conqueror, he thought only of his great lieutenant lying wounded on the field, and transferred to him all the honor of that illustrious day.

"I will be pardoned, I am sure, for referring to an incident which affords to my mind a most striking illustration of one of the grandest features of his character. On the morning of May 3, 1863, as many of you will remember, the final assault was made upon the Federal lines at Chancellorsville. General Lee accompanied the troops in person, and as they emerged from the fierce combat they had waged in 'the depths of that tangled wilderness,' driving the superior forces of the enemy before them across the open ground, he rode into their midst. The scene is one that can never be effaced from the minds of those who witnessed it. The troops were pressing forward with all the ardor and enthusiasm of combat. The white smoke of musketry fringed the front of the line of battle, while the artillery on the hills in the rear of the infantry shook the earth with its thunder, and filled the air with the wild shrieks of the shells that plunged into the masses of the retreating foe. To add greater horror and sublimity to the scene, the Chancellorsville House and the woods surrounding it were wrapped in flames. In the midst of this awful scene, General Lee, mounted upon that horse which we all remember so well, rode to the front of his advancing battalions. His presence was the signal for one of those uncontrollable outbursts of enthusiasm which none can appreciate who have not witnessed them. The fierce soldiers, with their faces blackened with the smoke of battle; the wounded, crawling with feeble limbs from the fury of the devouring flames, all seemed possessed with a common impulse. One long, unbroken cheer, in which the feeble cry of those who lay helpless on the earth blended with the strong voices of those who still fought, rose high above the roar of battle and hailed the presence of the victorious chief. He sat in the full realization of all that soldiers dream of— triumph; and, as I looked upon him in the complete fruition of the success which his genius, courage, and confidence in his army, had won, I thought it must have been from some such scene that men in ancient days ascended to the dignity of the gods. His first care was for the wounded of both armies, and he was among the foremost at the burning mansion where some of them lay. But at that moment, when the transports of his victorious troops were drowning the roar of battle with acclamations, a note was brought to him from General Jackson. It was brought to General Lee as he sat on his horse near the Chancellorsville House, and, unable to open it with his gauntleted hands, he passed it to me with directions to read it to him. The note made no mention of the wound that General Jackson had received, but congratulated General Lee upon the great victory. I shall never forget the look of pain and anguish that passed over his face as he listened. With a voice broken with emotion he bade me say to General Jackson that the victory was his, and that the congratulations were due to him. I know not how others may regard this incident, but, for myself, as I gave expression to the thoughts of his exalted mind, I forgot the genius that won the day in my reverence for the generosity that refused its glory.

"There is one other incident to which I beg permission to refer, that I may perfect the picture. On the 3d day of July, 1863, the last assault of the Confederate troops upon the heights of Gettysburg failed, and again General Lee was among his baffled and shattered battalions as they sullenly retired from their brave attempt. The history of that battle is yet to be written, and the responsibility for the result is yet to be fixed. But there, with the painful consciousness that his plans had been frustrated by others, and that defeat and humiliation had overtaken his army, in the presence of his troops he openly assumed the entire responsibility of the campaign and of the lost battle. One word from him would have relieved him of this responsibility, but that word he refused to utter until it could be spoken without fear of doing the least injustice.

"Thus, my fellow-soldiers, I have presented to you our great commander in the supreme moments of triumph and defeat. I cannot more strongly illustrate his character. Has it been surpassed in history? Is there another instance of such self-abnegation among men? The man rose high above victory in one instance; and, harder still, the man rose superior to disaster in the other. It was such incidents as these that gave General Lee the absolute and undoubting confidence and affection of his soldiers. Need I speak of the many exhibitions of that confidence? You all remember them, my comrades. Have you not seen a wavering line restored by the magic of his presence? Have you not seen the few forget that they were fighting against the many, because he was among the few?

"But I pass from the contemplation of his greatness in war, to look to his example under the oppressive circumstances of final failure—to look to that example to which it is most useful for us now to refer for our guidance and instruction. When the attempt to establish the Southern Confederacy had failed, and the event of the war seemed to have established the indivisibility of the Federal Union, General Lee gave his adhesion to the new order of things. His was no hollow truce; but, with the pure faith and honor that marked every act of his illustrious career, he immediately devoted himself to the restoration of peace, harmony, and concord. He entered zealously into the subject of education, believing, as he often declared, that popular education is the only sure foundation of free government. He gave his earnest support to all plans of internal improvements designed to bind more firmly together the social and commercial interests of the country, and among the last acts of his life was the effort to secure the construction of a line of railway communication of incalculable importance as a connecting link between the North and the South. He devoted all his great energies to the advancement of the welfare of his countrymen while shrinking from public notice, and sought to lay deep and strong the foundations of government which it was supposed would rise from the ruins of the old. But I need not repeat to you, my comrades, the history of his life since the war. You have watched it to its close, and you know how faithfully and truly he performed every duty of his position. Let us take to heart the lesson of his bright example. Disregarding all that malice may impute to us, with an eye single to the faithful performance of our duties as American citizens, and with an honest and sincere resolution to support with heart and hand the honor, the safety, and the true liberties of our country, let us invoke our fellow-citizens to forget the animosities of the past by the side of this honored grave, and, 'joining hands around this royal corpse, friends now, enemies no more, proclaim perpetual truce to battle.'"

The following are among the resolutions:

"The officers, soldiers, and sailors, of the Southern Confederacy, residing in Maryland, who served under General Lee, desiring to record their grief for his death, their admiration for his exalted virtues, and their affectionate veneration for his illustrious memory—

"*Resolved*, That, leaving with pride the name and fame of our illustrious commander to the judgment of history, we, who followed him through the trials, dangers, and hardships of a sanguinary and protracted war; who have felt the inspiration of his genius and valor in the time of trial; who have witnessed his magnanimity and moderation in the hour of victory, and his firmness and fortitude in defeat, claim the privilege of laying the tribute of our heart-felt sorrow upon his honored grave.

"*Resolved*, That the confidence and admiration which his eminent achievements deserved and received were strengthened by the noble example of his constancy in adversity, and that we honored and revered him in his retirement as we trusted and followed him on the field of battle.

"*Resolved*, That, as a token of respect and sorrow, we will wear the customary badge of mourning for thirty days.

"*Resolved*, That a copy of these resolutions and of the proceedings of this meeting be transmitted to the family of our lamented chief."

On the 29th of October a meeting was held to appoint delegates to represent the State of Maryland at the Richmond Lee Monumental Convention. After some brief remarks by General I.R. Trimble, and the adoption of resolutions constituting the Lee Monument Association of Maryland, the Hon. Reverdy Johnson addressed the meeting as follows:

HON. REVERDY JOHNSON.

"*Mr. Chairman and Gentlemen*: I am here in compliance with the request of many gentlemen present, and I not only willingly complied with that request, but I am willing to do all I am able, to show my appreciation of the character, civil and military, of Robert E. Lee. It was my good fortune to know him before the Mexican War, in those better days before the commencement of the sad struggle through which we have recently passed. I saw in him every thing that could command the respect and admiration of men, and I watched with peculiar interest his course in the Mexican War. It was also my good fortune to know the late Lieutenant-General Scott. In the commencement of the struggle to which I have alluded, I occupied in Washington the position of *quasi* military adviser to him, and was, in that capacity, intimately associated with him. I have heard him often declare that the glorious and continued success which crowned our arms in the war with Mexico was owing, in a large measure, to the skill, valor, and undaunted courage of Robert E. Lee. He entertained for him the warmest personal friendship, and it was his purpose to recommend him as his successor in the event of his death or inability to perform the duties of his high position. In April, 1861, after the commencement of hostilities between the two great sections of our country, General Lee, then lieutenant-colonel of cavalry in the Army of the United States, offered his resignation. I was with General Scott when he was handed the letter of resignation, and I saw what pain the fact caused him. While he regretted the step his most valuable officer had taken, he never failed to say emphatically, and over and over again, that he believed he had taken it from *an imperative sense of duty*. He was also consoled by the belief that if he was placed at the head of the armies of the then Confederation, he would have in him a foeman in every way worthy of him, and one who would conduct the war upon the highest principles of civilized warfare, and that he would not suffer encroachments to be made upon the rights of private property and the rights of unoffending citizens.

"Some may be surprised that I am here to eulogize Robert E. Lee. It is well known that I did not agree with him in his political views. At the beginning of the late war, and for many years preceding it, even from the foundation of this Government, two great questions agitated the greatest minds of this country. Many believed that the allegiance of the citizen was due first to his State, and many were of the opinion that, according to the true reading of the Constitution, a State had no right to leave the Union and claim sovereign rights and the perpetual allegiance of her citizens. I did not agree in the first-named opinion, but I knew it was honestly entertained. I knew men of the purest character, of the highest ability, and of the most liberal and patriotic feelings, who conscientiously believed it. Now the war is over, thank God! and to that thank I am sure this meeting will respond, it is the duty of every citizen of this land to seek to heal the wounds of the war, to forget past differences, and to forgive, as far as possible, the faults to which the war gave rise. In no other way can the Union be truly and permanently restored. We are now together as a band of brothers. The soldiers of the Confederacy, headed by the great chief we now mourn, have expressed their willingness to abide by the issue of the contest. What a spectacle to the world! After years of military devastation, with tens of thousands dead on her battle-fields, with the flower of her children slain, with her wealth destroyed, her commerce swept away, her agricultural and mechanical pursuits almost ruined, the South yielded. The North, victorious and strong, could not forget what she owed to liberty and human rights. We may well swear now that as long as liberty is virtuous we will be brothers.

"Robert E. Lee is worthy of all praise. As a man, he was peerless; as a soldier, he had no equal and no superior; as a humane and Christian soldier, he towers high in the political horizon. You cannot imagine with what delight, when I had the honor to represent this country at the court of Great Britain, I heard the praises of his fame and character which came from soldiers and statesmen. I need not speak of the comparative merits of General Lee and the Union generals who opposed him; this is not the place or time for a discussion of their respective successes and defeats; but I may say that, as far as I was able to judge of the sentiments of the military men of Great Britain, they thought none of the Union officers superior to General Robert E. Lee. Their admiration for him was not only on account of his skill on the battle-field, and the skilful manner with which he planned and executed his campaigns, but the humane manner in which he performed his sad duty. They alluded specially to his conduct when invading the territory of his enemy—his restraint upon his men, telling them that the honor of the army depended upon the manner of conducting the war in the enemy's country—and his refusal to resort to retaliatory measures. I know that great influences were brought to bear upon him, when he invaded Pennsylvania, to induce him to consent to extreme measures. His answer, however, was, 'No; if I suffer my army to pursue the course recommended, I cannot invoke the blessing of God upon my arms.' He would not allow his troops to destroy private property or to violate the rights of the citizens. When the necessities of his army compelled the taking of commissary stores, by his orders his officers paid for them in Confederate money at its then valuation. No burning homesteads illumined his march, no shivering and helpless children were turned out of their homes to witness their destruction by the torch. With him all the rules of civilized war, having the higher sanction of God, were strictly observed. The manly fortitude with which he yielded at Appomattox to three times his numbers showed that he was worthy of the honors and the fame the South had given him. This is not the first time since the termination of the war I have expressed admiration and friendship for Robert E. Lee. When I heard that he was about to be prosecuted in a Virginia court for the alleged crime of treason, I wrote to him at once, and with all my heart, that if he believed I could be of any service to him, professionally, I was at his command. All the ability I possess, increased by more than fifty years of study and experience, would have been cheerfully exerted to have saved him, for in saving him I believe I would have been saving the honor of my country. I received a characteristic reply in terms of friendship and grateful thanks. He wrote that he did not think the prosecution would take place. Hearing, however, some time after, that the prosecution would commence at Richmond, I went at once to that city and saw his legal adviser, Hon. William H. McFarland, one of the ablest men of the bar of Virginia. Mr. McFarland showed me a copy of a letter from General Lee to General Grant, enclosing an application for a pardon which he desired General Grant to present to the President, but telling him not to present it if any steps had been taken for his prosecution, as he was willing to stand the test. He wrote that he had understood by the terms of surrender at Appomattox that he and all his officers and men were to be protected. That letter, I am glad to say, raised General Lee higher in my esteem. General Grant at once replied, and he showed his reply to me. He wrote that he had seen the President, and protested against any steps being taken against General Lee, and had informed him that he considered his honor and the honor of the nation pledged to him. The President became satisfied, and no proceedings were ever taken. General Grant transmitted to the President the application of General Lee for pardon, indorsed with his most earnest approval. No pardon was granted. He did not need it here, and, when he appears before that great tribunal before which we must all be called, he will find he has no account to settle there. No soldier who followed General Lee could have felt more grief and sympathy at his grave than I would, could I have been present upon the mournful occasion of his burial. I lamented his loss as a private loss, and still more as a public loss. I knew that his example would continue to allay the passions aroused by the war, and which I was not surprised were excited by some acts in that war. I love my country; I am jealous of her honor. I cherish her good name, and I am proud of the land of my birth. I forbear to criticise the lives and characters of her high officers and servants, but I can say with truth that, during the late war, the laws of humanity were forgotten, and the higher orders of God were trodden under foot.

"The resolutions need no support which human lips can by human language give. Their subject is their support. The name of Lee appeals at once, and strongly, to every true heart in this land and throughout the world. Let political partisans, influenced by fanaticism and the hope of political plunder, find fault with and condemn us. They will be forgotten when the name of Lee will be resplendent with immortal glory.

"Mr. Chairman and gentlemen, in the course of Nature my career upon earth must soon terminate. God grant that when the day of my death comes, I may look up to Heaven with that confidence and faith which the life and character of Robert E. Lee gave him! He died trusting in God, as a good man, with a good life and a pure conscience. He was consoled with the knowledge that the religion of Christ had ordered all his ways, and he knew that the verdict of God upon the account he would have to render in heaven would be one of judgment seasoned with mercy. He had a right to believe that when God passed judgment upon the account of his life, though He would find him an erring human being, He would find virtue enough and religious faith enough to save him from any other verdict than that of 'Well done, good and faithful servant.' The monument will be raised; and when it is raised many a man will visit Richmond to stand beside it, to do reverence to the remains it may cover, and to say, 'Here lie the remains of one of the noblest men who ever lived or died in America.'"

HON. GEORGE WILLIAM BROWN

"*Mr. Chairman and Gentlemen*: The able and eloquent gentlemen who have preceded me have left but little for me to say. I rise, however, to express my hearty assent to the resolutions. Their broad and liberal views are worthy of the great and good man whose virtues and fame we seek to commemorate. He has passed away from earth, and our blame or censure is nothing to him now. The most eloquent eulogies that human lips can utter, and the loftiest monuments that human hands can build, cannot affect him now. But it is a satisfaction to us to know that expressions of the love for him which lives in every Southern heart—ay, in many a Northern heart—were heard long before his death, and that honor shed noble lustre around the last years of his life. He was the representative of a lost cause; he had sheathed his sword forever; he had surrendered his army to superior numbers; he was broken in fortune and in health, and was only president of a Virginia college, yet he was one of the foremost men of all the world.

"It has been said of General Lee, as it has been said of Washington, that he was deficient in genius. His character was so complete that what would have seemed evidences of genius with other men, were lost in the combination of his character and mind. He was always, and especially in every great crisis, a leader among men. During the four years of his education at West Point he did not receive a single reprimand. As a cavalry-officer, wherever he went he was a marked man; and when General Scott made his wonderful march to the capital of Mexico, Captain Lee was his right arm. At the commencement of the late war, though only a lieutenant-colonel of cavalry, he was offered the command of the armies of the United States. What a prize for ambition! Fortune, fame, and honors, awaited him. Where would he have been to-day? Probably in the presidential chair of this great nation. But he rejected all to take his chance with his own people, and to unite with them in their resistance to the vast numbers and resources which he knew the North was able to bring against them. There is nothing more remarkable in the annals of warfare than the success with which General Lee defeated for years the armies of the United States. Consider the six-days' battles around Richmond; the second battle of Manassas; the battles at Antietam, Fredericksburg, and Gettysburg; the wonderful contest at Chancellorsville; then again the remarkable battle of the Wilderness, in which it has been said by Federal authority that General Lee actually killed as many men as he had under his command; the defence at Cold Harbor, the prolonged defence of Richmond and Petersburg, and the admirably-conducted retreat with but a handful before an immense army. Well has he been spoken of as 'the incomparable strategist.' Did any man ever fight against more desperate odds or resources?

"But not merely as a great general is General Lee to be admired. He claims our admiration as a great man—great in adversity. I think there is nothing more admirable in all his life than his conduct in assuming the sole responsibility at Gettysburg. In the midst of defeat Lee was calm, unmoved, showing no fear where despair would have been in the heart of any other general, and saying to his officers and men, 'The fault is all mine.' Let the monument be raised, not merely by soldiers of General Lee, but by all men, no matter of what political feelings, who appreciate and honor that which is manly, great, and patriotic. The monument at Richmond will be the resort of pilgrims from the North as well as from the South, and the grave of Lee will be second only in the hearts of the people to the grave of Washington."

LEXINGTON, KY.

At the meeting at Lexington, resolutions were adopted similar to those already given. The meeting was addressed by General Preston and others.

GENERAL W. PRESTON.

"I am permitted to accompany the report with a few remarks, although I deem it unnecessary to use one word of commendation on the character of such a man. These resolutions are no doubt very short, but they will testify the feelings of every right-minded, noble-hearted man, no matter what may have been his opinions as to the past. Every true and generous soul feels that these resolutions are expressive of the sorrow entertained by the whole country. We speak not only the common voice of America, but of the world at this hour. It is no ordinary case of eulogy over an ordinary being, but over one who was the man of the century; a man who, by mighty armies commanded with admirable skill; by great victories achieved, and yet never stained by exultation; by mighty misfortunes met with a calm eye, and submitted to with all the dignity that belongs to elevated intelligence, and by his simplicity and grandeur, challenged the admiration of civilized mankind; and still more remarkable, after yielding to the greatest vicissitudes that the world ever saw, resigned himself to the improvement of the youth of the country, to the last moment of his mortal life, looking to the glorious life which he contemplated beyond the tomb. I must confess that, notwithstanding the splendor and glory of his career, I envy him the dignity of the pacific close of his life. Nothing more gentle, nothing more great, nothing more uncomplaining, has ever been recorded in the history of the world. By returning to Napoleon, we find he murmured, we find all the marks of mortality and mortal anger; but in Lee we find a man perfect in Christian principles—dignified, yet simple.

"I knew him first when he was a captain. I was then a young man connected with one of the regiments of this State, in Mexico, the Fourth Kentucky; and when I first saw him he was a man of extreme physical beauty, remarkable for his great gentleness of manner, and for his freedom from all military and social vices. At that time, General Scott, by common consent, had fixed upon General Lee as the man who would make his mark if ever the country needed his services. He never swore an oath, he never drank, he never wrangled, but there was not a single dispute between gentlemen that his voice was not more potent than any other; his rare calmness, serenity, and dignity, were above all. When the war came on, he followed his native State, Virginia, for he was the true representative of the great Virginia family at Washington. He was the real type of his race. He was possessed of all the most perfect points of Washington's character, with all the noble traits of his own.

"Scott maintained that Lee was the greatest soldier in the army. His discerning eye compared men; and I remember when, in some respects, I thought General Lee's military education had not fitted him for the great talents which he was destined to display. I remember when General Scott made use of these remarkable words: 'I tell you one thing, if I was on my death-bed, and knew there was a battle to be fought for the liberties of my country, and the President was to say to me, "Scott, who shall command?" I tell you that, with my dying breath, I should say Robert Lee. Nobody but Robert Lee! Robert Lee, and nobody but Lee!' That impressed me very much, because, at the beginning of the campaign, Lee was not prosperous; and why? because he was building up his men with that science which he possessed. His great qualities were discerned not after his remarkable campaigns; but, long before it, his name was regarded with that respected preëminence to which it did rise under that campaign. And I now say, and even opposite officers will admit, that no man has displayed greater power, more military ability, or more noble traits of character, than Robert E. Lee. Therefore it is that America has lost much. Europe will testify this as well as ourselves in this local community. Europe will weigh this, but after-ages will weigh him with Moltke and Bazaine, with the Duke of Magenta, and with all military men, and, in my judgment, those ages will say that the greatest fame and ability belonged to Robert Lee. But let us look to his moral character, to which I have already alluded. Through his whole life he had been a fervent and simple Christian; throughout his campaigns he was a brave and splendid soldier. If you ask of his friends, you will find that they adore him. If you ask his character from his enemies, you will find that they respect him, and respect is the involuntary tribute which friend and enemy alike have to pay to elevated worth; and, to-day, as the bells toll, their sounds will vibrate with the tenderest feelings through every noble heart. Public confessions of his worth and his greatness will be made through thousands of the towns and cities throughout this broad land; and, even where they are silent, monitors within will tell that a great spirit hath fled. This secret monitor will tell that a great and good man has passed away, who has left, in my opinion, no equal behind him."

REV. DR. HENDERSON.

"Since the announcement of the death of Robert E. Lee, I have been momentarily expecting the appearance of a call to pay some tribute to his splendid memory; but, if a notice had been given of this meeting, it altogether escaped my attention, else I would have been here freely and voluntarily. If I am a stranger in Lexington, and my lot has been cast here only during the last three weeks, yet I am happy that my fellow-citizens here have paid me such great respect as to call on me, on such an occasion as the present, to testify to the greatness and glory of General Robert E. Lee. Some public calamity is required to bring us into one great brotherhood. 'One touch of Nature makes the whole world kin.' Though you are all strangers to me, yet, in that common sympathy which we all feel, we are mourners together at the bier of departed worth.

"It does not become one of my profession to take any partisan view of the life of such a man, although it was my fortune to follow the same flag which he carried to victory upon so many fields. When it was furled, it was done with such calm magnificence as to win the admiration of his enemies and of the world. Yet I do not stand here to make any reference to that cause which has passed from the theatre of earth's activity, and taken its place only in history. But I do claim the right, from the stand-point which I occupy, of pointing to a man worthy of the emulation of all who love the true nobility of humanity; a man who was magnanimous to his enemies; who would weep at the calamities of his foes; who, throughout the sanguinary struggle, could preserve in himself the fullest share of human sympathy. History will challenge the world to produce a single instance in which this great man ever wantonly inflicted a blow, or ever wilfully imposed punishment upon any of his captives, or ever pushed his victory upon an enemy to gain unnecessary results—a man who, in all his campaigns, showed the same bright example to all the battalions that followed the lead of his sword. And now, since that flag which he carried has been furled, what a magnificent example has been presented to the world! It was said of Washington that he was first in war and first in peace, but, in the latter regard, Robert E. Lee showed more greatness than even the Father of his Country. He was struck down; the sun that had brightened up the horizon of hopes sank in dark eclipse to set in the shadow of disappointment. Calm and magnificent in the repose of conscious strength, he felt that he had lived and struggled for a principle that was dear to him. Though dead, it only remained for him to

184

be our example to the stricken and suffering people for whom he labored, and to show how magnanimously a brave and true Christian could act even when all he held sacred and dear was shattered by the hand of calamity. And, at the close of his career, he devoted his splendid capacity to the culture of the minds of his country's youth. He came down from the summit on which he had won the world's admiration, to the steady, regular duties of the school-room, to take his place in the vestry of a Christian church, and to administer the affairs of a country parish in the interest of Christianity. A man who, by his dignity and simplicity, preserved the constant admiration of his enemies, without even giving offence to his friends, such a man should receive a niche in the Pantheon of Fame.

"He stood in that great struggle of which as a star he was the leader, of unclouded brightness, drawing over its mournful history a splendor which is reflected from every sentence of its chronicle. He was an example of a man, who, though branded because of defeat, still, by his exalted character, gave a dignity and nobility to a cause which, doubtless, is forever dead, yet still is rendered immortal by the achievements of Robert E. Lee's sword and character."

NEW YORK.

"Services were held last evening," says a New-York journal, "in the large hall of the Cooper Institute, in commemoration of the life and character of the late General Robert E. Lee, of the Confederate States Army, with especial reference to his civic and Christian virtues. The call for the meeting stated that, although it was inaugurated by the Southern residents in the city of New York, it was 'yet to be regarded as in no sense born of partisan feeling, but solely from the desire to do honor to the memory of a great and good man—an illustrious American.' The attendance therefore of all, without reference to section or nationality, was cordially invited.

"There was no special decoration of the hall. Grafulla's band was in attendance, and, prior to the opening of the meeting, played several fine dirges. The choir of St. Stephen's Church also appeared upon the platform and opened the proceedings by singing 'Come, Holy Spirit.' The choir consisted of Madame de Luzan, Mrs. Jennie Kempton, Dr. Bauos, and Herr Weinlich. Mr. H.B. Denforth presided at the piano.

"Among the gentlemen present on the platform were General Imboden, ex-Governor Lowe, General Walker, Colonel Hunter, General Daniel W. Adams, Dr. Van Avery, Mr. M.B. Fielding, Colonel Fellows, General Cabell, Colonel T.L. Gnead, Mr. McCormick, Mr. T.A. Hoyt, etc.

"Mr. M.B. Fielding called the meeting to order, and requested the Rev. Dr. Carter to offer prayer.

"The Hon. John E. Ward was then called to preside, and delivered the following address—all the marked passages of which were loudly applauded:

"We meet to pay a tribute of respect to the memory of one whom the whole South revered with more than filial affection. The kind manifestations of sympathy expressed through the press of this great metropolis, this assemblage, the presence of these distinguished men, who join with us this evening, testify that the afflicted voice of his bereaved people has charmed down with sweet persuasion the angry passions kindled by the conflict in which he was their chosen leader. This is not the occasion either for an elaborate review of his life or a eulogy of his character. I propose to attempt neither. Born of one of the oldest and most distinguished families of our country—one so renowned in the field and in the cabinet that it seemed almost impossible to give brighter lustre to it—General Robert E. Lee rendered that family name even more illustrious, and by his genius and virtues extended its fame to regions of the globe where it had never before been mentioned. There is no cause for envy or hatred left now. His soldiers adored him most, not in the glare of his brilliant victories, but in the hour of his deepest humiliation, when his last great battle had been fought and lost—when the government for which he had struggled was crumbling about him—when his staff, asking, in despair, 'What can now be done?' he gave that memorable reply, 'It were strange indeed if human virtue were not at least as strong as human calamity.' This is the key to his life—the belief that trials and strength, suffering and consolation, come alike from God. Obedience to duty was ever his ruling principle. Infallibility is not claimed for him in the exercise of his judgment in deciding what duty was. But what he believed duty to command, that he performed without thought of how he would appear in the performance. In the judgment of many he may have mistaken his duty when he decided that it did not require him to draw his sword 'against his home, his kindred, and his children.' But Lee was no casuist or politician; he was a soldier. 'All that he would do highly that would he do holily.' He taught the world that the Christian and the gentleman could be united in the warrior. It was not when in pomp and power—when he commanded successful legions and led armies to victories—but when in sorrow and privation he assumed the instruction and guidance of the youth of Virginia, laying the only true foundation upon which a republic can rest, the Christian education of its youth—that he reaped the rich harvest of a people's love. Goodness was the chief attribute of Lee's greatness. Uniting in himself the rigid piety of the Puritan with the genial, generous impulses of the cavalier, he won the love of all with whom he came in contact, from the thoughtless child, with whom it was ever his delight to sport, to the great captain of the age, with whom he fought all the hard-won battles of Mexico. Some may believe that the world has given birth to warriors more renowned, to rulers more skilled in statecraft, but all must concede that a purer, nobler man never lived. What successful warrior or ruler, in ancient or modern times, has descended to his grave amid such universal grief and lamentation as our Lee? Caesar fell by the hands of his own beloved Brutus, because, by his tyranny, he would have enslaved Rome. Frederick the Great, the founder of an empire, became so hated of men, and learned so to despise them, that he ordered his 'poor carcass,' as he called it, to be buried with his favorite dogs at Potsdam. Napoleon reached his giddy height by paths which Lee would have scorned to tread, only to be hurled from his eminence by all the powers of Europe which his insatiate ambition had combined against him. Wellington, the conqueror of Napoleon, became the leader of a political party, and lived to need the protection of police from a mob. Even our own Washington, whose character was as high above that of the mere warrior and conqueror as is the blue vault of heaven above us to the low earth we tread beneath our feet, was libelled in life and slandered in death. Such were the fates of the most successful captains and warriors of the world. For four long years Lee occupied a position not less prominent than that of the most distinguished among them. The eyes of the civilized world watched his every movement and scanned his every motive. His cause was lost. He was unsuccessful. Yet he lived to illustrate to the world how, despite failure and defeat, a soldier could command honor and love from those for whom he struggled, and admiration and respect from his foes, such as no success had ever before won for warrior, prince, or potentate. And, when his life was ended, the whole population of the South, forming one mighty funeral procession, followed him to his grave. His obsequies modestly performed by those most tenderly allied to him, he sleeps in the bosom of the land he loved so well. His spotless fame will gather new vigor and freshness from the lapse of time, and the day is not distant when that fame will be claimed, not as the property of a section, but as the heritage of a united people. His soul, now forever freed from earth's defilements, basks in the sunlight of God.' *Pro tumulo ponas patriam, pro tegmine caelum, sidera pro facibus, pro lachrymis maria.*'" (Great applause.)

GENERAL IMBODEN

Rose and said:

"It is with emotions of infinite grief I rise to perform one of the saddest duties of my life. The committee who have arranged the ceremonies on this occasion, deemed it expedient and proper to select a Virginian as their organ to present to this large assembly of the people of New York a formal preamble and resolutions, which give expression to their feelings in regard to the death of General Robert E. Lee. This distinction has been conferred by the committee upon me; and I shall proceed to read their report, without offering to submit any remarks as to the feelings excited in my own heart by this, mournful intelligence:"

RESOLUTIONS.

"In this great metropolitan city of America, where men of every clime and of all nationalities mingle in the daily intercourse of pleasure and of business, no great public calamity can befall any people in the world without touching a sympathetic chord in the hearts of thousands. When, therefore, tidings reached us that General Robert E. Lee, of Virginia, was dead, and that the people of that and all the other Southern States of the Union were stricken with grief, the great public heart of New York was moved with a generous sympathy, which found kindly and spontaneous expression through the columns of the city press of every shade of opinion.

"All differences of the past, all bitter memories, all the feuds that have kept two great sections of our country in angry strife and controversy for so long, have been forgotten in the presence of the awe-inspiring fact that no virtues, no deeds, no honors, nor any position, can save any member of the human family from the common lot of all.

"The universal and profound grief of our Southern countrymen is natural and honorable alike to themselves and to him whom they mourn, and is respected throughout the world; for Robert E. Lee was allied and endeared to them by all the most sacred ties that can unite an individual to a community. He was born and reared in their midst, and shared their local peculiarities, opinions, and traditional characteristics; and his preëminent abilities and exalted personal integrity and Christian character made him, by common consent, their leader and representative in a great national conflict in which they had staked life, fortune, and honor; and in Virginia his family was coeval with the existence of the State, and its name was emblazoned upon those bright pages of her early civil and military annals which record the patriotic deeds of Washington and his compeers.

"By no act of his did he ever forfeit or impair the confidence thus reposed in him by his own peculiar people; and when he had, through years of heroic trial and suffering, done all that mortal man could do in discharge of the high trust confided by them to his hands, and failed, he bowed with dignified submission to the decree of Providence; and from the day he gave his parole at Appomattox to the hour of his death, he so lived and acted as to deprive enmity of its malignity, and became to his defeated soldiers and countrymen a bright example of unqualified obedience to the laws of the land, and of support to its established government. Nay, more. With a spirit of Christian and affectionate duty to his impoverished and suffering people, and with a high estimate of the importance of mental and moral culture to a generation of youth whose earlier years were attended by war's rough teachings, he went from the tented field and the command of armies to the quiet shades of a scholastic institution in the secluded valleys of his own native Virginia, and entered with all the earnestness of his nature upon the duties of instruction, and there spent the closing years of his life in training the minds and hearts of young men from all parts of the country for the highest usefulness 'in their day and generation.' By these pursuits, and his exemplary and unobtrusive life since the close of the great war in America, he won the respect and admiration of the enlightened and the good of the whole world. It is meet and natural, therefore, that his own people should bewail his death as a sore personal bereavement to each one of them. Those of us here assembled who were his soldiers, friends, and supporters, sharing all the trials and many of the responsibilities of that period of his life which brought him so prominently before the world, honored and trusted him then, have loved and admired him, have been guided by his example since; and now that he is dead, we should be unworthy of ourselves, and unworthy to be called his countrymen, did we not feel and express the same poignant grief which now afflicts those among whom he lived and died.

"Those of us who were not his soldiers, friends, and supporters, when war raged throughout the land, but who have nevertheless met here to-day with those who were our enemies then, but are now our friends and countrymen, and appreciate with them the character of Lee, and admire his rare accomplishments as an American citizen, whose fame and name are the property of the nation, we all unite over his hallowed sepulchre in an earnest prayer that old divisions may be composed, and that a complete and perfect reconciliation of all estrangements may be effected at the tomb, where all alike, in a feeling of common humanity and universal Christian brotherhood, may drop their tears of heart-felt sorrow.

"Therefore, without regard to our former relations toward each other, but meeting as Americans by birth or adoption, and in the broadest sense of national unity, and in the spirit above indicated, to do honor to a great man and Christian gentleman who has gone down to the grave, we do

"*Resolve*, That we have received with feelings of profound sorrow intelligence of the death of General Robert E. Lee. We can and do fully appreciate the grief of our Southern countrymen at the death of one so honored by and so dear to them, and we tender to them this expression of our sympathy, with the assurance that we feel in the contemplation of so sad an event that we are and ought to be, henceforth and forever, one great and harmonious national family, sharing on all occasions each others' joys and sympathizing in each others' sorrows.

"*Resolved*, That a copy of the foregoing preamble, and these resolutions, signed by the president and secretary, be transmitted to the Governor of Virginia, with a request that the same be preserved in the archives of the State; and that another copy be sent to the family of General Lee.

  "J.D. IMBODEN,
Ex. NORTON,
JOHN MITCHEL,
C.K. MARSHALL,
T.L. SNEAD,
NORMAN D. SAMPSON,
Wm. H. APPLETON,
Committee on Resolutions"

"On motion, the resolutions were unanimously adopted by a standing and silent vote, which was followed by a spontaneous outburst of hearty applause."

We have given but a small portion of the addresses which were called forth by this national calamity, and these, no doubt, have suffered injustice by imperfect reporting. But we have shown, as we wished to show, the standard by which our people estimate an heroic character, and how the South loves and honors the memory of her great leader.

A few extracts from the English press will show the feeling in that country:

THE PALL MALL GAZETTE.

"Even amid the turmoil of the great European struggle, the intelligence from America announcing that General Robert E. Lee is dead, will be received with deep sorrow by many in this country, as well as by his followers and fellow-soldiers in America. It is but a few years since Robert E. Lee ranked among the great men of the present time. He was the able soldier of the Southern Confederacy, the bulwark of her northern frontier, the obstacle to the advance of the Federal armies, and the leader who twice threatened, by the capture of Washington, to turn the tide of success, and to accomplish a revolution which would have changed the destiny of the United States. Six years passed by, and then we heard that he was dying at an obscure town in Virginia, where, since the collapse of the Confederacy, he had been acting as a school-master. When, at the head of the last eight thousand of his valiant army, the remnants which battle, sickness, and famine had left him, he delivered up his sword to General Grant at Appomattox Court-House, his public career ended; he passed away from men's thoughts; and few in Europe cared to inquire the fate of the general whose exploits had aroused the wonder of neutrals and belligerents, and whose noble character had excited the admiration of even the most bitter of his political enemies. If, however, success is not always to be accounted as the sole foundation of renown, General Lee's life and career deserve to be held in reverence by all who admire the talents of a general and the noblest qualities of a soldier. His family were well known in Virginia. Descended from the Cavaliers who first colonized that State, they had produced more than one man who fought with distinction for their country. They were allied by marriage to Washington, and, previous to the recent war, were possessed of much wealth; General (then Colonel) Robert Lee residing, when not employed with his regiment, at Arlington Heights, one of the most beautiful places in the neighborhood of Washington. When the civil war first broke out, he was a colonel in the United States Army, who had served with distinction in Mexico, and was accounted among the best of the American officers. To him, as to others, the difficult choice presented itself, whether to take the side of his State, which had joined in the secession of the South, or to support the central Government. It is said that Lee debated the matter with General Scott, then Commander-in-chief, that both agreed that their first duty lay with their State, but that the former only put the theory into practice.

"It was not until the second year of the war that Lee came prominently forward, when, at the indecisive battle of Fair Oaks, in front of Richmond, General Johnston having been wounded, he took command of the army; and subsequently drove McClellan, with great loss, to the banks of the James River. From that time he became the recognized leader of the Confederate army of Virginia. He repulsed wave after wave of invasion, army after army being hurled against him only to be thrown back, beaten and in disorder. The Government at Washington were kept in constant alarm by the near vicinity of his troops, and witnessed more than once the entry into their intrenchments of a defeated and disorganized rabble, which a few days previous had left them a confident host. Twice he entered the Northern States at the head of a successful army, and twice indecisive battles alone preserved from destruction the Federal Government, and turned the fortune of the war. He impressed his character on those who acted under him. Ambition for him had no charms, duty alone was his guide. His simplicity of life checked luxury and display among his officers, while his disregard of hardships silenced the murmurs of his harassed soldiery. By the troops he was loved as a father, as well as admired as a general; and his deeply-religious character impressed itself on all who were brought in contact with him, and made itself felt through the ranks of the Virginian army. It is said that, during four years of war, he never slept in a house, but in winter and summer shared the hardships of his soldiers. Such was the man who, in mature age, at a period of life when few generals have acquired renown, fought against overwhelming odds for the cause which he believed just. He saw many of his bravest generals and dearest friends fall around him, but, although constantly exposed to fire, escaped without a wound.

"The battles which prolonged and finally decided the issue of the contest are now little more than names. Antietam, Fredericksburg, Chancellorsville, and Gettysburg, are forgotten in Europe by all excepting those who study recent wars as lessons for the future, and would collect from the deeds of other armies experience which they may apply to their own. To them the boldness of Lee's tactics at Chancellorsville will ever be a subject of admiration; while even those who least sympathize with his cause will feel for the general who saw the repulse of Longstreet's charge at Gettysburg, and beheld the failure of an attempt to convert a defensive war into one of attack, together with the consequent abandonment of the bold stroke which he had hoped would terminate the contest. Quietly he rallied the broken troops; taking all the blame on himself, he encouraged the officers, dispirited by the reverse, and in person formed up the scattered detachments. Again, when Fortune had turned against the Confederacy, when overwhelming forces from all sides pressed back her defenders, Lee for a year held his ground with a constantly-diminishing army, fighting battle after battle in the forests and swamps around Richmond. No reverses seemed to dispirit him, no misfortune appeared to ruffle his calm, brave temperament. Only at last, when he saw the remnants of his noble army about to be ridden down by Sheridan's cavalry, when eight thousand men, half-starved and broken with fatigue, were surrounded by the net which Grant and Sherman had spread around them, did he yield; his fortitude for the moment gave way; he took farewell of his soldiers, and, giving himself up as a prisoner, retired a ruined man into private life, gaining his bread by the hard and uncongenial work of governing Lexington College.

"When political animosity has calmed down, and when Americans can look back on those years of war with feelings unbiassed by party strife, then will General Lee's character be appreciated by all his countrymen as it now is by a part, and his name will be honored as that of one of the noblest soldiers who have ever drawn a sword in a cause which they believed just, and at the sacrifice of all personal considerations have fought manfully a losing battle."

THE SATURDAY REVIEW.

This journal, after some remarks on the death of Admiral Farragut, continues:

"A still more famous leader in the war has lately closed a blameless life. There may be a difference of opinion on the military qualities of the generals who fought on either side in the civil war; but it is no disparagement to the capacity of Grant or of Sherman to say that they had no opportunity of rivalling the achievements of General Lee. Assuming the chief command in the Confederate army in the second campaign of the war, he repelled three or four invasions of Virginia, winning as many pitched battles over an enemy of enormously superior resources. After driving McClellan from the Peninsula, he inflicted on Burnside and Pope defeats which would have been ruinous if the belligerents had been on equal terms; but twenty millions of men, with the absolute command of the sea and the rivers, eventually overpowered a third of their number. The drawn battle of Gettysburg proved that the invasion of the Northern States was a blunder; and in 1863 it became evident that the fall of the Confederacy could not be much longer delayed. Nevertheless General Lee kept Grant's swarming legions at bay for the whole summer and autumn, and the loss of the Northern armies in the final campaign exceeded the entire strength of the gallant defenders of Richmond. When General Lee, outnumbered, cut off from his communications, and almost surrounded by his enemies, surrendered at Appomattox Court-House, he might console himself with the thought that he had only failed where success was impossible. From that moment he used his unequalled and merited authority to reconcile the Southern people to the new order of affairs. He had originally dissented from the policy of secession; and he followed the banner of his State exclusively from a sense of duty, in disregard of his professional and private interests. He might at pleasure have been Commander-in-Chief of the Northern army, for he was second in rank to General Scott. His ancient home and his ample estate on the Potomac were ravaged by the enemy; but he never expressed a regret for the sacrifice of his fortune. There can be no doubt that he was often thwarted by political superiors and by incompetent subordinates, but his equable temper and lofty nature never inclined him to complaint. The regret for his loss which is felt throughout the vast regions of the South is a just tribute to one of the greatest and purest characters in American history."

It will not be inappropriate to reproduce here the tribute which appeared in the London *Standard*, on the receipt of the news of General Lee's illness:

THE STANDARD.

"The announcement that General R.E. Lee has been struck down by paralysis and is not expected to recover, will be received, even at this crisis, with universal interest, and will everywhere excite a sympathy and regret which testify to the deep impression made on the world at large by his character and achievements. Few are the generals who have earned, since history began, a greater military reputation; still fewer are the men of similar eminence, civil or military, whose personal qualities would bear comparison with his. The bitterest enemies of his country hardly dared to whisper a word against the character of her most distinguished general, while neutrals regarded him with an admiration for his deeds and a respect for his lofty and unselfish nature which almost grew into veneration as his own countrymen learned to look up to him with as much confidence and esteem as they ever felt for Washington, and with an affection which the cold demeanor and austere temper of Washington could never inspire. The death of such a man, even at a moment so exciting as the present, when all thoughts are absorbed by a nearer and present conflict, would be felt as a misfortune by all who still retain any recollection of the interest with which they watched the Virginian campaigns, and by thousands who have almost forgotten the names of Fredericksburg and Chancellorsville, the Wilderness and Spottsylvania. By the South it would be recognized as a national calamity—as the loss of a man not only inexpressibly dear to an unfortunate people by his intimate association with their fallen hopes and their proudest recollections, but still able to render services such as no other man could perform, and to give counsel whose value is enhanced tenfold by the source from which it comes. We hope, even yet, that a life so honorable and so useful, so pure and noble in itself, so valuable to a country that has much need of men like him, may be spared and prolonged for further enjoyment of domestic peace and comfort, for further service to his country; we cannot bear to think of a career so singularly admirable and so singularly unfortunate, should close so soon and so sadly. By the tens of thousands who will feel as we do when they read the news that now lies before us, may be measured the impressions made upon the world by the life and the deeds of the great chief of the Army of Virginia.

"Whatever differences of opinion may exist as to the merits of the generals against whom he had to contend, and especially of the antagonist by whom he was at last overcome, no one pretending to understand in the least either the general principles of military science or the particular conditions of the American War, doubts that General Lee gave higher proofs of military genius and soldiership than any of his opponents. He was outnumbered from first to last; and all his victories were gained against greatly superior forces, and with troops greatly deficient in every necessary of war except courage and discipline. Never, perhaps, was so much achieved against odds so terrible. The Southern soldiers—'that incomparable Southern infantry' to which a late Northern writer renders due tribute of respect—were no doubt as splendid troops as a general could desire; but the different fortune of the East and the West proves that the Virginian army owed something of its excellence to its chief. Always outnumbered, always opposed to a foe abundantly supplied with food, transport, ammunition, clothing, all that was wanting to his own men, he was always able to make courage and skill supply the deficiency of strength and of supplies; and from the day when he assumed the command after the battle of Seven Pines, where General Joseph Johnston was disabled, to the morning of the final surrender at Appomattox Court-House, he was almost invariably victorious in the field. At Gettysburg only he was defeated in a pitched battle; on the offensive at the Chickahominy, at Centreville, and at Chancellorsville, on the defensive at Antietam, Fredericksburg, the Wilderness, and Spottsylvania, he was still successful. But no success could avail him any thing from the moment that General Grant brought to bear upon the Virginian army the inexhaustible population of the North, and, employing Sherman to cut them off from the rest of the Confederacy, set himself to work to wear them out by the simple process of exchanging two lives for one. From that moment the fate of Richmond and of the South was sealed. When General Lee commenced the campaign of the Wilderness he had, we believe, about fifty thousand men; his adversary had thrice that number at hand, and a still larger force in reserve. When the army of Virginia marched out of Richmond it still numbered some twenty-six thousand men; after a retreat of six days, in the face of an overwhelming enemy, with a crushing artillery—a retreat impeded by constant fighting, and harassed by countless hordes of cavalry—eight thousand were given up by the capitulation of Appomattox Court-House. Brilliant as were General Lee's earlier triumphs, we believe that he gave higher proofs of genius in his last campaign, and that hardly any of his victories were so honorable to himself and his army as that six-days' retreat.

"There have, however, been other generals of genius as brilliant, of courage and endurance hardly less distinguished. How many men have ever displayed the perfect simplicity of nature, the utter absence of vanity or affectation, which belongs to the truest and purest greatness, in triumph or in defeat, as General Lee has done? When Commander-in-Chief of the Southern armies, he moved from point to point, as duty required, with less parade than a European general of division, wearing no sword, attended by no other staff than the immediate occasion demanded, and chatting with a comrade or a visitor with a simple courtesy which had in it no shade of condescension. Only on one occasion does he seem to have, been accoutred with the slightest regard to military display or personal dignity; and that, characteristically, was the last occasion on which he wore the Confederate uniform—the occasion of his interview with General Grant on April 9, 1865. After the war he retired without a word into privacy and obscurity. Ruined by the seizure and destruction of his property, which McClellan protected, and which his successors gave up to ravage and pillage, the late Commander-in-Chief of the Southern armies accepted the presidency of a Virginia college, and devoted himself as simply and earnestly to its duties as if he had never filled a higher station or performed more exciting functions. Well aware of the jealous temper of the party dominant in the North, and anxious, above all things, to avoid exasperating that temper against his conquered countrymen, he carefully abstained from appearing in any public ceremony or taking any overt part in political questions. His influence has been exerted, quietly but steadily, in one direction, with a single view to restore harmony and good-will between the two sections, and to reconcile the oppressed Southerners to the Union from which he fought so gallantly to free them. He has discountenanced all regretful longings after the lost visions of Southern independence; all demonstrations in honor of the 'conquered banner;' and has encouraged the South to seek the restoration of her material prosperity and the satisfaction of her national feelings in a frank acceptance of the result of the war, and a loyal adhesion to the Federal bond. It was characteristic and worthy of the man that he was among the first to sue for a formal pardon from President Johnson; not for any advantage which he personally could obtain thence, but to set the example of submission to his comrades-in-arms, and to reconcile them to a humiliation without which the conquerors refused them that restitution to civil rights necessary to any effort to retrieve their own or their country's fortunes. Truer greatness, a loftier nature, a spirit more unselfish, a character purer, more chivalrous, the world has rarely, if ever known. Of stainless life and deep religious feeling, yet free from all taint of cant and fanaticism, and as dear and congenial to the Cavalier Stuart as to the Puritan Stonewall Jackson; unambitious, but ready to sacrifice all at the call of duty; devoted to his cause, yet never moved by his feelings beyond the line prescribed by his judgment; never provoked by just resentment to punish wanton cruelty by reprisals which would have given a character of needless savagery to the war—both North and South owe a deep debt of gratitude to him, and the time will come when both will be equally proud of him. And well they may, for his character and his life afford a complete answer to the reproaches commonly cast on money-grubbing, mechanical America. A country which has given birth to men like him, and those who followed him, may look the chivalry of Europe in the face without shame; for the fatherlands of Sidney and of Bayard never produced a nobler soldier, gentleman, and Christian, than General Robert E. Lee."

We may add to these the following just remarks upon the occupation to which General Lee devoted himself at the close of his military career, from

THE OLD DOMINION.

"Surely it should be a cause of thankfulness and encouragement for those who are teachers, that their profession has received this reflection of glory and honor from this choice of his, from this life, and from this death. And it is enduring honor for all the colleges of the South, and for all our schools—an honor in which all may share alike without jealousy—that this pure and bright name is inseparably connected by the will of him that bore it with the cause of education, and is blended now with that of Washington in the name of one of our own institutions of learning. We think that so long as the name of Lee is honored and loved among us, our Southern teachers may rejoice and grow stronger in their work, when they remember that he was one of their number, and that his great heart, that had so bravely borne the fortunes of a great empire, bore also, amid its latest aspirations, the interests, the anxieties, and the hopes of the unpretending but noble profession of teaching.

"To leave this out of the account would be, indeed, to do sad injustice to General Lee's own memory. And that, not only because his position in this profession was of his own choice, and was steadily maintained with unchanging purpose to the end of his life, but also because the acknowledgment of his service here is necessary to the completeness of his fame. In no position of his life did he more signally develop the great qualities of his character than in this; and it may truly be said that some of the greatest can only be fully understood in the light of the serene patience and of the simple and quiet self-consecration of his latest years. It was then that, far from the tumult of arms and from the great passions of public life, with no great ambition to nerve his heart, nor any great events to obscure the public criticism of his conduct, he displayed in calm and steady light the grandest features of his character, and by this crucial test, added certain confirmation to the highest estimate that could have been formed of his character and of his abilities. It was indeed a 'crucial test' for such a man; and that he sustained it as he did is not among the smallest of his claims to the admiration of his countrymen. No tribute to his memory can be just that does not take this last great service into the account; and no history of his life can be fairly written that shall not place in the strongest light his career and influence as President of Washington College."

And we may appropriately close with the following thoughtful words from the pen of

HON. ALEXANDER H. STEPHENS.

"In the darkest hour of our trials, in the very midst of our deepest affliction, mourning over the loss of the noble Lee, Heaven sends to us as consolation the best sign of the times vouchsafed in many a day. It addresses the heart, rent as it is in surveying the desolations around us, as the rainbow upon the breast of the receding storm-cloud when its power and fury are over.

"That sign is the unmistakable estimation in which the real merits and worth of this illustrious chieftain of the cause of the Southern States is held by all classes of persons, not only in the South, but in the North.

"Partisans and leaders, aiming at the overthrow of our institutions, may, while temporarily in high places, by fraud and usurpation, keep up the false cry of *rebel* and *traitor*, but these irrepressible outburstings of popular sentiment, regarding no restraints on great occasions which cause *Nature* to speak, show clearly how this cry and charge are regarded and looked upon by the masses of the people everywhere.

"Everywhere Lee is honored; not only as a *hero*, but as a *patriot*. This is but the foreshadowing of the general judgment of the people of the whole United States, and of the world, not only upon Lee, but upon all of his associates who fought, bled, and died in that glorious cause in which he won his immortality. That cause was the sovereign right of local self-government by the people of the several States of this continent. *That* cause is not dead! Let it never be abandoned; but let its friends rally to its standard in the forum of reason and justice, with the renewed hope and energy from this soul-inspiriting sign that it lies deeply impressed upon the hearts of the great majority of the people in all sections of this country.

"In these popular manifestations of respect and veneration for the man who won all his glory in maintaining this cause, present usurpers should read their doom, and all friends of constitutional liberty should take fresh courage in all political conflicts, never to lower their standard of principles."

THE END

Printed in Great Britain
by Amazon